Get Your IT Career in Gear!

*Practical Advice for Building a Career
in Information Technology*

Get Your IT Career in Gear!

Practical Advice for Building a Career in Information Technology

Leslie Jaye Goff

Osborne/**McGraw-Hill**

New York   Chicago   San Francisco   Lisbon
London   Madrid   Mexico City   Milan   New Delhi
San Juan   Seoul   Singapore   Sydney   Toronto

Osborne/**McGraw-Hill**
2600 Tenth Street
Berkeley, California 94710
U.S.A.

To arrange bulk purchase discounts for sales promotions, premiums, or fund-raisers, please contact Osborne/**McGraw-Hill** at the above address. For information on translations or book distributors outside the U.S.A., please see the International Contact Information page immediately following the index of this book.

Get Your IT Career in Gear! Practical Advice for Building a Career in Information Technology

1234567890 2CUS 2CUS 01987654321

ISBN 0-07-212683-3

Publisher	**Technical Editor**
Brandon A. Nordin	Rory Paredes
Vice President and Associate Publisher	**Copy Editor**
Scott Rogers	Chrisa Hotchkiss
Editorial Director	**Indexer**
Gareth Hancock	Jack Lewis
Project Manager	**Computer Designer**
Deidre Dolce	Happenstance Type-O-Rama
Project Editor	**Series Design**
Laurie Stewart	Maureen Forys, Happenstance Type-O-Rama
Acquisitions Coordinator	
Jessica Wilson	

This book was composed with QuarkXPress 4.11 on a Macintosh G4.

For Lele and Lucy.

Contents

Acknowledgments

I would like to extend my appreciation to the editors I've worked with over the years, many of whom had a hand in shaping the articles that eventually led to this book, including Jodie Naze of ITworld.com, Joyce Chutchian and Amy Malloy of TechTarget.com, and David Weldon, Anne McCrory, Kevin Fogarty, Melissa Solomon, and Ellen Fanning of *Computerworld*.

Thanks to *Computerworld* for permission to reprint articles and research.

Thanks to Gareth Hancock and Jessica Wilson of Osborne/McGraw-Hill for helping me bring this book to fruition. To say they possess infinite patience would be an understatement. Thanks also to Bob Bolick of McGraw-Hill for giving me this opportunity.

Many thanks to Denise Cox, Alan Feuer, Edwin Maldonado, Steven Boling, Michael Lillard, Matthew Thompson, Stephen Rudko, Jerry Weinberger, Louis Edwards, Sandra Green, and Mary Brandel for their encouragement, support, and feedback.

A big thanks to my parents, Sammie and John Goff, and to my entire family for forgiving my absence while working on this project.

And most of all, thanks to the countless IT professionals, managers, and executives who have graciously given me their time over the last 15 years, especially those whose insights and experiences contributed to this book.

Leslie Jaye Goff
1 May 2001

Introduction

In the relatively brief 50 years since the debut of the first programmable computer, a remote, mysterious behemoth that filled a large basement room, computers have become utterly indispensable to how the world operates, in both business life and personal life. The prodigious processor has undergone a Darwinian evolution in scale and power to become a handheld personal appliance that we can't live without, which keeps track of our appointments and address books, beams messages to our friends and associates, and remembers our brilliant ideas for us.

Technology touches us in every aspect of our lives. Every time we make a purchase, for example—online or down the block in the corner grocery—interconnected networks of computers have made the transaction possible, from the system on which the packaging was designed, to the one that controlled the manufacturing and assembly process, to the one that tracked its journey from its source to the distributor to the store, to the one that recorded the final transaction and relayed the information to the inventory management system. Before stock gets too low, that system initiates the process all over again. The data collected and stored in each of those computer systems can be collected, put together, pulled apart, looked at by brand, by customer, by store, by location, and ultimately used to draw conclusions about how to sell more of the right product to the right people in the right place at the right time.

The digital revolution powered the longest peace-time economic boom in history and has created a robust job market for qualified professionals. If you're looking for a career in which you'll be continuously challenged—making a visible difference in your company's bottom line, working with teams of diverse people solving problems and overcoming obstacles, and ever standing on the brink of something entirely new and different—then look no further than a career in IT. The forces of the new economy are driving companies to forge new ways of doing business, and in a world moving at Internet speed, IT is the enabler.

How far you can go in IT today is limited only by your imagination. Even in the face of economic uncertainty, IT professionals are among the best positioned to weather any major changes in the job market. And the plethora of available jobs is such that IT professionals can pick and choose a job that suits their individual lifestyle. The hours can be long and longer—it's not uncommon for an IT project manager to sweat out a 15-hour-plus day when rolling out a new software package or network upgrade. But in general, an IT career affords nearly unlimited options to choose where you live, how you structure your work week, and how you balance your personal and professional lives. The need for IT workers is so pervasive that IT professionals can find challenging work anywhere in the country.

Gary Cooper, who grew up on a chicken farm and now is chief information officer (CIO) of Tyson Foods, in rural Springdale, Arkansas, notes that he can live in the rolling hills of Northwest Arkansas and still have one of the best IT jobs in the country. Those who abhor the thought of traditional corporate life can take a chance with a dot-com or strike out on their own as independent consultants. And for IT pros who have an activist streak, even nonprofit organizations—often perceived as technological backwaters—are very often on the cutting edge of using web-based technologies. Whatever your career aspirations, workplace likes and dislikes, or lifestyle priorities, an IT career can provide you the chance to rise to your greatest potential.

Not only does an IT career offer countless options, it also offers ample employment opportunities. With average IT turnover rates hovering around 20 percent a year and new IT job creation increasing annually, the demand for IT talent outranks the supply by a significant margin. Exact supply and demand projections vary greatly. The U.S. Commerce department's Office of Technology Policy asserts that "there is no way to establish conclusively whether there is, or is not, an overall IT worker shortage." On the other hand, a frequently cited annual study by the Information Technology Association of America (ITAA), a lobbying group based in Arlington, Virginia, projects that U.S. companies will create 900,000 new IT jobs in 2001, and 425,000 of those will go unfilled due to a shortage of workers.

While the ITAA's research has sometimes been called into question, anecdotal evidence confirms that, even with dot-com closures and corporate layoffs, IT organizations will continue to struggle with filling both newly created positions and those vacated by attrition. The Sunday classifieds in major metropolitan areas across the country are dominated by IT job listings, and online IT job sites like Dice.com, ComputerJobs.com, and Techies.com, to name just a few, are growing larger with each passing month. Whether you're an entry-level IT candidate, an established IT professional looking for the next step up, or a career-changer who wants to take your skills and experience garnered in another field into the IT realm, the opportunities to carve out a fulfilling, resilient IT career are boundless.

College students approaching the IT job market can expect both ample offers and generous starting salaries. The supply-and-demand gap has made campus recruiting a top priority for even the most discriminating employers. Like any good NCAA scout who sits in the stands of junior high school football games looking for future Heisman Trophy winners, many IT department recruiters are identifying potential candidates early in their college careers and following them through to graduation. Employers are expanding IT internship programs, bringing in sophomores and juniors, as well as M.B.A. candidates, for try-before-you buy opportunities. And successful interns are starting their last year of school with job offers locked up. At the University of Texas, for example, IT graduates have the best placement rate of the university's entire business school, with nearly 100 percent landing jobs by the end of their final semester, says Dr. Eleanor Jordan, who heads up the faculty for the Management Sciences and Information Systems department in the College of Business.

Entry-level IT salaries offered to college graduates with IT-related business degrees increased 5.4 percent in the spring of 2001 to an average of $45,167 for jobs in systems analysis and design and programming, according to the National Association of Colleges and Employers (NACE), which surveyed the campus career offices at 350 colleges and universities. Computer science graduates fared even better, with average offers of $52,259, up 7.8 percent over spring 2000.

Established IT professionals have the chance to grow their careers faster and in more new directions than at any other time since the early days of the profession, when it was something like the old West—open, uncharted territory where people made up the rules as they rode along. Given the difficulties of recruiting in a tight market, and the increasing reliance on IT for competitive advantage, companies are going to great lengths to retain their IT professionals. They're offering perks like free breakfasts and dinners, concierge services, and business casual dress policies. And more importantly, from a career development perspective, they're offering bonuses for reaching project milestones, ensuring time for training, and creating formal career paths that allow IT staff members to rotate throughout a variety of jobs to stave off boredom and skills obsolescence.

The possibilities for reviving an IT career by changing employers are just as significant, with companies adopting aggressive tactics to recruit experienced IT professionals. While stories of new recruits getting BMWs as signing bonuses are largely urban myths, signing bonuses are fairly commonplace in IT today, as are highly personal relocation services, like helping to find a new doctor for a pregnant spouse or paying off a mortgage while a recruit looks for a home in the new city.

The IT field is also wide open to career-changers. Professionals who would seem to have only tangentially related skills can work their way into IT jobs with either a unique skill set or with some careful planning and retraining. For example, Agency.com, an e-business design and consulting company based in New York's Silicon Alley, hired a theme park designer from the Walt Disney Co. to spearhead creative services and assist with new business development. "We always wanted a theme park designer," says Kyle Shannon, Agency's chief people officer. "We hire for talent, not skills."

James Little, former CIO for the Arkansas State Economic Development Agency (EDA), Little Rock, Arkansas, started his career as a business journalist before becoming a network administrator, then a website developer. He became the EDA's CIO within only three years and later launched his own web-design consulting firm. And Anita Mital, 35, formerly a high school geometry teacher in the New Orleans public schools, took night courses at Tulane University, earned a second Bachelor's degree in Information Systems Technology, and is now an applications developer for an IT services firm.

So many are doing so well in IT because IT organizations today require more than just technology skills. This book delves into how you can leverage all of your skills and experience for a successful career in IT, offers an in-depth look at the myriad roles that IT workers play in meeting today's challenges, and discusses the long-term prospects that await novice and experienced IT professionals. You can rely on it to be more than just a primer on getting an IT job; use it as your complete guide to building and sustaining an IT career. At any stage of your career, you'll be able to identify potential IT positions that match your current skills and experience while also taking you in new directions. You'll learn how to sustain your IT career over the long haul by keeping your skills up to date and tapping into new markets. You'll acquire the perspective you need to evaluate new opportunities and to create your own. With this book as a guide, you'll be able to effectively manage your career at each turn in the road, even as IT is constantly changing. The engines are revved, the checkered flag is waving, and it's time to get your IT career in gear.

Part I

Brave New World

In this Part

Chapter 1

· ·

Dispelling the Myths of the IT Profession

Before he even finishes responding to his morning email, Eric Chang is getting an all too familiar feeling that there just won't be enough hours in the day to accomplish all that he wants to do. With three major applications development projects on his plate, the senior associate/team leader in UBS PaineWebber's information services division has to check in with his team members, consult with mutual funds managers and stockbrokers on the data they need to give them an edge in the market, update his managers on his team's progress and troubleshoot the systems running the applications. It will be late afternoon before he does any real programming. His job is all about multitasking, and the work is all about providing UBS PaineWebber's employees with tools and information that will enable them to serve customers better than their financial services competitors can.

This is not your father's computer programmer. The days when the typical information technology professional sat in a cubicle all day hunched over a keyboard, a can of Jolt Cola and a half-eaten Twinkie within arm's reach, seem about as quaint now as a genuine whistle-stop political campaign in the mass media age. Even hard-core programmers spend only a fraction of their day actually doing hands-on development work. (See "A Day in the Life" profiles throughout this chapter.) Ideally, today's IT professional is sitting in on departmental and corporate strategy meetings, interacting with workers across the company, and forging ties with management and top executives. Even the most mundane tasks in IT are geared toward helping to create competitive advantage for the company. To succeed, an IT professional—from the lowest rungs of the rank-and-file up to the executive suite—should be as much M.B.A. candidate as technical guru.

"IT is all business; it just so happens that our toolkit has wires and buttons attached to it," says Scott Heintzeman, vice president of knowledge technologies at Carlson Hospitality Worldwide in Minneapolis, Minnesota, which owns the Radisson Hotel and TGI Friday's restaurant chains. If you want to know what the most important IT initiatives are, take a look at what the most important business initiatives are. From operations to applications development, IT professionals need to understand what's going on in their companies. If your job is monitoring system performance to make sure you don't have a major computer failure, you need to have a sense of what's at stake if the system goes down. And if you are creating or managing databases or developing applications, you must understand fundamentally what the business purpose is, or even the most elegantly written program will never catch on with its intended users.

Despite IT's connection to business initiatives and processes, the image of the geeky IT gear-head who hasn't a clue or a concern about what's going on in the rest of the company has only recently begun to change. With the much-publicized IT skills supply-and-demand gap and the rush to join the dot-comming of the universe, IT jobs have acquired a cool factor. But even in the early nineties, when the transformation of IT into a business-driven organization was already in full swing, the IT profession was often fodder for jokes.

"When I got my first job, as a mainframe production coordinator at MCI, my friends would laugh at me because I liked it," recalls Abbie Plessman, now an IT project manager at the telecommunications firm MCI WorldCom. "They thought it sounded horribly dull because they thought of me as in a cubicle by myself in front of a computer screen eight days a week. But I wasn't. I was working with teams of people and troubleshooting major problems and coordinating groups that were collaborating on solutions to the problems. It was exciting because I had the opportunity to learn something completely new and different."

Now her friends are a lot less likely to be laughing, as the supply-and-demand gap has elevated the status—and earning power—of the profession. Plessman, Chang, Heintzeman and others, in their attitude, their job descriptions, and their day-to-day accomplishments, undermine the mythology surrounding IT careers:

Myth: All IT professionals are techie gear-heads with little interest in anything outside of technology.

Myth: IT professionals possess a complete disregard for business concerns.

Myth: Once you join the ranks of IT, you'll work in solitary confinement for the rest of your life, living only for weekend movie marathons on the SCI FI Channel.

Myth: If you don't understand acronym-speak, don't even think of conversing with an IT professional.

Myth: You must have a computer science degree to get a job in IT.

A DAY IN THE LIFE OF A CIO

Scott B. Heintzeman, vice president of knowledge technologies, Carlson Hospitality Worldwide (a division of Carlson Companies), Minneapolis, Minn.

Years in IT   Full time since 1993; directly involved in IT projects since 1985; joined Carlson in 1972.

Arrives at the office   About 7:30 A.M. "I clear my voice mail in the car on the way to the office—I've usually gotten calls from Europe or Asia or calls about issues that have occurred throughout the evening."

Morning   Check email. "I usually have messages like a proposal for a new initiative—a new way to analyze data, for example—or an invitation to speak at a conference or a status report on a current project. Then, I block two hours every morning for my own work: correspondence, setting my calendar, synching up with my staff, checking projects that I want to monitor personally. Today I'm working on our five-year strategic plan and getting ready to finalize it for a presentation at our upcoming [company] conference in Hong Kong. I can only count on that first two hours for my own work, and the rest of the day is out of my hands, usually spent in various meetings—or rather, dialogue sessions. I'm constantly discussing new projects people want to consider. Today, I'll be with our company president talking about the five-year plan; last week I went with him to evaluate a company that we are considering for an acquisition. We wanted to see if there's a technology fit."

12:00 P.M.   "By now I've had three or four meetings or conference calls and have given input on a project or untangled a vendor problem. I usually have a lunch meeting or lunch on the road."

Afternoon   More meetings and conference calls. "Among my 7 direct reports, we have 15 to 20 live projects cooking, and there are always a couple that aren't going well or need extra attention. If I have a gap between meetings, I'll go back to email, voice mail, or scramble through the papers in my in-basket. I also check my stocks on the Web a couple of times a day. I have an Excite page customized to monitor two things: my personal portfolio, and also a list of suppliers and vendors I am doing business with or contemplating doing business with."

Leaves the office   About 6:00 P.M. "I usually clear my voice mail again on the way home, and I take my laptop with me to take care of some email from home—but only if my family is busy. And I'll scan the trade magazines if they're occupied. But typically I read the trades on flights—I travel about once a week."

A DAY IN THE LIFE OF A CIO

Best part of the day "My higher-energy time for creative work is the morning, and that's why I block that morning piece for things I have to accomplish."

Worst part of the day "If I get hauled into a long, tedious meeting that isn't targeted to things that make a difference—if it's not strategic and just informative. If a meeting starts gong that way, I will typically bolt."

Most stressful part of the day "Oh, heavens. One of the things that happens is I find myself switching thoughts and priorities so fast. In a given day, I might be thinking through problems in 30 or 40 significant areas. And at the end of the day, that can be quite exhausting. When I go home and my eyes are crossed, the kids know Dad had a hard day. Yesterday was tough like that, so I called my wife and said, 'When I get home, have the kids fed, and make sure their homework is done so we can all go out and practice archery in the park together, because I really need a break.' So we all went out and took a few shots at the target together."

Plessman, on all counts, defies these commonly held notions of the profession. She majored in human development at Colorado State University in Fort Collins, Colorado, with plans to be a social worker. Without any direct experience in information technology, she garnered her first job on the strength of her outgoing attitude and willingness to enter foreign territory—two essential qualities in today's business-driven IT organization. Since her initial stint as a mainframe production coordinator, she has progressed through a series of new positions, including IT college recruiting coordinator, software release manager, and, in 2000, project manager responsible for the applications that support MCI's large corporate accounts. In each position, her can-do attitude, sharp communication skills, and business savvy have been as important—if not more so—than her technical aptitude.

"With each new job I've had to learn new technical skills, but I never have to code or log onto mainframe systems," Plessman says. "Primarily, the job is based on communication. I've had to understand the business requirements plus the job that programmers and software testers have to do so I can communicate between them and department heads and vice presidents in the business units."

Not all jobs in IT are as business-oriented as Plessman's, and certainly a fair share of them are primarily technical. Networking and operations, for example, are all about keeping systems and infrastructure up and running; security-related work requires in-depth technical expertise; database administration is largely technical and, sometimes, quite solitary. And programming, once all the functional requirements are settled on and the user interface is designed, still comes down to hands-on, heads-down coding. Technical gurus—the ones you can turn to with any question and they'll have the answer, who enjoy troubleshooting systems problems and posting technical solutions and bits of code to online discussion groups—have a place in every IT organization, and that's not likely to change. But because everything that goes on in the business world today is in some way connected to information technology, the very nature of the job belies the mythology and renders it obsolete.

The IT-Business Connection

The hybrid professional who possesses IT, business, and communication skills, who can arrive at creative solutions to problems and turn abstract ideas about a business process into a system that improves and facilitates the process, is the linchpin of an IT team, the one who IT executives are clamoring to get on board. The single-minded, tunnel-visioned, techno-speaking IT staff has evolved into a constituency of multi-taskers who can move with ease from a technical task to a management meeting, from network troubleshooting to organizational problem-solving.

"What's unusual about my job are the myriad issues I deal with. I can be working on a vendor contract one minute, resolving a human resources concern the next, and fixing a technical problem the next," says Eileen Cassini, director of IT services for Harrah's Entertainment, in Memphis, Tennessee, who has been in the field for 11 years. "It runs the whole gamut, so I have to be flexible and able to drop one thing and go on to the next. That's becoming the norm for IT as we become more critical to enhancing corporate revenues."

Harrah's, which owns casinos and hotels, has made a big push over the last several years in the customer service and marketing area. In the process, Cassini and her staff have not only had to figure out how to best leverage the power of database technologies, data warehousing and data mining, customer relationship management technologies, the Internet, and more, but have also had to expand their knowledge of the gaming industry, the hotel business, their customer demographics, and consumer preferences so they can exploit the technology to further the corporate goals. "Whereas at one time our job was more about dealing with one set of end-users," Cassini says, "now we are sophisticated business people." The IT organization is the joint that connects Harrah's to its customers, and the impact of the staff's efforts is felt not just by the customer service and marketing area, but across the entire company.

A DAY IN THE LIFE OF A MIDDLE MANAGER

Eileen Cassini, director of IT services, Harrah's Entertainment, Inc., Memphis, Tenn.

Years in IT   Since 1990, after joining Harrah's.

Arrives at the office   About 7:50 A.M.

Morning   Check email. "That's also the last thing that I do before I go to bed at night. We're all pretty addicted to email, so it's not unusual to have a bunch in the morning even though I checked it late the night before, like a change notice on a system that went down overnight. Then I check voice mail, and then my calendar for the day. I deal with a lot of IT human resources [HR] issues, so my schedule usually has an HR update; a conference call about a system going to a capital [spending] committee; a negotiation with a vendor for, say, an ecommerce project. Then I start responding to day-to-day stuff, like paperwork. We're a casual environment, so even though I usually don't have back-to-back meetings, my direct reports will pop into the office to give me a heads-up on a project, or ask for advice on a promotion, or let me know we need additional contractors for something. If I have any time in between everything else, I try to take some time for strategic planning, like research for a reorganization we're doing. I try not to make the whole day just about daily productivity but also to plan for things that will move the organization forward."

12:00 P.M.   "My boss and several of my peers are in Las Vegas, so I'm often on a conference call at lunch because it's 10:00 A.M. in Vegas, and they're ready to get down to business. So I'm usually eating during the call. It's rare that I actually have a 'lunch hour.' We have virtual meetings throughout the day because we have people in five locations, and we've gotten really good at working this way."

Afternoon   "That's when a lot of urgent things usually start popping up: There's a problem with a system, and I need to approve the fix; an unanticipated teleconference with a project manager on an applications development project; or a human resources issue like confirming a salary offer or sweetening a deal."

Leaves the office   Around 6:30 P.M. "It's about a ten-hour day. And since I have no time for reading at the office, I read for about two hours at home every night: *Computerworld*, *CIO*, *Fortune*, *The Wall Street Journal*, or maybe a proposal for a new project, a capital [spending] request, or a supplier contract I need to look over."

A DAY IN THE LIFE OF A MIDDLE MANAGER

Best part of the day   "The mornings. I take the mornings before work for myself to get some exercise. I have an in-house gym."

Worst part of the day   "During the lunch period, when maybe I didn't have time to eat, and I'm hungry, and I can't get away. I'm a vegetarian, so I just can't pick up a hamburger."

Most unusual day   "The day I won our 1999 Chairman's Award. I usually read my colleagues very well, and they can't pull the wool over my eyes. But they kept the award such a secret that I was completely shocked. We were on a company-wide conference call, and when they started describing the winner, I didn't even make the connection that they were describing me. I leaned over to a coworker and asked if they were talking about a friend of ours. It was a complete surprise."

Carlson Hospitality's Scott Heintzeman marvels at how IT's involvement in the business has deepened even since he stepped into his current position in 1993. "Three or four years ago, at the beginning of the year there might be five or six IT projects that people were thinking of for the year. This year, as I swept through the company, there were 75 or 80 projects," he says. "And it's not that we haven't been deploying lots of capability all along, but that now, every single business action or piece of information people want to analyze somehow touches an IT process. And so, whether it's that HR needs a tool so they can find all the people who have XYZ skill, or the sales organization wants to analyze clients by characteristic, or marketing wants to launch an email campaign offering points-based incentives—they're all deeply dependent upon IT."

It's a far cry from his start with Carlson in 1978, when Heintzeman used his bicycle to deliver hotel linens to the housekeeping department of the company's Radisson South property. His career path within Carlson vividly illustrates how the increasing connection between business and IT has altered the profile of the IT professional. From his first inauspicious job, Heintzeman moved into hotel operations, shifting around the country opening up new hotels, establishing management procedures, and training staff. His first encounter with IT in 1985, was as a business team leader on a project to develop an automated reservation system. The company owned only two or three PCs at the time, and Heintzeman had never even used one. But he knew the hotel business, and he knew how to mobilize a team of people to forge new processes.

After getting the reservation system up and running, Heintzeman spent the next eight years with one foot in hotel operations and one foot in IT decision-making, and in 1993, Carlson saw an opportunity to unleash his dual experience in the executive IT management arena. Today he is responsible for all of Carlson Hospitality Worldwide's IT services, including its distributed global network, systems in more than 600 hotels around the world, the customer information management systems, and office automation systems.

"Over the years I had gravitated toward the IT area because I enjoy organizing people and issues and solving problems through better processes and organization," Heintzeman explains. "And today, IT is at the center of those opportunities. The common denominator between my early career and my work in IT is that I still enjoy finding problems and making things better."

Diversity Counts

Heintzeman's job, like Cassini's, Plessman's, and Chang's, is hardly solitary, nor is it confined to IT or submerged in a world of arcane acronyms. The emphasis on business-focused problem-solving traverses all jobs in IT and inherently demands IT professionals who are multifaceted, possessing a diversity of experience and skills. The more you exercise both sides of your brain, the better positioned you'll be to reap the rewards of the IT profession, notes Christopher Smith, chief information officer (CIO) of furniture retailer HomeLife Furniture Corporation. Smith has been known to hire jazz musicians and master chess players; to him, the most appealing IT job candidates are those who have immersed themselves in a hobby outside of technology because it shows they regularly exert the right brain/left brain connection.

"I need people who can take abstract thoughts about what people are trying to achieve, where they want the business to go, and turn those thoughts into something systematic and process-oriented that fits into the [IT] architecture that we're putting together," explains Smith, whose hobby is restoring old houses. Smith pursued a three-pronged degree in college, encompassing business, IT, and philosophy. Of the three, he says philosophy has been the most advantageous to him on the job: "It helped with getting to the root of what you're really trying to say, to solving problems and organizing arguments."

Likewise, Frank Stolze, former chief technology officer at e-tailer iBeauty.com in New York and now an independent consultant, studied physics as an undergraduate. He earned an M.S. in Computer Science afterward but says physics has been a beneficial backdrop for his IT career: "You get the grand picture in understanding how different things relate to each other."

A DAY IN THE LIFE OF A PROJECT MANAGER

Abbie Plessman, project manager for development and testing of internal applications to support large corporate customers, MCI WorldCom, Colorado Springs, Colo.

Years in IT   Since 1995.

Arrives at the office   Between 7:00 and 8:00 A.M.

Morning   "I get in early so I can feel prepared for whatever will be beating down my door later on. As a project manager, every day is different. Once I've checked my email and voice mail, from there it's a free-for-all. I always have ongoing projects and daily meetings, but most every day is driven by the previous day's events or something completely unexpected. That's what makes it fun for me. I usually have seven different projects, so I have a lot of status reports to get out and my own staff meetings—lots of meetings, conference calls, informal discussions in people's cubes to find out what's going on with part of a project. And lots of fire-fighting—like when end-users decide to give us new functionality requirements a week before we're due to roll out a new system. I have to mitigate the risks of making those changes to our users and to the software release days before implementation. In IT we can't always change things at the drop of a hat."

12:00 P.M.   "I tend to eat lunch at my desk while I respond to email, catch up on voice mails, and prepare for my afternoon meetings. Maybe once a week I head out with friends to grab a bite offsite."

Afternoon   Almost identical to the morning. "As a project manager, you have a lot of accountability and responsibility. I'm the single point of contact that anyone outside of my team comes to with questions, issues, information, and documentation. I'm like a filter for my developers and testers so they can concentrate on doing their jobs and not have to deal with all the day-to-day issues. I field all the questions for them so they can make sure the deliverables don't slip."

Leaves the office   Between 4:00 and 6:00 P.M. "Occasionally I log on to email at night, and typically I do some catch-up work on the weekends, like finishing a status report or preparing documentation."

Best part of the day   "Knowing when I leave the office that I helped to make people's jobs better, that I increased the quality of our output, and that I did the best I could with the deadline pressures, etc., that I had that day."

Worst part of the day   "When I have eight hours worth of meetings and I get a phone call from an executive who needs answers to a question ASAP. It totally throws off my whole day."

Five-year plan   "I'd love to be the manager for a group of IT project managers. And I love the telecommunications industry. It's fascinating because companies rely on their phone lines, Internet access, pagers, cell phones, email. It's a need that will never go away."

Companies are so eager to hire well-rounded, big-picture-oriented, hybrid IT staff members that they often go to extraordinary lengths to find them, even devising special internal training programs to create them. The Tribune Company, in Chicago, started the Technology Leadership Development Program, a two-year business rotation program designed to produce up-and-comers who can bring technology skills to business projects and business savvy to IT projects. It works like a highly competitive "fellowship," taking only two or three people a year from a pool of 25 or 30 internal applicants, and rotating them through a series of three-to-six month projects in each of Tribune's divisions, including publishing, broadcast, and interactive. "It's like I earned a Master's degree in Tribune," says Nedra Plonski, who became a project manager in Tribune Media Services after completing the rotation in 1999. Today she's director of technology for the Tribune Media Services Multimedia group, within the publishing division. "It really opened my horizons, giving me a chance to keep my technology focus but learn more about the business issues."

UnitedHealth Group, in St. Paul, Minnesota, created the Learning Institute, an in-depth training program that accepts 50 to 80 non-IT people a year, both from within the company and without, and turns them into IT professionals. "We're creating IT people from scratch, like in the olds days," says Paul LeFort, UnitedHealth's former CIO and now a consultant to the company. "We're increasing the size of the gene pool instead of cannibalizing it." And by taking career changers into the Institute, United-Health churns out those elusive hybrids so critical to today's IT organization.

Entrenched IT professionals may greet the disintegration of their collective mythology with a certain amount of anxiety, finding a level of comfort in some of the misperceptions that have grown up around the IT profession. If you're an IT professional who has taken a singular, technology-oriented approach to your career, you may feel there's no clear-cut path to the challenge of acquiring a broader perspective on your role in the IT organization. If you haven't made a point of wandering beyond the IT department lately, you may feel out of touch with the new direction the profession is taking, and you may hear the death knell ringing for your career. But in reality, you're perfectly situated to take advantage of the new career opportunities emerging for hybrid IT professionals. Your breadth and depth of technology experience is irreplaceable and desired as much as business expertise, problem-solving, and verbal skills.

You can leverage that experience by identifying your personal interests and marrying those with your technology expertise. Fusing the two together creates opportunities to carve out an entirely new IT career path for yourself. Not only can you affect personal change and growth, but you're also likely to find that your individual contributions within your IT organization will have more resonance. And if you're seeking to change employers, with subject-matter expertise, you'll be better positioned to garner a new job.

Consider Jerry Weinberger, a Visual Basic programmer with a 20-year IT career behind him. Weinberger, who came up through the mainframe ranks after earning an M.F.A. in Creative Writing in 1977, was interested in writing a mystery novel. To help lend an authentic voice to his storyline, he signed up for a couple of criminology classes at John Jay College of Criminal Justice in New York to gain some background on law enforcement. To write the coursework off on his taxes, he chose classes that had an IT angle; he found them so compelling that he ended up enrolling for a degree.

In 1993, he earned an M.A. in Criminal Justice with a specialization in Information Technology, and he later parlayed that into a senior systems analyst position with the New York City Department of Correction. "It wasn't a plan—I just thought it would be interesting," Weinberger recalls. A change in management at his former employer, the NYC Department of Transportation, inspired him to go job hunting, and he was perfectly poised for the opening at the Correction Department. Weinberger believes he is more the rule than the exception, that what makes IT interesting, exciting, and successful is the multiplicity of the people involved in it. "IT pros are like taxi drivers: You never know who's going to be behind the wheel," he observes. "A salmagundi of people go into this profession."

Changing Stereotypes

The irony of workplace stereotypes is that they tend to arise from some degree of reality. Before the personal computer, very few workers outside of the IT department (or "MIS," as it was usually called in the pre-PC era, for "management information systems") had any idea what was going on down in the data center. And the data center guys—for they were most likely to be guys—liked it that way. They comprised a unique breed, set apart from the rest of the company, operating the big corporate mainframes, processing requests for data, coding, and running batch jobs. But as personal computers pushed more power—and technology—to the desktop, the MIS staff had to come out of the data center and face their users head on. The more users were able to do with their personal computers, the more demands they made for additional functionality. Why wait two weeks to get last month's sales data from an MIS report when they should be able to access the database themselves?

It made sense, but when the two groups would meet to hash out requirements, it was like the Tower of Babel: They seemed to be speaking different languages. If a marketing exec wanted to know how to get demographic information on all customers in the Pacific Northwest who had bought brand X shoes in the last 12 months, the MIS reply might have something to do with SNA connectivity snafus and DB2 errors. From the mid-eighties, the pressure was on MIS to evolve into a strategic partner focused on the organization it served, and as it began to meet that challenge, the management information systems nomenclature gave way to the more expansive information technology. IT professionals evolved into business professionals, and business end-users became more astute on the technology side. Nevertheless, the stereotype lingered of the *Star Trek* aficionado who speaks only in acronyms, nervously adjusting his pocket protector.

In the last several years, that has begun to change. As IT professionals' star has risen in the workplace, so has their presence in the popular media. The dot-comming of the world has gone a long way to making IT cool, hip, and happening, and a new image has emerged in everything from print ads to television commercials to prime-time programming to the movies. While 1984's comedy *Revenge of the Nerds* portrays young technologists as geeky but lovable misfits, 2000's *Charlie's Angels* portrays a gifted programmer as a worldly—if misguided and villainous—hip dude who wins the affections of ultra-chic Drew Barrymore. Even though the character of Eric Knox proves to be the bad guy, he isn't an object of ridicule.

The voice-over in a commercial for CDW, the computer equipment and supplies marketer, trumpets, "A typical day in the life of the IT manager..." and features the IT manager as a much-in-demand leader, pursued by clamoring employees who "want everything and want it now." An ad for the computer jobs site Techies.com portrays a database administrator on a scale with rock stars, a corporate celebrity deserving of red-carpet treatment. Even daytime television got into the act; the soap opera "All My Children" featured a story line in 2000 about a hunky young dot-com entrepreneur trying to take his nascent company public. The fact that IT pros have evolved to the point that they are featured as major characters in the mass media signals a major shift in the public's perception of the IT profession.

It's a natural evolution for IT pros to garner such attention in the culture, notes Steve Hayden, vice-chairman of ad agency Ogilvy & Mather, in New York, who was the copywriter for the infamous 1984 Macintosh commercial that aired during the Super Bowl. As creative director for IBM's e-business advertising campaign, Hayden has made his own contribution to the changing image of IT professionals. A 1999 series of ads featured IT pros as cool cucumbers, throwing the spotlight on the helpdesk guru, the Internet security analyst, and the network administrator on the job in real-life situations. "It's a lot different than when we made the 1984 Macintosh commercial," Hayden says. "Then IT people were invisible or perceived as a priesthood sort of worshipping the air-conditioned mainframe. And now they're showing up—mostly as heroes, sometime as villains—because they are the most important purchasing influence. If your brand doesn't rank with that group, you won't go anywhere."

Hayden likens the emergence of IT pros as ordinary Joes in the media to the appearance of racecar drivers, gas station attendants, auto company executives and mechanics as characters in the popular literature of the twenties. Prior to the debut of Henry Ford's Model T, the general public saw automobiles as luxuries that only the very privileged could afford. With the mass-produced, lower-cost Model T, car ownership became commonplace, and the folks who worked in the industry found their place in the mass media, Hayden explains. Likewise, as PCs and the Web infiltrated the home, realistic images of IT professionals infiltrated the mass media; they earned their place in the mainstream of public consciousness. "It's totally tied to the PC revolution," Hayden says. "Computers were always objects of mystery and power, threat and promise. But now, when the technology becomes personal, the entire infrastructure supporting that becomes part of the popular culture."

Of course the glamorization of IT, in turn, has given rise to its own mythology and stereotypes. "Meet the Yetties," an article by Sam Sifton in *Talk* magazine's March 2000 issue, featured an "anthropological study of the Yettie (Young, Entrepreneurial, Tech-based)." While tongue-in-cheek ("The Yettie's political opinions are likely to be die-hard libertarian, retrofitted to allow for his inevitable amassing of wealth," and Yetties are "between the ages of 24 and 50, but are probably 28"), the article captured in broad strokes many of the hallmarks of the typical dot-com kid. The pocket protector has given way to the Palm, the Jolt Cola to a Starbucks venti skim latte, and *Star Trek* fans to *Star Wars* fans. Well, as far as stereotypes go, you could call that progress.

A DAY IN THE LIFE OF AN ENTRY-LEVEL IT STAFFER

Eric Chang, senior associate/lead developer for three web-based applications, UBS PaineWebber, New York, N.Y.

Years in IT   Since 1997; Chang entered UBS PaineWebber's Information Services Division (ISD) Associates Program, a two-year IT training program for recent college graduates, after graduating from the State University of New York at Buffalo with a B.S. in Computer Science.

Arrives at the office   Between 8:00 and 8:30 A.M.

Morning   Check email and voice mail; scan system logs to check on jobs that ran the night before; hand off reports to manager; and scope out the day's meetings. "If I'm in the middle of a project, I try to do some development work in the mornings. If I'm in the project-planning phase, it means a lot more meetings—getting the functional requirements, meeting with end-users, doing test shots, determining hardware requirements, a range of things."

A DAY IN THE LIFE OF AN ENTRY-LEVEL IT STAFFER

12:00 P.M. "By now I've replied to email, scheduled more meetings, touched base with my team to see how our projects are going, and taken care of any hardware needs. I try to go out for lunch or go to the gym—we have one onsite—but if my day has been really busy, then I grab something downstairs and keep working at my desk."

Afternoon "I usually sit down with my team members to discuss development issues, problems, fixes. The afternoon is focused on resolutions and how we can take care of things that have come up. I spend the end of the day in development mode, using a range of tools, like Vignette, to create dynamic web pages. I look forward to that because it's a break from meetings, and I can clear my head and focus on the tasks I need to take care of."

Leaves the office Around 6:00 or 6:30 P.M. "I don't have too many late nights except toward the end of a project. When we're rolling out an application, I usually want to be there for support issues and anything that comes up.

Best part of the day Between 2:00 and 4:00 P.M., "when I have a list of problems that have occurred, and I'm just fixing them. That brings joy to me, knowing that I accomplished something for the day. For example, recently we had an in-house data feed—of financial reports, statistics, stock trends, etc.—that was failing. It's critical to our brokers and mutual fund managers, and we had to fix it because it loads 800 documents a day to our web servers. There was a database lock on one of the tables, so I had to work with our database administrators [DBAs], and we had the information loaded in a matter of hours."

Worst part of the day "Feeling like there aren't enough hours in the day to get everything done. I'm trying to be ambitious and move myself up the ladder, so I have a tendency to feel like I haven't gotten enough done even when I've probably gone beyond the call of duty."

Five-year plan "Hopefully, a VP of some sort of leading-edge development for web-based mobile/wireless environments, getting a handle on the latest technologies."

Chapter 2

· ·

Ten-Plus Applications that Shook the World

To understand where the IT profession is going in the future, it's worth taking a look back at the innovations that have brought us to where we are today. While the profession is relatively young in the big scheme of things—the first electronic computer, the ENIAC, made its debut on February 14, 1946—it has come a long way in a short time. In 50-plus years, it has developed from a profession with no organizational models, few formal job titles, and a fly-by-the-seat-of-your-pants approach to getting the job done to one that drives the economy and creates new functional roles and career opportunities with each new innovation. As new technologies—from mainframes to PCs to networks to the Internet—have been applied to solving business problems, the IT profession has steadily progressed and grown in stature. Today, IT is an integral part of business strategy; IT professionals have marched out of the data center to the front lines, becoming key contributors to gaining competitive advantage, finding and serving customers, lowering costs, improving business processes, and driving markets.

David Allison, an IT historian and chairman of the Information Technology and Society department at the Smithsonian Institution's National Museum of American History, sees three major waves of innovation since the debut of the ENIAC. First, IT was applied mainly to making business operations more efficient. Next, companies started to automate their databases of information and come up with industry-specific applications. And in the current wave, IT is being taken to the next level with customer-specific applications of technology. "It's not just one story, it's a whole lot of stories depending on the cost and power of technology at any given time," Allison says. "And within each wave you see different stages of innovation."

The IT innovations of the past have not only changed the businesses that came up with them, they've had a subsequent long-range impact on how we live and work today. In a first-wave innovation, on the night of the 1952 presidential election, television network CBS used the Univac, the offspring of the ENIAC, to project that Eisenhower would defeat Stevenson. The application itself wasn't earth-shaking, but the appearance of a computer in a significant national news broadcast was. It captured the imagination of the American public and signaled that computers could be applied to everyday events. (Moreover, reviewed in light of the 2000 presidential race between Al Gore and George W. Bush, it stands as one of the more ironic stories in the intersection of technology and politics.) Eight years later, in a development that heralded the transition from the first wave to the second, American Airlines shook up the airline business and created an indelible impact on the future of computing and consuming when it created the Sabre reservation system and gave birth to online transaction processing. A decade later, with the second wave well underway, a consortium of executives from supermarkets and food manufacturers spearheaded the development of the Universal Product Code (UPC)—commonly referred to as the bar code. What started in 1970 simply as an industry-wide move to cut costs led to an IT innovation that laid the foundation for lasting change in how companies move products and consumers acquire them. The UPC, in turn, gave rise to the third wave of IT innovation, enabling companies to collect and analyze sales and marketing data in ways that are still changing the way they relate to customers. As companies tie their businesses to the Internet, the humble bar code and the applications that have grown from it are at the heart of today's mission-critical systems for customer relationship management (CRM) and supply-chain management (SCM).

By looking back, we get a glimpse of the opportunities that lie ahead for IT professionals to shake things up even further, to make a difference to their companies and, ultimately, to how we will live and work in the future. Collectively, these innovations and the ones that built on them bring to light the momentum IT can create. They show that IT, smartly applied, can take on a life of its own, shaking our world and taking us places we never dreamed of.

Election Night, 1952: CBS and the "Electric Brain"

In one of the earliest uses of computers for competitive advantage, the broadcast news team at CBS tied its fortunes to information technology on election night 1952 when it became the first TV network to use a computer to calculate election returns. The Univac I was the only commercially available computer at the time, and the public had taken to calling it the "Electric Brain." CBS's use of it to score the outcome of the presidential race between Adlai E. Stevenson and Dwight D. Eisenhower on November 4, 1952, marked an early collaboration between non-technical users and a computer programmer to create an application to meet a business objective. It also proved to be an early lesson in the garbage-in, garbage-out syndrome.

The news team at CBS, led by Sig Mickelson, then director of news and public affairs, got acquainted with the Univac in August 1952 after Paul Levitan, CBS director of special events, lunched with a public relations rep from the Philadelphia-based Eckert-Mauchly division of Remington Rand. In the hyperbole that still distinguishes computer industry PR today, the rep told Mickelson the Univac could predict the outcome of the election. Ever the skeptical newsman, Mickelson said in a 1999 interview that he knew *that* wasn't possible, but he realized that the computer could enable CBS reporters to analyze the returns more quickly than their competition.

And that could put CBS ahead of its network rivals. In his 1989 book, *From Whistle Stop to Sound Bite: Four Decades of Politics and Television* (Prager Publishers, New York), Mickelson, who died in 2000, wrote, "If ... the program was properly written, we could in all probability announce the winner of the presidential race while our competitors were still floundering in a sea of unsorted data." Moreover, he thought the Univac could give CBS's coverage "the additional top spin that we needed to build our ratings to a level that would permit us to fight it out on even ground with the (at that time) far larger NBC."

With only three months to go to the election, the news team began working with Max Woodbury, a mathematician from the University of Pennsylvania, to gather the data and write the program that would make the Univac tick. Even in 1952, the great divide between a user's grand vision and what programmers can manage to produce in a short period of time was already emerging. Mickelson had wanted to collect historical data on 40 key voting precincts around the country that could be matched against the incoming 1952 returns. He was hoping to detect and analyze regional shifts in voting patterns since the previous elections. While such an application is commonplace today, "in 1952 it was a matter of plowing new ground in a time span that was too brief to allow it," Mickelson wrote in his book.

For starters, the national picture had already changed a lot since the 1948 elections, so it would be hard to give the Univac useful data for an apples-to-apples comparison. Americans had moved out of the cities into the suburbs, and the population shift would make the old data somewhat unreliable. Poll closing times had changed. In the end, all they had to go on were the 1944 and 1948 election returns reported by the wire services on the half-hour, and just getting those together into a useful database was a mountain of work.

The news team gave Woodbury what they could, including acetate disks of CBS's coverage of the prior two elections and the half-hour wire reports that they managed to secure from Associated Press and United Press (now UPI). Woodbury devised an "If X, then Y," program for the Univac to run against the data. The plan was that every half hour, he would feed the Univac the old returns and the new returns, run the program, and produce odds on the election results.

By the night of November 4, Woodbury and John Mauchley, the co-inventor (with J. Presper Eckert) of the ENIAC and the Univac I, were ensconced in the computer room at Remington Rand's Madison Avenue headquarters. Mickelson, legendary CBS news anchor Walter Cronkite, and CBS reporter Charles Collingwood, who would report on the Univac's analysis, were stationed several blocks away in the CBS newsroom in New York's Grand Central Station. Little did they know that not only would political history be made that night, but computing history as well.

Illinois governor Adlai Stevenson had been the front-runner in all of the preelection polls. But as early as 8:30 that night, with Woodbury feeding the initial returns into the Univac, the odds jumped to 100:1 in Eisenhower's favor. Mickelson, who was producing the CBS coverage, was in a quandary: Should CBS report what the computer was projecting even though it ran counter to popular expectations? It looked like his grand idea was a bust. Although they had all been confident that the Univac would come up with accurate projections, "because of the opinion polls, Woodbury had been pretty well convinced that Stevenson would run closer, if not win, so he was concerned about the odds that showed up," Mickelson recalled in 1999. He opted not to report the 100:1 odds, and asked Woodbury to run a new set of numbers. Woodbury did, and the odds came down to a more reasonable 8:7 for an Eisenhower victory. About 9:00 P.M., Collingwood broadcast those results to CBS viewers.

That's when the garbage-in, garbage-out syndrome came into play. Woodbury discovered that in the second set of numbers he crunched, he'd accidentally added a 0 to Stevenson's total number of votes in New York State. He corrected the error, and the odds leapt back to 100:1 on Eisenhower. "It isn't the machine—it's the mathematician writing the problem, which any computer specialist knows is the weakness," Mickelson said. "The machine isn't weak—it just does what it's told to do based on the information that it's given."

The Univac did, in fact, give CBS a competitive edge: CBS was the first network to call the race, and the odds generated by the Univac were nearly dead-on. The official electoral vote was 442 for Eisenhower, 89 for Stevenson. Based on the first set of numbers Woodbury ran, the Univac had predicted electoral totals of 438 to 93—an error rate of less than 1 percent. On the popular vote, the Univac came within 3 percent of the official vote totals. NBC, which had featured an electronic calculator dubbed "Mike-Mono-Robot" to analyze the raw numbers, eventually predicted Eisenhower's victory about three hours before Stevenson conceded. ABC had merely posted election results on a blackboard, according to an article in the *Journal of Communication*, "Broadcasting National Election Returns, 1952–1976," by Thomas W. Bohn (Autumn 1980, pgs. 140–153).

Q&A WITH WALTER CRONKITE: ELECTION NIGHT, 1952

How did you feel about using the Univac for election-night coverage?

The whole idea was fascinating, but slightly appalling. We thought of it more as a gimmick than a tool that would become essential to our coverage. We went to Philadelphia, and here was this computer the size of a living room, and I found it fascinating and mystifying and over my head, but very interesting of course.

The earliest admonition we had about the computer was to quit using the phrase "electric brain." The folks in Philadelphia tried to convince us that the Univac didn't have a brain, and that whatever we fed into it would determine what we got out of it.

What do you recall about the reports from that night?

It was decided that the manner in which we would use the machine would be in betting quotations on what the results would be, which in retrospect is a ridiculous way to perform. As it turned out, the election was a runaway, and the odds immediately jumped to 100:1 and stayed there, so there was no mystery in the numbers and no sense of what their deeper meaning could be.

When those 100:1 odds first came back, I recall they said we couldn't go with that. So they fed it some different numbers to get the odds down to something more reasonable, and in the end, 100:1 turned out to be more accurate. Our opinion about it was significantly influenced by the [recalculation of the results], and that took a lot of the seriousness out of it.

Did you have any sense that CBS's use of the Univac that night would have a lasting impact on election reporting?

I don't think any of us saw the long shadow in the newsroom at all. There was some fascination over the possible uses of the computer in the future, but the way it was being used, it didn't strike us as being that practical, I don't think. We saw it as an added feature to our coverage that could be very interesting in the future, and there was a great deal of pride that we had this exclusively. But I don't think that we felt the computer would become predominant in our coverage in any way.

 NOTE *An edited version of this interview appeared in* Computerworld *on January 25, 1999.*

Later, some viewers criticized the broadcast, and the use of the Univac, for predicting the election's outcome before the polls closed, Mickelson recalled in his book. And reporter James "Scotty" Reston of *The New York Times* created a series of tongue-in-cheek columns in which the narrator consulted an omniscient "Uniquac" on matters of public policy. But by the 1956 elections, all three networks were in the computer game, and from there on out, computers would forever change the way we interpret the world around us.

1960: Automated Reservation Systems Take Flight

Anyone who uses the Internet to make airline, car rental, or hotel reservations—or in fact, to make any purchase at all—owes a debt of gratitude to an enterprising group of American Airline employees and IBM programmers who in 1960 began collaborating on the first computerized transaction processing system. Online reservation systems and, in a larger sense, ecommerce, are the direct descendents of American's original Sabre airline reservation system; that system's debut in October 1962 heralded the age of online transaction processing (OLTP) and ushered in a new era in the IT profession.

Like many early commercial IT innovations, the Sabre technology grew out of a Cold War initiative by the Department of Defense with MIT, IBM, and others dubbed Semi-Automatic Ground Environment (SAGE). From its work on the SAGE project, IBM had developed processor technology and mass-storage systems that would support real-time computing, and the company was looking for what today might be called a "killer app," a way to exploit the technology in the commercial data processing market. The seeds for Sabre were planted during a fortuitous meeting—on an airplane, fittingly enough—between C.R. Smith, president of American Airlines, and Blair Smith (no relation), a pioneering IBM marketing executive. When the two found themselves seated next to each other on a cross-country flight, their talk turned to how computers might change the paper-intensive, largely manual process of reserving and issuing a plane ticket. Computers, they speculated, might reduce the work and the error rate.

American already had applied some technology to the reservations process. In 1946, it inaugurated the Availability Reservisor, an electro-mechanical device that could monitor seat inventory and flight information, but could not book a seat. In 1952, it upgraded that system with a random-access memory drum and arithmetic capabilities, creating what it called the Magnetronic Reservisor, which in addition to checking seat availability, could reserve a seat or cancel a reservation. Nonetheless, the reservations process was still primarily manual, requiring a string of phone calls, teletype messages, and paperwork to book flights. The error rate was 8 percent, recalls Cliff Taylor, who worked in American's reservations department in the days of the Reservisor and became one of four key functional designers on the Sabre project. The meeting between the two Mr. Smiths led to a joint IBM/American study, released in 1954, on the feasibility of further automating the process. Five years later, at the end of 1959, American gave the Sabre project clearance for takeoff, and early in 1960, American set off on the first leg of what would be a two-year effort to get Sabre off the ground.

To company outsiders—and even to some within American Airlines—the idea of spending millions of dollars on a computer system that could otherwise be spent on, say, a fleet of jets, seemed preposterous at the time. (The investment in Sabre's original development and deployment was somewhere between $40 million and $60 million, Taylor says. That's somewhere between $194 million and $285 million today, based on inflation rates.) But neither American nor its reservations employees were deterred by conventional industry wisdom. When the call went out for internal recruits who might be interested in working on such a project, a whopping 650 people applied for the handful of jobs.

Taylor had been tapped to help put together a team for the project, a formidable task considering that programmers weren't readily available off the street. The first computer science degree program was still two years off—it would be inaugurated at Purdue University in 1962—and the relatively small number of programmers at the time were employed either by the handful of computer companies or highly technical companies like aeronautics firms. There weren't even any models for who made a good applications developer. Taylor ultimately decided to hire in his own image. He was an old pro in the reservations department, and he logically intuited that the best folks for the job would be those who knew how the old reservation process worked and who would ultimately be using the system once it was finished. He reasoned that you probably couldn't train a bunch of programmers, in a timely fashion, in the ins and outs of putting passengers on airplanes, but you could train airline employees to program.

Taylor says he wasn't surprised by the applicants' enthusiasm for the project. Computers were still commonly referred to as "electronic brains," and public curiosity was still high, driven by effective government publicity, Cold War propaganda, increasing news coverage, and movies like the 1957 Spencer Tracy-Katharine Hepburn romantic comedy *Desk Set*. "Typically, the population of reservations departments are relatively youthful—they were old enough to have experience but young enough to be bold and want to go out into this field that was brand new to everybody," says Taylor, now retired. "The airline business was still a very romantic business to be in, and to be in computers on top of that was having our cake and eating it too. So there was an exuberance and excitement about it, and not much thought about failure."

Q&A WITH CLIFF TAYLOR: INVENTING THE SABRE SYSTEM

What kind of pressure were you under? What would be the consequences if the project failed?

It never occurred to anybody that the project might fail. That sounds ridiculous, but I don't ever remember discussing failure. We never even considered it. We were under great schedule pressure … from the user community and corporate management. They were nervous about all the money being spent—a Boeing 707 was about $4.5 million, so $p60 million was a lot to spend … on some mysterious boxes that would sit in a room somewhere. So a lot of people were convinced we were loonies, but we were supremely confident because we didn't know any better.

What was the day-to-day atmosphere like?

It was exciting and fun. There were long periods of time when it was just your routine going into the office, but always there was an anticipation that we were doing something special and doing things no one else was doing. A lot of people [at other companies] were getting in touch with us and asking questions, so there was an ongoing high from all of that.

Everyone was pulling in the same direction—there were no factions like you might have in a typical bureaucratic office. There were arguments and debates about concepts and issues, but we never had any doubts about where we were headed.... So it was a relaxed atmosphere, and we had lots of long, leisurely cerebral discussions about how the system ought to work. One of our favorite pastimes was playing chess—there was a lot of chess going on. And a lot of Hearts. It was the most laid-back atmosphere I've ever worked in.

What was one of the big challenges you thought you'd never get past?

I can think of one that typifies the best part of that time. Sabre was an event-driven system from the start, and the fundamental motivating event is the incoming phone call from a customer who wants to make a reservation. But sometimes, in the world of reservations, there are other motivating events—like another airline changes its schedule, and a passenger whose flight originates on American and transfers to that other airline's flight has to be notified. We had to sort out how to deal with that, and we had a whole series of conversations for a month trying to figure it out. In retrospect, it's simple, but at the time, we had to invent a solution.

Q&A WITH CLIFF TAYLOR: INVENTING THE SABRE SYSTEM

That was eventually solved by three of us—me, Dick Casey [Taylor's counterpart on the IBM side of the team], and Charlie Ammann, who ran the original research project and who was a dear man and a mentor for me. We were sitting around this one desk, with all our feet propped on it, leaning back in our chairs with our arms behind our heads, and 17 cups of coffee all over the place, and we were just musing on how to make this work. And one of us started off with an idea, and the next person said, "Yeah, then we could do this," and the next person added to that, and so forth, and in five minutes we had solved this problem that we'd been working on for a month.

It was sheer pleasure—the intellectual interaction of solving problems, of mapping out a solution that would be embodied not just in Sabre; some also ended up being fundamental to the development of ... transaction processing systems today.

Taylor ended up interviewing and testing all 650 applicants for the job. "We wanted people who understood the job to be done and who had the intellect to see around the corner—who could see how to use a new tool to do an old job," he recalls, sounding like a twenty-first-century IT manager. For the initial ramp-up, Taylor hired ten American Airline employees whom he sent for training in the 7090 Assembler language, plus some experienced programmers from aerospace and defense firms. (Their average annual salary was between $8,000 and $9,000, equivalent to somewhere between $45,000 and $51,000 today; upper-level managers on the project earned about $20,000, or about $113,000 today.) They would develop the high-level specifications for the various functions Sabre would perform, and a team of IBM and American programmers would do the actual hard-core coding.

Besides having no models for how to select a good programmer in those days, Taylor notes that neither were there widespread models for the process of developing such a massive application. "We had to invent all the techniques and approaches as we went along," he says. "No one had ever implemented a transaction-oriented system before—all the existing operating systems were based on classical batch processing." The IBM-American team fell into a rhythm of what would later be called "structured programming": Taylor and the other functional designers would write descriptions of each function the system should perform. Those descriptions were then passed over to the relevant end-user departments, such as reservations, ticketing, or terminal services, for their approval before programmers started coding any piece of the system. "We had a continual dialogue between the day-to-day users and those of us who had been until recently users, and all those functional specs got turned into program specs," Taylor recalls. "Sometimes we got into debates with them," but their approval at the start and finish of each function was key to the process, and in the long-term contributed to Sabre's longevity.

The Sabre system made a limited debut in October 1962, with a test run on terminals in Hartford, Connecticut, running off an IBM 7090 mainframe at the IBM data center in Briarcliff Manor, New York. "It was absolutely electric," Taylor says. "It was like [later] watching the first moonwalk. Everyone was holding their breath." And the system immediately crashed. But the team toiled away until Hartford was running reliably, and then slowly added more cities, a few at a time. By 1964, American had made a full cut-over to the Sabre system. The error rate in booking passengers dropped to just under 1 percent, and the company realized about a 30 percent savings in labor costs, according to Sabre, the American Airlines spin-off that now oversees the Sabre system. The present-day system, which has continued and grown out of the development that began in 1960, handles nearly 40 percent of all electronic travel reservations worldwide and gave birth to Travelocity.com, the first Internet travel site for consumers. In the first quarter of 2001, the site generated $833.6 million in travel bookings.

"When I look back on the intellectual and conceptual fingers that reached out from those sessions, it is with pleasure and humility and awe," Taylor says. "Because we were really inventing the world of computers."

1970: Step Up to the Bar Code

In Wal-Mart stores, when you need a price check on a tube of toothpaste or a bottle of detergent, there's no need to go looking for a salesperson to help you. You can just take the item to one of the small scanners located throughout the store, hold the series of black-and-white lines emblazoned on the item up to it, and voilà, you have the price. It's a convenience that we take for granted. But behind that small convenience is an IT legacy dating back to a Kroger's store in Kenwood, Ohio, circa 1970, where the first test of supermarket scanning took place. The test would precipitate the launch of an industry effort to come up with a UPC, a corresponding symbol to represent it, and a machine that could read it. And over the next 30 years, that would fundamentally change the way manufacturers, distributors, and retailers develop, sell, inventory, move, and market products of every ilk.

The Kroger test had grown out of turmoil in the supermarket business. By the late sixties, the industry's growth had hit a glacial plateau. Costs were going up, productivity had stagnated, and revenues were flat, notes Robert Aders, who was elected chairman of Cincinnati-based Kroger in 1970. (Aders later became acting Secretary of Labor in the Ford administration and is now chairman of the Advisory Board, an international consulting firm.) For the modern supermarket to survive, the chains had to cut costs and boost efficiency, and industry executives saw the checkout line as the most germane place to start. Taking a cue from the banking industry, which was starting to scan paper transactions, Kroger had joined with RCA Corporation in 1968 to codevelop a prototype scanner and a coding system that could identify products by category and price.

"We were watching for the technology to become sophisticated enough" to try using it in supermarkets, Aders says. "We did it to prove it could be done." Kroger and RCA came up with a bull's-eye-shaped code that could be read in any direction by an electronic scanner, and for the Kenwood, Ohio, test, Kroger employees affixed the bull's-eye to every product in the store. When the first customer passed through the checkout line that morning, the now ubiquitous bar code became a glimmer in the industry's eye. But there were still many hurdles to jump. Given the number of individual supermarket chains and food manufacturers, not to mention the number of products themselves, industry-wide cooperation on a universal technology was a must. It was simply impractical to permit each player to develop its own product codes, says Stephen Brown, general counsel for the Uniform Code Council and author of *Revolution at the Checkout Counter: The Explosion of the Bar Code* (1997, Harvard University Press, Cambridge, Massachusetts). The food manufacturers joined the initiative out of "the fear that they would be bombarded by requests from different supermarket chains for different coding schemes," explains Brown, who in 1970 was the lawyer for the Grocery Manufacturers of America. If that happened, "they'd have to segment their inventory to use different labels for each chain or else crowd their labels with many different symbols." Moreover, the manufacturers could become the targets of antitrust suits if their labels appeared to favor one supermarket chain's code over another's.

So a few months after the Kroger-RCA test, an historic meeting of ten CEOs (five from the supermarket chains, five from the grocery manufacturers) was held in a hotel at O'Hare Airport in Chicago, where they were presented an edict by the presidents of six industry trade groups: "Either find a common code … or tell us you can't do it," Brown recalls. Although the two industry segments were traditionally more given to sparring than cooperation, they agreed that their futures would profit from applying their combined muscle to the challenge. Within two weeks they established the Ad Hoc Committee on a Uniform Grocery Product Code, and they tapped management consulting heavyweight McKinsey & Company to helm the effort. Sub-committees set out to come up with a coding system and a symbolic representation, as well as to encourage hardware vendors to develop the scanners. As time went on, many of the executives on the committee began bringing their data processing managers into the planning process, and they became key members of the team, Brown notes.

"It has been described as the most significant development in supermarkets since the development of the supermarket," Brown says of the work that came out of the Ad Hoc Committee. "It's a model of an inter-industry project conducted by all parties where, to a remarkable extent, the parochial interests of the individual companies were put aside in looking at the benefits to the industry as a whole."

Nonetheless, we almost didn't have the bar code, Brown notes. It could have been the circle code, the bull's-eye code, the square code, or any one of about a dozen symbols taken under consideration. The bar code was submitted by IBM, and developed by George Laurer, whose work grew out of an idea patented in the forties by an earlier IBM researcher, Joe Woodland. "[Woodland] got the idea when he was lying on the beach one day making marks in the sand," Brown says, "and he had one of those 'Eureka!' moments." After a few Eureka! moments of its own, the Ad Hoc Committee released the specs for the bar code and the hardware, and NCR Corporation, the leading maker of cash registers at the time, developed the scanner. By June 1974, Marsh Supermarkets installed the NCR scanner in a store in Troy, Ohio. It was there, on June 26, that a ten-pack of Wrigley's Juicy Fruit gum was the first purchase scanned with the new technology and the UPC in place.

Even then, the future that the bar code would bring was unclear, Brown says. Few people envisioned its application outside of the grocery industry, and usage was expected to peak at 6,000 to 12,000 users. The Ad Hoc Committee had done an economic analysis, and estimated that the baseline hard savings could be as much as 33 percent, and over time the soft savings could be even higher. And yet, the larger chains like Kroger ended up holding back on their investment in the in-store systems; it turned out to be the smaller chains like Marsh, Ralph's, Pathmark, and Giant Foods that became the early adopters. The in-store systems didn't gain critical mass until about 1976, Brown notes. "I don't think we knew fully what we had in our hands," Aders adds. "We knew that the information capture component of it would be important, because we knew that was key to getting the food manufacturers on board, by making the scanned data available to them. But in terms of the full integration of systems that we have today, I think only the visionaries saw that. The rest of us were looking at the day-to-day reductions of costs."

Q&A WITH ROBERT ADERS: CREATING THE BAR CODE

What was the real driver for the development of a Universal Product Code?

Prior to that time, the growth of the industry from World War II to the early sixties was so fast—you just had to put up a good supermarket and you'd succeed. But by the late sixties we had to find ways to save money as well because of competition. So the main driver was greater efficiency, which would [be measured by] reduced labor costs and savings in inventory management costs.

The CEOs I knew by that time were starting to get into operations, especially decisions about productivity. They were looking at productivity measurements very closely—like the transaction rates at checkout. So they also saw it as a way to speed up [the checkout line] and increase accuracy. The notion of data capture and all that came along later.

In that landmark 1970 meeting, it sounds like the power of IT brought together an entire industry.

That was unique. There weren't that many people at the senior executive level who were technically competent, so that was unusual in that respect. I have been in many industry meetings where we cooperated mostly because we were under the gun. This was different— it was, "Gee whiz, here is a new technology emerging, and we want to play a part. We don't know what we're doing, but we're going to try." It was a nice feeling, but also a little scary because no one in the room had the least idea of what would happen. We knew where we wanted to go, but we didn't have a road map.

The most impressive thing to me at the time was that we all found something we could work on together, and neither side was mad, and that was unusual. Before that, there were always a lot of differences and posturing on many issues. But this was not a matter of seeing who had the most muscle. This was an industry uniting to see if all our muscle could be used on the same thing. It might have been an early recognition by the whole industry that instead of fighting for a piece of the same pie, by working together the pie could get larger.

When did you first have the sense that the potential of bar code scanning was bigger than just cutting costs and speeding up the checkout line?

When a parallel development happened ten years later—computer-to-computer ordering, or EDI [electronic data interchange]. The need for a common language was critical to that whole process. It was thought that if you could find a way to reduce all you knew about a product down to its 11-digit product code, then you would have a system that would transcend any single company's identifiers. During the previous ten years [the sixties] we had moved from an all-paper accounting system to punchcards and then to computer programming, and now we were ready for the technology that would permit the integration of all that [across the industry].

The bar code scanning systems had an immediate impact on the grocery business, and eventually they took on a life of their own, gaining momentum and clearing the way for some of the key IT innovations of the eighties and nineties. By the eighties, myriad industry alliances were underway across all segments of the economy to conduct computer-based business-to-business transactions, or electronic data interchange (EDI). In 1985, a startup ground shipping company called RPS (later acquired by FedEx and now known as FedEx Ground) began using bar codes to label its containers, and a year later, FedEx Corporation introduced a handheld bar code scanning system, dubbed the SuperTracker, that captured detailed package information. These uses of the bar code helped revolutionize the entire package transportation industry and helped forge FedEx's leadership position today. By the late eighties, Frito-Lay had embarked on developing a handheld bar code scanning system that would put just-in-time inventory management capabilities in the hands of those who were delivering its products to grocery stores, pushing decision-making out from headquarters to where it mattered most. And retailer Wal-Mart Stores has leveraged the bar code and its associated technologies to transform its entire operations, from how it works with suppliers to customizing inventory at each local store based on local buying trends to conducting all of its business-to-business transactions via EDI. The bar code's legacy has been the cornerstone of the company's success and lies at the heart of its ability to offer the pricing discounts that make it one of the world's leading retailers.

The applications developed by companies like FedEx, Frito-Lay, and Wal-Mart are just a few examples of how the UPC ushered in the third wave of IT innovation—enabling companies to gather and analyze data to identify and target customers by their brand preferences, shopping habits, demographic affiliations, and more. It has paved the way for renewed vigor in the area of managing relationships with customers.

"We were told that what we were doing could be compared to the development of computers—they were designed for a specific purpose, and they did that well. But bright people thought of uses for them that went beyond their original intent," Brown says of the UPC initiative. "And to an extent we believed that about the UPC. We foresaw that something big would happen; we just didn't know what it was."

1991: The World Gets Webbed

As discussed in Chapter 1, the IT profession took a quantum leap forward with the emergence of the personal computer and the shift of power and resources from the data center to end users. Although initially resistant to the shift, IT gradually gained more visibility as it evolved from a misunderstood cost center into a partner to the business. The transformation of the IT profession that started with the move to PCs, local area networks (LANs), and wide area networks (WANs) reached a whole new level with the arrival of the World Wide Web. The most significant IT innovation of the nineties—perhaps of the twentieth century—the Web has inextricably sealed the bond between business and information technology and raised the bar for the IT profession.

Like CBS's use of the Univac to beat the competition in calling the 1952 presidential race, American's Sabre system, and the bar code, the Web started with a practical idea that rooted, grew, and branched out. It did not, at least initially, rise from some grand vision of a new world order, nor did Tim Berners-Lee, its creator, anticipate its rapid-fire growth. Rather, the Web grew out of an attempt to solve an everyday problem, evolving from an application Berners-Lee began working on in 1980 dubbed "Enquire." As he writes in his autobiographical account, *Weaving the Web: The Original Design and Ultimate Destiny of the World Wide Web by Its Inventor* (1999, HarperCollins, New York), Enquire was Berners-Lee's attempt to keep track of the vast array of people, projects, and computers at the CERN research laboratory in Geneva, Switzerland, where he was a physicist and researcher at the time. Using Enquire, which he developed using the Pascal language, he hoped to store information about CERN's 5,000 scientists, what they were each working on, and the computers where all of their research and data resided.

Enquire worked, but it never quite satisfied Berners-Lee's ambition. The ideas behind Enquire stuck with him over the years, giving rise to the loftier idea of linking all information stored in any computer, anywhere. He believed, as he states in his book, that "...computers could become much more powerful if they could be programmed to link otherwise unconnected information." In October 1990, with CERN's support, he again took up the challenge of creating a program that would enable him to build what he envisioned as a web of information.

Using the NeXTStep development environment on a NeXT cube (a workstation developed by Steve Jobs' follow-up venture to Apple Computer), Berners-Lee began developing Hypertext Markup Language (HTML), a browser-editor to navigate the links generated with HTML, and the communications software defining the HTTP protocol and uniform resource locators (URLs). Berners-Lee had a prototype of what he now called the World Wide Web up and running on a test server by Christmas Eve of 1990, and in 1991, CERN hooked up what would become the first World Wide Web server. Within a year, the fledgling Web boasted 1 million hosts. In 1994, Berners-Lee founded the World Wide Web Consortium (W3C) to help guide the continued growth of the Web.

Q&A WITH TIM BERNERS-LEE: WEAVING THE WEB

How has the Web's growth rate, both in numbers of sites and users, measured up against your initial expectations?

I didn't have any initial expectations: no "five-year plan" for the Web revolution. But after three months of continuous 1,000 percent annual growth in the load on just the first Web server, I got used to that rate of steady explosion.

In your book, you say you have little time for the attitude that "commercially motivated material polluted the Web." What were your original expectations regarding the level of commercial activity on the Web?

The Web is universal—it allows for all forms of expression and social interaction. I didn't have any specific expectations about how much it was to be used—for commercial or any other use. For all I knew, it was going to collapse after a few months.

Cyberspace isn't a limited resource like land, which, if taken by a shopping mall, isn't available for a park. The free, the personal, and the academic sites are still there, and indeed, proliferating very much as well.

Where do you think the balance lies between commercial activity on the Web and your original motivation, as you write in your book, to enable "communication through shared knowledge…collaboration among people at work and at home"?

The balance does not have to be defined. In a balance, when commercial traffic goes up, collaborative traffic goes down. This is not the case; they are not competing. In fact, there is a huge commercial value in collaboration. The company which learns to use the Web to work together better may be the company that survives. This is true externally as well as internally. When a salesperson finds a deal with a buyer, they are working together to find a good solution to a problem, whether it is a new kitchen or an insurance policy.

When asked to define the website, hopefully the CIO will know that this is going to be a job of defining the company. It will involve internal staff areas, areas for working with partners, and external public areas, all interlinked. I used to hope that the Web would become an accurate mirror of an organization; now I realize that it is, in fact, becoming the organization, as more and more of the interactions which define a company actually happen on the Web.

 NOTE *Excerpted from an interview that appeared in* Computerworld *on October 18, 1999.*

Berners-Lee's work wasn't so much revolutionary as a new fusion of many ideas that had existed for a long time. The roots of the Web date back to the seminal 1945 essay "As We May Think" by computer pioneer Vannevar Bush, who wrote of the memex, a personal information "device in which an individual stores all his books, records, and communications, and which is mechanized so that it may be consulted with exceeding speed and flexibility." Influenced by Bush, in 1965, Ted Nelson, a radical thinker who was among the first to advocate the notion of computers for the masses, coined the term *hypertext* to describe an intuitive system of navigating through information stored on computers. And a few years later, Douglas Engelbart, inventor of the mouse, proposed in the late sixties that hypertext could be used as a tool for collaborative work. With the advent of the Internet—which launched in 1969 as Arpanet, a project of the federal government's Advanced Research Projects Agency to connect government and academic computers first in the United States and later worldwide—the necessary distributed network foundation was in place to tie all of these ideas together and turn the notion of linking not just computers, but information, into a feasible reality.

"I happened to come along with time, and the right interest and inclination, after hypertext and the computer had come of age," Berners-Lee writes in his book. "The task left to me was to marry them together." That marriage transformed the Internet from a research tool accessible only to those with the technical know-how to exploit it into a digital realization of Vannevar Bush's information appliance readily accessible to the masses. As the PC had pushed computing from the main-frame to the desktop, the World Wide Web pushed information and communication from corporate corridors into the homes of Joe Q. Public, and in so doing, fueled a new revolution in IT.

Building on the innovations that preceded it, companies are leveraging to bring a whole new dimension to their relationships with customers, suppliers, and employees. They can solicit real-time feedback about their products, tap into the consumer consciousness, sell merchandise without boundaries, and even customize product offerings for individual customers. Within a very brief time, the Web has profoundly changed how companies, and individuals, conduct their day-to-day business. And with society's increased reliance on the Web for information, transactions, and communication, the impact that IT professionals can make in the course of a career appears as limitless as the Web itself.

"I don't think the future has ever looked better," says Mark Cutsforth, chief technology officer of SPACE.com, based in New York's Silicon Alley. "If the Web has done anything, it has gotten many more people involved with computers on a daily basis, and leading from that, regardless of any [market] correction on the horizon, the landscape has been permanently changed. Everywhere you look, there will be IT in one form or another."

The applications of IT discussed here are certainly not the only ones that shook the world over the last 55 years. But they are representative of how IT professionals, with a little ingenuity, creativity, and chutzpah, can put their skills to work to have a profound impact on their fellow employees, their companies, and even society at large. Who could ask for a better profession than that?

Chapter 3

The House that IT Built

Deciding to pursue a career in IT begets a number of subsequent choices. Technology touches all aspects of business today, creating myriad doorways into the house that IT has built. Depending on your skills, the options for a career in IT are essentially boundless and can be shaped as much by your interests and work style as by your prior experience. You can take a well-defined role within a large corporate IT organization or be a jack-of-all trades in a small startup; serve external customers and internal users alike by going with an application service provider (ASP) or an Internet service provider (ISP); or go the consulting route as an employee of a Big 5 consulting firm or as a sole proprietor. Each IT environment offers its own unique rewards and has its own drawbacks to weigh as you choose the type of organization that's right for you.

Corporate IT Organizations

It's nearly impossible to imagine a company that could operate today without an internal IT organization. Every so often, reports emerge from market research firms and the halls of academia sounding the death knell for internal IT. But even with consulting companies, outsourcers, and ASPs all offering to take the IT workload off of companies whose core business is manufacturing cars or selling televisions, the corporate IT organization remains a thriving entity.

The simple truth is that even if a company opted not to own any of the hardware or software that ran its operations, it would still need IT leaders and project managers just to run the relationships with all the external service providers and to research the best solutions for a company's business needs. And some applications are so critical to a company's position in its industry that it wouldn't consider placing them in someone else's hands. What responsible retailer, for example, would try to get by without a customer relationship management system? It's safe to say that corporate IT is here to stay.

That said, it's worth noting that many significant companies operate with very small internal IT organizations or don't have one at all. Elvis Presley Enterprises (EPE), in Memphis, Tennessee, manages the estate of the King of Rock and Roll, runs Graceland, and oversees all licensing of his likeness, recordings, and films. That's a massive undertaking, and one that is information-intensive. Nevertheless, EPE outsources most of its information-technology-related activities, from the production and hosting of its website to the development and management of its call center and reservation system to its catalog sales and fulfillment systems. The U.S. Space and Rocket Center in Huntsville, Alabama, which runs such high-tech-oriented activities as Space Camp and the Aviation Challenge, only established a formal IT department in 1997, after 27 years in operation. Nonprofit corporations are nearly always likely to get by with as few IT professionals on-staff as possible, relying instead on tech-savvy workers or volunteers. And most startups, even in the high-tech industry, usually rely on workers to wear their own IT hats.

For the most part, however, corporate IT organizations are a critical part of most larger companies, and they offer an array of career opportunities. You might start out as a database administrator, get involved on a data warehouse project, move into data mining and analysis, and then branch out into the overall data architecture. The possibilities for sustained career development are best within companies where the overall IT mission is aligned with business strategy, and the focus is on bringing technology solutions to bear on business problems and objectives. A corporate IT organization that moves forward without any connection to the core business that it serves is one that will not be very highly valued and is a prime candidate for an outsourcing arrangement.

Internal IT organizations are generally organized into three basic functions:

► Applications development, which creates the software programs—or customizes purchased software—to support the day-to-day running of the business, competitive advantage, and strategic direction.

► Networking and infrastructure, which comprises implementing and supporting all the hardware and software used to interconnect the organization and support the flow of information across it.

► Operations and end-user support, which manages the data center, the call center, the helpdesk, and other behind-the-scenes functions.

Other key IT areas, which may be broken out into their own departments or operate as subgroups of a larger department, include web development and ecommerce, database development and administration, security, training, and IT research and development. Each IT segment must work in concert with the others, and IT staff members across all segments work closely with each other as well as with business end-users.

Because they cover so much terrain, internal IT departments make good starting points for entry-level IT professionals, who often get to rotate through several different assignments in their first couple of years on the job. They are also a logical starting point for career-changers who want to make a move into IT: What better candidate for a job developing marketing applications than someone who has had an established career in the marketing department and already knows the company's brands and product lines?

 TIP *If you're an IT professional who feels stuck in a legacy technology role in a corporate IT organization and you want to jumpstart your career in a new direction, you don't necessarily have to change employers. While IT management can be reticent to shift hard-to-replace workers into new positions, they're far more worried about losing an IT staff member who understands their business. Find a mentor in another area of your IT organization who would be willing to help you make the transition to newer technologies. You may have to show some initiative up front by doing some self-study in the new technology or by attending free seminars or user group meetings after work, but the IT supply-and-demand gap can definitely work in your favor if you're seeking a change.*

What It's Like to Work in Corporate IT

Kimberlee Sherman, director of production process services, Starbucks Coffee Co. (www.starbucks.com), Seattle, Wash.; November 1999.

TENURE Since 1992.

WHY I LIKE WORKING HERE "The pace. There's a lot of change, and that's very energizing. And I have a lot of respect for the company's values and the quality of what we do."

NUMBER OF IT EMPLOYEES 225.

TOTAL NUMBER OF EMPLOYEES 35,000 worldwide, including the cafes.

WHAT DOES YOUR JOB ENTAIL? "I'm leading a new self-managed work team that's implementing standard processes for IT project management, telecommunications, operations, and technical services."

WHAT'S UNIQUE ABOUT STARBUCKS IT? "We're a manufacturer, wholesaler, and retailer, and we have catalog and online businesses, so our systems run the gamut. We always have new requirements because the company is very entrepreneurial."

WHAT ARE YOUR MISSION-CRITICAL SYSTEMS? "POS [point-of-sale] systems in the stores; manufacturing and distribution systems at our roasting plants; and we're implementing ERP systems, including Oracle Financials and an SAP human resources system. We're taking a best-of-breed approach."

HOW DOES IT CONTRIBUTE TO THE SALE OF A BAG OF COFFEE BEANS? "It starts with tracking the green coffee beans all the way through the roasting process, where we have silo management systems and production control. Distribution systems track [the shipping of] the roasted beans and systems in the stores track receipt. Then the POS system feeds [sales data] back into corporate, where a replenishment order is generated. It's full circle."

DO YOU USE THE STARBUCKS STORE JARGON IN IT? "Yes, we use a lot of the same terminology in our design work. And in the IT budget...we classified the rates for contract programmers (from least expensive to most expensive) as short, tall, grande, or venti."

EXAMPLES OF IN-HOUSE IT TRAINING Unix, database query tools, AS/400.

IT CAREER PATHS "We don't have predefined career paths, but there is a lot of movement around. Before my current job, I was in the strategic architecture group."

COMPENSATION AND BONUSES "We try to keep salaries current with the market, but it's hard to do that systematically, so we have a performance-oriented spot bonus program in IT. There's an individual stock purchase plan as well as a Bean Stock program, in which everyone gets X number of options at the end of each year based on salary and company performance."

DRESS CODE Professional casual. "Nice jeans are appropriate, but not cruddy stuff."

WORK DAY "We're a 24-hour-a-day IT shop, so we have varying schedules and a flex-time program...to accommodate a life-work balance. We have a lot of workaholics who put in 12-hour days. I work a 32-hour week and am off every Friday. I wanted to spend more time at home with my kids. Anyone who works over 20 hours a week still gets full benefits, [but] your salary, bonus, and vacation are prorated."

MUST PEOPLE CARRY BEEPERS? CELL PHONES? "Yes. Anyone responsible for an application carries a pager." On-call support rotates weekly.

KIND OF OFFICES "Mostly cubes. We're in an old warehouse; it's four-and-a-half floors, and...IT is stacked on three floors. We tried to arrange each IT group with proximity to the user groups it supports."

DÉCOR "The same look-and-feel as our stores. A lot of the warehouse elements are still here, like wide-plank wood floors and [exposed] pipes. On the top floor there's a small coffee roaster. Sometimes they conduct coffee tastings up there."

FREE REFRESHMENTS "We have espresso kitchens in all corners of the building with espresso machines, and the refrigerators are fully stocked with milk and syrups and eggnog. Everyone is trained to make the beverages we sell in our stores. We have to keep people hyped up on caffeine or they'll never make it through the day."

OTHER ONSITE AMENITIES The Java Gym, a full-service gym with aerobics, kickboxing, and yoga classes, and a massage therapist once a week; mini putting greens throughout IT areas.

PERKS A free pound of coffee beans every week; a 30 percent discount in Starbucks cafes; post-project parties; quarterly "Celebrate Success" parties; monthly birthday parties.

 NOTE *An edited version of this interview appeared in* Computerworld *on December 20, 1999.*

ASPs, ISPs, and Outsourcers

While corporate IT organizations are alive and well, even the most robust are turning to service providers for certain competencies that it doesn't make sense for them to maintain in-house. Like consulting, working for an outsourcing services company, an ASP, or an ISP exposes IT professionals to a wide range of technologies and businesses, but generally without the excessive travel that consulting demands. On the other hand, the demands on IT professionals who work for service providers are intense. Because their clients are relying on them—and paying them—for 24/7 systems availability, employees can expect to be on call via pager or cell phone all the time.

Outsourcing has often been construed as a dirty word in IT professionals' vocabulary, as they frequently associate it with downsizing and layoffs. There's some truth in that: During the economic downturn of the early nineties, many IT organizations turned to outsourcing arrangements as a cost-cutting move, and internal IT employ-ees were either let go or transferred to the outsourcing firm. But a March 2000 study by the Cutter Consortium, an IT consulting, research, and training firm, found that these days the IT supply-and-demand gap is actually the biggest driver behind IT out-sourcing. In a survey of 154 companies on IT-business alignment, 29 percent said the difficulty of hiring skilled IT professionals had spurred their decision to outsource, and 20 percent said the decision resulted from a lack of skills in-house. Only 2 percent reported that downsizing was the driver.

Outsourcing arrangements usually involve farming out responsibility for an IT organization's data center and operations, maintenance of legacy applications that don't require continued updates, and sometimes integration of the legacy systems with newer systems. The term outsourcing is also sometimes used to refer to arrange-ments where an IT organization hires an outside company to do specialized applica-tions development with the intent that the IT organization will eventually take over responsibility for the finished application. The employees of the outsourced services provider may either work onsite at the client or offsite at a centralized data center maintained by the outsourcing vendor. While IT professionals who work for outsourc-ing providers will have opportunities to work with a wide variety of clients, they gen-erally work for only one client at a time. That can provide a sense of stability without sacrificing long-term diversity.

The Cutter Consortium expects outsourcing to generate over $150 billion in rev-enues by 2003, which translates into plenty of job opportunities for IT professionals who choose that path—especially those who have a background in operations, infra-structure, networking, or systems administration.

ASPs comprise another robust, growing IT job market: International Data Cor-poration, the IT market research firm, projects that IT spending on ASPs will reach $7.8 billion by 2004, up considerably from $300 million in 1999. The ASP model differs from outsourcing in that it is application-centric and is based on renting hardware and software, which the client's end-users then access via the Internet. ASPs offer IT organizations the advantage of not having to buy a technology that they may not envision as being a long-term core competency and, like outsourcing, ASP arrange-ments alleviate niche staffing demands.

The IT employees in an ASP may be organized along technology lines—supporting a core group of applications for several different clients at once—or along client lines. Either way, for applications developers and system administrators, network adminis-trators, database developers and administrators, and helpdesk analysts, working in an ASP offers tremendous variety as well as the challenge of always being on the cut-ting edge of new software releases and hardware platforms.

"In an ASP you always get the latest releases of technologies and beta code, and you really stay on the leading edge with your technology skills," says Julie Palen, president of InterNoded in Cambridge, Massachusetts. InterNoded is an ASP that hosts about 300 different applications in the Lotus Notes/Domino environment. "In a [corporate IT] organization, you risk being typecast; the organization can't take risks with its mission-critical infrastructure. Here we also have to keep things stable, but we're always pushing the envelope with the latest and greatest."

Working for an ISP is somewhat different than working for an outsourcing vendor or an ASP in that ISPs generally serve consumers as well as IT organizations. Anyone who needs access to the Internet from a home office uses the services of an ISP, be it a traditional, full-service ISP like Earthlink, a broadband access provider like the cable company, a digital subscriber line (DSL) service company, or the granddaddy of them all, AOL, which offers its own online community in addition to Internet access. Corporations also use ISPs for access to the Internet, as well as for website hosting services. So within ISPs, you're dealing with a much more diverse clientele, all coming to you with vastly different levels of experience and expectations. By its nature, working in an ISP is networking-centric; ISPs are generally looking for network and infrastructure specialists, operations expertise, helpdesk and technical support experience, and—it goes without saying—Internet expertise.

TIP If you're not comfortable serving two masters, working in the IT services environment may not be for you. On the one hand, you have to fulfill the client's expectations—the success of your employer depends on your ability to please the customer, and you will have an indirect reporting relationship to the client. But your direct line of reporting is to your employer, and you have to heed internal company policies and work within the realm of your employer's expectations. If you tend to have trouble compartmentalizing your loyalties or find it difficult to be the go-between, you may want to consider another type of organization.

What It's Like to Work at an ASP

Dr. Mike Remedios, senior vice president and chief technology officer (CTO) at ReSourcePhoenix.com, an ASP specializing in financial and back-office services and outsourced business and IT staffing, San Rafael, Calif.; February 2000. (In January 2001, Remedios joined e-tailer Bluelight.com as chief information officer [CIO].)

TENURE   Since September 1998.

WHY I LIKE WORKING HERE   "There's that *Star Trek* feeling here of going where no one has gone before. You have input at all levels. If there's an opportunity, there's no reason why we can't do it...The thing that most IT people come here for is the variety and depth of the technology. We get a lot of former consultants because they can get the best of both worlds—a variety of clients and applications, but no travel."

NUMBER OF IT EMPLOYEES   About 95 in two locations.

TOTAL NUMBER OF EMPLOYEES   About 250. "That's hard to figure out because we're hiring fast and furiously."

CLIENTS   Thomas Weisel Partners (investment bankers), GE Capital Aviation Services, The California Wellness Foundation, and others.

HOW DO YOU DEAL WITH IT'S NEED TO SERVE BOTH THE CLIENT AND THE COMPANY?
"We try to treat all users as clients, whether they're internal or external. We try to balance all the different requests and try to be proactive on the [client] side. We make sure that everyone, even the most junior programmer, understands who they support. Attitude is really important to us."

WHAT KIND OF ATTITUDE DO YOU WANT?   "Can-do, upbeat, and gung-ho without taking unnecessary risks. We want calculated risk-takers who are good at watching out for the things that can go wrong, and who don't try to take on everything by themselves."

DO YOU MANAGE IT BY FUNCTION OR BY CLIENT ACCOUNT?   "We have matrix management. We have functional teams because there are issues with cross-training. But we also have to be client-centric in our deliverables. So we have project managers who drive deliverables on the [client] side and functional project managers who look after different parts of the infrastructure. During a project for a particular client, we also have a project manager and a technical lead who are thinking just about that client."

IT TRAINING IN 2000   "A lot of the e-business-type training."

BONUS PROGRAMS   Quarterly bonuses based on company performance and occasional spot bonuses for exceptional (individual) performance.

DRESS CODE   "It has become a lot more casual. When I first got here, it was very much the accounting standard of white shirts, suits, and ties. And you couldn't get a programmer into a suit. So for IT, it became business casual, and it's more lax for the programmers and the data center staff."

WORK DAY   IT staff hours vary according to the users they support. "The accountants come in at 5:00 or 6:00 A.M., so the IT group supporting them comes in between 6:00 and 6:30 and leaves at 4:00 or 5:00 P.M., unless there's a big project. The [sales force automation] group comes in around 10:00 A.M. and works to all hours of the morning."

MUST PEOPLE CARRY BEEPERS? CELL PHONES?   "We have BellSouth interactive two-way pagers. They enable us to maintain contact with each other and with clients, so it's a productivity advantage."

TELECOMMUTING POLICY   "Nobody has the God-given right to telecommute. But if you can get the work done better at home and meet your deliverables, it's up to your manager."

AMBIENCE   "People like to hang out and chat, so we have table tennis and foosball and an exercise room. We try to keep it as lax as we can so people can let loose when they're feeling uptight. Quite often we go to lunch together. People look out for each other because we have team goals vs. individual goals, and that only happens when people socialize a bit together."

KIND OF OFFICES   "In IT we have cubes and open spaces and offices for those who really need them, whether they're managers or technicians."

DÉCOR   "Kind of a Marin-County feel. All the office doors are wood, and we can each choose the kind of wood furniture we want in our offices. I have mahogany, coming from my banking background."

PERKS   "We have frequent parties like barbecues, beach parties, a trip to Alcatraz. When we do those things, people drop their titles, and everyone is the same."

NOTE *An edited version of this interview appeared in* Computerworld *on March 6, 2000.*

Consulting

For many IT professionals, consulting is all they'd dream of doing. It offers exposure to a vast array of technologies, business problems and challenges, organizational structures, and end-users. And it offers a choice between joining a large stable company whose client roster crosses all industries or a smaller niche player that focuses on a vertical industry or specializes in a particular technology. You can choose one with a local or regional practice or one that covers the nation or the globe. You can also choose to go solo.

One of the great lures of consulting is that because clients are usually bringing in consultants to help with the adoption of newer technologies, consultants are more likely to be on the leading edge of the technology curve—as well as on the leading edge of the IT pay scale. Consultants tend to command respect as experts brought in to solve problems (although they can also be viewed with envy by IT staff members). And whatever your area of expertise—applications development, networking, databases, you name it—you can bring it to consulting. But as every privilege carries a responsibility, consultants have to put in extra time staying up-to-date with their technology skills, business acumen, project management skills, and interpersonal communication skills.

The larger management consulting firms typically have a strong, formal corporate culture that isn't as appealing to hard-core techies as it is to those who view themselves as business technologists. Their work with IT organizations is largely centered around redefining business processes and implementing the technology to support those processes, and it usually involves long-term commitments. Consultants in these firms have to keep up not only with new technologies, but also with business and industry trends. Moreover, consulting at this level requires top-notch communication skills and political savvy. You're not only building technology solutions to business problems, you're also building consensus and acceptance within the client's environment.

Joining a vertical-industry consulting practice, such as one that specializes in healthcare or human resources consulting (just two examples among many), affords you the opportunity to develop a particular business expertise—or apply your established business expertise if you're moving into IT from a prior career. Likewise, you can join a consulting firm that focuses on a specific technology, like database design and implementation or object-oriented programming, or that concentrates on a functional area, like enterprise resource planning (ERP) or supply-chain management (SCM).

Among the newer entrants into the consulting game are the e-consultancies, or e-strategists, as they sometimes call themselves. These are the companies that began life usually as a boutique website design firm and have evolved into more full-service consulting groups offering a soup-to-nuts approach to doing business over the Web. While each of the e-consultancies has its own distinct corporate culture, their cultures are generally somewhat looser than those of the big management consulting firms, owing to their roots as Internet startup companies. Walking through their offices, it's not uncommon to see mod Jetson-esque office furniture, collections of *Star Wars* toys in employee's cubicles, unusual paint jobs, or conference rooms with silly names. (At the New York–based e-consultancy Agency.com, for example, conference rooms are named after favorite cereals, like the Apple Jacks room, or Hitchcock films, like the Spellbound room.)

Independent consulting is also a viable option, and most of those who strike out on their own find it so satisfying that they say they can't imagine going back to work for anyone else. In addition to the freedom to choose their own clients and determine their own schedules, independent consultants also get to exercise more control over the direction of their own career paths and skills development.

The major drawback they cite is that, owing to tax regulations (the 1706 rules, also known as The 20 Questions), many potential clients are reluctant to contract directly with sole proprietors. Proving that the contractor is a freelancer and not a full-time employee can be a real hassle for corporations, so they opt instead for a preferred provider arrangement—a contract with an agency that supplies contingency staffing, which is a polite way of saying individuals who do work-for-hire. Independent consultants and contractors are practically unanimous in their disdain for these agencies, usually referring to them derisively as "body shops."

Anyone considering independent consulting should realize that going solo entails far more than just hanging out your shingle and lining up gigs. Should you choose to go out on your own, be prepared to accept all the responsibilities of running a business—from the tax burdens to the paperwork to the sales and marketing of your services—in addition to the actual IT work.

All consultants, whether they're employed in large management consulting firms or they're independent sole proprietors, should be prepared for downtime, when they are not engaged in any active project. The larger firms will usually offer their employees the chance to pursue new training and education opportunities when they're in between gigs. Smaller firms may be forced to cut people loose. Independents will usually fill the time scrambling to line up a new job, catching up on paperwork, attending training, or simply taking a breather if they have the cushion of money in the bank.

TIP *If you're just starting out in IT, you probably don't want to attempt independent consulting or contracting. To succeed on your own, you need a proven track record behind you, and you should have certification to substantiate your credentials. But joining a large Big 5 consulting firm can make a lot of sense for entry-level IT pros and career changers. They offer myriad training and career development opportunities, and because their clients cut across all industries, you have the chance to work on an array of business problems. If you're adverse to travel or long hours, however, you probably won't be happy with any kind of IT consulting.*

What It's Like to Be an Independent IT Consultant

Vanda Collis, independent consultant doing business as Waltham Park Resources International Inc., Ridgewood, N.J.; May 2000.

TENURE   Since 1999.

WHY I LIKE INDEPENDENT IT CONSULTING   "I'm working for myself, and I'm extremely happy as my own boss… I had wanted to do heavy-duty work in ecommerce, and New York City is the mecca for that. [In my previous job] I was doing some high-level ecommerce work, but I wasn't managing actual projects—I was more involved with the customer relationship management aspects."

THE WORST THING ABOUT IT IS…   "You're constantly on the go. You must know when to take a timeout, and sometimes that's pretty tough… It's easy for one of the balls to slip. Independent consultants don't really get sick days, so I try to stay as healthy as possible. And we don't do three-day weekends. Even when we have Mondays off from the office, we're still working."

RECENT CLIENT   iXL, an e-consultancy based in Atlanta, Georgia.; Collis, working out of iXL's New York offices, helmed the redesign of a website for a financial services company.

DAY-TO-DAY PROJECT WORK INVOLVES…   "Preparing and making presentations; updating the project management plan, preparing action plans, and working on project definition documents; confirming costs with suppliers; coordinating with other functional groups supporting the project; touching base with engineers and the creative department, nailing down details with project leaders on the team, and conducting project review sessions; assessing applicable best practices; and following up with the end-client."

PREVIOUS IT EXPERIENCE   Fifteen years in financial services with such employers as J.P. Morgan, The Chase Manhattan Bank, and, most recently, FleetBoston Financial, where she worked in retail banking IT.

SKILLS   IT project management; quality assessment and testing; applications development in mainframe, client/server, and ecommerce environments.

DRESS CODE   Whatever suits the client, from business to business casual.

WORK DAY   5:30 A.M. to 12:00 A.M. or later. "A typical day is a very rigorous day."

WHY SUCH LONG HOURS?   "I put in 50 to 60 billable hours a week. On top of that, as an independent, I have to be my own support team, sales team, business development team, the strategist and the implementer, the bookkeepers and the mailroom. I have to project-manage my life." After dinner and putting the kids to bed, Collis typically spends several hours in her home office answering email, doing research, and preparing for the next day's agenda. In addition, she spends time on the weekends on book-keeping and accounting as well as preparing proposals for potential new clients. Moreover, she's attending night classes in pursuit of a Ph.D. in Project Management.

AN IDEAL SCHEDULE WOULD BE...   "Working for clients Tuesday through Thursday; taking Mondays and Fridays to work on business development, bookkeeping, and the other administrative tasks of running the business; and having the weekends totally free for myself and my family."

PERKS   Being able to take time off for family events whenever she wants, such as a school play in the afternoon or getting ready for a family party. "I'm always there for them. That's the one exception I allow myself for not working."

 NOTE   *Excerpted from an article in* Computerworld *on July 21, 2000.*

Dot-Com Startups

You could almost hear the collective sigh of relief among corporate IT hiring managers in 2000 when the dot-com startup craze finally met its comeuppance. Large corporations had been competing fiercely with the dot-coms for IT talent over the last several years, and with countless dot-coms shutting down or hit by layoffs in 2000 and 2001, it would appear that the Goliaths now have the recruiting advantage over the Davids. Nonetheless, it was the dot-com revolution that brought a new glamorous appeal to the IT profession, and for some IT professionals, anything less than working within the Internet economy would be downright stifling.

If you can stomach the uncertainty, the long hours (dot-commers have been known to put in 20-hour days and longer), and the exchange of your personal life for a stimulating work life, dot-coms still have a lot going for them. Plus, they have a lot to offer career-wise. While you aren't likely to get company-paid training and may find it next to impossible to take a cell phone–free night off from the office, you may well learn more in six months than many people learn in a year.

James Henry, who graduated from business school Bentley College, in Waltham, Massachusetts, in May 2000, joined dot-com Fair Market, a provider of auction services for other ecommerce ventures, because the job would expose him to advanced software-engineering techniques and put him on the front lines of an exciting new business. He would get to rotate through three different software engineering departments, working with external customers, internal systems, and quality assurance (QA). The Woburn, Massachusetts–based company had already filed its initial public offering (IPO) in March, but getting rich off of stock options wasn't what interested Henry, who turned down job offers from John Hancock Life Insurance Company and Oracle Consulting.

"With a large corporation, I thought I'd be placed into a department where I was just doing a certain task and doing it consistently, and it would be hard to move up a level," Henry explains. "Whereas in a [dot-com], it's far easier to move up in position and ranking over the long run, to accrue a lot of knowledge that will make me useful to any company."

As far as the work environment, dot-coms have a lot going for them, especially for those just entering the job market or those who are fed up with corporate conservatism and bureaucracy. They may require a lot of hours, but they're usually flexible about when you show up; they are generally even more casual than business casual; and they're usually quite generous with perks like free meals, gift certificates, concierge services, and foosball on the premises.

Those may seem like small perks in the face of the risk that any dot-com could be gone tomorrow, but collectively, they create a sense that the company acknowledges the risk and is taking a personal interest in the well-being of its workers. While it always seems that the average dot-commer is somewhere in his or her mid-to-late twenties, given the recent market correction and the subsequent nose dives by those that lacked business experience, the survivors would be glad to get some IT staffers on board who have substantial corporate experience behind them.

TIP *If you yearn to be in a dot-com environment but aren't comfortable with the inherent risk factor of a startup, a viable alternative is to work in the ecommerce technologies group within a larger, more stable IT environment. At The Pillsbury Company in Minneapolis, Minnesota, for example, the company's e-business strategy is carried out by the development technologies group. It comprises 24 public websites promoting its brands (such as Pillsbury.com, GreenGiant.com, and HaagenDazs.com), as well as a number of business-to-business ecommerce sites and participation in industry-wide web initiatives. In the entertainment industry, many companies have established new divisions encompassing web-related work as well as CD-ROM production and gaming. MTV Networks, for example, has set up The MTVi Group, which produces MTV.com, VH1.com, online radio site SonicNet.com, and numerous other international music-oriented websites.*

What It's Like to Work at a Dot-Com Startup

Eric Kidd, CTO and vice president of engineering at Petsmart.com, a pet supply
e-tailer (www.petsmart.com), Pasadena, Calif.; July 2000. (In a move that illustrates
dot-com growing pains, Petsmart announced in November 2000 that it would acquire
an 81 percent interest in PetSmart.com and bring the business in-house as a subsidiary. Kidd no longer works at the company.)

TENURE   Since October 1999.

WHY I LIKE WORKING HERE   "I'm really impressed with…the way people come
together for a common cause and give so much of themselves just for the satisfaction
of work that's well done. I think the biggest motivation here isn't the potential to
become wealthy from stock options—although they very well could—but rather to
do great things."

NUMBER OF IT EMPLOYEES   About 33, divided into 5 groups—web engineering and
ecommerce engineering (both doing applications development), quality-assurance
engineering, operations engineering (including networking, database administration,
and systems and network administration), and IS (responsible for internal office
systems).

TOTAL NUMBER OF EMPLOYEES   110.

AVERAGE AGE IN ENGINEERING   About 27.

UPCOMING PROJECTS   "Enhancements to our content management and rendering system, which we built in-house, continued enhancements to [a new] order management
system, and we have some ideas for…personalization and dynamic content."

IT TRAINING PLANS IN 2000   "Solaris administration, Oracle, and new web technologies. Our main programming languages are Perl and Java, so we'll have some cross-
training in those."

COMPENSATION AND BONUSES   Stock options for all employees and "competitive
compensation." Spot bonuses include gift certificates and project completion rewards
such as a PalmPilot V and a trip to Las Vegas (awarded to each engineering team member at the end of a site relaunch project in fall 1999).

DRESS CODE   Casual. "I've never seen anyone wearing a tie to the office."

WORK DAY "On average, around 9 A.M. to 7 P.M. When we're not on a big project, it's about a 50-hour week. But we just came off of a big project with a very aggressive deadline, and we were easily putting in 80-hour weeks. People were here 12 hours a day, 7 days a week. Some put in an excess of 100 hours a week."

WHAT WAS THE PROJECT? "A redesign of our order management system. It also involved updates of the commerce functions on the website, like the shopping cart and checkout. We were working on it for four months, and the last month was completely QA testing. We didn't have much room for error because people get upset if there are discrepancies in how we fulfill an order or charge their credit cards."

WHY WAS THE DEADLINE SO AGGRESSIVE? "We intentionally pushed ourselves...to start reaping the business benefits. As always happens, we had some requirements changes during the course of the project, so typically we were doing three weeks' worth of work in one week."

FAVORITE STRESS-BUSTERS "Rubber band wars. There was a big war between network engineering, ecommerce, and QA, and I have seen a lot of innovation in the design of rubber band weapons."

HOW DID YOU REWARD PEOPLE FOR THE HOURS THEY PUT IN? "During the project we gave everyone $100 American Express gift certificates. We had a champagne uncorking at the launch...and [later] we had a party to celebrate, with margaritas, Mexican food, and mariachis. And we [gave] people some time off. We [spent] $1,500 to $2,000 per person to take the team for a Paint Ball day, a trip to [a local theme park], and other [individual] rewards."

KIND OF OFFICES Open space. "We don't have any cubes or offices. All of the executives sit out with their teams."

DÉCOR "Modern-industrial. All of the walls are different colors—yellow, purple, green, eggshell, and black—which is a good break for the senses when you're working long hours. We have a nice view of the San Gabriel Mountains. In the middle of the suite, we have a kitchen area with a banana-shaped bar. And we have a lot of stuffed animals in our reception area."

FREE FOOD "Cereal, oatmeal, yogurt, fruit, candy, chips, Ramen noodles, soft drinks, and coffee. During project periods, we [bring] in lunch and dinner for the team every day."

FAVORITE IT SNACK FOOD   Slim Jims and licorice whips.

WHAT EVERYONE COMPLAINS ABOUT   "That we don't have cots for them to sleep on."

OFFICE MASCOT   Millie, the CEO's dog.

PERKS   "A Bow-Wow every two weeks, where we have beer and chips and salsa and celebrate birthdays with a cake."

WOULD EMPLOYEES FEEL COMFORTABLE EMAILING THE CEO?   "Yeah. They feel comfortable shooting rubber bands at the CEO."

 NOTE   An edited version of this interview appeared in Computerworld *on July 31, 2000.*

High-Tech Startups

For some people, the real appeal of an IT career is the possibility of starting the next Microsoft Corporation or Sun Microsystems. Working at a high-tech startup offers the chance of creating new technology that will directly touch customers, and that prospect creates a distinct environment, whether you're working in product development and engineering or providing internal IT support. Silicon Valley success stories are legendary (like the company founder driving into the parking lot in a brand new Ferarri after going public), as are the measures high-tech startups will take to recruit ace programmers (extraordinary signing bonuses).

Even before success is certain, working in a startup can be extremely gratifying, despite the tortuously long hours and the high level of risk. Many go out of their way to provide loads of touchy-feely perks, like onsite yoga classes, regular visits by a massage therapist, or concierge services. Workers tend to have a lot more autonomy and responsibility, as well as the opportunity to wear many hats—a software engineer developing the company's product might also do internal database development and administration, some network administration, and sit in on marketing and sales meetings.

Career-wise, though, IT professionals should consider that, as with dot-coms, taking a job in a high-tech startup has some tradeoffs. One, of course, is that you can count on putting your personal life on hold for a year or more while the company gets up on its feet. And you can pretty much count on not getting any company-provided formal training. Startup capital typically goes more to day-to-day operations than to the long-term career development of its staff. Even if the company is willing to throw training dollars at its staff, IT employees aren't likely to have the time to go for a two-day training session. Instead, IT managers in high-tech startups like to use phrases like "knowledge transfer" and "internal cross-training" to describe their continued education efforts. In other words, when you need to get up to speed on something new, you're going to be asking the software engineer in the next cubicle or looking it up in a book or on the Web.

Then there's also the possibility that the very aspects that drew you to a startup—risk, independence, freedom—could disappear overnight if the company is snatched up by a larger concern. Company priorities may shift, having an impact on workers' assignments or eliminating certain jobs altogether. Relocation or frequent travel might be required. If you were on-board early in the game, you might profit nicely from the acquisition, at least from a financial perspective. But if you joined later, your stock options will be fewer and your only "reward" might be ending up in the very type of company you were trying to avoid in the first place.

Worse still is the very real possibility that your fledgling firm's venture capital (VC) could dry up, leaving you in a Chapter 11 mess or desperately looking for a suitor to save the day. While the VC market seems to be more patient with high-tech startups than pure ecommerce plays, joining any startup is a risk that has to be weighed, whether you're a newcomer to the field or an old pro.

On the other hand, for people in a personal position to bear a long-term risk or who simply thrive on being on the edge, few experiences are as crammed full of daily on-the-job learning as working at a high-tech startup. Not only do you have to work through and solve your own technical challenges, but you get some valuable business lessons that many say are better than any M.B.A. program could ever supply. Live it, learn it, love it.

TIP *If you're a young entry-level professional with little to lose in terms of your professional credentials, financial security (i.e., you don't have a mortgage weighing you down), or family stability (no dependents), you're probably in a good position to take a flyer on a job with an IT startup. If it tanks, you may be back to ground zero, but you haven't really lost anything because you were starting from scratch anyway. Likewise, if you're an IT pro with a long resume behind you—a proven quantity whose future reputation wouldn't be jeopardized by a venture gone sour—and your financial house is in good shape, joining a startup could be just the thing you need to put a sense of excitement and passion back into your career, to remind you of why you went into IT in the first place.*

What It's Like to Work at a High-Tech Startup

Brian Scott, director of information technology, Epicentric (www.epicentric.com), a provider of packaged web portal and infrastructure software and content management services, San Francisco, Calif.; April 2000.

TENURE   Since April 1999.

WHY I LIKE WORKING HERE   "I come from a very corporate background, and that is a very different pace. The fast pace here is the big difference—being able to move ahead on the things you want to do."

NUMBER OF IT EMPLOYEES   12; 4 dedicated to internal IT infrastructure, desktop support, and systems administration, and eight to external hosting and content management services. "We'll more than double our staff this year."

NUMBER OF PRODUCT DEVELOPERS   40 (all Java developers).

TOTAL NUMBER OF EMPLOYEES   120 (up from 30 to 40 in January 2000).

MAJOR IT INITIATIVES   Working on the IT infrastructure and "ERP-type initiatives that would work down the middle of our internal and external operations."

IT TRAINING PLANS IN 2000   Training on an as-needed basis. "We try to pass on skill sets internally, and if we have skills needs that are not being met internally, we'll send them out."

COMPENSATION AND BONUSES   "We have to be competitive with salaries and stock options." The company gives all employees stock options, plus employee-referral bonuses.

DRESS CODE   Casual.

WORK DAY   Twelve-hour days, usually starting between 9:00 and 10:00 A.M.

MUST PEOPLE CARRY BEEPERS? CELL PHONES?   Yes. "Most of the IT staff carries a beeper, but only very rarely do you get called back to the office after-hours. We provide DSL service in all their homes so they can work remotely."

ONSITE AMENITIES   A dedicated concierge works for the engineering staff (including IT and product developers), "who does all the things they aren't able to do because they're working 12-to-16-hour days," including getting lunch and dinner, paying bills, dropping off and picking up dry cleaning, etc. "[Once] I had a flat tire, and she fixed it." Others include yoga classes at 8 A.M. on Tuesdays and Thursdays; massages on

Thursdays, scheduled in 15-minute blocks; three refrigerators fully stocked with snacks, fruits, vegetables, candy, and sodas; lunches and dinners paid for by the company.

HOW DOES THE IT STAFF MAKE TIME FOR YOGA CLASSES AND MASSAGES? "Everybody needs to take a break; I don't expect anyone to stare at their computer screen for hours on end."

HAVE THESE PERKS EVER INTERFERED WITH PRODUCTIVITY? (Laughs.) "We have a really good group of people, so there's never been a problem with people over-relaxing. We have a lot of work to do, and if someone needs an hour or two to regroup or to grab a couch and take a nap, I have no problem with that because I have full confidence that people are doing their job."

FAVORITE ITEMS IN THE REFRIGERATORS "Anything caffeinated."

OTHER PERKS Full healthcare plan, stock options, subsidized membership at a local gym, monthly birthday parties, and movie nights on Thursdays. "We take a weekly poll and get a DVD movie and bring pizza in. [Our first was] *The Matrix*. What else would you watch at a software company?"

WHY SUCH GENEROUS PERKS? "We wanted to create our own atmosphere, one that makes work comfortable for people. Certainly, wanting to be an employer of choice plays into it. But from the inception, we wanted to create a company that would be fun for people to come to every day."

KIND OF OFFICES A mix of cubes and open space on one floor in a refurbished factory. "Most of the engineering team is in a cubed environment because they need privacy to focus on a project. Those who are more collaborative, like marketing and sales, are in a more open environment."

DÉCOR Exposed pipes and cables; carpeted floor. "We have lots of big windows with a great view of the Bay Bridge and the San Francisco Bay."

WOULD EMPLOYEES FEEL COMFORTABLE EMAILING THE CEO? "Yes. We have an open-door policy for any manager in the company."

NOTE *An edited version of this interview appeared in* Computerworld *on April 17, 2000.*

Part II

Start Me Up

In this Part

Chapter 4

· ·

Start Me Up in Applications
Development and Database Jobs

Applications and databases are the face of IT throughout an enterprise. As the core tools that the majority of workers use to get their jobs done, they are the most visible aspect of IT. And from a pure IT perspective, creating and supporting access to applications and databases are the raison d'être for networking, infrastructure, operations, and end-user support.

Consequently, applications development and database jobs are among the most high-profile positions in IT. While corporate employees couldn't get much done without the hard work of network administrators, mainframe systems programmers, infrastructure architects, and other key behind-the-scenes IT professionals, it's the apps development teams that grab the spotlight. After all, applications are the programs that enable users to carry out their work—from ubiquitous productivity apps like word processors, web browsers, and email managers, to larger custom apps that create customer lists by demographic characteristics or facilitate catalog order fulfillment. Databases are the engine underneath the application's hood, the collection of records and files—from sales transactions to product inventories and customer profiles—that applications run off of. And data warehouses capture the records stored across multiple databases in a format that users can query, extract, and massage for detailed business analysis.

Working in concert on integrated teams, applications developers and database professionals create new software, databases, and data warehouses; refine and maintain existing ones; customize shrinkwrapped packages; and develop the interfaces between myriad systems so they operate as a seamless whole. Their impact on an organization is immeasurable, and the demand for them is nearly insatiable.

New applications development, customization of shrinkwrapped software, application integration across business functions, and development of data warehouses and data-mining applications are driving IT budgets and priorities in 2001, according to various industry reports. *Computerworld*'s 7th Annual Technology Skills Survey, published in December 2000, found that 70 percent of the 307 IT managers who responded planned to hire or train staff in programming languages, web-development tools, and object-oriented programming tools in 2001. Specifically, 30 percent of IT shops reported that they would hire or retrain staff for Internet applications development, 28 percent for ecommerce applications development, 18 percent for data warehousing and data mining, 12 percent for customer relationship management (CRM) systems, and 10 percent for enterprise resource planning (ERP) systems.

These findings are consistent with the results of a survey conducted by AMR Research, in Boston, that polled 900 IT professionals in U.S. companies across 13 industries. The study, published in October 2000, projected that spending on applications in 2001 would range from 17 percent to 21 percent of the total IT budget among manufacturers and from 13 percent to 20 percent among services companies. AMR found that ERP systems would lead with 32 percent of the applications budget; followed by ecommerce applications, 23 percent; CRM, 14 percent; and supply-chain management (SCM), 10 percent.

Taken together, the *Computerworld* survey, the AMR study, and other industry research indicates that the demand for applications developers and database pros will outpace the supply. Although new object-oriented programming tools, an increased reliance on off-the-shelf software, and automated database tools occasionally raise speculation that the role of the programmer and the database administrator (DBA) will diminish, it has never proven true. As the work becomes more automated, it simply frees developers and administrators up to focus on more strategic problems within the IT organization and the business at large.

Applications Development Jobs: A Sampler

Applications Developer

JOB TITLE VARIATIONS   Programmer, programmer/analyst, systems analyst, lead developer.

JOB DESCRIPTION   Applications developers are the artists of the IT organization. Although they're creating something that can't be seen, heard, or touched, their process is akin to that of a novelist, painter, musician, or sculptor. Starting from a blank screen—with an end goal in mind and a roadmap of requirements—bit by bit, they craft the intricate code that will eventually culminate in an application that will empower end-users to carry out the corporate mission, from identifying

SPOTLIGHT ON AN APPLICATIONS DEVELOPER

Anita Mital, 35, lead applications developer at Entergy Corp., New Orleans, La.

Entergy, a major southern utility, outsources all of its IT organization to Science Applications International Corporation (SAIC), which in turn has subcontracted with The Highland Group. Mital, who has been in IT since 1997, is actually a Highland Group employee.

Overall responsibilities   To develop and maintain two key homegrown applications, Rail Car Repair (RCR) and the Rail Car Management System (RCMS), within Entergy's Coal Applications Group.

Day-to-day responsibilities   "Right now, I'm converting the RCR application, which has a PowerBuilder front end, and putting a VB front end on it because there are certain capabilities that users had been promised that the application never could do. Both of these apps were started five years ago and were never completed. For example, the RCR app was supposed to calculate the labor and material costs [for repairing rail cars] correctly, and it doesn't. Five years and $5 million later, they still don't have an app that they can use the way they want it. So I'm doing a lot of coding right now to get the new screens to mesh with the existing database and stored procedures, and spending a lot of time with my users, in Houston, to get their requirements and wishlists. I've also had a lot of application maintenance issues lately. For instance, the application generates two invoices, and then one has to be backed out of the database, which is not an easy process. Or something is processed incorrectly, and I have to go in and correct it. The databases are very cumbersome, and users want to get rid of a lot of clutter. It took me four days just to cull through and eliminate all the clutter."

Technologies and technical skills required   Programming with VB and PowerBuilder; basic Oracle database maintenance; troubleshooting.

Other skills required   Project management; good communication skills for dealing with end-users of the applications. "My users have a lot of knowledge of the railroads and the coal mines, and they're the ones who are feeding me their requirements when I have to enhance or update the application. So I have to be patient, translate technical issues into nontechnical language, and be able to decide what is doable and what's not and then steer them in the direction that's appropriate for their application."

What I like most about this job   "The problem-solving aspect. There's a problem, and I have to figure out how to make it work, whether it's fixing something in the database or rewriting the application."

SPOTLIGHT ON AN APPLICATIONS DEVELOPER

What I like least about this job "Probably having direct contact with my client—all the time. There's no buffer. Whenever they do the least little thing wrong, instead of calling the helpdesk, they call me right away because that's what they're used to. The job requires a lot of handholding, and it just gets tiring after a while. They're very good customers, but when I'm on the phone eight hours in one day, it becomes a bit much. It impedes you from making progress on the work at hand."

Career path leading to this job Mital is a career changer who embarked on her IT career after several years of teaching geometry in the New Orleans public schools. She took night classes while teaching and joined The Highland Group in 1997 after completing a Bachelor's degree in Information Systems Technology at Tulane University. Her first IT job was in Entergy's desktop software group, where she was in charge of electronic software distribution (ESD). As head of ESD, she was responsible for ensuring—through QA testing—that any new applications rolled out to end-users' desktops didn't clash or interfere with existing applications. Also, using Microsoft's Server Management System (SMS), she wrote the scripts that would automatically deploy the applications to end-users consistently and correctly. When she transferred into applications development in May 1999, she had to learn PowerBuilder, an object-oriented programming tool, and to familiarize herself with Oracle, the underlying database for the coal applications. She took formal classes in PowerBuilder and brushed up on Oracle through self-study: reading books and playing with the database on an Entergy server.

How I landed in this position "One of the people I had worked with in desktop engineering had moved to the Coal Applications Group, and when a new opening came up, he offered it to me because I was very good at dealing with clients. We had worked closely together on a new desktop release, so he knew how I worked and wanted to add my skills to the group. Entergy has 500-plus applications, so I'd been dealing with a wide range of users, solving problems, engineering different software releases, and working with developers as part of my job in ESD. I'd studied programming and knew Visual Basic."

Advice to other IT pros interested in applications development "Work well with your coworkers because you never know where that might take you later. I landed in this position because of a good working relationship with a colleague, and it gave me more overall responsibility, plus it took me into a much higher salary bracket."

new markets to managing inventory to dealing with customers. Responsibilities include identifying business requirements and selecting the most appropriate tools to apply to automating business processes and workflow. This is a deadline-driven job that requires constant user contact as well as cooperation with other members of the development team, including DBAs, business analysts, and quality assurance (QA) testers.

EDUCATION AND CERTIFICATION REQUIREMENTS   While stories abound of whiz-kid programmers who forge highly successful IT careers without college (ever hear of Bill Gates or Steve Jobs?), traditionally, a college degree is required, usually in computer science or in business with a Computer Information Systems (CIS) or Management Information Systems (MIS) concentration. With the emergence of object-oriented front-end tools like Visual Basic (VB) and PowerBuilder, more and more people are moving into applications development from other fields. A strong background in math is recommended. Also, a background in music, with its mathematical foundation, or foreign languages, with their clear parallel to computer languages, are suitable academic credentials. Certification isn't usually required, but it can certainly be a distinguishing factor on a résumé. Most major language and tool vendors offer a variety of different certification programs.

TECHNICAL SKILLS REQUIRED   Proficiency in at least one programming language, and preferably more, plus various development environments and front-end tools; a thorough knowledge of the underlying operating systems; and an understanding of the constraints of hardware platforms. While many developers tend to have a favorite language and toolset—and in fact tend to be quite opinionated about what constitutes the most elegant solution—intense partiality to one skill set can be dangerous for programmers. The most successful developers are those who demonstrate technical breadth as well as depth.

OTHER SKILLS REQUIRED   Strong oral and written communication skills; the ability to translate abstract concepts into concrete ideas; documentation skills; business knowledge; troubleshooting and problem-solving skills. Also essential is the ability to put oneself in the end-user's shoes, understanding their work processes and how technology can be applied to automate and/or improve them.

POTENTIAL CAREER PATHS   The progression through the applications development ranks usually starts with a job as a programmer or junior programmer, followed by programmer/analyst (or systems analyst), lead developer (or team lead), and

APPLICATIONS DEVELOPERS: THE MANAGEMENT PERSPECTIVE

Christopher Smith, vice president and chief information officer, HomeLife Furniture Corp., Hoffman Estates, Ill.

Aside from technical skills, what's the most important attribute you look for in applications developers?

The ability to pull requirements, needs, and a sense of what really needs to be accomplished out of an organization that doesn't really understand what it needs. It's a connection between the left and right brains, so you can take creative, abstract thoughts about what people are trying to achieve, and where they want the business to go, and can turn that into something systematic, something that can be organized, that's process-oriented.

Why is the left brain-right brain connection important in applications development?

It saves development time and yields better results. You end up getting a more creative solution, and usually a more accurate solution—a more resilient solution that doesn't just meet the need today, but one that lasts longer and weathers situations that might not occur to you if you're just programming to specific specifications.

Here, because we're a relatively new company, we're developing a lot of things from scratch, and it's very easy to develop them the wrong way if you just take users' ideas at face value. We have to figure out what they are trying to do overall and how that fits into the architecture of what we're putting together. We only want to develop things once, the right way. Since we don't have to follow any old ways of doing things, we really have to figure out what the organization wants to achieve so we can find the new best way of doing things.

Can you cite an example that illustrates this attribute in action?

When we first started talking to our people—after spinning off from Sears—about what they needed to do in their new jobs, the person in charge of inventory had inventory systems requirements, the transportation person was worried about how to track our trucks, our CSR [customer service representative] manager was worried about CSR systems, and so on. If we had just listened to each of them, we would have developed these separate small systems and then tried to interface them.

APPLICATIONS DEVELOPERS: THE MANAGEMENT PERSPECTIVE

But by changing the conversation to "What are we as an organization really trying to accomplish?" we found that instead of creating individual processes for each of those groups, we could create a process that had a much larger, more cross-functional identity. It wasn't a series of processes each owned by individuals, but one geared toward the best way of meeting customer needs. The system we came up with was "Customer Entry Through Merchandise Receipt." Instead of focusing on individual requirements, we focused on the entire process that takes place from the time a customer enters a store until the merchandise arrives at their home.

How can applications developers cultivate the right brain-left brain connection?

When I'm hiring people, I look to see if they have any hobbies or interests that show they regularly exercise both sides of the brain. For example, our enterprise architect is a jazz musician—that's mathematical in its basis, but it's also very creative. I once hired a chess master, who was good at thinking strategically and also at thinking many steps ahead, which helps produce resilient [IT] systems. So develop your other interests, whatever they are. Find a creative outlet.

 NOTE *Excerpted from an interview that appeared previously on the website www.leapit.com.*

project manager (PM). The PM's job can be a stepping stone into IT management roles, such as director of applications development, vice president of technology, and so forth. (See Chapter 8.) Or PMs who prefer a more hands-on, in-the-trenches technical career can move serially from project to project, advancing in stature and salary by taking on increasingly complex, high-profile projects. Good springboards into applications development can include the helpdesk, quality assurance and testing, or database administration.

IS THIS POSITION FOR YOU? If you want an IT job that is creative and has a highly visible impact on the business, and if you like problem-solving, mathematical problems, musical composition, and/or foreign languages, you are well suited for applications development. You must work well on teams as well as alone.

Business Analyst

JOB TITLE VARIATIONS   End-user liaison.

JOB DESCRIPTION   Business analysts are the key players in gathering systems requirements from end-users in the business units and communicating those to the programmers and database pros on the project team. Typically, they are assigned to a particular area of the company, like the marketing department or human resources, and they work closely with functional users in their area to identify new applications needs and additional functionality for existing applications. They may also do some coding, but their primary job is to gather the business requirements and work with applications developers to translate those into systems requirements. Business analysts are true hybrids who must understand the business processes and workflow of their users as well as the constraints and limitations of the technology and the IT environment.

EDUCATION AND CERTIFICATION REQUIREMENTS   Ideally, business analysts have a mix of technical and business education. The ultimate candidate has a techno-M.B.A. Project management training is a definite plus. As for certification, the same rule of thumb applies as for applications developers.

TECHNICAL SKILLS REQUIRED   An overall familiarity with key programming languages and environments, operating systems, and IT infrastructure.

OTHER SKILLS REQUIRED   The ability to translate techno-speak into plain English and to translate business priorities into technology requirements is essential. To gain credibility with both their business and IT constituencies, business analysts must be able to speak both languages—without a hint of condescension. An ability to prioritize strategic projects and daily tasks is also key, as business analysts will nearly always have several balls in the air at once. As with all development-related jobs, problem-solving skills are a must.

POTENTIAL CAREER PATHS   Given the hybrid nature of the job, business analysts can move fluidly about the company, going deeper into IT or into the business units as they desire. For the more technically inclined, the business analyst's role offers prime experience for the trek to the chief information officer office.

IS THIS POSITION FOR YOU?   If in college you couldn't decide whether to major in general business or MIS/CIS, you'd be well-suited for the business analyst role. You should like interacting with people on a variety of different levels, enjoy having several different things going on at once, and be as intrigued by the business as by the technology.

Quality Assurance Tester

JOB TITLE VARIATIONS   Quality control analyst, software tester, QA engineer, QA analyst.

JOB DESCRIPTION   Software QA professionals are responsible for testing both prototype applications and the final version to ensure that when an application is deployed, it functions as intended without causing conflicts and glitches with other applications on the network. While they play a key behind-the-scenes role in development and deployment, they nonetheless work closely with business users to determine where errors and problems are occurring as well as to solicit feedback regarding usability. In addition to identifying and correcting existing problems, QA testers must also anticipate and head off potential future vulnerabilities.

EDUCATION AND CERTIFICATION REQUIREMENTS   A degree in computer science or information technology is required. Certification in quality assurance and control and/or technical certifications are recommended but not required.

TECHNICAL SKILLS REQUIRED   QA pros need depth and breadth in all technologies related to applications development, including basic programming and database skills (VB, Java, C, C++, SQL, etc.) and web technologies. They also need an understanding of the IT infrastructure, client/server and multitier applications environments, networking, hardware constraints, and key operating systems such as Unix, Windows NT, Windows 2000, and mainframe operating systems. Familiarity with the development life cycle and structured development methodologies is key, as well as experience with automated testing tools like WinRunner and LoadRunner.

OTHER SKILLS REQUIRED   QA professionals must be detail-oriented, tenacious, and resilient. You need excellent troubleshooting and problem-solving skills, as well as vision. Project management skills are a must—even if you are not the QA lead, you must apply project management techniques to your daily workload. Communication and documentation skills are a must, as is the ability to work well on teams and foster cooperation among testers, developers, and users.

POTENTIAL CAREER PATHS   A next step following QA work is applications development. Or those who enjoy both could alternate between the two roles as they work on different cross-functional teams. QA pros also could conceivably move into operations or technical support, given their troubleshooting and problem-solving skills.

IS THIS POSITION FOR YOU? If you enjoy detail-oriented work and complex problem-solving, are tenacious enough to keep searching for the cause of a problem without giving up, and forward-thinking enough to anticipate potential future problems, you have what it takes to succeed in this position.

Applications Development Technologies Checklists

Programming Languages and Tools

✓ AS/400 RPG

✓ C, C++, Visual C++

✓ CGI

✓ Cobol

✓ Extensible Markup Language (XML)

✓ Groove (peer-to-peer development environment)

✓ Java, JavaBeans, Enterprise Java, JavaScript

✓ Lotus Notes/Domino

✓ Microsoft Exchange

✓ Perl

✓ PowerBuilder

✓ Universal Modeling Language (UML)

✓ Visual Basic (VB)

✓ Wireless Application Protocol (WAP)

Operating Systems

✓ AS/400 OS

✓ Linux

✓ Novell NetWare

✓ PalmOS

✓ Unix (including Sun Solaris, IBM AIX, Hewlett-Packard HP/UX, etc.)

✓ Windows 2000

✓ Windows CE

✓ Windows NT

Database Jobs: A Sampler

Database Administrator, Database Analyst, Database Developer

JOB TITLE VARIATIONS   While there are no real variations on the titles, there are variations in the definitions of the various roles. While larger organizations may have sufficient need and staff to segment each of the three roles quite clearly, in many midsized and smaller IT organizations, the DBA has a hybrid role that includes design and development work, or a developer may also do database analysis. In startups, one person may be called on to fulfill all three roles.

JOB DESCRIPTION   Extending the metaphor of applications developers as artists, database developers and administrators supply the words, the paint, the notes, and the clay with which application developers create their works of art. The specific job description depends on the degree to which the DBA, database developer, and database analyst roles are segmented within an organization. In the strictest sense, DBAs are responsible for the overall performance of the database, focused on maintenance and archiving, monitoring, and fine-tuning. Database developers work closely with business analysts and applications developers to determine the best database design based on applications requirements, and they create the underlying databases for applications. The database analyst is involved with requirements and design, as well as extracting data from the database to create reports. DBAs who have a hybrid role will also take on database development, design, and analysis, maintain and manage data models, and work with application architects to introduce new functionality.

EDUCATION AND CERTIFICATION REQUIREMENTS   A college degree is usually required, as well as formal training in a leading relational database. The key certifications for the two leading relational databases are the Oracle Certified Professional (OCP) DBA certification and the Microsoft Certified Database Administrator (MCDBA) for DBAs who have been working with SQL Server for at least one year. With database jobs ranking among the most difficult to fill in IT, certification is rarely required.

SPOTLIGHT ON A DATABASE ADMINISTRATOR

Steve Dlubala, 53, DBA, Johns Hopkins Medical Institutions, Baltimore, Md.

Overall responsibilities To maintain, monitor, and tune Oracle databases, plus develop new databases or extend existing ones to meet new applications requirements. "My customers are applications developers rather than end-users. Part of the DBA's job is to bridge the gap between applications developers and technical support," Dlubala says.

Day-to-day responsibilities "I'm usually juggling two to four projects at a time. After an applications developer gathers end-user requirements and analyzes them from a developer's perspective, I look at those and translate them into database structures. Usually I try to extend an existing database to fit their needs. If a new database is necessary, here the development responsibility is part of the DBA's role. The work is partly solitary and partly team-based. I have to review what I'm doing with other members of the project team to ensure that it will integrate correctly with the application.

"There's also ongoing database maintenance, monitoring, and tuning to ensure topflight performance of the database. Tuning requires a lot of effort; we have some fairly sizeable databases, and response time is critical in healthcare. The real drudgery types of tasks are repetitive, so you can set up processes to run automatically, and you just check them. Also, we have a data warehouse, and on a scheduled monthly basis, I'm responsible for extracting data from the mainframe or midrange applications systems and loading that data into the various databases in the data warehouse. That involves checking to make sure those databases aren't overloaded and performance is still reasonable."

Recent projects The Electronic Patient Record, a PC-based clinical application that pulls a patient's lab results, radiology reports, clinical notes, surgical notes, and other information from myriad disparate systems to present doctors with a single, complete view of a patient's history. The application, which is powered by the Patient Master Database (in DB2), won a *Computerworld* Smithsonian Award. "If we didn't have this, a doctor would have to sign on to one application to look at labs, then another to look at surgery notes, etc.," Dlubala says. "It was a complicated, multilayered project that has been around for a while, and we are still expanding it." Recently Dlubala has been working on integrating several new sources of data into the system, such as patient allergies and medications.

SPOTLIGHT ON A DATABASE ADMINISTRATOR

Technologies and technical skills required   A thorough understanding of relational database theory and development and experience with specific databases, including Oracle, Sybase, and DB2; basic programming expertise; plus depth and breadth in various operating systems, including Unix, VMS, and Windows NT. "You must be able to navigate through not just the database piece, but whatever other pieces are involved in building or tuning the databases," Dlubala explains. "If the database is running on Unix, you need to understand how to navigate through Unix directories and files."

Other skills required   "Intuition, forethought, and common sense. Also, detective skills are good—problem-analysis and determination. If you're doing monitoring and tuning, it's always good to snoop around and look for things that could be perform-ance bottlenecks but aren't necessarily obvious. Communication skills are somewhere between moderately and very important. Most of my projects require life-cycle docu-mentation that's read by IT directors and sometimes end-users, so you need to be able to write plain-English documentation."

What I like most about this job   "The variety of things that I do. And as far as spe-cific tasks, I like problem-solving more than new planning and development. To a cer-tain extent, I like the solitary aspects of it, but when you get embroiled in a problem, it helps to start a conversation with someone and get their opinion because they may have seen the problem before."

What I like least about this job   "As I'm getting older, I would say the hours. Because we're a large 24/7 environment, when we do changes to applications or install new things, it's usually done between 4:00 A.M. and 6:00 A.M. on Thursday mornings. That time slot is part of our negotiated service agreement with end-users. Fortunately, we don't have to do it every week."

Career path leading to this job   Dlubala joined Johns Hopkins in 1982 as an MVS systems programmer working on IBM mainframes. He gained his first relational data-base experience following an IT reorganization in the late eighties that moved him into the Unix area, where he did a combination of applications and database develop-ment work. Several years later, "the pendulum swung back to the mainframe," he says.

SPOTLIGHT ON A DATABASE ADMINISTRATOR

Johns Hopkins renewed its focus on mainframe applications development and installed IBM's mainframe-based relational database DB2. Dlubala was involved with migrating several Unix databases to DB2, and because he had prior mainframe programming experience, he moved back into applications development with a focus on DB2-related apps. In 1997, he moved back into the database group, working with Oracle.

Advice to other IT pros interested in database administrating   "A fairly even temperament and the ability to work well under pressure are assets in this job. The pressure we have is not constant, but some things occasionally require immediate attention for a couple of hours, so be flexible in terms of your day and your workflow. Persistence is also a good attribute to have."

TECHNICAL SKILLS REQUIRED   A solid grounding in relational database theory and concepts plus direct experience with a leading database; depth in at least one major operating system, and preferably several; familiarity with various database utilities and performance tools; experience with report generators, online analytical processing (OLAP) tools, and data-mining software. Programming skills are a big plus.

OTHER SKILLS REQUIRED   Troubleshooting and problem-solving skills; detail-oriented; oral and written communication skills for dealing with different members of the IT organization and creating documentation; working well with others as well as alone.

POTENTIAL CAREER PATHS   The most natural extension of DBA skills is to get more involved in database development, including data warehousing and data mining. Because DBAs work closely with applications developers, moving into a programming role or business analyst role is also a viable career path. Another option is to move over to technical support or operations.

IS THIS POSITION FOR YOU?   If you like a balance between teamwork and detailed solitary work, getting hands-on with the inner workings of technology, and uncovering and resolving painstaking problems that others might find tedious, you would find the database role challenging. Because of its close relationship to applications development, it also has strong creative aspects.

Data Warehouse Architect

JOB TITLE VARIATIONS   Data warehouse engineer; data warehouse application architect; senior data warehouse project manager.

JOB DESCRIPTION   The buck stops here in the design, development, and implementation of a data warehouse. The architect establishes an overall technical architecture that is consistent with the IT architecture and infrastructure, and oversees the complete construction of the warehouse and associated applications. Responsibilities include requirements-gathering and analysis, defining the architecture, setting standards, creating a web-based strategy for applications to run off the data warehouse (such as decision support systems, CRM systems, and knowledge management systems), and evaluating hardware, database software, middleware, data-mining tools, and required network capacity and infrastructure. This position typically requires substantial prior experience—ranging from seven to ten years in database and applications development, including exposure to data warehouses, data mining, decision-support systems, etc. But in smaller IT organizations, three to five years of data warehouse–related and project management experience may suffice.

EDUCATION AND CERTIFICATION REQUIREMENTS   A Bachelor's degree in Computer Science or in Business with an MIS/CIS concentration is usually required. Project management training and/or certification is preferred, if not essential, and change management training is also applicable. Any database or programming-related certification would be a plus.

TECHNICAL SKILLS REQUIRED   Command of applications development languages and tools such as Universal Modeling Language (UML), C, and Java; experience with database technologies including Oracle, SQL, DB2, and extract, transform, load (ETL) tools such as Informatica; prior use of data-mining, data-analysis, and data-modeling tools (such as OLAP tools and Cognos); and knowledge of Unix and/or network operating systems such as Windows NT or Windows 2000.

OTHER SKILLS REQUIRED   Because the implementation of a data warehouse requires the cooperation and support of cross-functional teams of IT professionals and business unit managers and end-users, excellent communication and negotiation skills are a must. The ability to manage and lead change is key because a data warehouse— and the applications it supports—will significantly transform business processes and workflow; to be successful, users must buy into the system and feel a sense of ownership in the project. A solid understanding of business priorities and processes, plus the ability to articulate a vision for how a data warehouse can contribute to those, is also essential.

DATABASE ADMINISTRATORS: THE MANAGEMENT PERSPECTIVE

Ian Drury, former chief technology officer (CTO), MVP.com, Chicago, Ill.

At the now defunct ecommerce startup MVP.com, which shut down in January 2001, the database administrators had a hybrid role, performing not only the traditional DBA duties of maintaining, monitoring, and fine-tuning the database, but also designing, developing, and analyzing databases. Here, the company's former CTO, who came up through the database ranks, discusses what it takes to succeed as a database professional.

What kind of skills and experience do you look for when hiring DBAs?

On the technical side, the DBA needs to be an expert in SQL [Structured Query Language] and how to improve the performance of SQL statements and queries. They may be analyzing performance-degrading queries, and they have to think about how to rewrite a query to bring back the same data but more efficiently from a performance perspective. Specifically, [at MVP.com] we wanted experience with Microsoft SQL Server, with three-to-five-years' experience designing and operating complex transactional databases, preferably in an ecommerce environment. And we wanted someone who had been forced to live with bad [database design] decisions so they would have that experience.

Our DBAs also needed to be grounded in the fundamentals of data modeling and understand the pros and cons of denormalization—taking two separate tables and combining them. You get some duplicate data, but you also get some performance advantages. We also wanted two to six months of applications development and coding experience so they could understand the viewpoint of the apps development team.

Aside from technical skills, what are the key attributes you look for in a DBA?

Interpersonal skills are important because the DBA is often at the center of things— working on one side with the applications development team and on the other with the operations team that is trying to keep things stable in the production environment. So good communication skills to bridge between those two areas, plus the ability to stay cool under pressure are essential.

How do DBAs contribute to the IT mission?

[In an ecommerce environment] we live and die every day by the performance of [the] site, and the site only works if the database is working well. So [the] revenue

DATABASE ADMINISTRATORS: THE MANAGEMENT PERSPECTIVE

stream is dependent on the database functioning well. Also, many ecommerce players have ever-changing business development deals and an ever-evolving business model, and the database has to support [the company] through that process. The design can either be an enabler or an inhibitor of our revenue streams, and the DBA has to think ahead and anticipate potential directions the business might go in and include [flexibility to adapt to change] in the design.

The DBA is particularly important in cases where you have developed a custom application. If you're using an off-the-shelf package, the database is included in that, and it's been tested and proven. In an environment where you're using a custom ecommerce app, it's even more critical to have a strong DBA.

Can you cite an example of the impact the DBA can have on a company?

We were in the middle of a pretty critical customer segmentation analysis project to identify new directions we should take our business in and how to satisfy those [target] customers. It would have been pretty difficult to pull the type of data we needed straight out of our production database, so we needed some tools to massage the data.

One of our DBAs jumped right in, and within a day, he had installed a fairly economical OLAP tool and was extracting data from the production database. Within two more days, he had pulled together over 50 reports that enabled us to complete the customer segmentation and analysis. That analysis drove a major site redesign, and the redesign resulted in increased conversion of shoppers into buyers, and thus an increase in revenue.

Is the DBA role as critical in larger, more traditional environments as it is at a startup?

I was a DBA for five years and very much felt that I made an impact. I spent part of that time developing the database for a custom billing system for Telstra [a teleommunications firm] in Australia. And that was a very similar situation, where the database was really the heart of the application. The database had to perform well in a production environment so customers could get answers to their questions about their accounts, but it also had to support new business directions that Telstra wanted to take.

DATABASE ADMINISTRATORS: THE MANAGEMENT PERSPECTIVE

In general, how can a DBA make an outstanding individual contribution on the job?

By really demonstrating a solution-oriented, can-do approach to attacking business problems, stepping outside the technical viewpoint, and understanding the business and how your contribution can have a bottom-line impact. Get involved early in the development life cycle so that you are contributing to the solution.

Create and communicate a plan and regular processes for how you'll support the development and production environments, including how often you'll introduce changes to the data model and execute utilities like backups, how you approach performance monitoring. And plan ahead for crises. Identify the worst things that can happen in a production environment, and document how you would respond to those situations. The time to think about it is when you have plenty of time to think clearly and exhaustively, not when the crisis happens.

NOTE *Excerpts from this interview appeared previously on the website www.leapit.com.*

POTENTIAL CAREER PATHS   Time spent in this position could lead into just about any applications development or database-related management path. Next steps could include manager or director of applications development, an e-business-related management position, leading advanced technology research and development, and others.

IS THIS POSITION FOR YOU?   If you have at least several years of database experience, including participation on data warehouse projects, and are looking for a growth position, becoming a data warehouse architect is a logical move for you. But, you must be willing to take on at least project management responsibility; depending on the IT organizational structure, the position often ranks above PMs. This position is available as a permanent job or a consulting gig.

Database Technologies Checklists

Databases

✓ IBM DB2

✓ Informix

✓ Microsoft Access

✓ Microsoft SQL Server

✓ Oracle 8i

✓ Sybase

Reporting Tools

✓ Crystal Reports

✓ Impromptu

✓ Oracle Reports

✓ SAS Enterprise Reporter

Online Analytical Processing Tools

✓ IBM Intelligent Decision Server

✓ Microsoft SQL Server OLAP Services

✓ SAP Business Information Warehouse

✓ SAS Software

Data Warehouse and Data-Mining Tools

✓ Cognos Scenario

✓ Cognos Visualizer

✓ IBM Intelligent Miner

✓ Oracle Darwin

✓ SAS Enterprise Miner

Chapter 5

· ·

Start Me Up in Networking and Infrastructure Jobs

Networking and infrastructure are the torso and limbs of IT; they move data and applications throughout a company and connect one part to another.

The differences between what constitutes the network and what constitutes infrastructure can be fuzzy, and the distinction between networking and infrastructure and operations is even blurrier. To borrow from the commonly used analogy of the Internet as a superhighway, networks are the streets, avenues, county and state roads, and interstates over which applications and data travel; the infrastructure comprises the traffic lights, intersections, bridges, overpasses, and entrance and exit ramps.

In technical terms, networks are a series of interconnected nodes—the large computers, servers, PCs, and other devices attached together—while infrastructure refers to the connecting hardware, software, and transmission media, including routers, hubs, cables, telephone lines, and so forth. Responsibility for networks and infrastructure typically falls to a dedicated group, but it sometimes seeps into the operations area; at the very least, the two groups must work closely together. (See Chapter 6.)

Day to day, the prime objective in networking and infrastructure is to ensure 24/7 uptime and availability of the network. In commercial enterprises, downtime can very quickly translate into lost revenue; there are not only the indirect losses stemming from the impact on user productivity, but with a growing dependence on Internet-based revenue streams, there can be a direct hit on the bottom line. Even in organizations whose revenues aren't dependent on network uptime, high performance and throughput are vital to daily operations.

Consider the research network for the National Energy Research Scientific Computing Center (NERSC Center) division of the Lawrence Berkeley National Laboratory, in Berkeley, California. It supports the efforts of about 2,500 scientists and researchers worldwide, who use the network to exchange information and access the lab's supercomputer to do the intensive calculations required in their research. "We're the largest unclassified computer center in the world," says Brent Draney, a network analyst at NERSC. "Where most companies measure things in gigabytes, we measure them in terabytes, and we're currently working toward a petabyte of online storage—that's 1,000 terabytes. So I'm constantly dealing with our ability to have the best possible throughput. If you look at the amount of data we're capable of dealing with, it does no good if people can't get it to us."

So in any networked environment, performance degradation or an outage are critical events. It falls to the networking and infrastructure team to ensure that they don't happen and to recover as quickly as possible when they do. Long term, the mission in networking and infrastructure is to anticipate future resource requirements, scale for growth, and optimize network performance. Demand for top-notch networking professionals, therefore, is extremely high. Securing the physical network and the data that travels over it is the other significant part of both the day-to-day and long-term objectives in networking and infrastructure, although there's a growing—and fiercely debated—trend to parcel out the responsibility to a corporate security department. Wherever the responsibility falls, network security is the hot growth area for networking professionals.

Networking and Infrastructure Jobs: A Sampler

Network Administrator

JOB TITLE VARIATIONS   LAN administrator, NT administrator, network infrastructure administrator.

JOB DESCRIPTION   Network administrators keep local area networks (LANs) up and running, and as such, they are among the most in-demand IT professionals. Every company that has a network must have at least one network administrator. Depending on the size of the company and the IT organizational structure, network admins may be assigned to a specific LAN for a department, business unit, or division, or several LANs throughout the company. The job mainly entails managing and updating network operating systems, but it can also encompass these tasks: providing server management, maintenance, and updates; granting user-access rights and passwords; providing security administration; providing end-user support directly or in conjunction with a helpdesk; documenting procedures and problem resolutions; and ensuring that applications on the network are running properly.

SPOTLIGHT ON A NETWORK INFRASTRUCTURE ADMINISTRATOR

Jason Bornstein, 30, team leader for NT infrastructure support, Entergy Corp., New Orleans, La.

Entergy, a major southern utility, outsources all of its IT organization to Science Applications International Corporation (SAIC), which in turn has subcontracted with The Highland Group. Bornstein, who has been in IT since 1994, is a Highland Group employee who works onsite at Entergy.

Overall responsibilities   To manage and maintain the infrastructure for the Windows NT environment, including troubleshooting, diagnosing, resolving, and preventing technical problems. "It's a roll-up-your-sleeves-and-get-in-there kind of job. I'm in charge of infrastructure support for SMS [Microsoft Systems Management Server] and MS-SQL, plus planning and support for the NT domain infrastructure. SMS and SQL Server work hand-in-hand: SMS inventories all of Entergy's workstations and enables electronic software distribution, and all the information about the applications inventory, location, etc., is stored on SQL Server."

Day-to-day responsibilities   "It's more or less waiting for something to break. And I do a lot of preventive maintenance—running database consistency checks, some minor coding like writing Perl scripts to see if the databases need to be expanded, and managing the (applications) inventory data. Sometimes I'm involved in an ongoing project, like an operating system upgrade or a reorganization of network infrastructure components like Wins and DHCP [Dynamic Host Configuration Protocol]. I hardly ever deal with end-users—I can't remember the last time I did. But I do have customers—field support staff and other IT groups—whenever they have problems with their servers. I'm part of a team [that builds and maintains NT servers], but I'm the only person on my team who does what I do, which is a bit of an honor but also a bit of a burden when things go wrong."

Technologies and technical skills required   Windows NT, SMS, SQL Server, storage area network (SAN) solutions, and Perl scripting. "When we're hiring new people, analytical skills are what we look for most—technical skills can be taught. I didn't have a lot of formal training; I'm mainly self-taught through books and magazines. I took all my MCSE tests in an eight-week period about five years ago, but I've let my certification lapse. I just don't find it helpful. In this job it's more about demonstrating what you know day-by-day than having a piece of paper that says you're qualified. Even degrees don't matter that much. But I'm currently going to school at night for a Bachelor's in Information Systems Technology at Tulane University."

SPOTLIGHT ON A NETWORK INFRASTRUCTURE ADMINISTRATOR

Other skills required   General troubleshooting and analytical skills. "I don't have to know exactly how everything works as long as I know how to break it down into its component parts and can troubleshoot which part is failing. It requires a lot of improvisation. I'll fix something, and someone will say, 'How did you know to do that?' Well, I didn't know—I just tried it."

What I like most about this job   "The flexibility. I can set my own direction, choose what I want to learn, and take on new tasks in my downtime. Right now, I'm reading up on Windows 2000, more complex uses of Perl, and thinking about getting Linux certification. I have a Linux box on my desk, and part of my downtime plan is to learn that."

What I like least about this job   "There's not anything I seriously dislike except that after you get the hang of [this job], it gets kind of boring. After you've faced your first few big issues, the day-to-day operations are easy to handle. A good day is actually when something goes wrong because that makes it interesting. When things are running smoothly, sometimes you're bored out of your mind. So I just keep reading up on new technology, trying to stay ahead of the curve. I'd like to remain in infrastructure, but maybe under a different umbrella, like Linux or Unix."

Career path leading to this job   Bornstein got his start in IT just by clowning around—literally. After buying his first computer, he realized he had a knack for troubleshooting and problem-solving, and he started doing small maintenance and setup jobs for small businesses. But he was supporting himself by working as a clown at local events, and he fortuitously ended up working a large banquet at a computer convention. "I was going from table to table, and at one I noticed that they had these IBM tambourines as favors. So I started making these obscure technology jokes, and one of the attendees asked me what I did for a day job." When he told her PC troubleshooting, she was impressed enough by the knowledge his jokes had demonstrated to suggest he apply for a job with her company, a small outsourcing firm. A few weeks later, he had his first full-time IT job doing field support and troubleshooting for PCs and LANs for the outsourcing firm's local clients, including Entergy. There he met the president of The Highland Group and joined the firm in 1997.

Advice to other IT pros interested in IT infrastructure   "You should be very open-minded about the technology. There are a lot of egos in IT, a lot of technical arrogance. Sometimes you'll get into a contest with a coworker over who knows more about how a problem should be resolved. So you have to be willing to put your ego aside and try not to react to the attitudes around you."

Basic network administration can be an entry-level position, but it usually requires two-to-three-years' work experience. Theoretically, the migration to Windows 2000 may reduce the number of network administrators needed in larger companies. With older network operating systems such as Novell NetWare and Windows NT, each separate LAN domain requires a dedicated administrator. In Windows 2000, Active Directory centralizes domain management, so depending on size, Windows 2000 networks can be administered by a few or even one network admin.

EDUCATION AND CERTIFICATION REQUIREMENTS   A Bachelor's degree in Computer Science or other IT-related degree is required. Equivalent work experience may substitute, especially if combined with certification, such as the Microsoft Certified Systems Engineer (MCSE) or Novell's Certified Network Engineer (CNE). Certification is almost always listed as a requirement in job descriptions, and while the right qualifications can substitute, it is nonetheless highly recommended. The number of network administrators with the MCSE has grown so substantially that it may be needed just to even the playing field with other job seekers. Certification in complementary operating systems such as Unix and Linux is a huge plus, as are the Cisco Certified Network Associate (CCNA) or Cisco Certified Network Professional (CCNP) credentials.

TECHNICAL SKILLS REQUIRED   Network operating system expertise (especially command of the user domain structures), including Windows 2000 Server, Windows NT, Novell NetWare, Sun Solaris or Linux; Internet technologies expertise; knowledge of server software such as Microsoft Internet Information Server (IIS), Microsoft Exchange, Lotus Notes/Domino, etc.; basic network security know-how; an understanding of network hardware, such as routers, switches, and hubs; and a working knowledge of the applications running on the network. Familiarity with the latter is needed to help troubleshoot whether the cause of a problem is at the applications layer, server layer, or network-operating-system layer, as well as to provide helpdesk and field support to end-users. Network administrators should also understand different network topologies and how the LAN connects into the wide area network (WAN). Some basic programming or scripting skills are recommended.

OTHER SKILLS REQUIRED   Troubleshooting and problem-solving, patience in dealing with end-users, ability to do detailed documentation in clear and precise language, and the wherewithal to quickly research solutions to problems. Although perceived as a backroom position, network admins must nonetheless possess good communication skills for dealing with end-users, IT coworkers, and management.

POTENTIAL CAREER PATHS   Network administrators can progress up the chain of command in networking and infrastructure, advancing to network engineer or network architect, for example. Other logical moves include security administration, systems administration, and operations.

IS THIS POSITION FOR YOU?   If you want a hands-on technical job that offers a good view of the overall IT organization, holds the promise of growth into a variety of areas, and offers tremendous job security, network administration is a good choice.

Network Engineer

JOB TITLE VARIATIONS   Infrastructure engineer, network analyst, network manager, network designer.

JOB DESCRIPTION   Whereas network administrators are focused on LANs, network engineers work on the WAN. Generally, network engineers deploy, configure, test, monitor, maintain, and manage the WAN infrastructure, such as routers, hubs, switches, and software. But this can be a catch-all job title that entails different responsibilities in different organizations, including capacity planning, administration, and analysis, design and testing of the WAN, virtual private networks (VPNs), the intranet, and connections to the Internet. Depending on the IT environment, the network may integrate voice, data, video, email, voice messaging, and transaction systems in a seamless whole. Network engineering may also encompass developing and managing automated network management systems. Given their complexity, network engineering positions usually require two to three years of network administration experience.

EDUCATION AND CERTIFICATION REQUIREMENTS   A Bachelor's degree in Computer Science or a related engineering discipline is usually required, although equivalent work experience can substitute. Cisco's CCNA or CCNP or a vendor-neutral certification in networking hardware is highly recommended, as are certifications in network operating systems such as Microsoft's MCSE, Novell's CNE, or a Linux or Unix certification.

TECHNICAL SKILLS REQUIRED   Knowledge of all major network operating systems and server software (see the "Network Administrator" section); experience with network hardware, especially Cisco equipment, including routers, brouters, hubs, switches, cabling, etc.; an understanding of the different types of WAN topologies and their benefits and uses, including Ethernet, VPNs, frame relay, asynchronous transfer mode (ATM), digital subscriber line (DSL), T-base, IBM's Systems Network Architecture (SNA), and more; an understanding of network protocols, such as Transmission Control Protocol/Internet Protocol (TCP/IP) and the OSI reference model (a de facto standard description of the seven layers of technology required for two computers to communicate); Internet technologies; network management techniques and standards, such as Simple Network Management Protocol (SNMP), and products such as Computer Associates' Unicenter, Hewlett-Packard's OpenView, etc.; and a thorough understanding of network security techniques and procedures, including firewalls and best practices for incident response and recovery. Basic programming and/or scripting skills are recommended if not required.

OTHER SKILLS REQUIRED   Communication and documentation skills; troubleshooting and problem-solving; ability to work well on teams; and persistence.

POTENTIAL CAREER PATHS   Network engineers can advance through the networking and infrastructure ranks in roles such as infrastructure project manager and network architect, and then move into networking or operations management. A transition into network security is also an option. These jobs are plentiful and high-profile within Internet service providers (ISPs) and application service providers (ASPs), as well as telecommunications and cable companies.

IS THIS POSITION FOR YOU?   If you live and breathe computer networking, enjoy a hands-on technical role that has growth potential on both a technical track and a management track, and are detail-oriented without sacrificing the big-picture perspective, network engineering is one of the most challenging and critical roles in IT.

TIP Network engineering job titles and descriptions sometimes feature the word "telecommunications." Its meaning was at one time very clearly focused on voice communications or on jobs within telecommunications providers, such as RBOCs and long-distance carriers. But as voice and data networks have merged, and the telecom industry has gone through myriad changes, telecommunications has a much broader meaning. It is sometimes synonymous with infrastructure, sometimes refers to computer-telephony (networks and applications that integrate phone networks and computers, such as in call centers), and sometimes refers to the WAN topology (i.e., a frame relay, ATM, or DSL network may be referred to as a telecommunications network). Before you rule out a job opportunity that includes "telecommunications" in the title or description, read the job requirements closely. It may be just what you're looking for.

NETWORK ENGINEERING: THE MANAGEMENT PERSPECTIVE

Oriya Pollak, cofounder and vice president of technology and network operations, iNYC.com, a DSL service provider and high-end web hosting service, Brooklyn, N.Y.

Pollak is one of those quintessential self-made IT career fast-trackers. He interned for a website design and development startup during high school and earned his first certification—the A+ PC Technician Certification—right after he graduated. With that under his belt, he started doing small consulting jobs to gain experience and pursued the MCSE in Windows NT. Driven by an entrepreneurial spirit, he cofounded iNYC, one of the first DSL service providers, in May 1999.

Not content to rest on his laurels, he subsequently garnered the Microsoft Certified Trainer (MCT), the MCSE+I (Internet specialization), Cisco's CCNA and CCNP, as well as Red Hat's Linux certification. Today, he manages a staff of 12 network engineers and oversees operations for a wide area DSL network with 7 point-of-presence servers connected to the national Internet backbone and 3,500 nodes.

What are the major differences between working in an ISP and working in the networking group of a corporate IT organization?

The major difference is that in internal IT, your responsibilities are very specific—you're dealing with a limited number of operating systems and server types and applications, so you need to master a few things really well. In an ISP, you're dealing with a whole lot of different things—multiple hardware platforms and operating systems, and every client's environment is different. So you must be a good overall network engineer because you'll be exposed to a lot more technologies. You need to know all the network and Internet protocols because in an ISP, you have a lot of different networks connected together, and then those are connected into the nationwide backbone.

In my group, our internal network administration is only 5 percent of what we manage. It's only 50 nodes. Whereas my ISP network has 3,500 nodes to manage, and many different topologies—ATM, frame relay, IP, etc. So, you just have a lot more going on.

Aside from technical skills, what are the key attributes you look for in a networking professional?

I make sure that they are not afraid of the technology and don't have any technology biases. I don't like to hire people who say they're strictly into Solaris or Linux or NT—they have to like learning new things. And just as important is that the candidate is a people person. Even though networking pros are supposedly backroom people, they have to know how to talk to people, how to have a conversation.

NETWORK ENGINEERING: THE MANAGEMENT PERSPECTIVE

Why are those attributes important in networking?

If engineers are limited technically, it will limit your business. If there's a new technology out there that can help your business, you need to be ready to go forward with it, and if someone is afraid of learning a new technology or has biases against certain technologies, they won't be able to help you move forward.

People skills are important because if the network isn't working, then you have to send an engineer to the client site, and if they can really talk to users, that improves the whole process of troubleshooting. If they can establish a relationship with the users, then you can start to provide proactive support—the user will feel comfortable calling and asking how we can prevent the possibility of future problems. That kind of proactive support is important for us as an ISP because we're trying to generate revenue and earn a profit. But that service ethic is just as important in a corporate networking organization because it bridges the gap between IT and the business.

What technical skills and experience do you look for?

At a minimum, you must know IP networking, all the basic operating systems like Windows NT and 2000, and you should know your way around Unix or Linux. Actually, most of the network administrators we hire are Linux pros, because if you can do Linux, you can handle Windows 2000 or Windows NT. They should be able to demonstrate an understanding of everything from the IP level to the application level.

If someone has experience as a network administrator, that's great. If they have no prior networking experience but have been curious enough to, say, set up a Linux box in their living room, that can be okay, too. I just hired a guy for network technical support who had never done the job before, but he has a network at home with two NT boxes and two Linux boxes. He clearly isn't afraid of learning new things because he's been playing at home. He had worked in customer service for a high-tech vendor, so he knows how to talk to people. He told me straight out that he didn't know anything about Cisco, but said, "Give me a book and let me learn it." He just made me feel confident in him.

You yourself have a lot of technical certifications—do you expect the people you hire to have them, too?

I look for experience, and if I can afford to hire the person with the best experience, then I don't care about certification. But if I can't afford the most experienced person, then a piece of paper is good because it shows that the candidate is a hard worker who's dedicated, goes out and reads the books, and is ready to learn new things.

NETWORK ENGINEERING: THE MANAGEMENT PERSPECTIVE

I definitely recommend that people finish college, because this industry is crazy. I've been lucky, but I urge people not to mess around with their education because you never know what's going to happen. Get some real knowledge behind you, and get hands-on experience at the same time. Go for internships, volunteer to work for free—that's a great way to learn because you're allowed to mess up when you're new and not getting paid.

What kind of temperament do you need to succeed in networking?

You need to be calm, focused, and sharp. You must be curious, but know when to be cautious. And a sense of humor is really important. It's a big plus because you'll take things more lightly and won't get angry when things are going crazy around you. You'll be dealing with a lot of crises and have four people on hold who all need something and need it now. So you have to stay calm, and help calm them down, and then stay focused on what you have to do.

What's your advice to networking professionals?

Invest time in learning new skills and getting certified. You're working hard, and on the weekend you want to go out or just kick back. But stay in and study. And don't delay your test. Take it right after you study, and if you fail it, take it again the next day and study all night. You'll never know everything, but you'll know enough.

Don't do what you don't like. Don't take Cisco certification just because it pays well. If you prefer Linux administration, take that because if you like it, you'll be more productive. Focus on what you like, and try to be the best at it. Give yourself a time table—two weeks to learn this, four weeks to learn that—and write it out.

But keep in mind that you should branch out beyond just your core expertise. If you specialize in Windows NT administration, take time to learn about Cisco routers and TCP/IP and other operating systems. Books are your best friends. You should be reading three or four hours a night. Don't get stuck on one topic—get books on Cisco, ATM, Windows, Linux, SQL—because in networking, you'll deal with many different users, many different scenarios, many different technologies, and you need to at least be familiar with what a technology is supposed to do.

Network Architect

JOB TITLE VARIATIONS   Network designer, lead network engineer, infrastructure architect.

JOB DESCRIPTION   The network architect's role is definitely a management position, but how high-ranking it is depends on the size and structure of a given IT organization. It can range from a high-level project management role to a director- or VP-level position; it may also be initially given to a consultant who gradually hands the reigns over to an internal network engineer. But regardless of management rank, the network architect's role is to oversee the design, deployment, and long-term growth management of a company's entire network infrastructure, including LANs, the intranet, Internet connections, VPNs, and the WAN.

Responsibilities include analyzing network requirements now and in the future, performing capacity planning, evaluating and selecting network hardware, ensuring that new systems and software are compliant with the technical architecture, and designing and deploying the network management scheme. The network architect works closely with security, operations, and applications development management in assessing long-term needs, as well as with business units regarding the types of applications and number of employees to be added to the network in the future. If a company lacks a dedicated security architect, that responsibility will also fall to the network architect.

EDUCATION AND CERTIFICATION REQUIREMENTS   At least a Bachelor's degree in Computer Science or a related field is required; a techno-M.B.A. is a plus. Certifications such as Cisco's CCNA and CCNP, Microsoft's MCSE, and others will put candidates on a fast track for this position.

TECHNICAL SKILLS REQUIRED   The network architect possesses all the technical skills of the network administrator and network engineer, with greater depth and breadth. The most qualified candidates have spent time in both positions, as well as in a security-related capacity and operations. Direct experience in applications architecture is a huge plus; at a minimum the network architect has a solid understanding of applications requirements.

OTHER SKILLS REQUIRED   Forecasting and planning skills; ability to do detailed documentation; communication and negotiation skills; ability to lead and manage change; project management skills; and staff management and budgeting skills.

POTENTIAL CAREER PATHS   This position is definitely a stepping stone into upper IT management within networking or operations. Another possibility is moving into a technology research and development (R&D) management position. In the long term, experience in this position can lead to chief network officer in companies where that position exists or the chief technology officer. High-level consulting is another option.

IS THIS POSITION FOR YOU?   If you have come up through the networking ranks and are looking for a management-level position that is strategic while still hands-on technical, the network architect's role is one to aspire to. But you must be ready to manage staff and deal with top-level managers across IT and within business units.

Security Administrator

JOB TITLE VARIATIONS   Network security analyst, security specialist, network security engineer.

JOB DESCRIPTION   With viruses, denial of service (DOS) attacks, network break-ins, data theft, and other security incidents on the rise, this is one of the fastest-growing and most demanding jobs in all of IT. Security administrators are focused on detecting, reacting to, and preventing all types of security breaches, requiring them to operate in both a reactive and proactive capacity at all times. Moreover, in addition to ensuring the security of the physical network, security admins are also concerned with the security and integrity of the data on the network. Responsibilities include staying up-to-date daily on new threats, flaws, and vulnerabilities; downloading, testing, and installing software patches to tighten up network security; monitoring network traffic for unusual events; conducting other intrusion detection tests; establishing incident recovery procedures; helping determine and enforce corporate security policy; educating users; establishing user access rights, and more. In reactive mode, once an incident is detected, administrators follow an incident-handling process—such as those used by emergency response teams—for clarifying the problem and its cause, fixing it, and restoring the system.

EDUCATION AND CERTIFICATION REQUIREMENTS   A Bachelor's degree in Computer Science is preferred, if not required. A few undergraduate and graduate degree programs have emerged offering an information security specialization, which, if combined with the right experience, would certainly move a candidate to the top of the

SPOTLIGHT ON A SECURITY ADMINISTRATOR

Leon Rosenstein, 25, security/network administrator, "The Montel Williams Show," New York, N.Y.

Overall responsibilities   "Intrusion prevention, detection, and recovery. Hopefully, the recovery part isn't necessary, for obvious reasons. There's no such thing as perfect security. It really comes down to risk management, and every organization has different risks. We worry about other shows finding out the topics for our shows, for example. That's our intellectual property. I have to set our security policy and educate users. I also do network administration and serve as the helpdesk. We have about 80 systems here—mostly Macs, plus an NT server and a Linux box—so I'm almost past my limit of what I can keep up with on my own. I'm managing to stay on the bucking bronco, but it's not an easy ride."

Day-to-day responsibilities   "It depends on how big a day it is in the security world. The first thing I do is read all of the day's security alerts—I'm on about ten different mailing lists. It's a lot of research into new vulnerabilities. If there are new flaws, there will be a patch issued, and I have to deal with determining whether we're vulnerable, and if so, downloading, testing, and installing the patch. I check my firewall and server logs every day—that's very important because it lets me know the traffic going in and out every day—plus make sure the backup is working and audit user actions. For example, if a user login fails three consecutive times, I'll log in and see what's going on. It's a proactive measure because that's a sign of a potential threat. It could be an indication that someone is trying out passwords illegally.

"As a network admin, I'm basically a firefighter. For example, if there's a problem with a printer, I have to redirect traffic to avoid it. Or we like to see photos of people before we put them on the show, and sometimes their pictures come over in weird file formats, so I have to straighten that out. But sometimes there are major net admin issues—like making major topology changes to the network. In terms of helpdesk support, I get a lot of questions about Microsoft Office, especially PowerPoint and Publisher."

Technologies and technical skills required   "Here we run an NT network, but I need to know as many operating systems as possible—NT Server, Windows 2000, Linux, Macintosh (Mac OS 8 or 9.1)—plus Microsoft Internet Information Server, Exchange Mail Server, TCP/IP, IDS [Intrusion Detection System] for traffic analysis, and PGP [Pretty Good Privacy] encryption. I also do some Perl scripting, although I'm not as fluent as I should be. I can only write very basic stuff or download Perl scripts from the Web and make changes to them."

SPOTLIGHT ON A SECURITY ADMINISTRATOR

Other skills required "You have to work well under pressure and must have people skills. Users will try to circumvent your security policy if it becomes restrictive, so you have to be able to teach them, coax them, in plain English. You need to be charismatic. Multitasking is important because within one two-minute span, I might get a security alert that the version of the firewall I'm using has a fatal flaw, and I need to download a patch for it, and at the same time Montel's manager calls and says her computer isn't working, and I have to take care of both ASAP. And troubleshooting and problem-solving; there may be fewer issues to troubleshoot, but they're much more dramatic."

What I like most about this job "I just love everything about security. It's just all so fascinating. I love the reading and the constant learning and the 'me vs. them' state of mind. There's a kind of mysticism to the security culture; I love the whole challenge of the good guys vs. the bad guys."

What I like least about this job "Sometimes it's very overwhelming. We haven't had any security incidents here, but traffic analysis is very intensive—it's searching for the needle in the haystack. It can be very draining mentally, and you're in the middle of it and that's when something on the network breaks down that needs your immediate attention. Sometimes there's a lot of pressure. In one job that I did as a consultant, there were so many back doors into the client's network it was ridiculous. Fighting off a DOS attack is very time-consuming because it involves so much coordination with others, and everyone has their own agenda. Or sometimes you have clashes between programmers and security administrators. A developer may write a CGI [common gateway interface] script that's not secure, and the net admin won't put it on the network, and then there's a playground stand-off. So there can be a lot going on at once."

Career path leading to this job "About three years ago, I was working as a network administrator at an entertainment payroll company, and one day we just had no Internet access. We couldn't figure out the problem, and when we called the ISP, no one there could figure it out either—not even the VP of technology. It turned out to be a DOS attack, and the ISP eventually realized it, but only after days and days of looking at logs. It was a targeted attack against our company launched from a computer on another continent. And once we got our service restored, they attacked us again two hours later.

SPOTLIGHT ON A SECURITY ADMINISTRATOR

"I just found the whole thing so interesting—the forensic aspect of computer crime is very different from regular crime. There's evidence, but it's not physical evidence. There's this spy-counterspy aspect. So I started trying to immerse myself in intrusion detection and the computer security culture. Security had always interested me because I'd read about these 14-year-olds who would break into corporate networks and steal credit card numbers. And it seemed so extreme that someone so young could outwit someone more than twice their age who's earning a six-figure salary. So when I went through that DOS attack, I just decided to take the plunge.

"I've always been self-taught, so I started reading all the books and getting fairly good at it. I joined all the mailing lists—Bugtraq was particularly helpful—and focused all my attention on security. I have four networked computers in my apartment, and I would break into my own computers and infect them—which is legal because they're mine. And I learned by doing. I simulated real situations by putting on software with real vulnerabilities, and then I'd look at what happened and how to restore the system. Then I started doing penetration testing, where you try to get into the mindset of a hacker and try to break into other computers. I got my friends to let me break into their computers, and then I started getting professional references to small businesses. By then I started to feel that I could put security skills on my resumé—it probably took me about two years to feel competent. This is my first job as a dedicated security admin."

Advice to other IT pros interested in network security   "Read as much as you can, and when you think you've read enough, you've just gotten started. When new patches come out, test them and apply them. Don't procrastinate. If you're a network administrator and you're interested in security, bring it up with your manager. Volunteer to start logging certain events, and slowly take on more responsibility. Set up a network in your home, and attack your own systems as a test. There's no substitute for real-life experience."

list. Certification is highly recommended, and not just the MCSE. A number of vendor-specific security programs are available, but an independent, vendor-neutral certification—such as those from the Global Incident Analysis Center (GIAC) or the International Information Systems Security Certifications Consortium (ISC2) will ensure the most thorough training.

TECHNICAL SKILLS REQUIRED   Experience as a network or systems administrator plus in-depth knowledge of as many operating systems as possible, including Windows 2000, Windows NT, Unix in all its flavors, Linux, and Macintosh OS; experience with common server software running on top of the OS, such as Microsoft IIS, Microsoft Exchange, Lotus Notes/Domino, and other server software; an understanding of major networking protocols (TCP/IP), various network topologies, and different types of telecommunications networks, such as Ethernet, frame relay, ATM, Integrated Services Digital Network (ISDN), DSL networks, and others; Internet technologies; familiarity with Secure Sockets Layer (SSL), email filters, firewalls, VPNs, data encryption programs like Pretty Good Privacy (PGP), and other security techniques and standards.

OTHER SKILLS REQUIRED   Troubleshooting, problem-solving, logical thinking, and communication skills are essential. Sometimes just detecting an intrusion is a challenge—they aren't all obvious. And once detected, security administrators must assess the effects of the intrusion, how to block it, and how to recover from it, all of which involves observation, hypothesizing, deduction, and collaboration with others. Imagination is a huge asset if not a requirement. Security administrators should be able to get into the mindset of intruders and anticipate what they might want to do and how they would do it.

POTENTIAL CAREER PATHS   Security experts are in such high demand that security administrators with depth and breadth of experience can pursue consulting; companies frequently hire outsiders to do penetration testing or to contribute to developing the network security architecture. Staying within the corporate fold, options include moving up the management ranks in security and network infrastructure, shifting focus from physical network security to customer/data privacy, or applying security expertise in other network, infrastructure, or operations roles, such as network architect or director of operations. Security administrators who want to take up the cause of incident survival, vulnerability research, and security education should consider joining a response team organization (such as CERT, GIAC, or others). Those usually hire the crème de la crème, so your skills and experience must be top-notch.

NETWORK SECURITY: THE MANAGEMENT PERSPECTIVE

Jeffrey Carpenter, technical manager at the Computer Emergency Response Team (CERT) Coordination Center, Pittsburgh, Pa.

Carpenter manages a team of 25 security analysts and administrators at the CERT Coordination Center, part of the Software Engineering Institute's Networked Systems Survivability Program. CERT was formed by the Defense Advanced Research Projects Agency (DARPA), the U.S. Department of Defense agency that developed the Internet. It was December 1988, only two months after the now-infamous Morris Worm crippled about 10 percent of all computers connected to the Internet, drawing attention to the need for standard practices for surviving network attacks. In addition to its original mission of providing incident response services to networks that have been breached, CERT also studies Internet vulnerabilities, publishes security alerts and best practices, provides security training, and helps launch other response teams.

In terms of day-to-day work, how is working in the network security area distinct from other areas of IT? What's the mission?

The mission is to react to spontaneous security problems and work to ensure long-term security, but if there are differences between network security jobs and other IT jobs, that shouldn't be the case. Security needs to be stressed more in all IT jobs—that's why we're in the predicament we're in now. Security is not a one-time thing where you go in, secure your machines, and then you're done. It must be ongoing, in short-term reactive mode, long-term proactive mode, and short-term proactive mode.

Security is more than just dealing with viruses and hackers. On an abstract level, it's about guaranteeing that your sensitive information is only accessed by authorized users. You have to go beyond the machines themselves and make protecting the data, ensuring data integrity, and monitoring access part of your business processes so that data is secure at a high level. There needs to be a top-down approach so that you can prioritize what is valuable and important to the company and then determine the adequate level of security.

NETWORK SECURITY: THE MANAGEMENT PERSPECTIVE

Aside from technical skills, what's the most important attribute you look for in network security professionals?

Problem-solving skills and communication skills are extremely important, and when I conduct interviews, I ask questions to probe candidates' abilities in both areas. It's often some time into the interview before I ask a specific technical question. To determine problem-solving skills, I'll give a scenario that doesn't have a single right or wrong answer, and ask the candidate to talk through how they'd solve the problem so I can measure the steps they go through and how they speculate what the problem might be. Sometimes, I deliberately don't give enough information so I can see what kind of discovery process they go through. I judge their communication skills all throughout the interview, but I may also ask about how they would handle hypothetical situations that would show me how they interoperate with other people [end-users and coworkers].

They must be very strong technically, but security professionals must also have business knowledge and understand a company's products and services so they can determine what is valuable information: Intellectual property? Customer data? Every business has to evaluate what their valuable assets are because they're different for each organization, and that's how you formulate the appropriate security plan. It requires much more than technical knowledge to do that. You can't just hire a systems administrator or net admin to do that—it has to involve people who understand business processes.

What kind of prior experience do you like to see on a candidate's résumé?

Most security knowledge today is gained through experience—you can't read a book and be a security expert—so an entry-level person is unlikely to get a security job. There aren't enough degree-granting programs that focus on security. As a nation, we have a big deficiency there. I would consider someone who has an undergraduate or graduate-level education specifically in a security-related program—as long as they fit the other criteria—but there just aren't that many out there. Most of the people we have here started as systems administrators or net admins, and that's the best avenue available today. You start there and try to increase your security responsibilities within that position.

NETWORK SECURITY: THE MANAGEMENT PERSPECTIVE

So I look for experience that shows they've demonstrated problem-solving skills, have significant technical expertise, and have experience working on teams and/or directly with end-users. I like to see what actual jobs they've done and projects they've completed. And in the interview, I'll measure them against how much technical expertise they should have based on what's on their résumé. I also look for evidence that they're creative and have initiative.

Why are creativity and initiative important in network security?

They're actually important for any IT job, but especially in network security. Creativity takes problem-solving to another level. It's important here at CERT because one of our responsibilities is to give [IT shops] advice on what they need to do to defend their networks against what may happen tomorrow. So you have to be innovative to anticipate what the eventualities might be, and then figure out how they can protect themselves from those—in addition to today's problems and yesterday's.

That's where you need initiative. It's about having the tenacity to see a problem through and to figure out how, in addition to what you're already doing, you can have a greater impact. It's thinking beyond your day-to-day responsibilities and looking at security in a proactive way.

What's your advice to IT pros who want to establish a network security career?

Look within your organization for ways you can add security responsibilities to what you're doing. When I was a systems administrator, I didn't initially have any security responsibilities, but by the end I did because I looked for opportunities to add security aspects to everything I did. Over time, that became part of my job.

I can't recommend enough reading to help get a better understanding of security. Certainly, if there's a university near you that has an information security program, that's certainly worth looking at. And a number of professional organizations and conferences address security in tutorials and conferences. Those also enable you to network and meet others in fields that you can learn from.

IS THIS POSITION FOR YOU?   If you like whodunits, are drawn to themes of good vs. evil, enjoy brainteasers, and have strong powers of deduction, all combined with a technical orientation, security administrator could be the job for you. Part detective, part IT pro, this position will only continue to grow in stature in the long term.

TIP Quite often, the responsibility for security administration falls into the hands of the network administrator. But the number of new security incidents is growing at such a rapid rate that it is difficult for network admins to keep up with all the new information and perform their regular duties, notes Stephen Northcutt, director of GIAC at the SANS Institute, in Baltimore. "Major new exploits come up every couple of weeks, and dealing with them requires fairly specialized skills," he explains. He recommends that larger organizations have one or two dedicated security administrators who are part of the network administration group. Network or systems administrators looking for a next step up in their career should propose that their company break out the security admin function or consider looking for an employer that already does.

Information Security Architect

JOB TITLE VARIATIONS   Director of information security, network security architect.

JOB DESCRIPTION   Sometimes a middle-management role, sometimes higher, the security architect is in charge of developing and deploying the overall IT security plan, architecture, and strategy, and managing the security staff activities. Depending on the corporate organizational structure, this position may be part of the IT network and infrastructure group or a separate corporate security department. Either way, the security architect will work closely with managers across all of IT as well as business unit management to set security priorities and policy, develop recovery procedures, assess and manage risk, and ensure both physical network and data security. Prior experience in security-related jobs is required; other relevant experience includes disaster recovery, operations, networking, and systems integration.

EDUCATION AND CERTIFICATION REQUIREMENTS   At a minimum, this position requires an IT-related college degree. An advanced degree with a specialty in networks and information security is a plus. Independent, vendor-neutral certification—such as the GIAC or ISC2 programs—is highly recommended, if not required.

TECHNICAL SKILLS REQUIRED   A minimum of five years' security experience plus other IT experience is the norm for the security architect's position. Generally, security architects come up through the technical ranks, and they should have depth and breadth in all aspects of networking and security.

OTHER SKILLS REQUIRED   Because setting security policy and procedures requires understanding what constitutes a company's most valuable information, assets, and intellectual property, security architects must have a solid understanding of a company's products and services, marketplace and competition, and business processes. Companies will typically look within to fill this position, or if they recruit from outside, will look for prior experience in their industry niche. Communication, documentation, and negotiation skills are a must, as the security architect must foster cooperation with other IT and business departments and at times will have to navigate through turf battles. Prior experience managing project teams is a must.

POTENTIAL CAREER PATHS   If executed successfully, this job can be a stepping-stone to the executive suite, including the CTO or CIO office. Another emerging high-level title is the chief privacy officer, who oversees the protection of customer data. Security architects can also carve out careers as high-level security consultants.

IS THIS POSITION FOR YOU?   If you're a security expert who enjoys looking at the big picture and you're interested in climbing the management ranks, the security architect's role will be a key strategic career move. You must be interested in managing people as well as security.

Network and Infrastructure Technologies Checklists

Operating Systems, Server Software, and Applications

✓ Email software

✓ Linux

✓ Lotus Notes

✓ Microsoft Exchange

✓ Microsoft Internet Information Server (IIS)

✓ Novell NetWare

✓ Unix (including Sun Solaris, IBM AIX, HP/UX, and others)

✓ Web browsers (Netscape Communicator and Microsoft Explorer)

✓ Windows 2000

✓ Windows NT

Network Hardware

✓ Bridges

✓ Brouters

✓ Cables (Fiber optic, coaxial, twisted-pair, etc.)

✓ Hubs

✓ Modems

✓ Networked storage devices

✓ Routers

✓ Switches

Local and Wide Area Network Technologies and Protocols

✓ Active Directory (part of Windows 2000)

✓ AppleTalk/AppleShare

✓ Domain Name System (DNS)

✓ Ethernet

✓ File Transfer Protocol (FTP)

✓ IBM's Systems Network Architecture (SNA)

✓ Internetwork Packet Exchange (a Novell networking protocol)

✓ OSI reference model

✓ Peer-to-peer networking

✓ Simple Network Management Protocol (SNMP)

✓ Storage area networks

✓ Sun's Network File System (NFS)

✓ TCP/IP (the key Internet and private network protocol)

✓ Token Ring

✓ Virtual private network (VPN)

✓ Wireless Application Protocol (WAP)

✓ X.500 Directory Services—including Directory Access Protocol (DAP) and Lightweight Directory Access Protocol (LDAP)

Security

✓ Antivirus software

✓ Data encryption/cryptography (including PGP, 128-bit encryption, data encryption standard, and public key cryptography)

✓ Digital certificates

✓ Firewalls (Checkpoint, Nokia, etc.)

✓ Internet Protocol Security (IPsec)

✓ Secure Sockets Layer (SSL)

✓ Sniffer programs for network monitoring and analysis

Telecommunications Technologies

✓ Asynchronous transfer mode (ATM)

✓ Digital subscriber line (DSL)

✓ Frame relay

✓ Hybrid Fiber Coaxial (HFC) networks

✓ Integrated Services Digital Network (ISDN)

Chapter 6

· ·

Start Me Up in Operations and End-User Support Jobs

If applications and databases are the face of IT, and networking and infrastructure its torso and limbs, then operations and end-user support comprise its heart and vital organs. As the group responsible for monitoring and maintaining system performance, availability, capacity, and recovery across the entire enterprise, the operations area is critical to the smooth operation of the business. End-user support, including the helpdesk, desktop support, and IT training, are like the diplomatic corps for the IT organization. Because most of what goes on in these areas happens behind the scenes—and is visible only when something goes wrong—professionals working in operations and user support don't always get the credit they deserve from end-users. But those who have made their careers in these areas say they find it extremely gratifying.

"There's a lot of satisfaction and a lot of responsibility in what we do, and with that comes a lot of [technical] authority," says Anthony Falanga, systems programming section manager at UPS in Mahwah, New Jersey. "What you do in operations can dramatically improve the way applications run, and for me that's tremendously satisfying. While applications are sexy and get all the attention, they don't mean anything unless operations is going smoothly. There are so many different things going on behind the scenes that people don't see but that are all there to help [systems] operate in the best way possible."

In the last decade, the visibility of the operations area has increased dramatically as computing power and responsibility has moved out of the exclusive domain of the data center and into decentralized IT and individual business units. Distributed computing, such as client/server architectures and, more recently, Internet-based computing, has shed new light on the importance of operations. At the same time, the organizational structure of operations has shifted somewhat, and the delegation of technical responsibilities varies from company to company. In some companies, operations is quite distinct from networking and infrastructure, while in others, there's an overlap of responsibility. (See "Operations: The Management Perspective" later in this chapter.) Some companies have corralled the three into one large group.

Working in end-user support may be the most under-appreciated job in IT. Support pros hear all about it when users are unhappy but seldom reap any of the praise when PCs and applications are functioning smoothly. Moreover, their role is key in conveying the good will of the IT organization and creating user buy-in to systems and applications. If you can take the heat, end-user support is an ideal launch pad for an IT career, as it is the window into an organization's entire technology infrastructure.

While both operations and end-user support are largely hands-on, technology-driven areas, like any other part of IT, they must be business-focused; the goal of optimizing mainframe systems performance isn't to demonstrate the machine's technical prowess but rather to optimize corporate productivity. The objective of user support isn't to demean users but to empower them to get their jobs done. So, even though operations and user support professionals will inherently be more technology-focused than their counterparts in applications development, they must be just as in tune with corporate goals and strategy.

Operations Jobs: A Sampler

Systems Programmer

JOB TITLE VARIATIONS   Mainframe systems programmer.

JOB DESCRIPTION   The systems programmer job should not be confused with applications development; rather, the focus is on mainframe operating systems and related system-level software, as well as the integrity of the hardware. Primary responsibilities include installing, configuring, maintaining, and upgrading systems software, plus documenting system changes and troubleshooting and resolving software problems. Systems programmers work closely with other operations teams such as performance monitoring, storage management, capacity planning, disaster recovery, and the helpdesk, as well as applications developers and networking staff. Advanced systems programmers will also evaluate and select new software. Depending on the size of the operations staff, systems programmers may also monitor and track performance. Systems programmers are typically required to be on an on-call rotation.

SPOTLIGHT ON A SYSTEMS PROGRAMMER

Anthony Falanga, 44, systems programming section manager, UPS, Mahwah, N.J.

Overall responsibilities   Configuring, installing, maintaining, and supporting mainframe hardware (including computers and peripherals), operating systems and software; designing, maintaining, and supporting an architecture that provides maximum flexibility and contingency.

Day-to-day responsibilities   "We're exclusively an IBM mainframe shop, with 15 machines, mainly IBM 9672s with G6 processors. Mainframe integrity is my primary responsibility—performance [tuning] is handled by another team. My job is to make sure the hardware and software are always running to near perfection. On the software front, I keep very busy. We have over 100 mainframe software products, and in any given year, at least two-thirds of those must be upgraded or modified. I also get involved with [software-related] problem resolution when it's not an applications problem. On the hardware front, a lot of processors have to be upgraded or replaced to keep up with technological improvements our vendors have made."

Technologies and technical skills required   OS/390 [an evolution of the MVS operating system], Assembler [a mainframe systems programming language that generates source code], JCL, and C ("which is becoming a universal language for applications and for systems programming"). "It's rare that systems programmer would be your first job in operations—you need some other kind of mainframe-related experience first, in the performance area or applications or machine operation. [The latter is] the most prominent because that's where you learn the ins and outs of the machines by interfacing with them every day."

Other skills required   Communication, organization, and teamwork skills. "This group regularly serves as a hub for a lot of activity that has to be coordinated with a lot of other support groups that deal with the mainframes. We have many different levels of systems programmers, and the higher you go, the more enhanced communication skills you need. It's generally true that we are dealing with other IT people most of the time—with other support teams 75 percent of the time and applications developers 25 percent of the time—but you also have to deal with, say, applications managers who want to know about our facilities and the features that mainframes can provide. That's when communication skills come in the most."

SPOTLIGHT ON A SYSTEMS PROGRAMMER

"You have to be well organized because you might be taking on many tasks at a time. And you have to be good at teamwork—especially at UPS—and support each other and bring each other technical knowledge. That's what makes the systems programming group work so well."

What I like most about this job   "As much as it sometimes seems like things don't change, there is always a tremendous amount of change going on. The mainframe has evolved tremendously, and the hardware can never be beat for reliability. They're capable of doing all those things now that you can do on other platforms. For example, a lot of web applications run on Unix and use DB2 data. So before you'd have a platform in the middle to serve as a translator or interpreter to replicate the DB2 data and put it in a different format. In today's world, you can go right to the mainframe with your web application, retrieve the data straight out of the DB2 database, and it's all transparent to the end-user."

What I like least about this job   Sometimes you have to make some tough decisions about taking dramatic steps to fix problems—like deciding whether to do a complete reboot of the operating system, which would mean taking the mainframe offline. And mainframes are capable of running a tremendous amount of work, so taking them offline impacts everybody. So sometimes I'd rather not have to make those decisions, but if something critical happens, you have to. We've come a long way toward minimizing outages, but we're not perfect."

Career path leading to this job   Falanga graduated from college in 1978 with a degree in chemical engineering and went to work for a large engineering firm. Following an industry downturn, he lost his job in 1983 and was out of work for a year. During that period, he enrolled full-time in a mainframe training program at the Chubb Institute, and in 1984 he secured a job with a large insurance firm in New York as a mainframe applications programmer. "We had only a few people supporting the application, so I was doing not only [application] coding but also supporting the system code. That's how I broke into learning about systems programming." When the company moved its headquarters to North Carolina in 1985, Falanga joined UPS as an MVS systems programmer. "I started as your typical grunt, and now I'm in management—this area offers tremendous growth."

SPOTLIGHT ON A SYSTEMS PROGRAMMER

Advice to other IT pros interested in systems programming   "First, you have to accept that systems programming will not be your first job in operations. So get into a position that will give you the opportunity to get there—like storage management or performance tuning or operations analyst. And take it upon yourself to keep learning and training. I'm a firm believer that if I hadn't motivated myself [to acquire new skills], I wouldn't be where I am today.

"Predictions of the demise of the mainframe are dead wrong—their growth is as robust as it has ever been. We have 15 of them, and they're not small ones. What other platform could handle 5 million package-tracking requests in a day? I can't imagine working in any other area."

EDUCATION AND CERTIFICATION REQUIREMENTS   As with many operations jobs, the right experience is considered more important than a degree. At least three-to-four-years' prior experience, usually in applications development or another area of operations, is required. Anyone aiming for this job should go through systems software training early in their career.

TECHNICAL SKILLS REQUIRED   Depending on the IT environment, exposure to a range of mainframe and midrange platforms can apply, including the IBM S/390, IBM AS/400, Hewlett-Packard 3000 or 9000, DEC VAX, IBM plug-compatible mainframes, and others. Experience with the following is a plus: Job Control Language (JCL), Assembler, Customer Information Control System (CICS), DB2, and Virtual Telecommunications Access Method (VTAM). Knowledge of communications protocols such as Systems Network Architecture (SNA), Systems Application Architecture (SAA), and Transmission Control Protocol/Internet Protocol (TCP/IP) helps too, along with knowledge of various mainframe software products from Computer Associates and others.

OTHER SKILLS REQUIRED   Because systems programmers regularly interact with other areas of IT, interpersonal communication skills are essential. Written communication skills are also required for documentation. Troubleshooting and problem-solving skills, as well as the ability to stay cool under pressure, are a must.

POTENTIAL CAREER PATHS   Because the responsibilities involved in this position cut across all segments of operations, it can easily lead to an IT management track within the operations area. Other options include moving into applications development management or into the networking and infrastructure area.

IS THIS POSITION FOR YOU?   If you thrive in a position of tremendous responsibility, enjoy being behind the scenes in a roll-up-your-sleeves capacity, and can handle the pressure of constantly dealing with new and unique problems, this is one of the most challenging jobs you can have in operations. It is especially suitable for those who prefer interacting with other IT professionals more than end-users. But even though you may not deal directly with users, you must nonetheless have a good feel for the business and how IT contributes to both day-to-day business operations and long-term business strategy.

Systems Administrator

JOB TITLE VARIATIONS   Systems engineer, senior systems administrator.

JOB DESCRIPTION   Systems administrators perform a role similar to that of systems programmers but are focused on Unix platforms such as Sun Solaris, Hewlett-Packard's HP/UX, IBM AIX, and others. Depending on the organizational structure, they may be responsible for all the Unix servers in a company or department, regardless of the specific version of Unix, or they may they specialize on a single platform type. Responsibilities include performing regular system administration and maintenance, including installation, configuration, backup, performance monitoring, and upgrades. Systems administrators are also responsible for ensuring system availability and providing technical support to other IT teams that come in contact with the server, such as applications development, e-business, and networking and infrastructure. In senior-level positions, they will also make new technology recommendations, evaluate and test architectural changes, and participate in overall systems and network management.

EDUCATION AND CERTIFICATION REQUIREMENTS   A Bachelor's degree in Computer Science or a related field is required, or a non-IT degree combined with technical training can substitute. Relevant work experience can also substitute for a degree. Certification on one or more Unix platforms is highly recommended.

TECHNICAL SKILLS REQUIRED   In-depth knowledge of at least one flavor of the Unix operating system plus experience in the client/server environment, knowledge of systems management tools like Hewlett Packard's OpenView and others, and working familiarity with applications, databases, scripting languages, networking protocols, and file structures (such as TCP/IP, SNA, DNS, NFS, and others), network security techniques such as firewalls, and storage management. Familiarity with Linux is a plus as more companies start to bring the new operating system into the server mix.

OTHER SKILLS REQUIRED   Troubleshooting and problem-solving skills, communication skills, ability to stay cool under pressure, and ability to manage self-directed work as well as cooperate on teams.

POTENTIAL CAREER PATHS   Systems administrators can advance through various levels of responsibility within the administration role, eventually graduating to an operations management track, or they may make lateral moves into other areas of operations, network administration and management, or IT security-related positions. Depending on their long-range interests, systems administrators can move into IT architecture roles, and eventually toward an executive-level position such as chief technology officer.

IS THIS POSITION FOR YOU?   If a highly technical, behind-the-scenes role like systems programming appeals to you, but mainframes do not, this could be the position you're looking for. You must have a love of technology and understand the inner workings of servers, but be prepared to keep one eye on business goals and objectives, especially at the senior level. While you must be comfortable with solitary work, you must also have a team orientation because this role touches many areas of IT.

Operations Analyst

JOB TITLE VARIATIONS   Equipment operator, operations administrator.

JOB DESCRIPTION   As the title implies, this entry-level position is responsible for the routine hands-on operation of mainframe, midrange, and Unix systems and subsystems, plus technical support within the data center. Responsibilities include overseeing timely data-processing production, monitoring system status, interpreting error messages, and reporting system malfunctions. In some cases, operations administrators may also be responsible for performance monitoring and tuning as it relates to systems availability.

OPERATIONS: THE MANAGEMENT PERSPECTIVE

Jim Jahrling, manager of information systems (IS) operations, HomeLife Furniture Corp., Hoffman Estates, Ill.

What is the overall mission in operations?

To provide the day-to-day administration and support for all the systems, to provide enhancements to those systems, and work on developing new systems that will make the business run more efficiently and profitably. Here we support the systems in head-quarters and in 130 stores nationwide.

How is working in the operations area different today than in the past?

Before we were pushing buttons, watching monitors, doing batch processing. Today, we're much more interactive, working with other people in IT and the company and more involved in the development of systems. Operations is no longer this glass house for IT—it's another business unit that interacts with all the others. There is not a slow day, and you aren't chained to a cubicle or a desk.

We also have a lot more movement in and out of operations today than, say, 10 or 15 years ago when it was a data center job. From operations you can go into any area in which you want to apply yourself. I don't see a lot of operations staff go into programming, but net-working and infrastructure are definitely kindred spirits. You can also move into other areas of the company, like business operations, if you have a good feel for how IT works with the business.

How do you delineate what operations is responsible for and what falls under net-working and infrastructure?

In our company, since we're small, a lot of our responsibilities bleed into other areas. So operations is responsible for the routers and switches because they're all in the computer room, and we have to make sure that we have the correct configuration files, etc. We acquire, install, and maintain the networking gear, but the networking and infrastruc-ture group would make the recommendations and do more of the high-level architecting and conceptual design. Operations is more the hands-on side.

What skills and experience do you look for in filling operations jobs?

Within our company, we look for people who have a well-rounded background in our operating systems—NT, Unix, and Windows 2000. They don't necessarily need

OPERATIONS: THE MANAGEMENT PERSPECTIVE

degrees or certifications, but rather some experience that demonstrates growth between where they started and where they are today. We consider how well we feel they can acquire and apply new skills, whether they enjoy technology and want to move along with it. We also like to see that they've had project management and soft-skills training or are willing to do that.

Aside from technical skills, what are the key attributes you look for in operations professionals?

Communication skills, because you deal with people at all levels, from administrative assistants to the CEO. I'll pick an English major who can communicate well. I also look for an ability to work well with others, and someone who's organized and can put together a plan for why we should do things a certain way. You need a strong work ethic—a willingness to go beyond just the 8:00 A.M. to 5:00 P.M. job. This is a 24/7 operation, and you can get called off-hours. We can all log in from home and can pretty much do 90 percent of the support remotely except for things like pushing buttons or pulling a cable.

What kind of temperament is needed to do well in this area of IT?

In any IT position, you are always dealing with last-minute changes, but even more so in operations because you're dealing with all the business units and the operations unit staff. So you must be flexible, able to handle multiple projects, and literally able to think on your feet because you encounter a lot of new stuff daily.

I won't hire people who want to sit at a desk all day. You need to be extroverted and deal with people, and maintain your manners and a good demeanor regardless of what other people are saying. There can be a lot of finger pointing—a user reports a problem, and a programmer concludes that it's a hardware problem, and then the person who runs the hardware says, "No amount of hardware will compensate for poor programming." It's a my-way-or-no-way attitude. We try to keep a lid on that and work those things out privately.

Why would you recommend pursuing a career in operations?

If you're looking to learn a lot about a company, operations is a great place to be because you're interacting with the entire company.

EDUCATION AND CERTIFICATION REQUIREMENTS A college degree or completion of a technical training program is preferred, if not required, but some companies will train candidates for this role.

TECHNICAL SKILLS REQUIRED Knowledge of major hardware platforms and operating systems, including IBM S/390 mainframes and OS/390, midrange systems such as the IBM AS/400 or DEC VAX, and Unix-based systems such as Sun Solaris servers.

OTHER SKILLS REQUIRED Documentation, communication, and troubleshooting skills.

POTENTIAL CAREER PATHS A stint as an operations administrator can lead to supervisory positions managing other operators, such as shift supervisor. It also provides the necessary foundation for moves into other areas of operations such as performance monitoring, capacity planning, storage management, or systems administration. A move into network administration is another option.

IS THIS POSITION FOR YOU? If you anticipate a career in the operations area, this is a solid first step that will prepare you for a range of future positions. It also offers a viable path into IT without a college degree, although some technical degree or certification, such as an Associate's degree or certification from a technical training institute, is a preferred or necessary substitute. Career advancement may be slower without a degree behind you.

TIP A job title that frequently comes up when searching for operations jobs is "systems analyst" or "business systems analyst." This can be confusing because systems analyst is a job title with a different meaning in the applications development area. When used in operations, it usually represents an amalgamation of operations functions, such as performance monitoring and tuning, capacity planning, and machine operations.

Storage Management Specialist

JOB TITLE VARIATIONS Data storage administrator, storage area network (SAN) support specialist, SAN administrator.

JOB DESCRIPTION As data warehouses send corporate storage requirements into and beyond the multiterabyte range, storage management is becoming an increasingly critical function in the operations area. In response to the increase in storage needs, the last several years have seen a number of new storage technologies emerge, such as SANs, near-line tape (NLT), Fibre Channel technology (a communications technology that connects devices on a SAN), and more. Effective storage management is essential to overall system performance and responsiveness, and it is a key component of disaster recovery planning. Storage specialists ensure efficient input/output (I/O), contribute to data integrity, and work to guarantee 24/7 data access. Responsibilities include creating file sets, spanning logical data over physical disks, performing data archiving and backups, troubleshooting, doing systems administration as it relates to storage functions, and more.

EDUCATION AND CERTIFICATION REQUIREMENTS   A Bachelor's degree in Computer Science is preferred, but not required. Certification in some storage-related discipline is recommended, such as the EMC Proven Professional Certification Program.

TECHNICAL SKILLS REQUIRED   Experience with leading storage management solutions, such as the EMC storage systems and software products (including Symmetrix, Connectrix, and others) and Computer Associates Unicenter storage management suite; an understanding of SAN architecture; familiarity with a range of different storage devices; and knowledge of major operating systems and networking protocols, as well as storage-specific communications technologies like Fibre Channel.

OTHER SKILLS REQUIRED   Solid interpersonal skills, an orientation for teamwork, organizational skills, methodical approach to work, troubleshooting, and problem-solving.

POTENTIAL CAREER PATHS   Logical steps after working in storage management are data warehouse management, systems administration, systems programming, or, if you have the requisite prior experience, disaster recovery or capacity planning.

IS THIS POSITION FOR YOU?   If you are comfortable in a job that not many of your colleagues in IT really understand, that is highly technical and hands-on, that is critical yet frequently underestimated, and that provides a good stepping stone to systems programming and beyond in operations, consider a stint in storage management. Further up the operations management ladder, having this position on your résumé will speak volumes about how well rounded you are.

Capacity Planner

JOB TITLE VARIATIONS   Capacity planning analyst, performance and capacity planning analyst.

JOB DESCRIPTION   This complex position entails monitoring and tracking daily systems performance and availability to forecast future system capacity requirements. By keeping statistics on past and present resources usage, capacity planners come up with projections for future systems and peripherals needs. Depending on the size and structure of the operations group, the capacity planner may be a manager whose team handles systems performance and availability monitoring, while the planner focuses on statistical analysis and forecasting, or the capacity planner may be directly responsible for both aspects of the job. Responsibilities include building applications capacity models, designing and implementing measurement and forecasting processes, assisting applications developers with stress testing, and creating and implementing long-range capacity plans. This position must work closely with business managers, applications developers, and networking and infrastructure teams.

EDUCATION AND CERTIFICATION REQUIREMENTS   A Bachelor's degree in Computer Science, MIS, or Statistics is usually required; a strong math and statistical background is recommended. Previous experience in performance measurement and system tuning is a must.

TECHNICAL SKILLS REQUIRED   Experience with statistics packages such as SAS; previous operations experience with mainframe, midrange, and Unix systems and subsystems; proficiency in major operating systems; working knowledge of I/O and bandwidth constraints; an understanding of network architecture; and some programming experience.

OTHER SKILLS REQUIRED   Strong communication skills, project management and organizational skills, math and statistical skills, analytical skills, and troubleshooting and problem-solving skills.

POTENTIAL CAREER PATHS   Capacity planning experience can be leveraged on a management path or technical track, leading to jobs in networking and infrastructure, the higher levels of operations, and, ultimately, the chief information officer or chief technology officer.

IS THIS POSITION FOR YOU?   If you're secretly a shade-tree mechanic on the weekends who enjoys pushing the performance of your automobile to its extreme limits and clocking your speed on the highway, you will probably enjoy the performance management aspects of this job. If, on top of that, you enjoy tracking and comparing performance statistics, you likely have the right disposition for capacity planning. If you have your eye on top-level operations management or the IT executive offices, spending time in this critical IT position can be a definite plus.

Disaster Recovery Analyst

JOB TITLE VARIATIONS   Disaster recovery specialist, business recovery analyst, contingency planning analyst.

JOB DESCRIPTION   In the event of major system outages caused by a catastrophic event, contingency plans must be in place to restore functionality and systems access. The disaster recovery analyst works with various teams across the entire IT organization to determine critical resources and formulate and test a comprehensive plan for bringing systems, data, and applications back online in the shortest time possible following large-scale damage to a data center. Plans must be modified and retested each time the IT environment undergoes change, such as when new technologies are added or systems are upgraded or phased out. In the event that the plan must be executed, the disaster recovery team oversees implementation.

EDUCATION AND CERTIFICATION REQUIREMENTS   A Bachelor's degree in Computer Science, Business Information Systems, or related degree is preferred, but equivalent on-the-job experience can substitute. Certification such as Certified Business Continuity Planner (CBCP) or Associate Disaster Recovery Planner (ADRP) is highly recommended.

TECHNICAL SKILLS REQUIRED   A well-rounded technology background, including experience in the client/server, Internet, and mainframe environments; specific technology skills preferences vary according to the environment. Prior experience in the operations or infrastructure area is recommended. This is not an entry-level position; it requires substantial exposure across all areas of IT.

OTHER SKILLS REQUIRED   Organizational skills, a methodical approach to anticipating and planning for each possible contingency, excellent communication and documentation skills, and an understanding of internal corporate business processes.

POTENTIAL CAREER PATHS   Given that planning and executing a successful disaster recovery plan is mission-critical, and that the process encompasses all of IT, this is a position that can lay the groundwork for a management path to the executive suite. Disaster recovery specialists are well positioned to continue upward in operations or networking and infrastructure.

IS THIS POSITION FOR YOU?   If you are comfortable having the burden of the entire company on your shoulders, enjoy planning as much as implementing, and are at ease marshalling all resources available to you toward a single cause, this could be an exciting, career-building IT position for you. But you must live with the fact that in the best-case scenario, the results of your efforts will never be implemented.

Operations Technologies Checklists

Hardware

✓ DEC VAX

✓ HP 3000 and HP 9000 servers by Hewlett Packard

✓ IBM AS/400

✓ IBM S/390 mainframes

✓ Sun Enterprise servers

✓ Unisys ES7000 and ES5000 servers

Operating Systems

✓ IBM MVS

✓ IBM OS/390

✓ IBM OS/400

✓ Linux

✓ Unix (including HP/UX, Sun Solaris, IBM AIX, etc.)

Storage Management Systems

✓ EMC (various tools)

✓ IBM (various tools)

✓ Microsoft Storage Management System

✓ Storage area networks (SANs)

✓ Unicenter Storage Management Suite by Computer Associates

Disaster Recovery Planning Tools

✓ ComPAS by Comdisco

✓ Comprehensive Business Recovery software by SunGard

✓ ePlanner by SunGard

✓ Living Disaster Recovery Planning System (LDRPS) business continuity planning software by Strohl Systems

✓ Systems Professional Business Impact Analysis (BIA) software by Strohl Systems

✓ Tivoli Disaster Recovery Manager

Capacity Planning Tools

✓ Distributed Sniffer System/RMON network management tools by Network Associates

✓ SAS/STAT statistical analysis tools

Systems Management Tools

✓ IBM (various tools)

✓ OpenView by Hewlett Packard

✓ Unicenter by Computer Associates

End-User Support Jobs: A Sampler

Helpdesk Analyst

JOB TITLE VARIATIONS Helpdesk technician, technical support analyst.

JOB DESCRIPTION Helpdesk analysts are the front line in end-user support, the ones who spend their days troubleshooting and diagnosing problems for frustrated end-users, who are typically at their wit's end by the time they contact the helpdesk. Problems are classified as Level 1, Level 2, or Level 3 based on severity, whether it is an isolated incident or a network-wide problem, and troubleshooting difficulty. Helpdesk analysts usually handle Level 1 problems; Level 2 calls and higher are assigned to desktop support staff or to another area of IT. If a Level 1 problem can't be resolved in 15 minutes or less, it is usually kicked up to the next level to free the helpdesk analyst to take another call; the amount of time allowed for each call may be shorter during times of high call volume. With intranets in place, some companies have adopted a self-service helpdesk model—giving users basic problems and solutions online—in an effort to reduce their helpdesk costs. In the self-service model, helpdesk analysts may also be responding to user problems via email and/or chat.

EDUCATION AND CERTIFICATION REQUIREMENTS   A Bachelor's degree in Computer Science is preferred, but a degree in business or liberal arts is acceptable if coupled with technical training and/or certification. Substantial technical expertise can substitute for a degree. Helpdesk certification programs are available, but more important are technical certifications such as the Microsoft Certified Professional (MCP), the Microsoft Certified Systems Engineer (MCSE), the Lotus Notes Certified Lotus Principal (CLP), and other applications-related certifications.

TECHNICAL SKILLS REQUIRED   Thorough knowledge of desktop operating systems, applications, and hardware, plus devices that attach to PCs, including Windows 2000, Windows NT, Microsoft Office, Lotus Notes/Domino, Microsoft Exchange, web browsers, etc., plus internal corporate applications. Prior experience using helpdesk or call center software programs is a plus.

OTHER SKILLS REQUIRED   Analytical skills, troubleshooting and problem-solving, superb communication skills, the ability to listen without interrupting, documentation skills, visualization skills (the ability to project what the user is seeing on his or her screen), patience, resilience, and the ability to keep your cool and lay back when others are blowing off steam.

POTENTIAL CAREER PATHS   If you want to pursue a career in end-user support, the helpdesk is your first stop on the way to desktop support, helpdesk manager, director of user support, and on up the management chain. Moreover, the helpdesk analyst's job is a springboard into just about any area of IT, including network administration, operations, or applications development.

IS THIS POSITION FOR YOU?   If you are seeking an entry-level IT position but haven't yet decided which area of IT you ultimately want to pursue, the helpdesk is an excellent starting point. But you must enjoy interacting with users, troubleshooting and solving problems, and possess the patience of a saint.

SPOTLIGHT ON A HELPDESK MANAGER

Liz Anderson, 27, helpdesk manager at a large investment banking firm, New York, N.Y. Anderson is an employee of Shamrock Computer Network, which provides helpdesk outsourcing services.

Overall responsibilities   Manage the helpdesk (including nine helpdesk analysts and five desktop support staff members serving 3,500 users), schedule the staff rotation for coverage from 6:00 A.M. to 11:00 P.M. Monday through Friday, handle "client escalations" (situations in which a user is dissatisfied with the helpdesk service), and manage ad hoc projects, such as configuring and installing PCs for new users or scheduling support for new applications rollouts.

Day-to-day responsibilities   "Managing the wait queues and keeping an eye on the automated call distribution system to ensure that our performance is up to par. On average, we answer calls within 10 to 15 seconds. If I see that call volume is high and everyone is tied up, I log in and answer calls myself. A big part of performance measurement, unfortunately, is metrics. So you may have solved a huge problem, but if it took too long—if it occurred during a high-volume call time, and you spent a long time on it—it could be detrimental. You also have to keep in mind who the top clients are—here it would be traders and managing directors. For example, if a trader can't see his stock ticker, that could mean lost revenue. In other companies, your priority clients would be the top-level executives.

"Dealing with client escalations is a big part of my day. For example, a trader has called the desk several times and hasn't gotten a response during critical trading hours, so they leave me a message about not getting a response in a timely manner. By the time we talk, they're pretty aggravated. First I let them speak and say whatever they have to say before I even open my mouth. I take notes on the key portions and make a mental note of where we failed and where the user may need some education. When they've had their say, I apologize for the thing that the desk failed on and state that we'll address it, whether it was a process or a person that failed. And then I let them know what they did wrong—but I don't put it that way. Once you've let them speak and you haven't interrupted them, they've let off a good amount of steam, and that gives you a chance to admit to doing something wrong and apologize. And you do that first so that then they're ready for the reeducation, the redirection. They're a little more open-minded."

SPOTLIGHT ON A HELPDESK MANAGER

Technologies and technical skills required   Microsoft Office, Windows NT, Lotus Notes, and network administration skills. "We're willing to train people in the helpdesk package [Remedy] because our screens are customized anyway."

Other skills required   "Great communication skills—written as well as verbal because you have to document incidents. You need the ability to really listen and ascertain what the user is saying. For example, they might say, 'I can't get into my application' or 'I can't get onto my machine.' And depending on the person, that could mean many different things—they can't actually power on, or they can't log on via NT, or they can't open the application they use every day. And as a helpdesk technician, I have to pinpoint where their problem is really occurring. There's a set of generic questions you ask: Are you new to the location? Have you used this application before? Have you been assigned user rights? But you're winging it every time.

"You also need great visualization skills—you have to be able to visualize the problem someone is describing or you'll never be able to pinpoint the cause. You have to visualize what they are seeing on the screen, which goes back to knowing the applications really, really well.

"People tend to underestimate this position. They think it's mundane and that helpdesk pros don't have a brain, and that's not true. You can acquire the applications and networking knowledge, but the communication, troubleshooting, and visualization skills have to come naturally."

What I like most about this job   "The interaction with the clients—the trouble-shooting aspect and the satisfaction of knowing you helped someone."

What I like least about this job   "The fact that you have restrictions—you can only go so far to troubleshoot the problem, and then you have to send it to the group that has direct oversight for [the source] of the problem. So, for example, if a user can't access an application, and the problem turns out to be that they haven't been granted user rights, we can't just take care of that. We have to send them to the LAN administration group to grant them rights. I'd like to provide the solution all the way, provided it wouldn't cause any problems with our stats."

SPOTLIGHT ON A HELPDESK MANAGER

Career path leading to this job   While attaining a B.S. in Computer Science from Pace University in New York, Anderson did an internship in desktop support, "which was great because you have a lot more rights to see the problem through to the end, and you have more of a one-on-one relationship with users." After graduating, she joined Shamrock as a helpdesk analyst and was promoted to helpdesk manager three years later. In the future, she anticipates continuing on a management track, but she wants to remain directly involved with technology as well. "Right now, I like that I'm still involved in hands-on support as well as management. For me, that's the best of both worlds."

Advice to other IT pros interested in the helpdesk   "The helpdesk can be a good entry-level point into IT organizations, depending on whether the helpdesk's role is a hands-on model or an operator model. In the hands-on model, you're actually trouble-shooting and solving problems, dealing with the user yourself. You have a lot of rights to resolve the problem. Then it's a great way to learn a company's technologies and make the right IT contacts to help you get to the area of IT where you ultimately want to be. Career paths after the helpdesk really vary. I've known people who went into desktop support, LAN administration, systems administration, applications development, the e-business group. It's just a matter of building up your contacts and keeping up with certifications and technical knowledge.

"But on some helpdesks, you just answer the phone, ascertain the problem, and write up a ticket for a call back from the appropriate group. In that model, you just need to be able to answer the phone; sometimes you don't even need to know enough technology to figure out where to send the ticket because you're just passing it on to a generic user support group. And unfortunately, a lot of people's perception of the helpdesk is based on that model. So don't take a job like that because you'll go nowhere. You can determine what model a company uses during the job interview. Ask them what responsibilities you would have and how many rights the helpdesk has to resolve a problem. Fortunately, the operator model is being phased out, and the hands-on model is becoming more pervasive."

Desktop Support Technician

JOB TITLE VARIATIONS   Desktop support analyst, field support technician, user support specialist, field engineer.

JOB DESCRIPTION   This position, which usually follows a stint on the helpdesk or related experience, is akin to a technical ambassadorship. Desktop support technicians spend time in the business units, solving desktop PC problems one-on-one for users whose problems can't be resolved by the helpdesk (referred to as Level 2 or Level 3 calls). They also set up and configure PCs for new users, handle upgrades, and may be involved with new applications rollouts. Depending on the IT organizational structure, they may be assigned to a specific department or floor and be colocated with their users or may work from the helpdesk area, going out into the departments as needed. Remote offices such as sales offices, manufacturing facilities, and other branches or divisions usually have at least one local desktop support technician.

EDUCATION AND CERTIFICATION REQUIREMENTS   A college degree or equivalent experience is required. As with the helpdesk analyst position, technical certification in a company's primary applications and operating systems is highly recommended for advancement.

TECHNICAL SKILLS REQUIRED   In-depth expertise in PC hardware, operating systems and applications, including Wintel, Macintosh, and Unix platforms; peripherals; Windows 2000, Windows NT, various flavors of Unix, and Novell NetWare; email applications, groupware, web browsers, and internal corporate applications. Basic programming and networking skills are highly recommended.

OTHER SKILLS REQUIRED   Ability to communicate technology terms and concepts in plain English, troubleshooting and problem-solving skills, patience, and a customer-service orientation.

POTENTIAL CAREER PATHS   Becoming an end-user trainer would be a natural extension of experience gained as a desktop support technician. In the long run, time spent in this position can be a good backdrop for continued upward movement in the end-user support organization as well as moves into operations, applications development, or networking and infrastructure. The regular interaction with workers in business units, the problem-solving aspects, the hands-on technology experience, and insight into frequently occurring problems can be leveraged across the board in IT depending on where your interests lie.

IS THIS POSITION FOR YOU?   If you have an eye on continuing up the ladder in end-user support or operations, have great problem-solving skills, enjoy dealing with end-users and translating technology into nontechnical terms, and are looking for a hands-on, roll-up-your-sleeves IT position but want to gain exposure to your company's business units, you would prosper in this job. But it is essential to have the right attitude toward end-users: You must be friendly, patient, and never condescending.

IT Trainer

JOB TITLE VARIATIONS   Applications trainer, technical trainer, instructional designer, courseware designer.

JOB DESCRIPTION   IT trainers lead technical courses for end-users, IT professionals, and other trainers. They work for a variety of different organizations, including internal corporate training departments, third-party training vendors, the training arms of high-tech vendors, online training organizations, and courseware developers. Their primary responsibility is to teach, but they may also be involved with setting curriculum standards, designing courses, and producing training guides for other trainers.

EDUCATION AND CERTIFICATION REQUIREMENTS   A college degree is preferred, but equivalent experience will substitute. You must have on-the-job, hands-on IT experience in the area that you will be teaching, such as three years of experience as an applications developer or network administrator. Certification is highly recommended, and most certification programs offer a training track.

TECHNICAL SKILLS REQUIRED   In whatever area you wish to teach, your technical skills must not only be up-to-date, but also somewhat ahead of the curve. You also should have complementary skills. For example, if you will be teaching end-users Office 2000, you must also be skilled in Windows 2000. If you will be teaching Java to applications developers, you should be knowledgeable in Java, JavaBeans, JavaScript, and Java2 Enterprise Edition (JEE2), as well as object-oriented databases and other programming and scripting languages frequently used in conjunction with Java. Trainers who want to get involved with courseware development should also have experience with multimedia production and authoring tools.

END-USER SUPPORT: THE MANAGEMENT PERSPECTIVE

Laurie Davis, director of customer support, Girl Scouts U.S.A., New York, N.Y.

What is the overall mission of the end-user support organization?

The end-user support organization is a company's window on technology. A helpdesk analyst is the first person you speak to when you have a problem. If you have a good helpdesk system, when the analyst logs in the user's telephone extension, all of their information [e.g., name, title, location, PC configuration, etc.] pops up on the screen. You try to get all the information you can about the problem, including error messages they've received, and figure out what the problem is. You set limits of about 15 minutes for the resolution, and if after 15 minutes you can't resolve the problem, it goes to the second level. Or, if you have more than three users calling with the same problem, then you know it should be escalated to the top because a lot of people are affected.

Some companies are set up so that the helpdesk person goes into the user community. I personally don't agree with that model because then you're leaving yourself open to not having the phones answered. That won't work in a midsized-to-large company. People don't like voice mail—they want a live person on the phone. If everyone is leaving the desk to take care of a problem, you may not have anyone manning the phones. A better model is to have a [desktop support] person for each department, and then you can put the problem into a queue if it needs to go to the next level. Helpdesks are very sophisticated about transferring calls.

What skills and experience do you look for in end-user support?

There are so many new technologies that the helpdesk needs to be familiar with, and you have to stay up-to-date on all of them—Palm Pilots, operating systems, applications, everything. Having corporate standards helps a lot because then the helpdesk knows what standard products they must support. But if someone is technical, you can always teach them more technical skills. There are helpdesk certification programs, but I don't require certification because it's kind of like a college diploma—just because you have it doesn't prove you can do the job.

END-USER SUPPORT: THE MANAGEMENT PERSPECTIVE

The most important thing with any tech support job is personality. You must be very friendly, very customer-oriented. I always like to interview potential candidates on the phone to see if they're articulate and friendly. And follow-up skills are key, because users want to be kept informed and know what's going on to fix their problem. And you have to be able to prioritize.

The helpdesk is usually a stepping-stone to other areas of IT, so I love to find someone who has made a decision to stay in the support area. It's an extremely stressful job because you're getting yelled at all the time, and about the longest you can stay on the job without burning out is 12 to 18 months.

If you want to stay in end-user support, what can you do to stave off burnout?

I try to give them some incentive for growth, like rotating off the desk and going out into the field to handle Level 2 calls or putting them on special projects. I might assign them to work on creating processes for the helpdesk to get them off the phone for a few hours one or two days a week or make them a project manager in charge of building a knowledge base [of common problems and resolutions].

What kind of temperament do you need to do well in end-user support?

People are yelling at you all day, so you have to remember that they aren't really yelling at you, they're yelling at the situation. But you get to know everyone, and if you can make people happy, they do appreciate it. But mainly you only hear complaints because computers are our livelihood, and when they don't perform, you can't earn your livelihood.

What's your advice to someone interested in working in end-user support?

It's great experience for someone who wants to get into IT or desktop support. And it's a great field because you're always learning, you're never bored, and technology is the future, so you're on the cutting edge of everything.

OTHER SKILLS REQUIRED   The ability to inspire enthusiasm for technology, excellent presentation skills, and a knack for simplifying complex concepts into building blocks that can be easily understood by others of lesser experience, listening skills, and patience.

POTENTIAL CAREER PATHS   Time spent as a trainer can take you in several different directions. Continuing on the training track, you could move from training end-users to training other IT professionals to training other trainers, as well as from instruction into instructional design—developing courseware, live classes, online training programs, and curriculum. You could also leverage training as a transitional step into teaching if you pursue the necessary teaching credentials. Trainers can step back into hands-on IT within their specialty area or, if you find the evangelical aspects of training appealing, you could even consider applying your presentation skills to move into high-tech sales and marketing.

IS THIS POSITION FOR YOU?   If you ever considered teaching as a career, but your love of technology drew you into IT instead, the IT trainer role would enable you to bring the two avocations together. But you must enjoy making presentations and being in front of a crowd, and you must have an enthusiastic personality that will ignite the interest of others. Moreover, you must be able to put yourself in your students' shoes; remember that everyone learns at a different pace, and be willing to do whatever it takes to bring all of your students up-to-speed.

End-User Support Technologies Checklists

Helpdesk Call Center Applications

✓ Action Request System by Remedy

✓ Heat by FrontRange Solutions

✓ Support.com by Support.com

✓ Support Magic by Network Associates

✓ TrackIt! by Blue Ocean Software

Troubleshooting Utilities

✓ Carbon Copy by Compaq Computer Corp.

✓ PCAnywhere by Symantec Corp.

✓ ReachOut Enterprise by Stac

Common End-User Operating Systems, Applications, and Hardware

✓ Corel

✓ Email

✓ Lotus 1-2-3

✓ Lotus Notes

✓ Mac OS

✓ Macintosh

✓ Macintosh applications

✓ Microsoft Internet Explorer

✓ Microsoft Office

✓ Netscape Communicator

✓ Palm OS

✓ Palms

✓ Photoshop

✓ Windows 2000

✓ Windows NT

✓ Wintel PCs

Chapter 7

Start Me Up in E-business and Internet Jobs

The Internet has arguably done more to stir up the IT profession than any other technological innovation since the emergence of the computer. It has stimulated the creation of new jobs on a massive scale, and even with escalating layoffs in the dot-com sector throughout the second half of 2000, the Internet will continue to drive the IT job market. Opportunities for both new and established IT professionals to work in e-business and Internet-related jobs will grow as so-called "old economy" companies increase their reliance on the Internet as an enabling tool for business and a source of revenue streams.

Information technology professionals hold 28 percent of all Internet-related jobs in the new "Internet economy," according to a recent study by the Center for Research in Electronic Commerce at the University of Texas (UT). The study, "Measuring the Internet Economy," found that the Internet economy now directly supports more than 3 million workers, and it generated $830 billion in revenue in 2000. Moreover, the report indicates that the dot-com demise is hardly the harbinger of the end of Internet-related job growth. In fact, pure-play dot-coms comprise only 9.6 percent of the overall Internet economy. The contribution of traditional "offline" companies "...to the Internet economy revenue and job estimates far exceeds that of dot-com companies," the report noted.

Even with all the media coverage surrounding the closures of many high-profile dot-com companies, interest in e-business IT jobs remains high. "When we do college recruiting, every single intern wants to work in ecommerce," says Leo Timmons, senior manager of the Ebusiness Applications Development Group at The Pillsbury Company, in Minneapolis, Minnesota. "They have no idea what it really means, but they know it's what they should ask for." The Internet has created such a swell of interest in IT that a number of M.B.A. programs have begun to offer specialized e-business tracks, as have undergraduate business schools and continuing education programs. These new courses signal not only increased interest among students and established professionals, but also a nearly insatiable demand by corporate IT organizations and dot-coms for qualified employees.

That demand is welcoming new entrants into the IT job market and creating opportunities for established IT professionals to forge new career paths. Traditionally, IT professionals entrenched in older technologies have had a tough time gaining a spot on projects involving new technologies, but e-business is the great equalizer. When it comes to web-enabled applications development, database analysis, and network support, legacy skills are often seen as a plus. In the corporate world, public websites, intranets, and extranets must tie into existing backend systems, requiring substantial expertise in systems integration and a depth of knowledge about a company's business processes. And as dot-coms move to batten down the hatches and make greater strides toward profitability, they are placing more value on IT professionals with proven track records.

While *ecommerce* is certainly the Internet buzzword of note, Timmons notes that job seekers should make a distinction between ecommerce and e-business. "Ecommerce involves transactions," he explains, "whereas e-business is anything having to do with using Internet technologies for business objectives, transaction-oriented or not, including marketing, recruiting, information delivery—any business that's conducted over the Internet." And although the adage "Content is King" sometimes seems to get lost in the rush to make money over the Internet, plenty of IT opportunities remain in content-oriented ventures such as entertainment, research, and portal sites, nonprofit organizations, academia, and government. And in the wireless world, the definition of Internet-related IT jobs is expanding as corporations and dot-coms alike move to port their applications and content to any device connected to the Internet, such as personal digital assistants (PDAs) and cell phones.

E-business, whether conducted by offline corporations or pure-play dot-coms, entails largely the same IT requirements as any other business activities. The primary Internet-related IT jobs, therefore, run parallel to traditional IT jobs—applications developer, database administrator/developer/analyst, network administrator, security analyst, network architect, systems administrator, etc. But they generally require specialized skill sets.

Moreover, the Internet has created some new job titles, such as site producer, web developer, and ecommerce architect, to name a few. In many cases, dot-coms have come up with their own spin on traditional IT titles. For example, the word "engineer" is frequently used, such as software engineer (applications developer), web engineer (site designer), or systems engineer (systems administrator). Whereas the top IT executive in a corporate IT department is usually the chief information officer, in a dot-com, it is typically the chief technology officer, reflecting the dot-com's emphasis on technology as a driver as much as an enabler. (See Chapter 8.)

As these titles demonstrate, the differences between working in a corporate e-business group and a dot-com are largely cultural. This chapter focuses on the unique aspects of IT jobs and responsibilities in each environment and the new job titles created by the Internet.

NOTE *For a full discussion of the differences between working in a dot-com and a corporate IT organization, see Chapter 3.*

Corporate IT E-business and Internet Jobs: An Overview

The e-business group within a corporate IT organization combines the fast-paced excitement and new experience of working on Internet-related projects with the stability and job security of working for an established company. That's not to say it is without risk. E-business projects are among the most mission-critical, highly visible projects going on in IT today, and project failures will garner as much attention, if not more, as successes.

The department's overall responsibilities usually encompass a company's public websites, the intranet, and supplier- and customer-facing extranets, plus industry exchanges and marketplaces. Individual job descriptions are usually more segmented and specialized in the corporate environment than in a dot-com. Project management, applications development, and database-related positions are the most prevalent in a corporate e-business group. Architects, site designers, and web developers are a given, as are system administrators to manage the various web servers. The networking function, as it relates to e-business, may be contained within the group or may be handled by the centralized networking department. (See "Corporate IT E-business Jobs: The Management Perspective" later in this chapter.) While spending time in the e-business group may fast-track your career relative to the typical corporate IT job progression, you will likely advance at a more measured pace than you might within a small dot-com startup.

As companies move to web-enable all business processes, the day will come when the e-business group won't be cordoned off into its own niche because everything the IT department does will be somehow tied to the Internet.

"The Internet is increasingly becoming part of the basic business model for many companies," notes the UT study. "The Internet is rapidly becoming an integral part of the traditional economy—like telephones, elevators, and personal computers over the years—leading to the day when there will be no separate measure of the Internet economy."

CORPORATE IT E-BUSINESS JOBS: THE MANAGEMENT PERSPECTIVE

Leo Timmons, senior manager, Ebusiness Applications Development Group, development technologies department, The Pillsbury Co., Minneapolis, Minn.

 NOTE *In July 2000, General Mills in Minneapolis, Minnesota, announced that it would acquire The Pillsbury Company from food and beverage conglomerate Diageo plc; General Mills shareholders approved the deal in December 2000, but as of this printing, the acquisition was still pending.*

How are the IT jobs in a corporate IT e-business department different from those in a pure-play dot-com?

The scale is different. In a dot-com company, there are fewer people, so you may do more things—you may design the logo, reboot the servers, and write the [applications] code. In corporate IT, there's more specialization—one person's job is to do server maintenance, one's is to code, one's is to do creative design.

How are responsibilities delegated in the Pillsbury e-business group?

Our overall responsibility is e-business applications development, and there are three tracks. A business-to-consumer track is concerned with our public Internet sites—like Pillsbury.com and HaagenDazs.com—and customer relationship marketing. There's a business-to-business track that's focused on electronic procurement, industry exchanges, and marketplaces. Then there's a business-to-employee track focused on the intranet and the creation of the corporate portal for communicating internally with employees, and that also incorporates the knowledge management [KM] area—tracking internal skill sets like who knows how to bake bread, who knows what's inside a can of soup, etc.

What about the network responsibilities? Does that fall under your group or another department in Pillsbury IT?

We've created an Internet infrastructure team that's responsible for the perimeter—domain registrations, firewalls, intrusion detection, etc. Then in the Pillsbury IT operations group, there's a networking group focused on Internet and EDI [electronic

CORPORATE IT E-BUSINESS JOBS: THE MANAGEMENT PERSPECTIVE

data interchange] infrastructure that takes care of routers, cabling, etc. They're like an internal ISP to us, and we get our Internet networking services from them.

Some companies have their own end-to-end teams for Internet infrastructure and development. We cut the other way for historical [organizational] reasons, but it would be simpler to have an end-to-end organizational structure.

Given the cultural differences between a dot-com and corporate IT, what's your take on hiring former dot-commers?

The only trepidation I would have about hiring a dot-commer would be their motivation—were they of the get-rich-quick motivation? Are their perceptions of IT that everyone works 18 hours a day and never goes home? Or are they looking for more job security and stability? If it's the latter, then they would make a great hire for the corporate culture because they know the grass isn't greener in dot-coms. As far as skills go, a dot-commer would bring great experience with them, even if the dot-com was a failure. But my experience is that those folks tend to bounce from one dot-com to another and haven't sought out the corporate culture very often.

I usually hire either a young entry-level person with no prior experience, or, for jobs that require more experience, I like to hire from within the company—someone who may have no e-business experience but they have extensive legacy systems experience.

What kind of temperament do you need to do well in this area of IT?

E-business exaggerates the need for people who can multitask and work very quickly. A lot of the applications that we do are temporary—like a sweepstakes offered at a website that only lasts 30 days. Some may only run for a day—like an online chat that only lasts an hour. So it's not like working on systems that run for ten years in a legacy environment. Also, the ability to get along with others is critical. When I'm hiring for our team, it doesn't matter how smart you are if you can't get along with other people. Everything we do is intensely collaborative, and I can't just set a programmer in a corner by themselves.

IS WORKING IN A CORPORATE E-BUSINESS GROUP FOR YOU?   Yes, if you want to be on the leading edge of where IT is headed in the future, but you prefer job security over the risk of working for a dot-com. If you are already employed in a corporate IT organization, it may be easier—and more prudent—to transfer into the corporate e-business group instead of joining a dot-com. But if you thrive on the frantic pace and do-or-die atmosphere of a startup environment, you might get more satisfaction out of a dot-com, and you can use a stint in a corporate e-business group as an intermediate step to that goal.

TIP Non-IT professionals looking for a stepping stone into IT can leverage their business/ functional expertise to transfer into the e-business group. If you're in marketing or communications, for example, start by seeking a content-oriented role, learn a front-end editing tool like FrontPage to move into site design, and then gradually move into programming by mastering Visual Basic (VB) or Active Server Pages (ASP). Or if you're a human resources professional, sign up to work on the HR intranet team as a functional expert, and then start gaining the technical skills you need to get more deeply involved in the IT end.

Dot-Com E-business and Internet Jobs: An Overview

Aside from the cultural differences between working for a dot-com vs. a larger, traditional company, the IT environment is distinct. For one, the IT pros in a dot-com are inherently the rock stars of the company. The company would not exist without them. While many dot-coms have fallen because the technology vision lacked a foundation in a sound business plan, the fact remains that because a dot-com's business exists only in cyberspace, technology is king.

The IT jobs in a dot-com cover the gamut—applications development and site design, database development, administration and analysis, quality assurance and testing, and networking and internal IT support. The latter is usually assigned to only one or two people responsible for the internal network and end-user support. And supporting other IT professionals has its challenges: "You can't confuse them with techno-speak; they're much more demanding and knowledgeable than your average user," says Rick Cecil, director of NT operations at iBeauty.com, a cosmetics e-tailer in New York. Conversely, because they have a firsthand understanding of what you're up against, "they're much more forgiving when they can see that something is out of your control."

DOT-COM IT JOBS: THE MANAGEMENT PERSPECTIVE

Gregor Cranz, chief technology officer, iBeauty.com, New York, N.Y.

Cosmetics e-tailer iBeauty.com has moved beyond the classic startup phase, with several rounds of venture capital funding behind it and shiny new offices in Midtown Manhattan (a big step up from an overcrowded, musty Chelsea loft in its earlier stages). But, Cranz notes, "We still act like a startup."

How is working in a pure-play dot-com different from a corporate IT e-business department?

There's a very fundamental difference in the commitment to technology as an investment. Older companies tend to add e-business on as another division, whereas dot-com companies bring it in as a foundation, so they're faster to spend money on IT and don't have to go through as much bureaucracy to get an IT plan paid for and implemented. Ecommerce is our business model—we sell things online—so IT comes first, and it's easier to get IT money out of dot-com companies. That goes for salaries as well as budgets, but you'll work harder for it in a dot-com. You are all things to all people.

What are the differences between working for a content-oriented dot-com and an ecommerce-oriented dot-com?

Technically, it's not as challenging to do content sites. There aren't the same security issues and transactional backend issues, like fulfillment systems and reconciling credit reports, etc. An ecommerce dot-com is doing all the same things as a content-driven site, plus sales and marketing.

I see content sites as a failing business model. They won't go away, but they'll change a lot. We already see a trend where once upon a time the Net was all about free information—it was a means for universities to post a wealth of information. And now, slowly, more and more content is being put behind tollbooths—a pay-per-view model. For example, at a site like Guru.com, you pay a fee to chat with an expert on a subject. That's what newsgroups were always for, and those are free. But things are slowly shifting that way.

DOT-COM IT JOBS: THE MANAGEMENT PERSPECTIVE

How are the IT responsibilities delegated in a dot-com?

We have five disciplines: web engineering, or applications development; database services, which is separate from development because of the backend issues and reporting; operations, including networking, infrastructure, and systems administration; quality assurance; and the desktop group, which provides internal IT support. That's a fairly typical model.

If you've been working in a corporate IT e-business group, how can you get on board with a dot-com?

Learn as much as possible. In corporate IT, you have much greater access to training, so get yourself trained. Also, you should be represented by a recruiter. I've gotten every single job I've had through an agency, and as a manager, I can justify using the high-end agencies to find candidates. So select a high-end agency—not your typical mail-merge type that's just trying to collect a commission. If you're highly technical and lacking in people skills, it helps to have a recruiter who can negotiate for you.

Will corporate IT pros have to overcome any biases against them among dot-com IT folks?

I don't see a bias—it just means that people have solid experience. Dot-coms are stricter with their hiring guidelines because they want people with the most experience that they can pay the least amount of money. Corporations just want to pay the least amount of money.

What kind of temperament is needed to do well in a dot-com?

In general, you need to violate the stereotype of the snotty tech guy. There's a skit on "Saturday Night Live" called "Your Company Computer Guy," and the character is as condescending as humanly possible. You need to break that mode because people don't tolerate it anymore, and people in a dot-com are pretty tech savvy so they especially won't stand for it. Also, try to think outside your field of vision, because it's not like dot-coms are overstaffed and there are people sitting around twiddling their thumbs. There's so much to do in a dot-com that things can fall through the cracks. If you grab them and take care of them, then you're really going to help the company. Don't be a corporate leech.

You can expect to wear many hats in a dot-com IT position. You may be an applications developer, but you could be called on to help out with something as mundane as data entry when the company is up against a deadline. While initiative is prized in any type of IT organization, self-motivation, enthusiasm, and a willingness to volunteer for projects in a dot-com can turn an administrative assistant into a project manager in a relatively short time.

IS WORKING IN A DOT-COM IT JOB FOR YOU?   Yes, if you want to be on the cutting edge of Internet technology and are able to accept a high level of risk. Just because a dot-com has longevity doesn't mean your job will be secure—consider that even such well-funded companies (with well-trafficked sites) as Amazon.com and The Motley Fool have had layoffs. If you're a career changer looking for an entrée into IT, sheer chutzpah and ambition may land you an opportunity within a dot-com, but mastering the new skill sets will be up to you. Allocating time and money for training is not usually a high priority in dot-com startups.

New Internet-Related IT Jobs: A Sampler

Ecommerce Architect

JOB TITLE VARIATIONS   Applications architect, Internet architect, site architect.

JOB DESCRIPTION   As the name implies, this is a mid- to high-level design position, responsible for constructing the overall functional and technical design of an ecommerce site. Duties can include selecting the ecommerce platform, defining and designing site navigation, gathering business requirements, working with product and marketing departments to establish branding strategy, mapping the processes and workflow, storyboarding, determining the traffic patterns and volume the design must support, and developing an applications framework.

EDUCATION AND CERTIFICATION REQUIREMENTS   Minimum of a Bachelor's degree in Computer Science or MIS, plus training and experience in a software development methodology. Certification in key Internet technologies is a plus (such as the Sun Certified Architect for Java Technology), as is project management certification. Vendor-neutral certifications in e-business (such as the Sysoft Certified E-business Professional program) can help provide the necessary background for this job.

TECHNICAL SKILLS REQUIRED Breadth and depth in major Internet development languages and tools, including Java, CORBA, VB, and XML; Oracle or another relational database, ColdFusion and SQL; operating systems such as Windows NT, Windows 2000, Sun Solaris and others; familiarity with major ecommerce platforms such as Vignette and ATG Dynamo; and a sound, overall understanding of network architecture and web security. You should have substantial IT experience behind you in applications development, project management, and Internet-related positions. Experience on an enterprise-wide development project is essential.

OTHER SKILLS REQUIRED An understanding of business processes and workflow; project management skills, problem-solving skills; strong communication skills, including the ability to deal with end-users, business unit managers, and IT staff and management, plus the ability to translate business requirements into technical requirements; ability to multitask; and ability to navigate between looking at the big picture and concentrating on details.

POTENTIAL CAREER PATHS Owing to both the breadth and depth of skills this position requires, it can mark a significant step into upper IT management, such as infrastructure architect, systems architect (with responsibility across all of IT), management positions in applications development or advanced technology, and on up to the IT executive suite.

IS THIS POSITION FOR YOU? If you are solutions-oriented, enjoy figuring out how to apply technology to business processes, and prefer applications design to actual programming, you would be well-suited for this job. You must have an appreciation for the big picture as well as the finer details.

Information Architect

JOB TITLE VARIATIONS User interface designer.

JOB DESCRIPTION This design job is concerned with the user experience at a website—anticipating how a user will navigate through the site's content, and mapping out the content and design accordingly. The end result is a balancing act between the intended experience or message (whether the purpose is entertainment, informational, branding, or transactional), and how web surfers will use the site. The information architect works closely with both the content/editorial team and site designers and developers to translate functional requirements and goals into an overall technical architecture for the site. He or she also develops the look and feel of the user interface, including screen flows, storyboards, site maps, and navigational rules. Other responsibilities include usability testing, presentations, and team management.

EDUCATION AND CERTIFICATION REQUIREMENTS A Bachelor's degree is required (some employers prefer a Master's degree), but a number of different educational backgrounds can be brought to bear on this job, including psychology, behavioral sciences, human factors, industrial design, instructional design, library science, writing, multimedia, graphic design, and more. Formal education or certification specifically related to this position has not yet emerged. Required experience includes digital production, website design and development, interface design, usability testing, and project management.

TECHNICAL SKILLS REQUIRED Familiarity with an array of web development and design languages and tools such as Java, JavaScript, HTML, Dynamic HTML (DHTML), common gateway interface (CGI), Perl, ASP, VB, C++, Flash, Shockwave, etc.; and an understanding of operating systems and networks. Technology skills, while required, are not the most important ones for this position.

OTHER SKILLS REQUIRED Creative problem-solving skills; analytical skills; ability to anticipate how people think and respond to stimuli; strong communication skills, including presentation, writing, and documentation skills; leadership skills; and content-management skills.

POTENTIAL CAREER PATHS Information architects who want to get more deeply involved in the technical side could foray into applications development and applications or systems architecture—and continue moving up the management ladder in applications development or e-business. Just like many career paths can lead into this position, myriad paths can grow from it.

IS THIS POSITION FOR YOU? If you want to be involved in an IT position that is multidisciplinary and leverages a diverse range of skill sets, and you have an affinity for the human factors in technology and have a creative bent, this could be an ideal position for you. If you are breaking into IT from a creative field, education and training, or a similar multidisciplinary profession, this is an appropriate stepping stone.

Site Producer

JOB TITLE VARIATIONS   Web producer, interactive producer, multimedia producer, creative director, web project manager.

JOB DESCRIPTION   This job title is most common in content-oriented ventures such as entertainment industry websites that involve extensive use of streaming video, audio, graphics, and interactive features like games and contests. The site producer functions essentially as a project manager and must feel comfortable dealing with IT professionals, the creative department, writers and editors, marketing, and other areas. While little or no programming is involved, a producer must nonetheless have a solid understanding of web programming languages and site development and design tools; in some cases, producers will be responsible for some basic HTML coding. Primary responsibilities include leading content generation, overseeing digital production, tracking assets to be used in the site, scheduling project deadlines, and monitoring progress. The producer also coordinates the efforts of departments such as art, editorial, development, marketing, and merchandising, from initial conceptualizing of the site through the launch and maintenance.

EDUCATION AND CERTIFICATION REQUIREMENTS   A college degree is a stated requirement, but the right experience would garner consideration in lieu of a degree. Prior experience as a team leader or project manager on an Internet-related project is required; formal training and/or experience in a creative field such as CD-ROM production, art, graphic design, advertising, or entertainment is preferred. Web-related certification is a plus, as is project management certification.

TECHNICAL SKILLS REQUIRED   Thorough familiarity with web development and design tools such as HTML, DHTML, JavaScript, Flash, Shockwave, etc.; web server operating systems, such as Sun Solaris, Windows 2000, and Linux; web server software such as Microsoft Internet Information Server, Microsoft Exchange, or Lotus Notes/Domino; database development; and networking. Experience with a project management package such as Microsoft Project is a plus.

OTHER SKILLS REQUIRED   Creative skills, leadership skills, strong communication skills, and analytical skills.

POTENTIAL CAREER PATHS   Site producers who develop strong technical skills could go into project managing an e-business site or other applications development projects;

those with an aptitude for business processes and workflow could pursue a business analyst role; and those more focused on the human factors and user experience could pursue the information architect position.

IS THIS POSITION FOR YOU? If you have a creative liberal arts background and leadership skills, and you want to be involved with the Web but lack in-depth technical experience, this job is a good transitional step into IT. It also provides valuable experience to those who want to pursue a dot-com management track but not necessarily through the technical ranks. Site producers could also go on to get more involved in multimedia production such as gaming or instructional CD-ROMs.

SPOTLIGHT ON AN INTERACTIVE PRODUCER

Jesse Martinez, 28, interactive producer for a New York–based broadband media services company that develops websites and interactive products for the entertainment industry.

Martinez (a pseudonym) arrived in New York's Silicon Alley from New Orleans just before the dot-com market correction of March 2000. Dot-coms were still in a hiring frenzy, and within three weeks, she garnered several job offers, settling on one that leveraged both her educational background in film studies and her web production experience with a small consulting firm. But by the end of the year, the dot-com climate had changed considerably, and Martinez was let go just before Christmas—along with nearly all of her coworkers—as the company began evaluating alternate business models. Below she discusses the job she held and how the role is changing in today's shifting dot-com market.

Overall responsibilities "It's basically a project management role, with responsibility for scheduling, requirements gathering, tracking client assets like graphics, video, and other elements for the site, and managing the development staff for each project. My projects included producing websites for the company as well as for external clients. For example, internally I oversaw the development and upgrading of the corporate website, managed the website development for several independent films, and managed the animated logo used on all the company's film and video products. External projects included designing Flash and HTML websites and the user interface for an interactive application for a handheld device.

SPOTLIGHT ON AN INTERACTIVE PRODUCER

Day-to-day responsibilities "Usually I would juggle three to four projects of different scopes and at different stages at the same time. So on a typical day I'd be checking the status of each project; checking in with designers and developers to see if they're on schedule and if there were any new issues to resolve; communicating the project status to the client and getting clarification on their needs or feedback and approval on deliverables. I also spent a lot of time trying to get the assets in, revising copy, getting legal approvals, etc."

Technologies and technical skills required "HTML, Microsoft Project Manager, Visio for diagrams and flowcharts, Photoshop, and basic knowledge of how web servers work, FTP [file transfer protocol], and web production. You have to be very comfortable working within a networked environment and understand file sharing, and know enough about web capabilities that you can talk intelligently to your clients and schedule production appropriately.

"Producers come from all different backgrounds, and some have more technical experience than others. I have a little more than some because I came up through the production ranks, while some come to it from other disciplines like video or print production, and they've picked up the web skills along the way."

Other skills required Project management and organizational skills, working well with others, and communication skills. "You have to be able to negotiate and be diplomatic with the client, as well as manage your team."

What I like most about this job "The people. It's a creative, unique environment with a lot of smart, creative personalities. You're trying to push the envelope of design and technology. I also got to work on my technical skills and become a better manager. Getting things done gives you a certain satisfaction—understanding client requirements, solving problems, and getting the design to go with that. And the projects themselves are interesting—since it's entertainment-related you have more leeway in the creativity."

What I like least about this job "The constant attention to details on a very mundane level. Problem-solving is fun, but some problems are very banal, like figuring out how to schedule something. A lot of that is very dry—who's going to do what, the budget. Those are good skills to have for any job, but I'm more interested in using my conceptual skills."

SPOTLIGHT ON AN INTERACTIVE PRODUCER

Career path leading to this job   "I had one year's experience as a producer at a smaller website design firm in New Orleans, and I was a web production staff member for about nine months before that. I first started getting web experience in graduate school, where I was a teacher in the computer lab. I got an M.A. in English with a specialization in film and media studies, and that related to this particular job."

How I landed in this position   "I targeted the New York market specifically because I'd heard great things about working in Silicon Alley. In smaller markets it's really hard to find producer jobs like you can in New York, where there are so many connections to different industries. I wasn't exactly sure that I wanted to continue to be a producer—my long-term goal is to move more into an information architect role, working out the user interface and navigation design. But I knew that my producer experience was the best entry into the New York job market, and I focused my message for prospective employers and recruiters as a producer. It helped that I had previous web production experience, I knew HTML, I was familiar with graphics programs, and I had worked on a variety of platforms—Windows, Unix, and Macintosh. I wasn't a Johnny-come-lately."

Advice to other IT pros interested in interactive producing   "From what I've seen, it's harder now to find a producer position if you don't have the web experience. Earlier in the game, dot-coms would take anyone who could manage a project, but now they want people with definite web experience, not just project management experience. Experience with traditional IT projects would definitely get you in the door."

Web Administrator

JOB TITLE VARIATIONS   Intranet administrator, NT/web administrator, Internet Information Server (IIS) administrator, Domino administrator.

JOB DESCRIPTION   The web administrator's role is essentially the same as a network administrator or systems administrator, but with a focus on servers connected to the Internet. Sometimes the job also entails administration and support for the corporate intranet and/or extranet. Responsibilities include establishing and refining operating procedures, updating directories, monitoring and tuning server performance, troubleshooting, and making modifications and upgrades to the operating system. (See Chapter 5 for more information about the network administrator's role and Chapter 6 for more information about the systems administrator position.)

EDUCATION AND CERTIFICATION REQUIREMENTS   A Bachelor's degree in an IT-related field is required, and certification, such as the Microsoft MCSE+I, is highly recommended. Cisco Certified Network Associate (CCNA) or Cisco Certified Network Professional (CCNP) certification is recommended for those who want to stand a cut above and who intend to make a career in networking. Web-related certification would be a big plus.

TECHNICAL SKILLS REQUIRED   In-depth knowledge of Internet server platforms such as Internet Information Server, Windows NT, Windows 2000 Server, SQL Server, Sun Solaris, Lotus Notes/Domino, etc.; experience with major ecommerce platforms and email systems may also be required. Knowledge of web development languages and tools, such as HTML, VB, ASP, and ColdFusion is also desired but not required.

OTHER SKILLS REQUIRED   Troubleshooting abilities, attention to detail, task-oriented disposition, ability to stay calm under pressure, and good communication skills.

POTENTIAL CAREER PATHS   This job is a good position for growth in many different directions, including web applications development, network or systems administration, database administration, applications development, or operations. It can be useful experience for those who choose an IT management track but is an equally good choice for those anticipating a purely technical track.

IS THIS POSITION FOR YOU?   If you prefer a structured, task-oriented job that is highly technical and hands-on, this is an excellent choice, although the web administrator's role may be less structured than a traditional network or systems administrator role.

Web Developer

JOB TITLE VARIATIONS   Web designer, HTML programmer.

JOB DESCRIPTION   The web developer is a key team member who brings an eye for page design and navigation, storyboards, graphic design, and content presentation to a web-based project. Responsibilities include generating logos and other graphical elements, participating in the storyboarding process, knowing HTML programming or using HTML editors to generate web pages, and acting as a liaison between business units and the applications developers. Web developers, who may work on intranet or extranet sites as well as public websites, usually report to the project manager, but must also do some project management themselves.

SPOTLIGHT ON A WEB DEVELOPER

Debbie Lynch, 46, web developer, Harrah's Entertainment, Memphis, Tenn.

Overall responsibilities Site design, programming, and graphics development for various Harrah's internal and external websites, including the corporate site (www.harrahs.com), an eProcurement site for the Harrah's intranet (where employees can purchase supplies and services), and a human resources department intranet (where employees can access information about their vacation time, insurance benefits, performance reviews, and more).

Day-to-day responsibilities "It depends on what stage of the project we're in, and I'm always juggling multiple projects. Typically I have three to four at a time in different stages. A typical day is a combination of hallway communication, formal meetings, and hands-on work. I may have several consecutive days of meetings and teamwork, followed by several days of heads-down, hands-on work.

"In the development stage, there's a lot of storyboarding—working with users to find out what their desired outcome is, understanding all the steps in the process that we're bringing to the Web, all the possible scenarios that could occur in the process, and determining what can and can't be done. Programmers have to understand the process so they can design the navigation and the back end properly. Once the storyboards are done and we have consensus, we move into the design phase. That's where I come into play more, working on the look-and-feel and designing logos and art elements. Then we have to take it into the budget-approval process, and that involves making presentations. Once we get budget approval, then the actual design is completed and tested prior to launch. After launch, the team takes care of maintenance, but in other organizations, that could fall to a desktop deployment team."

Technologies and technical skills required HTML, JavaScript, FrontPage, Flash, Shockwave, and various graphics software packages. "Networking is a huge part of it. I have to know the fundamentals of networking, but that's not the part that thrills me. I'm focusing on the design and programming side."

Other skills required "A lot of creative skills, and this is where I have a leg up on most web developers—or so I've been told—because they often don't have the design capabilities. The creative design is usually handed off to someone else, so if you have both the technical skills and the design capabilities, that's a plus. The ability to multitask is important, and I definitely have to use my people skills to communicate with all levels of management and not have a fear of making suggestions about what might

SPOTLIGHT ON A WEB DEVELOPER

work better than what they're thinking of. And I have to translate technology to users and user requests to technologists. I work on teams with several other people, and you have to keep everyone in the flow and happy."

What I like most about this job "From a career standpoint, with the way the technology is growing, the Internet is a roller coaster that I want to be on. Every time I get into a new project, I start learning something new. And I know it's not going away tomorrow—ten years down the line, it will still be here, and it will evolve and I can evolve with it."

What I like least about this job "The networking side. In networking there's so much information that you have to memorize and be on top of all the time. It's very structured and straightforward, and I'm more interested in the creative aspects of the job."

Career path leading to this job The role of web developer leverages Lynch's previous experience in documentation and graphic design. She spent nine years in the Harrah's IT department as an internal graphic designer with responsibility for designing newsletters, brochures, presentations, team logos (such as the Y2K team logo used on t-shirts and posters), recognition rewards, and more. Prior to working at Harrah's, Lynch had been involved in IT as a documentation specialist at a high-tech company in California.

Retraining required Lynch spent about 15 days in training in 2000 learning HTML, JavaScript, and FrontPage. She also pursued the Certified Internet Webmaster certification program developed by ProsoftTraining.com Inc. "Getting certified helps others see me as not just 'Debbie the graphics person,' but as someone who's helping lead our Internet development. And it builds my own self-confidence." Lynch's training plans for 2001 included Flash and Shockwave classes.

Advice to other IT pros interested in web development "There will be sustained demand for web developers in corporate IT. There's still a lack of talent even with the dot-com demise, and companies can't fill the positions available now. And with [front-end] editors available like Microsoft FrontPage and Dreamweaver, you don't even have to know a lot about HTML—although it will benefit you to learn it—as long as you have an eye for design and a feel for developing web pages. And once you have a foot in the door, you can go more in-depth into the programming end with Visual Basic and Active Server Pages."

EDUCATION AND CERTIFICATION REQUIREMENTS A college degree is a stated requirement, but the right background and experience could substitute. That would include experience in the graphic arts, design, writing, or programming. Web-related certification is a plus.

TECHNICAL SKILLS REQUIRED Basic web development languages and tools, including HTML, Flash, Shockwave, etc.; experience with HTML editors such as Microsoft Front-Page or Dreamweaver; a thorough understanding of web servers, operating systems, and networking; and a grounding in more complex development languages such as Java, JavaScript, VB, or ASP is desired, as it will facilitate communication with web applications developers.

OTHER SKILLS REQUIRED Strong communication and presentation skills, a team-oriented work ethic, visual/graphics skills, ability to multitask, creativity, and analytical skills.

POTENTIAL CAREER PATHS This is an entry-level position in the Internet category, so depending on personal preferences—are you more interested in the creative aspects or the technical aspects of the job?—web developers can progress to the roles of applications developer, web administrator, project manager, site producer, creative director, or information architect.

IS THIS POSITION FOR YOU? If you are an entry-level programmer with a creative bent or you come from a creative background and have a technical bent, this is an ideal entry point into an Internet career. You must enjoy working on teams and be deadline-driven.

TIP One Internet job title that has faded from use is webmaster. Once the catch-all title of choice for the person who was in charge of a website—who was responsible for the programming, the graphic design, the server, the database, you name it—"webmaster" became an ultra-cool status symbol in the early Wild West days of the Web. If you were a webmaster—or web mistress, web Guru, or any other variation—you were on the leading edge. But as websites became more complicated, requiring more than just rudimentary HTML programming and colorful graphics, the jobs surrounding websites become much more specialized. When the title is used today, it usually refers to someone doing site maintenance and maybe some troubleshooting of the HTML code or content management. Sometimes it still turns up in job descriptions or is added on to another job title as an afterthought, mainly for recruiting purposes because it has widespread name recognition. At the IT job search site Computer-jobs.com, a search for "webmaster" in early 2001 turned up only 103 jobs nationwide, and those were most frequently development and engineering jobs where a recruiter had tacked on "webmaster" to cover all the potential search terms.

E-business and Internet Technologies Checklists

Applications Development and Database Technologies

✓ Active Server Pages (ASP)

✓ ATG Dynamo Server Suite

✓ CGI

✓ ColdFusion

✓ Dynamic HTML (DHTML)

✓ HTML

✓ Java

✓ Perl

✓ Visual Basic

✓ Wireless Application Protocol (WAP)

✓ XML

✓ Lotus Notes/Domino

✓ Microsoft Exchange

✓ Microsoft SQL Server

✓ Oracle

Operating Systems and Server Software

✓ Linux

✓ Microsoft Internet Information Server

✓ Sun Solaris (and other versions of Unix)

✓ Windows 2000

✓ Windows NT

Website Design Tools and Standards

✓ Dreamweaver

✓ Flash

✓ IP Multicast

✓ Microsoft FrontPage

✓ Real Networks Streaming Media

✓ Shockwave

Common E-business Platforms

✓ Ariba B2B commerce platform

✓ ATG Dynamo e-business platform

✓ CommerceOne

✓ Customer Interaction Software by Blue Martini Software

✓ E-business application platform by Vignette

✓ InterWorld commerce suite

Content Management Tools

✓ Content Management Server by Vignette

✓ TEAMS software suite by Artesia Technologies

E-business-related Applications

✓ i2 Supplier Relationship Management Suite

✓ Siebel Systems e-business applications (customer relationship management)

✓ Unified CRM Solution by Chordiant Software

Networking and Security Technologies and Protocols

✓ Cisco routers and switches

✓ Emerging Internet2 standards

✓ Firewalls

✓ PGP encryption

✓ Secure Sockets Layer (SSL)

✓ TCP/IP

Chapter 8

Start Me Up in IT Management

In the anatomy of IT, management could be viewed as the brain of the organization. That's not to say that IT managers are smarter than their subordinates (and, in fact, many subordinates would insist that they most definitely are not). But it is management that makes the decisions that, in the best-case scenario, will align IT with the business and enable business strategy. For some, moving up the IT management ranks represents the ultimate opportunity to make an impact on their companies; others view it as the death knell for their technical skills.

It's true that with each step up in management, you gradually give up direct involvement at the implementation level. You expand your focus to the big picture of how IT interacts with and supports the business, and how prepared your organization is to meet the challenge in terms of skills, staffing, and overall direction. Naturally, as you take on responsibility for strategic planning, recruiting and hiring staff, shaping subordinates' career paths, budgeting, performing return on investment (ROI) analysis, and other management-level duties, you will be less and less involved in hands-on IT work. Instead of attending an advanced Java seminar, you're more likely to attend a Gartner Group Symposium on "Managing IT for Sustained Competitive Advantage." Nonetheless, those who have chosen the IT management track say it brings the satisfaction of feeling more connected to business strategy and that leading the IT vision and developing staff offers a sense of making a profound and lasting contribution.

"I certainly enjoyed being more technical, but I found that I wanted greater challenges. I wanted to take a step out and be a real leader," says Joe Plaster, vice president of e-business technology at V.F. Shared Services, the wholly owned IT subsidiary of apparel manufacturer V.F. Corporation, in Greensboro, North Carolina. "Certainly there are some monetary benefits, but my real motivation was the challenge and my feeling that I could make a difference to the success of IT."

Giving up the hands-on work and delegating tactical technology decisions to staff members is inherently difficult for many talented IT pros as they move into management. Kevin Book, senior director of technology at The Motley Fool, Alexandria, Virginia, says his biggest management mistake to date was "suppressing the best ideas of the people around me by being adamant about a technical decision." His staff was working on the backend system supporting news content on the company's financial research website (www.motleyfool.com), and Book made an ill-fated design decision that a younger, less-experienced staff member challenged. "He said my technique wouldn't work well on the Microsoft platform, but I had applied some tried-and-true design principles and I was convinced I was right," Book recalls. "Later we ended up having to rewrite the system the way the other programmer had suggested." As a result, Book temporarily lost the confidence of his staff. He recovered, he says, by acknowledging that he'd been wrong; moreover, he demonstrated true leadership ability by taking a hard look at how he'd handled the situation and resolving to modify his approach in the future. "I learned a big lesson about forcing my opinions down people's throats. That was when I really learned to ask my staff about the best ways of doing things."

Although you're further removed from the technology itself as you advance up the management ranks, that doesn't mean you relinquish your technology skills. You may not be programming or troubleshooting a network-security problem, but you will bring your knowledge of technology to bear on the long-range planning and decision-making you'll face as an IT manager. Staying on top of key technologies is essential to the strategic aspects of the job. John Plummer, information technology division manager for Corning's Controls and Connectors division, in Corning, New York, regularly attends executive-level technology training such as a course delineating the commonalities and differences between various enterprise resource planning (ERP) systems like SAP, PeopleSoft, and Baan, and a high-level networking course explaining the various communications protocols.

"A technology-trends focus is important," Plummer says. "You can't be a technician after a certain point—you won't be the guy putting in hubs and routers and loading software—but you need to be aware enough of technology so that you aren't snowed by your technicians. You have to continue to study, pay attention to journals, interact with the right leaders, attend conferences, and know enough about changes in technology to be able to translate current technical jargon into business language and make [strategic technology] decisions."

Even as you reach the IT executive suite, when perhaps it's been years since you wrote a line of code or tuned a database, you must remain conversant in the technology at all levels to gain the trust of your staff and encourage them to sustain an exchange of ideas with you. "Having reached my position by coming up in IT in the applications and operations areas allows me to have a dialogue with most of the individuals in my organization," explains Cecilia Claudio, senior vice president, chief information officer (CIO), and chief transformation officer at Farmers Insurance Group in Los Angeles. "I can provide advice at a pretty low level."

When a programmer consulted her about a problem he was having with a legacy system because the Assembler code wasn't documented, she suggested that "rather than going back and documenting the code, it would be better at this point to understand the function that this part of the code delivers, develop something in a 4GL [fourth-generation language] that achieves the same function, and replace those bits of Assembler code module by module." Being able to offer that level of concrete advice on a technical problem, Claudio notes, has been key to garnering the support of her staff. "They know they can come to me with low-level questions or high-level questions; they know my passion and intensity and support for what they do."

A big part of IT management involves acquiring responsibility for your people, not only managing their day-to-day work, but also playing a role in mentoring their career development. You approve their training plans, their promotions, their salary increases, and their bonuses. You help set the tone for how well they all work together. You resolve the conflicts among them. You create the litmus tests for new job candidates and decide who gets hired and who doesn't. Sometimes you decide who gets fired. And you establish the policies that may determine whether your staff is happy on the job or not.

"Moving up requires a huge change in focus," Plaster says. "You must have more social skills, more people skills. As a project manager, maybe you have five or six people to worry about, and then suddenly you have a lot more people and a lot more involvement with them."

For example, when André Mendes, former CIO at the Public Broadcasting System (PBS) in Alexandria, Virginia, first joined the organization as director of client/server development in 1998, he not only had to chart a new IT strategy, he also had to map out individual career paths for each of his 45 staff members within the new strategy. He had to create incentives for them to buy into the new IT mission and adapt to new ways of doing their jobs. Mendes says he couldn't just throw money at them—that would have been merely a short-term solution, and as a nonprofit, PBS couldn't compete with private industry anyway. Instead, Mendes had to think beyond financial inducements and take a holistic approach. The transformation of the IT department was successful, he says, because he considered their personal goals and aspirations as well as the organizational objectives; each person's new mission was tied to the greater mission of aligning IT with the business of PBS. What's more, as he addressed their long-term career concerns, he also took into account their quality-of-life issues.

"I tried to build an atmosphere where people feel appreciated, and like they're part of a family as opposed to part of a team," says Mendes, who in April 2001 became chief operating officer of Pluvita Corporation, a biotechnology firm in Bethesda, Maryland. "I implemented a three-pronged strategy: invest in their training in the latest technologies, promote from within exclusively, and make sure that they have a sane lifestyle. We're not working 40-hour weeks, but we're not working 70-hour weeks either. Everyone goes home at a reasonable time."

Mendes successfully inspired the support of his staff at PBS. But the magnitude of such staff-related issues is frequently what's most overwhelming for many IT professionals as they try to transition into management: "For IT managers to be effective, we have to focus on soft skills, and a critical soft skill is the ability to develop other people and help them achieve their best," Plummer says. Not everyone is equipped for that part of the IT management role; as noted in "IT Leadership: A Roundtable Discussion" at the end of this chapter, effectual IT leadership hinges on possessing an internal sense of benevolence and generosity toward others. That must be balanced by objectivity and an ability to make the tough decisions that are best for your organization even when they may hurt individuals you care about.

"Nothing is more difficult than changing someone's life negatively," says Bob DeRodes, CIO of Delta Air Lines, in Atlanta, Georgia. DeRodes recalls a time in a previous management position at another airline when financial problems caused by a flight attendant strike forced the company to make IT staff cuts. "The toughest thing in the world is sitting down and telling people that their jobs have been eliminated," he says. "But true leaders behave the same in bad times as they do in good times—you deal in the facts, stay honest, tell the truth, show compassion, and then work harder than ever before to maintain the esprit de corps."

Divorcing yourself from the day-to-day technology issues and accepting the responsibility of managing people both serve the greater goal of IT management: to create a vision for how IT can support and lead the business. As you move toward the CIO's office, the passion for technology that drew you into IT in the first place should transform into a zeal for business as well. "You need a passion for business because ultimately, you're focused on the same things they are," Plummer says. And it takes a distinct perspective to carry out the responsibilities of the top spot in IT. "One of the keys to success for any CIO is to be able to both find the constellation in the stars—create vision—and to be able to find the fly specs in the pepper," DeRodes says. "You have to navigate the full breadth of the challenge of the enterprise. Some people are great visionaries, but they don't see the details, and some are the opposite. As CIO it's essential to do both well, and it has to be an ongoing process. You must always be thinking about vision and strategy *and* spending time reviewing the details of where you're going."

How you progress through management depends on the degree of hierarchy in the IT organizational structure. The project manager's role is the universal first step into management, and it typically comes after four to six years of IT experience, with team-leader experience on at least one or two prior projects. In very large IT organizations, a typical path after project manager might be manager, director, vice president, and senior vice president and CIO or chief technology officer (CTO). At each level along the way, you may make two or three lateral moves, gaining visibility and responsibility with each. For example, you may move from director of applications development, managing current development strategy, to director of advanced technologies, where you'd be more involved in setting goals for future IT strategy. Depending on the company, there may be more layers, such as senior manager or senior director. In smaller companies and startups, there tends to be fewer layers; you could hop from project manager to director to CTO in a dot-com, for example.

Unfortunately, as you get closer to the executive level, you may find new IT management opportunities begin to be fewer and further between. Not everyone can be the CIO, notes Dave Opton, founder and CEO of ExecuNet, a Norwalk, Connecticut–based executive recruiting firm. "All organizations are hierarchical, and there's only one person at the top of the pyramid."

Following is a look at the project manager's role, IT executive titles, and potential IT management paths to the top.

IT Management Jobs: A Sampler

Project Manager

RANK IN THE IT MANAGEMENT HIERARCHY   Entry level. The project manager (PM) role is the first real step into management, and for many, time spent in this role leads to a decision that joining the management ranks is not for them.

JOB DESCRIPTION   In a nutshell, the PM runs the project and is accountable for completing the final product— whether an application, a data warehouse, a network upgrade, or any other IT deliverable—on time and on budget. A large part of the PM's role is nontechnical, dealing with scoping the project requirements, scheduling each piece of the project, tracking each team member's progress, managing changes and updates, and keeping stakeholders and IT management informed on project status. The PM also takes on at least partial responsibility for creating user buy-in and fostering acceptance of the end product. Concurrent with the management responsibilities, the PM may also do some of the hands-on technical work of the project, especially at the final deployment. Once the initial product is completed and deployed, the PM will oversee the next iteration, which will be based on user feedback and acceptance and will include late changes that weren't allowed in the initial project.

EDUCATION AND CERTIFICATION REQUIREMENTS   A college degree or equivalent on-the-job experience; pursuing certifications in the technologies you use every day will give you a leg up toward this position; and project management certification is highly recommended if not required.

SKILLS REQUIRED   Depth and breadth in your area of expertise (whether applications development, networking and infrastructure, or operations and end-user support); effective communication skills and finesse with coworkers and end-users; ability to multitask; proficiency in at least one project management tool, such as Microsoft Project; an understanding of how IT supports business objectives; and budgeting and/or ROI analysis skills are a big plus.

EXPERIENCE REQUIRED   While there are no hard-and-fast rules, it typically takes four to six years of IT experience to become a PM. You need a proven track record of working well in a team environment, as well as making outstanding individual contributions to successful project completion. You will need to serve as a team leader on at least one successful, high-visibility project before being entrusted with the PM role. As team leader, you must demonstrate that you can hit your deadlines and foster the support and cooperation of your team members.

WHERE CAN YOU GO FROM HERE?   Continuing on the management track, after serving as PM on a number of projects of increasing complexity and visibility, the next move up would be a manager's position responsible for a number of concurrent projects (each with their own PM reporting to you) within your domain of expertise. A PM in the networking area, for example, might become manager of network engineering. Project managers who opt to remain on a technical track will typically continue rotating through consecutive PM positions, gaining visibility and stature by taking on new technologies and larger projects. For example, a PM in the applications development area might move into data warehousing by first helming a data mart project and then a data warehouse project.

Director

RANK IN THE IT MANAGEMENT HIERARCHY   Middle to upper management. Depending on the number of layers in the IT organizational chart, the director level is somewhere between manager/senior manager and the VP level. But the exact title and level of responsibility varies. Some companies may not use the "director" title, instead promoting senior managers directly to vice president.

JOB DESCRIPTION   A director/vice president has responsibility for a specific IT functional area, such as director of applications development or director of operations. The exact job description depends on the IT area and the position's rank on the IT organizational chart. In general, the director is accountable for budgeting, conducting ROI analysis, handling staffing and human resources issues, managing vendor negotiations and relationships, ensuring that project plans are aligned with corporate IT strategy and overall business goals, and maintaining corporate IT standards. The director reports to a VP (or, if the middle-management layer is considered VP level, the VP/director would usually report to the CIO or a senior VP).

EDUCATION AND CERTIFICATION REQUIREMENTS   As you move into this level of management, it's definitely time to consider obtaining a techno-M.B.A. (if you don't have a computer science background) or M.B.A. (if you have a strong technical background). While it's not required, it will clearly set you apart from the rest of the IT management pack. (See Chapter 12.) At the very least, you will need to take some management and leadership seminars to reach this level.

SPOTLIGHT ON A MIDLEVEL MANAGER

Joe Plaster, 38, vice president for e-business technology, V.F. Shared Services, the wholly owned IT subsidiary of apparel manufacturer V.F. Corp., Greensboro, N.C.

Overall responsibilities   "I'm responsible for all web applications development crossing the Internet, extranets, and the intranet, and leveraging the technology investments made in V.F. across all of our business units. V.F. has made some large investments, for example, in i2 Technologies software [a supply-chain management system], and I'm not directly responsible for that system but for incorporating it into a supply-chain marketplace that V.F. is participating in called the SoftGoodsMatrix.com marketplace. I'm also responsible for reducing the costs of development. For example, we have many different websites, and we want to use common components across each one so that

SPOTLIGHT ON A MIDLEVEL MANAGER

we're not paying for same things over and over. And I'm responsible for putting my organization together: hiring, recruiting, retention, etc."

Day-to-day responsibilities   "I usually have multiple meetings with my project leaders, and I'm in contact with different business stakeholders throughout V.F., as well as my manager. I also participate in various project meetings, whether it's a scoping exercise, a requirements review, or meeting with business units to see if there are opportunities for new projects. I often have to delegate responsibilities and rely on my direct reports—you can't be in every single meeting. I don't really do any hands-on implementation. I'm very close to it, but not sitting in on it every day. There has been a gradual letting go of implementation responsibilities as I've come up from project manager to director to where I am now."

Notable differences as I've moved up the IT management ladder   "As a VP, I have much more visibility and contact with the senior managers at V.F. than I did as a director, and I have more direct reports. As a director, I was certainly involved in keeping costs down and managing people, but I wasn't the stakeholder/owner like I am now. The buck doesn't stop here, but it slows way down. I'm shepherding what's next and setting priorities. The project-manager role is really the first step into management, and you are focused on a single project at a time, whereas as you move up, you have a wider range of projects and issues to deal with."

Technologies and technical skills required   "You bring your technical skills with you, but as you move up, people skills and financial skills definitely start to take over. There's a huge change in focus. It's hard to separate your technical responsibilities from your management responsibilities, and the mix changes every day depending on what's going on. Is there an implementation in progress? Is it budget time? Is there a reorganization going on? There is a fear that you'll lose your technical side, but the reality is that you're moving from a technical job where you're there because of your technical skills into a leadership role where you're there because of your leadership skills."

Other skills required   "People skills—getting consensus, team-building, etc. There's a sales aspect to managing people: the hiring, attracting people to the organization, and bringing it all together. You're always thinking about the makeup of your organization.

SPOTLIGHT ON A MIDLEVEL MANAGER

And as you move up, you rely more on financial knowledge, like how to do budgets. I had a background in math, but I don't have an M.B.A. I had the opportunity to work with good people who mentored me along in this area. I took it as a challenge to learn it all."

What I like most about this job   "The visibility is part of it, and being able to multi-task on concurrent projects. I find it challenging, and there are a lot of different opportunities."

What I like least about this job   "The duration of the budgeting process—it goes on a long time. But I wouldn't say it's a huge dislike. It's a core part of my responsibilities. Also, I'm getting 50 emails a day from vendors. That's a nuisance."

Career path leading to this job   Plaster has worked at V.F intermittently for over 15 years. He first joined the company fresh out of college in 1985 in a technical support role for a V.F. business unit. In 1988, he left for a Customer Information Control System (CICS) programming position at Wachovia Bank in Winston Salem, North Carolina. Five years later, he returned to the same V.F business unit as an applications developer and got involved in an SAP R/2 implementation project, working his way up to lead architect. Following the project, he tried his hand at SAP consulting for six months until V.F. lured him back as director of the company's Common Systems Technical Support group, providing infrastructure support for a common suite of applications across the company, including the i2 supply-chain planner, SAP R/3, Logility Forecasting, and Gerber's web product data management (PDM) apparel industry software.

The e-business-related experience he gained in that role—such as dealing with security issues, firewalls, servers, and applications integration—as well as the management experience put him in line for his current position, which is focused on extending the company's common systems architecture out to retail partners, customers, suppliers, and vendors. He was promoted in March 2000. To come up to speed in his current position, Plaster has attended management training classes and high-level management conferences, as well as strategic ecommerce seminars.

Advice to other IT pros interested in IT management   "It's not an easy path. Taking a step out to leadership isn't a clear, straight path, and it requires a lot of confidence in your abilities. If you don't get it right the first time, try again."

SKILLS REQUIRED   Proven leadership ability; strong oral and written communication skills; business expertise; and breadth and some depth of technical skills in the relevant discipline.

EXPERIENCE REQUIRED   A college degree is generally preferred but equivalent work experience may substitute; a substantial history (ten years or more) in the relevant IT discipline, including proven success in managing projects and people; and some complementary experience in a related IT discipline is a huge plus (e.g., experience in applications development for a director of operations or experience in operations for a director of network engineering).

WHERE YOU CAN GO FROM HERE?   It isn't necessarily a straight shot up the ladder from a single stint as a director. You may make several lateral moves first. At this level, it's important to leverage your management skills to move into various complementary areas of IT to foster a broad view of the entire IT organization and its relationship to the business. A director of operations may become director of network infrastructure, for example. Depending on your background and experience, and the org chart in a given company, you might become a director or vice president (or CTO) of a business unit, division, or subsidiary, or you may move to the next level of management within the corporate IT organization.

Chief Information Officer

RANK IN THE IT MANAGEMENT HIERARCHY   The top spot. The IT buck stops here.

JOB DESCRIPTION   It falls to the CIO to establish a vision for IT that is aligned with business objectives, and to communicate that effectively to senior corporate management, as well as divisional and business-unit management, IT management, and the rank-and-file. As such, the CIO sets the tone for how the IT organization is perceived throughout the company. In a sense, the CIO must be all things to all people, as comfortable in the boardroom as in the computer room, making strategic and tactical decisions about technology direction, IT products and services, and IT organizational structure and management.

EDUCATION AND CERTIFICATION REQUIREMENTS   A college degree is required, and an M.B.A. is preferred, but substantial strategic IT experience can substitute for an advanced degree. In addition, the CIO should have attended at least one—and preferably more—high-level executive leadership development course or seminar.

SKILLS REQUIRED   Business expertise, but also a passion for business; the ability to create vision as well as concentrate on the details; top-notch communication and presentation skills; an ability to translate business objectives into IT strategy and vice versa; and strong leadership skills, including the ability to provide strategic leadership as well as day-to-day motivation and direction.

EXPERIENCE REQUIRED   It typically takes a minimum of 20 years to land the CIO's job; 25 to 30 years would be average. Time spent in a business management role or in strategic IT management consulting can put you on a fast track for the top. CIOs can come up through the ranks in any area of IT, but cross-over experience is essential. For example, if you establish yourself initially in applications development, make a point of spending time in operations as well; if you start out in operations, be sure to rotate through networking and infrastructure and/or applications. And for up-and-coming CIOs these days, experience in e-business is paramount.

WHERE CAN YOU GO FROM HERE?   For the majority of CIOs, this is often the last stop before retirement. Depending on your age and ambition when you reach this level, you may occupy the CIO spot at several different companies, or you may consider leveraging the position to move into executive business management. Your experience could qualify you to aim for the CEO's job or executive vice president of corporate planning, for example. Other options include becoming a CIO for hire, taking acting CIO positions at companies in transition that have special short-term needs, or founding your own management consulting firm.

Chief Technology Officer

RANK IN THE IT MANAGEMENT HIERARCHY   That depends; this is a relatively new and still growing job title. In some large companies, the CTO position may be the top IT management spot within a large division or subsidiary; in others it's a corporate position that reports directly to the CIO, while in some smaller companies and startups it's the title of choice for the most senior-ranking IT executive. The CTO as the top IT executive is more common in IT industry companies, dot-coms, startups, and small-to-medium businesses.

JOB DESCRIPTION   While the CIO's role is visionary, the CTO's role is more tactical. The CTO is responsible for helping set IT strategy and aligning the IT direction with business objectives, but is also more likely to take a hands-on role in technology implementation and deployment. The CTO in a dot-com, startup, or small company may be given more free reign to make independent decisions about IT than the CIO of a large company, who works more closely with executive business management. Nevertheless, the CTO must still bear the responsibility for fostering cooperation between IT and business management and creating buy-in for IT's support of the business strategy. The CTO also makes IT organizational decisions regarding structure and staffing.

EDUCATION AND CERTIFICATION REQUIREMENTS   A college degree is required; a techno-M.B.A. or other relevant advanced degree is preferred, but equivalent on-the-job experience can substitute. Like the CIO, the CTO should have completed management and executive leadership training.

SKILLS REQUIRED   The CTO, like the CIO, must be part visionary, part day-to-day IT leader. But, as the title implies, the CTO typically has a heavier focus on the technology itself and, in some cases, a closer, hands-on relationship to IT staff members and project teams. Proven leadership and communication skills are essential, as well as the ability to translate business objectives into technical requirements and to match technology direction to corporate strategy.

EXPERIENCE REQUIRED   At the divisional level, the CTO spot generally requires at least 10 to 15 years of IT experience; at the corporate level, a minimum of 20 years of experience is typically necessary. However, in both cases, it depends on the definition, responsibilities, and reporting relationship of the role. In a dot-com organization, for example, the CTO may have fewer years of experience but deep technical expertise on the leading edge of Internet and web technologies.

WHERE CAN YOU GO FROM HERE?   Again, that depends. If you've been CTO for a division or subsidiary of a large company, you should be in line for a senior corporate IT position such as vice president of IT reporting to the CIO, or perhaps even CIO or corporate CTO. If you rotate through the CTO spot within several different divisions or subsidiaries, managing a larger organization each time, then you could walk directly into the CIO position. A CTO for a dot-com company who transitions into the corporate IT world will likely move into the middle management level, such as senior manager, director, or vice president, depending on years of experience and track record.

MOVING UP IN IT MANAGEMENT: THE MANAGEMENT PERSPECTIVE

John Plummer, information technology division manager, Controls and Connectors division, Corning, Inc., Corning, N.Y.

Plummer, a 15-year IT veteran at Corning, has had a multifaceted career at the company, working in various business units as well as within the corporate IT department. Partly owing to the Corning culture, which is noted for moving people around the organization and promoting from within, and partly to his own drive, Plummer has moved steadily upward from mainframe applications developer to his current position leading IT for a large diversified division:

> **Corning Consumer Products division plant, Green Castle, Pennsylvania, 1986–1989** Mainframe applications developer (PL/1, Assembler, Cobol, RPG), 1986; database analyst (Computer Associates Datacom mainframe database), 1987.

> **Corning Corporate IT, Corning, New York, 1989–1998** DBA (CA Datacom), 1989; team member, Decision Support and Executive Information Systems (building data warehouses before they were called "data warehouses," using early client/server technologies), 1991; manager, Decision Support and Executive Information Systems, 1992; manager, Information Resources Management group (IRM, a group he created and spearheaded to plan, deliver, and manage Corning's data architecture), 1993; IT transfer manager (planning and managing the separation of IT assets and systems associated with the sale of Corning's Consumer Products division), 1997.

> **Steuben division and Corning Museum of Glass, Corning, New York, 1998–2000** Information technology division manager, 1998.

> **Controls and Connectors division, Corning, New York, 2000–present** Information technology division manager, 2000.

Plummer's interest in IT management grew from a belief that "the role if IT is to partner with the business," he says. "And to facilitate that, it was more important to take the management track. It affords you more opportunity to align IT with business strategy." Moreover, having spent 12 years as a human resources professional before going back to school for a degree in computer science, Plummer has an interest in and talent for developing other people, a key trait in successful IT managers. Following, he discusses what he looks for in up-and-coming IT managers and how he has managed his own IT career path.

MOVING UP IN IT MANAGEMENT: THE MANAGEMENT PERSPECTIVE

What skill sets do you look for as you evaluate potential up-and-coming managers?

I look for seven specific things: an awareness of and interest in technology and technology trends; a passion for business; a passion for developing other people, especially subordinates; good strategy development skills—people who can think at 10,000 feet but also aren't afraid of the details; good planning skills; good decision-making skills; and good communication skills—can they make a one-hour presentation on why implementing an ERP system is necessary as well as deliver an elevator speech? That is, if you bump into the CEO in the elevator and he asks what you do, you have three minutes to tell him, and you can't waste words or shoot from the hip.

What kind of temperament and personality do you look for in up-and-coming managers?

You have to learn to be a bit of a politician—that's a key difference between the management and technical tracks. Diplomacy is very important. You need a relatively thick skin. You'll get into heated discussions with [business-unit] managers who are focused on P&L [profit and loss], and your idea may be sound and balanced, but if it conflicts with their P&L, they may not buy into it. That's when the ability to communicate effectively and sell your idea is crucial: it takes a certain amount of salesmanship. And a sense of humor is a good thing because you're working with human beings, and humor is the great equalizer.

As an IT professional moves up the management ranks, what are the career options?

It's not unusual to move laterally over into, say, the marketing or sales area with an interest in a [business] manager's role. But if you stay within the IT management track, you would continue to rise toward CIO.

It seems that, given the dot-com phenomena, many younger IT professionals expect to reach the top within ten years. In your experience, how long does it usually take?

A 30-year career, or about 50 years of age, is about average for becoming a CIO or CTO. I don't doubt that there are 30-year-old CTOs, but it takes a while to really

MOVING UP IN IT MANAGEMENT: THE MANAGEMENT PERSPECTIVE

learn and adopt the kinds of practices and behaviors necessary to lead at that level—to understand strategy development, communications, planning, and decision-making. You can take courses on technique, but the actual practice of it takes practice and experience.

You've had a diverse array of jobs as you've come up through the IT management ranks. How typical is a career path like yours?

As I've talked to other managers in other companies, I get the sense that my process may not be that typical. Many others appear to stay focused in a narrower scope as they move through the management track. They may not get exposure as broad as is typically expected here at Corning. It may have to do with the business diversity of an employer. Corning is very diverse and has a lot of channels for broad exposure.

What would you say has been the common thread through all of your jobs?

They've all been about the delivery of quality information. In each role, I've been interested in making sure IT is an enabler and that employees have the quality information they need to make the decisions that they make. In terms of my function, responsibilities, and technology platforms, I've had tremendous diversity—the techniques and skills necessary for each of these roles has been different.

You actually created one of your key management roles yourself by convincing Corning's upper IT management to form the Information Resources Management (IRM) group and put you in charge. How did you go about creating that opportunity for yourself?

I spent a lot of time researching the issues associated with not having a structure for our information and looked at the costs and benefits associated with [putting a structure in place]. I did benchmarking studies with other companies to see what they had in place and the benefits to them. We were benchmarking an Executive Information System [EIS], so that afforded me the opportunity to benchmark IRM. I also did a lot of research on my own time, reading material from industry leaders, and I joined associations like the Data Administration Management Association and the Data Warehousing Institute. I got involved with the mainstream of people who were becoming the experts in the field. Then I submitted a 15-page proposal that I wrote on my own time.

MOVING UP IN IT MANAGEMENT: THE MANAGEMENT PERSPECTIVE

I believed in it; I believed it was important. And besides, it was fun for me. I enjoy writing, and it isn't something I shy away from. The Corning culture really encourages people to introduce new ideas—the company has built its reputation on innovation. I certainly felt the normal fear and trepidation associated with presenting something new, but you have to take some measure of risk.

What kind of management training have you had on your way up?

At Corning, we have Supervisor Effectiveness courses, a set of courses given over a few days where we're taught a variety of techniques for managing conflict, identifying critical skills, and assessing staff competencies, plus regulatory issues such as OSHA [Occupational Safety and Health Administration] rules and antidiscrimination guidelines. We also have work/life balance training to learn how to help ourselves and our staffs strike a balance between on-the-job effectiveness and outside effectiveness. And I've had training focused on oral and written communication and budgetary training to understand fundamental financial practices and language as you develop a budget around IT.

What's your advice to people considering an IT management career?

Be honest with yourself about your skills and interests. Far too many people jump into management because they think that's the glory track in IT, and they don't stop to evaluate their skills and interests. If you take an honest assessment of yourself and find that you're neither interested nor do you possess the right skills, I would question whether you want to move this way. It's not all glitz and glitter, and mastering the soft skills is a lot harder than people think.

TIP *Every so often, as new trends emerge in IT, a new three-letter executive IT title crops up for a while; sometimes it lasts and sometimes it doesn't. When the CIO job title first emerged, for example, it was "an early recognition of the strategic impact of technology on the objectives of a business as opposed to technology for the sake of back-office productivity," notes Dave Opton of ExecuNet. But the title was dismissed by many who didn't yet have a sense of how IT would evolve to become a strategic business partner. It wasn't until the mid-nineties that the title became ubiquitous. The CTO title has emerged from the dot-com world, to give the top IT executive "more of an R&D or 'inventor' flavor," Opton adds.*

Another title that made a brief appearance in the mid-nineties was chief knowledge officer (CKO), responsible for capturing and organizing a company's vast array of information assets. The verdict on the CKO spot remains to be seen, but a number of companies are adopting the lower-level "knowledge architect" position. Yet another new executive IT title that has the potential to catch on is the chief security officer. The CSO role has emerged from the increased emphasis of the Internet age on the security of networks and data, as well as data-privacy concerns. In some cases, this is an IT-related position responsible for coordinating all internal and external network-security efforts and reporting to the CIO; in others, it's a much broader role encompassing not only IT security, but also corporate security and reporting to the CEO. Finally, another one to watch—one that may stand alone or be rolled into the CSO's job—is chief privacy officer (CPO), responsible for protecting the privacy of customer and employee data.

IT Management Career Paths: A Sampler

There are as many roads to the IT executive suite as there are to drive from New York to Los Angeles. You can take a traditional, straight-up-through-the-IT-ranks path or a more circuitous route in and out of IT and business roles; you can focus on specializing in a particular industry, or wander in and out of a variety of market niches. Keep in mind that, depending on the types of organizations you work for and how often you change employers, you may advance quickly or at a fairly measured pace, so you shouldn't get too preoccupied with timetables. Just don't expect to get there overnight; roll down the windows and enjoy the drive. Following are some sample roadmaps to the promised land.

Coming Up Through Applications Development

Junior Programmer
You gain proficiency in Visual Basic, Java, or C++ as you work on maintaining a sales-and-marketing application; take a course in object-oriented programming concepts.

Programmer/Analyst
You continue to refine your programming skills as you take on responsibility for analyzing user requirements; rotate through one to three projects to add new functionality to existing sales-and-marketing applications; take courses in structured programming and

full life-cycle development methodologies and/or complete a certification program in a key programming language. *After two to three years with your first employer, you might start to consider hitting the job market; if so, try to identify new opportunities that will leverage both the technical and functional experience you've gained so far.*

Business Analyst

Recognizing that you won't advance to IT management on technology skills alone, you take a break from hands-on programming to act as liaison between project-development teams and business-unit end-users (in sales and marketing, where you've already been working, or in a related business area such as merchandising or order fulfillment); your job is focused on gathering and analyzing user requirements, and because you have programming experience, you volunteer to help with coding when the team is in a pinch; take a business course or seminar that relates to the business unit you're working in. *If, after three to four years in applications development you find that your career growth is stalling, you either need to take a critical look at your skills and on-the-job performance or start looking for a new employer.*

Team Leader

Your initiative in pursuing training and certification and your finesse with users and coworkers have been noticed; take responsibility for gathering user requirements for the front-end of a new order-fulfillment system; you coordinate the programming responsibilities among team members and take on some yourself; you report to the project manager; take a project management course and start getting your ducks in a row for project management certification. Next, having worked on the front-end of the order-fulfillment system, you ask to be assigned to a project on backend integration with the inventory management and distribution systems; you gain exposure to the bigger picture of how applications interoperate, acquire more complex development skills, get a view into the operations area, and leverage your front-end skills to act as a key liaison between the front-end developers and the systems-integration team; start working on project management certification (if you haven't already) and take a backend applications technical course.

Senior Team Leader

With exposure to sales-and-marketing and order-fulfillment applications, on both the front end and backend, you're assigned to a new web-enabled customer relationship management (CRM) application project; coordinate the development efforts of team members and work closely with database analysts on defining the data structures and how the CRM application will interact with the data warehouse; you report to the project manager but also have contact with the data architect, applications development managers, and business unit managers; complete your project management certification, take an advanced SQL course, and attend seminars on developing e-business applications.

Project Manager

After gaining substantial team leader experience, you get a much deserved promotion to project manager; because you'll have a learning curve on the management aspects, you initially stick with an application area you're familiar with, like CRM; you're still doing some hands-on implementation work, but instead of focusing on discrete parts, you have to oversee all aspects of a project from determining and analyzing user requirements to development and testing to deployment to backend integration, plus you are responsible for scheduling each piece of the project; you learn how to start delegating more and relinquish much of the hands-on work you're accustomed to doing yourself; while your stints as a team lead gave you some direct experience in resolving conflicts, you now take on greater responsibility for your direct reports and for interviewing and hiring new developers; as your managerial skills come up-to-speed, you switch from CRM to something new, like web-enabled supply-chain management (SCM), followed by work on a business-to-business (B2B) industry marketplace; identify your weakest soft skills areas and take the appropriate courses to overcome your personal development obstacles, plus take a B2B ecommerce course; start considering the possibility of getting a techno-M.B.A. *Project management experience will give you greater leverage in changing companies; if you're unsatisfied with your current employer or want to get experience in a new industry, this would be a good time to start shopping around, but take into account that you may want an employer that offers tuition reimbursement because you may soon pursue a techno-M.B.A.*

Applications Development Manager

Your soft skills have come a long way fast, you've shown an ability to master both new technologies and business concepts quickly, and you're respected by IT management and staff alike; the promotion into middle management acknowledges your growth and puts you solidly on the way toward upper IT management; you are responsible for a number of project managers and teams, and your duties encompass recruiting and hiring, performing employee reviews and goal-setting, budgeting, managing vendor relations, participating in strategic planning, and more; you report to the director of applications development and are in regular communication with your counterparts in e-business, operations and end-user support, and networking and infrastructure;

you start developing a big-picture view of how different IT areas work in concert; take a finance and budgeting course, take management-level seminars on enterprise-wide applications strategies and development, and start working on a techno-M.B.A.

Applications Architect

Having demonstrated both your technical and business savvy and a commitment to working on your soft skills, you now take on more strategic responsibility for the overall applications architecture, a position that puts you in day-to-day contact with executive IT management across the organization; you continue to have staff management and budgeting responsibilities; knowing you will soon need to move into another area of IT to develop greater breadth, you take IT operations-related seminars or courses, such as intro to capacity planning or intro to disaster recovery (which will also help you get your current job done); finish up your techno-M.B.A. *You start networking for an operations position during this period; if your employer isn't open to moving you into operations, you might want to consider an outside opportunity to make the next step; however, if you received tuition reimbursement for your techno-M.B.A., you may be obligated to remain with your current employer for a specified amount of time or be charged back for the reimbursement; also, because you are now climbing the management ladder, you may want to factor how many job hops you've previously made into your decision—at this point, you should be demonstrating some sense of corporate loyalty.*

Capacity Planning Manager

After spending time in the applications development arena, you transition to the operations area; while you've made a lateral move in terms of rank, you have a considerable learning curve in this challenging new position, which will be critical to your drive for executive-level responsibility; you bring your experience as an applications architect to bear directly on your new mission and leverage the knowledge gained in those operations seminars, but you also refine the skill of knowing when and how to solicit information and feedback from both subordinates and mentors as you come up to speed; the strategic planning skills you've demonstrated helped land you in this position, so you play to your strengths and compensate for your weaknesses through delegating and information-gathering, which illustrates your management savvy; you gain greater exposure to the networking and infrastructure area and deepen your relationships with business unit managers; take a statistical analysis refresher course early in the transition or at least review materials from your M.B.A. studies, attend training in your company's statistical software, and take a management-level overview of network architecture. *If you joined a new company in order to garner an operations position, you will have the additional challenge of forging new relationships with fellow IT managers and business-unit managers, plus learning the ropes in a new environment and corporate culture; in other words, you'll have your work cut out for you, and it may take a little longer to move to the next step than if you had started out in the role as a known quantity.*

Senior Manager of E-business Operations

The hard work you did learning the ropes in capacity planning is rewarded with a foray into the e-business group where you return to an applications-oriented comfort zone but also bring your newly polished operations experience into play; with responsibility for day-to-day operations in the e-business area, you oversee applications development, planning and architecture, network performance and security, front-end and backend systems integration, vendor relations, and strategic planning for the Internet, intranet and extranets; you have a number of direct reports and a variety of teams under you, and because this is a strategic position, you report directly to the vice president of IT; given that staff turnover can be high in this area of IT, you map out a new recruiting and retention strategy and pay close attention to the individual career goals of your staff; take a management-level course in staff-development techniques, attend a number of strategic e-business seminars and management conferences, and start sitting on panels and/or making speeches and presentations at industry trade shows; you may want to join a Toastmasters group if you need help refining your presentation skills.

Director of Capacity Planning

When the director of capacity planning gets promoted, you come in as the replacement, leveraging your previous experience in capacity planning and getting a boost up in the management ranks in the process; while there is always more to learn, you've spent time in this area already and don't want to stay too long, so you start developing a potential successor early on; use this opportunity to forge tighter alliances among applications development, operations, and networking and infrastructure, and come up with processes and procedures to minimize turf battles; take an executive-level conflict-resolution course.

Senior Director of Advanced Technology

With experience in both applications development and operations, and solid experience in strategic planning, you now head up the IT R&D department, identifying potential new technologies that will meet company and IT needs in the future; you enjoy being immersed in technology again, but you make the position a strategic one, constantly matching new research projects to future business direction and becoming an evangelist for advanced technologies across the organization; you take the opportunity to research the staffing needs that new technologies will create and develop a forward-thinking recruiting, hiring, and retention strategy to meet the needs of the IT organization in the future; you prepare a management report detailing your suggestions and present it to the CIO; attend a number of executive briefings and industry conferences on emerging technologies, as well as seminars and conferences on the future of the IT organization; continue making speeches and appearing on industry panels.

Vice President, IT Strategy and Planning Practice at a Management Consulting Firm

You've worked in corporate IT organizations your entire career, you have a techno-M.B.A., and you've started to develop a higher profile in the field; you cap that off by entering the management consulting arena, where you'll gain—in a relatively short time—greater exposure to a wide variety of IT shops in different industries; the move has the residual benefit of increasing your professional networking potential tenfold, as you work with CIOs and CEOs across the country; you bring all of your past experience to bear on advising IT organizations on strategic planning for future technology and organizational needs; work with a coach or mentor to refine any lingering weaknesses in your management style; continue making public presentations.

Vice President of IT

Thanks to a synergistic relationship you've formed as a management consultant with a soon-to-retire CIO, you accept a position as the designated heir apparent; you spend a good deal of your time in the number 2 spot to learn the company's corporate culture, get to know IT management and staff, build their confidence, inspire their trust in you, and ensure a smooth transition when you take the CIO reins; you also spend time in the company business units, divisions, and subsidiaries, learning the company's business and forging ties with business executives; working with the CIO, you create a vision that encompasses the strategic direction already in place as well as new insights that you bring to the table.

Senior Vice President and CIO

You've arrived at last; but, as in any of your previous roles, you must continue to prove your value every day; now you start wondering whether you just might be CEO material.

KEYS TO A MANAGEMENT CAREER

Keep in mind that the career path described above represents only one potential route to the top. But it is representative of a basic model that you can apply to designing your own IT management career path, whether you're coming up through applications and database development, operations and end-user support, networking and infra-structure or e-business. The keys to carving out a management career are the following:

✓ Get a solid grounding in technical skills early on.

✓ Pursue certifications to demonstrate your commitment to career development.

✓ Look for early opportunities to interface with the business as you gain visibil-ity in IT.

✓ Acquire business functional expertise along with technical expertise.

✓ Rotate through several different positions in one IT department, and then look for an opportunity to move into a different but related IT area (e.g., in the sample above, from applications development into operations).

✓ Identify opportunities to work on e-business projects as well as offline proj-ects, and prepare for the time when the entire IT organization will be an e-business organization. (See Chapter 7.)

✓ Hone your soft skills such as communication and presentation skills, conflict resolution, etc.

✓ Take project management courses and seriously consider project management certification.

✓ Consider obtaining an M.B.A. or techno-M.B.A., or at least take some business and management classes, as well as leadership and professional development seminars.

✓ Build up a network of professional contacts and mentors who can provide career guidance, advice on resolving problems (technical and otherwise) at work, and connections with potential new job opportunities.

✓ With each new role you accept, make sure you continue learning even as you leverage the experienced you've gained so far; if you seem to plateau at the vice-president level, consider taking a role in business management or in IT management consulting, and parlay that experience into the CIO or CTO spot.

Coming Up Through Operations and End-User Support

Helpdesk analyst

↓

Network administrator

↓

Systems administrator

↓

Senior systems administrator

↓

Senior storage network administrator

↓

Systems programmer

↓

Senior systems programmer

↓

Disaster recovery project manager

↓

Systems programming manager

↓

Capacity planning manager

↓

Senior manager, IT operations

↓

Director of IT operations

↓

Director of infrastructure

↓

Vice president of operations

↓

Senior vice president of operations and infrastructure

↓

Senior vice president and CTO

Coming Up Through Networking and Infrastructure

Helpdesk analyst

↓

NT administrator

↓

Team member, network infrastructure upgrade project

↓

Network engineer

↓

Security analyst

↓

Team lead, firewall installation and network security testing project

↓

Senior security analyst

↓

Senior project manager, network integration project (resulting from a merger)

↓

Network architect

↓

Director of networking and infrastructure

↓

Divisional CTO

↓

Vice president of networking and infrastructure (corporate)

↓

Senior vice president and CTO

TIP *How often you should change employers is really a matter of personal choice. On the one hand, your career—and salary—will likely advance more quickly by changing companies; on the other hand, excessive job-hopping may make you appear overly opportunistic. Yet another school of thought is that you will ultimately stagnate by staying with one employer for a large portion of your career, while some say that if you're intent on scaling the management ladder, you need to demonstrate some sense of corporate loyalty. Ultimately, "Your intuition will tell you when your personal growth is slowing or stopping and your job satisfaction is different than it was before," ExecuNet's Dave Opton says. "Follow that internal thermostat," he advises. In fact, contrary to prevailing trends, it's not uncommon for IT professionals to remain with a single employer for their entire careers (for example, Scott Heintzeman, vice president of knowledge technologies at Carlson Hospitality Worldwide, Minneapolis, Minnesota, who is profiled in Chapter 1, joined Carlson at age 17. John Plummer, the divisional information technology manager at Corning who's featured in this chapter, has spent his entire IT career at Corning). If a company remains an IT leader and proactively commits to your career development, you may not feel a need to jump ship.*

SPOTLIGHT ON THE TECHNICAL TRACK: WHY I GOT OUT OF IT MANAGEMENT

Jerry Weinberger, 48, senior systems analyst, New York City Department of Correction, New York, N.Y.

IT management isn't for everyone, and fortunately, the demand for strong technologists is robust enough that you can opt to pursue a purely technical track. After a brief stint as a project manager, leading the development of a mainframe-based claims management application at Blue Cross, Blue Shield of New York in the mid-eighties, Weinberger concluded that if he never had to manage another team, it would be too soon. He took a long hard look at his skills and temperament and decided he would be happiest continuing in a hands-on applications development role. "In IT, they're always dangling management jobs in front of you," says Weinberger, who launched his IT career in 1980. "They think anyone who's not in management wants to be. But I actively avoid it."

Why did you feel you were unsuccessful as a project manager?

I don't like telling people what to do, and I'm really impatient. I don't suffer fools gladly, and I was told that when I went into project management mode, I became Stalin. I was tyrannical. I didn't like delegating, so I would just do things myself that I should have given to team members. Whenever I felt that someone was taking too long or that I could do a better job, I'd get frustrated, and I would try to take it over and force them to let me do it.

SPOTLIGHT ON THE TECHNICAL TRACK: WHY I GOT OUT OF IT MANAGEMENT

What did you find was the most difficult part of managing?

Hiring people. I wasn't good at it because I just assumed anyone who walked in the door could do the job. I didn't think you had to be a braniac, so I would find people who I thought were interesting and who I thought I'd enjoy working with. I hired one guy because he liked the Talking Heads and Andy Warhol films. He was extremely intelligent, and when he would work, he did a great job. The problem was, he turned out to be a junkie, and if he showed up at all, he spent a good part of the day asleep. He ultimately was fired, and it was emotionally traumatic for everyone in the group because we all liked him and felt sorry for him. That's about the time I decided not to be in management.

What did you learn about yourself from the experience?

The Peter Principle is true. You reach your own level of incompetence, and for me, it was management. I'm a good technician. That's where I belong.

How is the technical track satisfying career-wise?

In applications development, it's creative. You start with nothing and you end up with something. You're God. Of course, being God can be tedious.

Does opting for a technical track have an impact on your career financially?

Yes. You make less money, because management ultimately hires and sets salaries, so inevitably, management is paid higher salaries than the technical set. But my suspicion is that if I'd stayed in that project management role, my salary would be much less, because I'd be teaching now. I'd have given up IT altogether.

What's your advice to others who choose to pursue a technical track instead of a management track?

You'll always be marketable if you don't get locked into a useless piece of software. To stay up-to-date with your skills, keep changing projects, either within your organization or by leaving. Let your boss know you want to join a new project, and if he says no, consider greener pastures. Find a nonthreatening way to let your boss know just how unhappy you are and what the consequences could be. Usually, when you're really good at working with a particular language or application, management wants to keep you on it. If that software is something marketable, fine. But if it's not, consider your options.

IT Leadership: A Roundtable Discussion

What qualities distinguish effective IT leaders? Do you have what it takes to become a CIO? Below, four CIOs who were named to *Computerworld*'s "2001 Premier 100 IT Leaders" list share their perspective on the essential ingredients of successful IT leadership. They are (in alphabetical order)

▶ Cecilia Claudio, senior vice president, CIO and chief transformation officer, Farmers Insurance Group, Los Angeles, California

▶ Bob DeRodes, CIO of Delta Air Lines and president and CEO of Delta Technology (DT), the company's wholly owned IT subsidiary, Atlanta, Georgia

▶ Rickie Hall, vice president and CIO, ANC Rental Corporation, Ft. Lauderdale, Florida

▶ André Mendes, vice president and CIO, Public Broadcasting System, Alexandria, Virginia (In April 2001, Mendes joined biotechnology firm Pluvita Corporation, in Bethesda, Maryland, as chief operating officer.)

What are the keys to effective IT leadership?

DeRodes: Deal in facts, tell the truth, show compassion and caring, and maintain the esprit de corps. You lead by example, so you have to think about what kind of example you set. As CIO you only have one chance to be trusted, and if you lose that chance, then from that point on you can't be effective.

Mendes: You have to walk the talk. Your staff will scrutinize what you do and say on a daily basis, and it's extremely important that all you do and say is consistent with the message that you're giving employees. Beautiful speeches last a half hour, but a commitment lasts a lot longer. You have to deliver on your commitment.

Claudio: I have to remind myself every day that my success depends on the people around me, and that I'm also responsible for their success. They can't develop a sense of pride if they're just executing what I say. They have to come to conclusions, take risks, fail and succeed on their own, and if I don't give them the opportunity to do that, I am failing them as their leader.

Can leadership skills be taught or does leadership have to exist within a person?

Claudio: From my perspective, it's a combination of both. There are some leadership traits that you are born with, and no matter how many classes you take or books you read, you are not going to become something you're not. It's part of your DNA. So some people who may not think of themselves as leaders could be, but they just haven't gone through leadership training. When they do, they find their inner leader; they find that all along they were always acting as a leader. But I don't think you can take someone without those key traits and make them a leader. It's 70 percent DNA, 30 percent education.

Mendes: There is an equal component of nature and nurture in leadership, but I can't remember ever not wanting to be a leader. That's a very strong command from within.

DeRodes: I would agree that there are some innate leadership skills that cannot be taught—you can learn lessons about them and can improve on them, but some you just have to be born with. For instance, some people care about people and some don't. Strong leaders have to care about their people. And in [IT], people are often solution-oriented and not necessarily compassion-oriented. And you can't change that DNA.

What are some other essential, innate leadership qualities?

DeRodes: One is drive—the old fire in the belly. At DT, we give out what we call the Jalapeño Award to people who demonstrate fire in the belly. It's hard to fake that drive, energy, and excitement—it's either there or it isn't.

Claudio: Extreme drive. Obstacles don't stand in the way of leaders—leaders will find ways to eliminate them. Also, ambition, a sense of purpose, being a risk-taker, being an explorer, being curious—those are inherent traits of leadership that one shows at a very early age. You can't learn those things.

Mendes: It comes down to believing or not believing in yourself and your ability to lead. I don't think most people want to lead. A lot of people are comfortable with someone else defining a vision and selling it to them, and then being led through it.

How do IT leaders gain the support of their staffs?

Hall: By listening, hearing the multiple sides to a situation. No one is ever completely right or wrong, and you have to put yourself in their shoes and say, "Hmm, I can see where you got that perspective. I hadn't thought of that before." When I first got here, and there was a lot of frustration over an outsourcing deal that wasn't working out, I had to be sensitive to the fact that they'd been through a lot, that maybe I wasn't aware of all the nuances of what had happened. So I had to make sure I heard each person's version of events. And they wanted to share that with me and fill me in. They needed to vent.

Mendes: If you try to cram something into people, even if you succeed, and even if it's the best thing for everyone, there will be resentment. People like to reach consensus—that's just human nature. We all want to be winners and have the best ideas. So, as a leader, you just try to point out the salient factors in all decisions and hope that the best solution prevails. It doesn't always work, but you still have to allow people to reach consensus by a careful analysis of the facts.

IT is constantly undergoing change, both technological change and organizational change. How do IT leaders affect and create support for change?

Claudio: Most people naturally have a resistance to change. We like things to be predictable, to go the way that we expect them. We don't like surprises, we don't want our world to turn upside down. Change is very disruptive and stressful and something most people will not sign up for. So you have to paint a compelling picture and show why change is needed in an organization.

DeRodes: You have to begin with the end in mind. You clearly articulate that end picture to people and create a future stake for them so they understand why things need to be different. Then you begin working on people individually. There are good change agents, and good change targets. So you identify people who are struggling with change and ask someone to work with them in a buddy system to help them adjust to the change. The other keys are consistency and open, honest dialogue around the change itself. It's okay for CIOs to stand up in front of an organization and say, "Well, it looks discouraging, and we're not getting there as quickly as we'd like, but let's stay the course."

A CIO operates at a very high level, with executive-level responsibilities. To what extent can you remain hands-on and in touch with your organization day to day?

Mendes: I actually deal with just about all of my folk's daily. I walk around once or twice a day and interact with the helpdesk, systems administrators, and database administrators. If nothing else, I can gauge the atmosphere and their morale; I can find out what's keeping them up at night.

DeRodes: I like to know the name of every employee in DT, and I very much enjoy walking around and sitting down at people's desks and understanding what they're doing. I always learn a lot about us as a company when I do that. You have to go to the newest entry-level workers in the organization and understand what they do every day and how they do their work, and you have to do that all the way up to your VPs. You have to navigate throughout the whole organization—that's not optional. CIOs should be seen as engaged, as understanding both employees and customers, and not simply as boardroom execs.

Hall: You have to be accessible; you can't be all the time, but you try to be at the right times. On a recent project we were putting in some long hours, and I would join the team after hours and say, "It's been a while since I programmed, but how can I help you?" It's rolling up your sleeves and being available to help, letting them know that [you're] living through the same experience they are.

As CIO you are the voice for IT throughout the enterprise. How do you gain support for IT among business-unit management and staff?

Claudio: I've made it a stress point in the IT organization that we cannot be perceived as a black box. We need to be completely open and welcome people from all parts of the enterprise to come in and see what we do and how. It's about making the IT organization more receptive to, and not threatening to, other parts of the company because a lot of [business users] still see IT as a group that doesn't understand the business, speaks a different language, and spends a lot of money without delivering a lot of value. We have changed how our business partners see us because they can ask any question, and anyone can come in and make suggestions and recommendations or work in our group for a while.

Mendes: Every chance I get I drop in on business unit managers and make sure that my perception from within IT of how their systems are working matches their perceptions. For example, I'll check in with the fulfillment manager in our video sales unit and get a read from her on how batch processes are working and if there are glitches between the ecommerce system and the order-fulfillment system. And in discussions with heads of business units, I like to quote something I've read to elicit a conversation about their strategic direction and where IT should be going next.

Hall: When I meet with business unit managers, the first thing I ask them is, "What comes to mind when I say IT?" And they'll say, "My PC, the network, the helpdesk." And then I make sure that they understand that IT is really a collection of people who have all the same joys and challenges as any other team. I make sure they know what IT does and how it benefits the business. We're not implementing technology for technology's sake. We rent cars, and I show them how IT contributes to that, how IT impacts revenue and all aspects of the company.

Part III

Hot Pockets

In this Part

Chapter 9

....

Hot Projects

To grow your IT career, it is essential that you participate in high-visibility projects that contribute to your company's bottom line and sustainable competitive advantage. As business requirements change and markets shift, so do the high-impact projects. As we move full-steam ahead into the twenty-first century, businesses are struggling with how to make faster, more accurate business decisions; leveraging their relationships with customers and acquiring new customers; tying their ecommerce efforts into their regular business operations; efficiently managing inventory planning and forecasting from the supplier through distribution and sales; getting the right information to the right people at the right time; and managing their infrastructures so that all of these new network-dependent applications operate unfettered by technical constraints.

More than ever before, IT is proving invaluable to the success of these efforts, and IT professionals who spend time providing solutions to these challenges will remain marketable for the foreseeable future. Following is a look at what you need to know and what it's like to work in each of these key areas: data warehousing, customer relationship management (CRM), web-to-backend systems integration, supply-chain management (SCM), knowledge management (KM), and network management.

TIP Significant project experience in data warehousing, web development, enterprise resource planning (ERP), CRM, and other development environments can add a premium of between 20 percent and 50 percent to your base salary, depending on your responsibilities and impact on a project, notes David Foote, president of Foote Partners LLC, which conducts quarterly salary and skills surveys of IT organizations nationwide. The premium may be paid as part of a team bonus or a combined individual and team bonus.

Building a Data Warehouse

BUSINESS OBJECTIVE   To turn data stored in various systems across a company into information that can support strategic business decisions. "A data warehouse allows you to collect data from multiple, disparate transactional systems, combine all that data, and present it back to the business in a unified method," explains José Porro, director of information resources in the sales decision support group at Marriott International, in Bethesda, Maryland. For example, data collected from sales, payroll, CRM, and general ledger systems could be combined in a data warehouse "to start putting together a picture of how much business are we doing with a specific customer, how much effort are we applying to that customer, and what the net effect is in terms of profit margins," Porro says. "So we get a better picture, and then we can make better decisions, which is really the end goal."

HOW IT CONTRIBUTES   In a way, IT has created the problem that data warehousing solves, Porro notes, because IT built the disparate systems in the first place. Now it falls to IT not only to amalgamate the data from each system into one real-time environment, but also to put the data into a single, consistent format. "When you start collecting all that data, you find that the ways it is represented in each individual system clash with each other, so you have to start a process of cleansing the data. For example, I may be listed as 'Jporro' in one system, 'Porro, José' in another, and 'José Porro' in another. We have to determine if that is three different people or one person and rectify all the data. That's one of the biggest problems IT has to solve in a data warehouse project."

What It's Like to Work on a Data Warehouse Project

In 2000, Porro served as project director for a web-based data mart that contains all the information for about 2,200 different Marriott properties worldwide. A *data mart* is akin to a miniwarehouse—whereas a warehouse contains a variety of different data from across the enterprise, a data mart is generally subject-specific. Marriott's Property Data Mart has transformed the company's ability to provide accurate, up-to-date information about each of its hotels and resorts to corporate sales managers, travel agents, and individual travelers booking reservations through its call centers and the website (www.marriott.com).

WHAT WAS THE PURPOSE OF BUILDING THE PROPERTY DATA MART?   We wanted a web-based application that property managers could use any time to update and maintain information about their property, in real-time on an ongoing basis. The information includes, for example, what amenities each property offers—free coffee in rooms, a pool, newspapers in the morning—as well as local attractions, local businesses, and more. The sales and marketing department uses the data for things like promoting our properties in travel guides and contracting special rates with corporate customers.

Before the data mart, each manager would put all the information into a spreadsheet on a diskette and mail it to headquarters once a year. Then at headquarters, all those spreadsheets would be filed into a master database, and it was a huge effort each time, and there was only that one chance a year to get it right. If the sales department was preparing a proposal to offer corporate discounts to a large company, they'd have to contact each property each time to get the latest data. Now we can get those proposals together very quickly. With the data mart, we have one central real-time repository that can be used by all of our sales channels, including the website and our reservations system.

WHAT'S INVOLVED, AND HOW HAS THE PROJECT PROGRESSED? The first phase of the project was focused on web-enabling the application so everyone can access it and getting the information from our hotels. Now we're working on integrating the mart with a wider array of systems across Marriott and cleansing all the data, and later we'll start adding different kinds of properties to the mart, such as our vacation clubs and senior living services properties.

WHO IS INVOLVED ON THE PROPERTY DATA MART PROJECT? On the IT side, myself as the director, a project manager, some business/systems analysts, some web developers, some database architects, network administrators, and web administrators. On the business side, the stakeholders are in our knowledge management department, and during the requirements gathering and testing phase, property managers, sales managers, and general managers were involved in a project pilot group to provide input about how the system looked and how it met business needs.

WHAT TECHNICAL SKILLS AND PRIOR PROJECT EXPERIENCE WERE YOU LOOKING FOR IN STAFFING THE PROJECT? From a development standpoint, the key was having people with web development experience. We're using Microsoft InterDev as the development platform, which is a Visual Basic–like language. We also needed people with database skills, specifically Oracle. The network administrators needed Windows NT as well as HP/UX because our database server is an HP/UX box, and the web administrators needed Microsoft IIS [Internet Information Server] as well as firewall experience.

In terms of project experience, we needed people with experience maintaining the property information in all of the systems in our portfolio so they could understand our existing world and see what we were trying to fix, and what kinds of things we needed to target as we brought all the data together and cleansed it to give it one consistent face. In any warehouse project, there has to be a core group that's very intimate with the existing process, from the technology side and business sides. To succeed, you have to understand where you're coming from. One of the reasons a lot of warehouses fail is because the project starts off without the business knowledge of where they're coming from or why they're doing it.

WHAT KIND OF BUSINESS PROCESS AND/OR TECHNICAL TRAINING DID THE TEAM HAVE TO GO THROUGH?   The IT folks sat with the business folks to understand the business process and how it was being conducted, the vocabulary being used on the project, and the hot buttons we were trying to address.

WHAT WERE A COUPLE OF THE MAJOR CHALLENGES—FROM A PROJECT PERSPECTIVE AS WELL AS A PERSONAL PERSPECTIVE—AS YOU BUILT THE DATA MART?   On a project of this nature, there are many groups that have to be involved, and I don't have control over those groups but I have to influence them. And that's always a challenge when you're trying to impact a great number of groups within a large organization. Getting everyone to feel invested in the project is the big issue. A lot of times, everyone has so many other priorities, it can be difficult to get their attention because we are already so busy. So the challenge for me is, how do I get them to buy into the data mart and work with me to get it done on my time frame vs. being at the back of the line of their priorities?

HOW IS WORKING ON A DATA WAREHOUSE PROJECT VALUABLE TO AN IT PROFESSIONAL'S CAREER OVER THE LONG TERM?   From a technology perspective, data warehousing is a big and growing area in IT right now. But beyond that, one of the things that makes you successful on a data warehousing project is that you have to understand the business, know what's going on, why one system does something one way and another system does it another way, and find the common ground. If you do that successfully, you'll know more about the business than the business does, and then you will become really valuable in terms of the business knowledge that you can bring to other projects. You'll be a true asset, and that will open the door for you to focus on business issues more than on technical issues, which is very important in IT today.

WHAT ARE SOME LOGICAL NEXT STEPS FOR IT PROFESSIONALS AFTER THEY'VE WORKED ON A DATA WAREHOUSE PROJECT?   After you've collected all this information in one place to produce a common set of reports, you want to start doing predictive analysis based on the data, so data analysis and data mining are logical next steps. After that, you might move into EIS [Executive Information Systems]—those have a lot to do with data warehouses. If you want to leave the data warehouse area, you can launch into any of the areas that you have collected data from, such as financial systems or sales systems or CRM.

Also, you'll have a good overall perspective of the business because in building the warehouse, you'll have touched on several different business areas. So it's a good stepping stone to the IT executive suite because of the business exposure. If you are ever going to make it to the executive suite, you must understand that IT is here to solve business problems, and that message often gets lost as we worry about the latest technical gizmo. If you solve a business process, you become a hero, and you'll make it to the top faster than pure techies.

WHAT'S YOUR ADVICE TO SOMEONE WHO WANTS TO GET INVOLVED WITH DATA WAREHOUSES?   Well, this is not going to be an entry-level project. You should take at least a course in understanding the fundamentals of data warehousing, because they're very different than transactional system fundamentals or building a database. Just because you've built a payroll system doesn't mean you're qualified to work on a data warehouse that will draw from the payroll system—you must understand the broader concepts. Also, SQL database exposure is imperative for all positions on the team, and project management training is important for the PM [project manager] and the team leaders.

 INDUSTRY FACT IT spending on data warehouse software and tools will increase from $5 billion in 1999 to $17 billion in 2004, representing a compound annual growth rate of 26 percent, according to International Data Corporation, Framingham, Massachusetts. The market research firm's projections indicate that data warehouse job opportunities for IT professionals will remain strong as companies move from the initial deployment of warehouses to mining the data and delivering information for strategic decision-making and competitive advantage.

Building a Customer Relationship Management System

BUSINESS OBJECTIVE   To deliver to customers what they want, when they want it. "Through CRM, I know who our customers are, and I can market to each one directly via our catalog or our website," says Paul Fusco, chief information officer (CIO) at Jcrew, in New York (www.jcrew.com). For example, the company sends out 1.6 million email messages every two weeks to active shoppers whose activities have been analyzed by the CRM system. That's the kind of marketing effort that has a direct impact on the bottom line, Fusco says: "It generates more sales, pushes more product through." Ultimately, CRM systems should give companies a complete historical picture of each customer's interaction with the company, which creates opportunities for targeted sales campaigns, proactive customer service, and increased customer loyalty. CRM systems also help with the ever-critical job of inventory forecasting, Fusco notes. "We start buying merchandise for Christmas in May or June, so we must have a very good handle on what we think customers will buy," he explains.

HOW IT CONTRIBUTES   "CRM is a blending of technology with marketing and segmentation," Fusco says. "There are two edges to the CRM sword—knowing the customers and giving them what they want and when, and being able to market to the customer. That's where the P&L [profit and loss] comes in." CRM applications capture the critical data that allows a company to define and identify its customers, and facilitate one-on-one marketing based on an analysis of that data.

To that end, the Web has been the great enabler in CRM. For example, as a customer surfs the site, the company is able to ascertain key facts such as where that customer is located, the customer's gender, and other information. And by capturing each click of the mouse that the customer makes during a site visit, the company knows which type of merchandise the customer is interested in.

Using that information, the company can later directly target that customer, via email, with an ad or special likely to generate a sale. "The email system lets you segment, and then you can personalize your efforts by looking at their shopping and buying habits. We can capture every click, and at the end of the day, the week, the month, we know how successful an ad was."

What It's Like to Work on a Customer Relationship Management System

As CIO, Fusco oversees the implementation of a CRM system that integrates Jcrew's three sales channels—its website, its catalog call center, and its retail stores. The first iteration of the system has enabled the company to personalize its email marketing campaigns and its website according to specific customer demographics and shopping habits. Such capabilities will be key as the company moves forward with new business initiatives, such as its line of children's clothing launched in March 2001. "From a CRM standpoint, we should be able to put [male and female] customers together in a household, and more often than not, know whether they have children, and market directly to them," Fusco explains. "That's the power of a good CRM system."

WHAT WAS THE PURPOSE OF YOUR CRM SYSTEM?   CRM is an ongoing project. Our first implementation, in 2000, was in the dot-com space, managing our email system and website to do direct targeting by market segmentation. For example, we don't want users in Minnesota logging on to the site in October to be presented with bathing suits, nor do we want [to market] winter coats to users in Florida. Next, we rolled CRM into the catalog space, and now we're looking at the retail space to tie it all together. We're currently extending the CRM system with a data warehouse, capturing data from the dot-com systems, the call-center systems, and retail systems. If we know who the customer is and what they're buying and which colors and sizes, we have a big opportunity for upselling.

WHAT'S INVOLVED, AND HOW HAS THE PROJECT PROGRESSED?   Each implementation is small and targeted—we're keen on deliverables that are six months out, nothing more, with additional business functionality delivered in increments of every three months after that. Some of the software is developed from scratch and some is prepackaged. Most of the work was done internally around the database design and development. And on the front-end is our email system. So the reporting software ties into the database to help us generate segmented marketing lists, like people in Florida who bought swimsuits last year, and then we can construct and send out an email campaign to those customers.

WHO IS INVOLVED ON THE CRM PROJECT?   There are about 12 to 15 people, including IT and the business sponsors. We're the blueprint engineers, but the business sponsors own the project—they pay the bills. On the IT side, there's the project manager; a system architect who plans the hardware platform, database and programming language; a networking/communications person for voice and data because we have to tie the call center into the topology; and three to five applications and database developers. On the business side, there's the COO [chief operations officer], marketing people, and creative people. And I'm very hands-on.

The project manager owns the project from cradle to grave. The systems architect and networking person are involved for 30 to 35 percent of the project lifespan. And the developers are active on it for about five months. From day 1 to implementation is about six to eight months, but the system is never actually done. So people rotate in and out of the CRM project and other projects we have going on, such as a large SAP initiative, an HR initiative, and a large project to automate a distribution warehouse. As we go into each phase of the CRM project, we look at our pool of people who have worked on it before and put them on it again.

WHAT TECHNICAL SKILLS AND PRIOR PROJECT EXPERIENCE WERE YOU LOOKING FOR IN STAFFING THE PROJECT?   I wanted people who had done CRM before. There's one person who had done CRM in the credit card industry, and I had done two other CRM projects before at an insurance carrier and at a large media company. But the retail market is very different because it's hard to figure out who the retail customer is, plus in retail you have higher buying volumes.

I also needed someone who had heavy transaction processing experience because you don't want to hold the customer up while you're processing data on them. So you need someone who knows how to design a system that will serve up data very, very quickly. The networking person needs to have prior experience designing high-volume, redundant, fault-tolerant networks. And in terms of specific technical skills, we needed Sun Solaris, Oracle, and Java. Everyone on the team has at least five to six years of experience.

WHAT KIND OF BUSINESS PROCESS AND/OR TECHNICAL TRAINING DID THE TEAM HAVE TO GO THROUGH?   We take IT people and put them into the business for two to three weeks. For example, we'll put them on the floor packing and shipping orders so they can see how that's done, and put them into the marketing and creative departments so they can see how people access those systems. It's a walk-in-my-shoes-for-a-day kind of thing. There wasn't any specific technical training—our IT people spend roughly three to five weeks a year in training.

WHAT WERE A COUPLE OF THE MAJOR CHALLENGES—FROM A PROJECT PERSPECTIVE AS WELL AS A PERSONAL PERSPECTIVE—AS YOU BUILT THE CRM SYSTEM?   The biggest challenge is the sheer volume of data. Just think of how many clicks of the mouse one person makes as they navigate through the site, how many emails we send out in a year. We have terabytes of data gathered on individual customers in one year, and we have three years of historical data. So the challenge is managing that volume and turning it into a decision-making tool.

From a business perspective, the challenge is impatience. Most businesses just don't have a grasp of the volumes of data and what it takes to ensure that you get the data right. You only get one kick at the can—if you don't get the data right, a rebuild is very, very costly. Also, when you put the COO and the chief design officer together in a meeting, they talk apples and oranges. With the COO the world is black-and-white, and with the creative folks, it's all gray, and it's hard to put an IT person in the middle. So communication is a big challenge.

HOW IS WORKING ON A CRM PROJECT VALUABLE TO AN IT PROFESSIONAL'S CAREER OVER THE LONG TERM?   You get to see more than you would in just a warehouse automation project, for example. CRM is the kernel of the business—it's all about your customer, and IT gets to see every facet that touches the customer—marketing, creative, and the call center. And you also see the financial impact of dealing with that customer. So you become more valuable to the company and don't get pigeonholed on financial systems or payroll systems, or whatever. Not that there's anything wrong with those.

WHAT ARE SOME LOGICAL NEXT STEPS FOR IT PROFESSIONALS AFTER THEY'VE WORKED ON A CRM PROJECT?   To cross over into the business, or from the business side into IT. We've done it both ways, and it works. We had a marketing person who helped us build the customer segmentation part of the system. He spearheaded the selection of the third-party software—the business logic piece that sits on top of the database. And then we thought, who better to implement that product than the one who led the vendor-selection process and came up with the system requirements? So we got him technical training in high-level Oracle database design, and in a year or so, we'll probably move him into the analytical side. He'll become a data analyst who can get data from our [data] warehouse very quickly in an informative way.

Working on a CRM project can be very long and very frustrating, but it's also a lot of fun and very rewarding. It has really come in to its own over last year or two, and the tools are really there to support it—Informatica, Siebel, Oracle, and SAP all have great tools. So CRM is in its prime and will remain on the horizon for the next three to five years.

WHAT'S YOUR ADVICE TO SOMEONE WHO WANTS TO GET INVOLVED WITH CRM PROJECTS?
Get into data warehousing, marketing systems, high-volume transactional systems, and analytical systems. Look for data-mining experience, work with data transformation tools. Get experience on CSR [customer service representative], POS [point-of-sale],

or financial systems with high volumes. I look at project experience a lot more than technical skills—I can teach them the technology.

INDUSTRY FACT *More than two-thirds of companies that have implemented CRM systems are seeing a substantial return on investment (ROI), AMR Research, in Boston, reported in March 2001. In a survey of 100 companies, 68 percent of respondents said CRM is generating ROI. Survey respondents said the systems have improved customer satisfaction and retention (78 percent), reduced the cost of services (71 percent), increased sales and revenue (59 percent), aided new customer acquisition (57 percent), reduced the cost of sales (52 percent), and reduced headcount (50 percent). With results like these, IT professionals can count on continued job opportunities in the CRM arena.*

Integrating a Website with Backend Systems

BUSINESS OBJECTIVE   When ecommerce websites are tightly integrated with backend systems such as order fulfillment, inventory management, financial and other systems, it improves a company's operational effectiveness, customer service efforts, and financial-reporting capabilities, notes Paul Halstead, chief technology officer (CTO) of click-and-brick travel agency Cheap Tickets, in Honolulu, Hawaii. "You want the sales activity from your website to be managed through your normal business reporting and financial systems, and to let your web transactions flow through your regular fulfillment processes," Halstead explains. "From a financial-reporting perspective, it's important because it allows you to see the business as a whole, and from a customer service perspective, it reduces potential errors and eliminates additional costs of fulfilling an order."

HOW IT CONTRIBUTES   The IT department has an opportunity to become leaders of change throughout the company, Halstead says. In analyzing the requirements for a web-to-backend systems integration project, IT is in the unique position of identifying new business processes that leverage the best capabilities of both the web frontend systems and the legacy backend systems. "In many ways we've become the change agents because you get to go back and evaluate what you're doing for its applicability today," he explains. "The strange thing about legacy systems is that they tend to hang onto business rules that were in place when they were implemented even though those business rules don't apply anymore."

For example, owing to the business logic in its order fulfillment system, Cheap Tickets (www.cheaptickets.com) was unable to book reservations and issue tickets for customers who wanted to place orders less than five days before the start of their trip. Through the course of integrating its website with its backend order fulfillment system, IT was able to reduce its delivery turnaround to 24 hours. "That helps increase our overall revenue," Halstead adds. "In that case, IT actually had an impact on the bottom line in addition to streamlining our systems."

What It's Like to Work on a Web-to-Backend System Integration Project

Cheap Tickets has been in business since 1986 and has a substantial base of mission-critical legacy backend systems. The company launched an online reservation and sales system in 1997, and it now transacts about 40 percent of its total sales over the Web. That has necessitated a substantial project to tie the web sales channel into its existing backend systems, and CTO Halstead, who has significant travel industry experience, is serving as program manager for five concurrent projects. "I'm hands-on up to my elbows," he quips. "I've stepped back into the fray." Among the five projects to integrate the website with backend systems is a business-process redesign that will change the way Cheap Tickets processes the data required to issue tickets to customers, speeding up order fulfillment and improving its financial reporting.

WHAT WAS THE PURPOSE OF YOUR WEB-TO-BACKEND SYSTEM INTEGRATION PROJECT?
We're currently replacing what is pretty much a manual process with workflow and order management software. Today, when an order is placed online or over the phone, a PC-based system reviews the reservation data, validates the correctness of each field, and issues the ticketing command. In cases where that system can't process a ticket because there are missing fields or incorrect codes, the order gets put into a queue where it's processed manually. The new workflow management system will eliminate all of that and tremendously reduce instances where manual intervention is required.

A senior business analyst got us started on this path. She's the one who pulled us out of the box of simply recreating the process we currently have and put us onto a new concept of how to automate this piece of our business.

WHAT'S INVOLVED, AND HOW HAS THE PROJECT PROGRESSED? We are combining Oracle Workflow [a module in Oracle Financials] with an order management package—that we're still shopping for—and tailoring them to our specific needs. All the data that we put into a reservation to set it up for ticketing and accounting will be stored in the workflow system. It's a lot of internal accounting information—like product codes, vendor codes, sales channel codes—that later are used in financial reporting. With the new order-management application, our customer service representatives won't have to know the codes; we're writing our own front-end for it, and they'll have pull-down menus and be able to enter information in plain English, so we won't have as many errors. The order will then go into the workflow management system, which will automatically assign the codes to be dumped into the financial system.

So we're configuring and extending the packages' capabilities. We'll write some custom code ourselves that will manipulate some of the data, but we're not changing any of the [source] code that we're buying. That allows us to take advantage of future releases of the software without having to do a big project.

WHO IS INVOLVED ON THE WEB-TO-BACKEND SYSTEM INTEGRATION PROJECT?

The business analyst, a systems analyst who is helping evaluate which systems to purchase to ensure smooth integration, and a team of three developers working on the front-end pieces that we need to write. One of the developers is a database architect/database analyst who is defining the data structures and validating the data sources.

There aren't any networking or operations people involved yet, but there will be at the end. Since this is sitting on our corporate WAN [wide area network], the networking infrastructure is in place; it will just be a matter of adding another node to the infrastructure. The operations team will ensure that we have the server capacity to support these applications, and if not, they will extend our capacity. They'll also define the operational procedures, like backup and recovery. And we have a disaster recovery consultant on retainer who will come in at the end and add this to our disaster recovery plan.

WHAT TECHNICAL SKILLS AND PRIOR PROJECT EXPERIENCE WERE YOU LOOKING FOR IN STAFFING THE PROJECT?

The business analyst had a lot of reservation system experience as well as financial system and ERP implementation experience. Her skills makeup is 30 percent technical, 60 percent business, and 10 percent creative problem solving. She's truly someone who can look at the same problem everyone else is looking at and see a different way to think about it. If you get the right business analysts on your staff, half your job is taken care of.

In terms of technical skills, we needed Oracle for the database work and Java, Visual Basic, and some C for developing the user interface.

WHAT KIND OF BUSINESS PROCESS AND/OR TECHNICAL TRAINING DID THE TEAM HAVE TO GO THROUGH?   There wasn't any business process training, but we sent the team through training on Oracle Workflow, and when we purchase our new order management software, there will be some training on that.

WHAT WERE A COUPLE OF THE MAJOR CHALLENGES—FROM A PROJECT PERSPECTIVE AS WELL AS A PERSONAL PERSPECTIVE—AS YOU DID THE INTEGRATION?   On a personal level, it's just keeping up the energy level to keep this all going. We are changing a lot of things in the company very quickly, so we're at a point where this needs to cycle down; we need to come to some sort of conclusion so we can have a quiet period for a while. The project challenge is taking our internal customer groups through this process of change. Users find it intimidating that we are changing the way they do their jobs, and there's a lot of fear that after the new system is in place and working, that we won't need as many people in [the order processing] department as we have in the past. So that builds up some levels of resistance.

HOW IS WORKING ON A WEB-TO-BACKEND SYSTEM INTEGRATION PROJECT VALUABLE TO AN IT PROFESSIONAL'S CAREER OVER THE LONG TERM?   The exposure to these types of technologies is valuable in and of itself. Oracle Workflow is going to be a growth area, so that's an excellent technical skill to have. But it's also a great addition to a résumé to be able to say you've implemented a system that reduced operations costs, eliminated customer service issues, and increased sales.

WHAT ARE SOME LOGICAL NEXT STEPS FOR IT PROFESSIONALS AFTER THEY'VE WORKED ON A WEB-TO-BACKEND SYSTEM INTEGRATION PROJECT?   If you do well on a project of this scope, management is definitely an opportunity. From a technical perspective, you could go into a data warehouse or executive information system project because a system like this is all about the collection and transition of data into a financial system. So you learn about data origins, and data cleansing, and what a piece of transactional data means. Once you understand data on a transactional basis, you can pull it into a repository and start doing data analysis and data mining with this pool you helped create. One of the most valuable assets in data warehousing is someone who really understands the transactional basis.

WHAT'S YOUR ADVICE TO SOMEONE WHO WANTS TO GET INVOLVED WITH WEB-TO-BACKEND SYSTEMS INTEGRATION?   Just working on a website is not enough to qualify for a project like this. You need significant experience, preferably in enterprise-wide systems like ERP or CRM, or experience working on any one of the individual systems that the integration project is going to tie together. I look for someone who has a proven track record of delivering based on customer requirements and whose résumé speaks to the importance of interfacing with users throughout a development project. In terms of the technology, strong Oracle skills are important.

Building a Supply-Chain Management System

BUSINESS OBJECTIVE   Supply-chain management systems can give companies more control over the sourcing, manufacture, sale, and replenishment of their products by enabling collaboration among suppliers, manufacturing plants, and distribution channels to improve inventory planning and management. "You want to integrate the supply-and-demand processes to eliminate cost, waste, and time from [the process of getting a product from] the supplier into the distribution network and onto store shelves," says Steve St. Thomas, senior systems manager at Harley-Davidson (www.harley-davidson.com), in Milwaukee, Wisconsin.

HOW IT CONTRIBUTES   In addition to developing the software solution, IT can bring its experience to bear on the business solution, identifying new workflow management scenarios that reduce the amount of time required to source parts, put a product together and ship it, St. Thomas notes. "Working in this world, you pick up business knowledge just by being involved, so we deliver not only the program to support the process but also help direct where the process goes," he says. "We can certainly help contribute to the business rules and the design of the business process."

What It's Like to Work on a Supply-Chain Management System

St. Thomas, who started his IT career as an applications developer in 1986, has been involved with supply-chain management since 1997, when Harley-Davidson launched its current SCM system to manage inventory forecasting and planning for its line of motorcycle parts and accessories. While the initial project gave the company a view into which products were moving out of its warehouses, the company in 2001 began extending those capabilities to its retail channels. The idea is to get a complete picture of customer demand to better exercise inventory control and manage its supplier relationships based on more accurate inventory forecasts.

WHAT WAS THE PURPOSE OF YOUR SCM SYSTEM?   In 1997 and 1998, we did a pretty traditional implementation of Manugistics software for inventory planning and forecasting based on the level of demand we see at our warehouses. We are now extending
that capability, in a pilot project, to the entire supply chain beyond our company bor-
ders. Whereas before we could do forecasting and planning by being able to see what
was moving in and out of our warehouses, now we'll have a view of what's moving in
and out of retail.

But in addition to that, we're adding an element of collaborative planning; we'll
be able to get input and feedback from our dealers to determine the appropriate level
of product replenishment and restocking. For example, at the retail level, a dealer in
a particular location might be selling a lot of Part X, and if you just looked at that, the
sales of that part, you might conclude that it needs replenishment. But the reality
might be that the dealer had been discounting the part to get rid of it because it
hadn't been selling well and they don't want to carry it anymore. So you have to have
a level of collaboration with the dealer to make truly accurate decisions about replenishment and forecasting.

WHAT'S INVOLVED, AND HOW HAS THE PROJECT PROGRESSED?   It is a continuously
evolving project. We're always adding to what we started in 97–98. All of these SCM
software products have some sort of collaboration module that you can add, and that
has been the big thing in the SCM market in the last two years. We're sticking with
Manugistics and are in the process of implementing the collaboration module, which
will let us feed the retail data into our demand-forecasting program in addition to the
wholesale data.

With most of these SCM modules, you don't have to do what we would have called
customization in the past. You're doing more configuration work—making settings in
the software so the process works the way you want it. But you're not actually changing code; the modules are highly configurable and give you a lot of options. It's a huge
cost issue when you customize too much because then it's much harder to upgrade.

WHO WAS INVOLVED ON THE SCM PROJECT?   On the IT side, this is a more analyst-
heavy project because there's less development work, and you have to nail down the
[business] process design to do the configuration of the packaged software. So there
aren't a lot of programmers, but more business analysts and systems analysts. There's
a project manager. There isn't a full-time DBA [database administrator] on the team—
we interface with the database team as needed. On the business side, there are many

stakeholders. We have not only our internal inventory planning and replenishment staffs, but also our business partners—the Harley dealerships and third-party parts-and-accessories dealers own part of the process, and our internal manufacturing units, which we consider suppliers, own part. Right now, the system doesn't extend back to external suppliers, but in another area of IT, they are doing an SCM project that does.

WHAT TECHNICAL SKILLS AND PRIOR PROJECT EXPERIENCE WERE YOU LOOKING FOR IN STAFFING THE PROJECT?   In implementing the Manugistics collaboration module, the technical skills are a little [different] because this is more of an integration effort than a development effort.

So you must understand the hardware and software infrastructure and the network infrastructure; for example, as we put this software in place, what does it mean for the infrastructure from a network-platform and computing-platform perspective? You have to make sure you are hooking all the pieces together correctly—they tend to be database-intensive and processor-intensive—so you must have adequate network throughput and sizing of the processors, and you have to worry about the new software causing unanticipated glitches with existing systems. In terms of specific technical skills, usually the integration with these prepackaged products is done through some kind of scripting language, so here Perl is important.

As for project experience, it depends on the level of the person. From a project manager standpoint, SCM systems are complex projects with a lot of different stakeholders, so prior experience on a big enterprise-wide project is a plus. With developers, you need someone who's familiar with how to configure a shrinkwrapped package. There's much less programming from scratch, and more configuring and testing based on how the processes will work. Here we grew our team from scratch, but having a traditional inventory planning and forecasting system background would be a huge help because then you would understand the functionality. We brought in some consultants who are familiar with Manugistics, and most of the internal team members have been here a long time.

WHAT KIND OF BUSINESS PROCESS AND/OR TECHNICAL TRAINING DID THE TEAM HAVE TO GO THROUGH?   We didn't do business-process training, but we all went through the same training on Manugistics as our end-users so we could understand how the product worked from an end-user perspective. And then we had some additional Manugistics technical training specific to implementing the software.

WHAT WERE A COUPLE OF THE MAJOR CHALLENGES—FROM A PROJECT PERSPECTIVE AS WELL AS A PERSONAL PERSPECTIVE—AS YOU BUILT THE SCM SYSTEM? By their nature, SCM projects tend to have a lot of stakeholders—the suppliers, the dealers. It isn't just wholly contained within your organization. And with each stakeholder, there are business process issues and different expectation. So you have to make a business case for the system that balances a number of different perspectives.

For example, the parts dealers will see a benefit from the system down the line, but we're actually asking them to do work that they've never had to do before—to take ownership for the system. And we have the same problem with every organization that the system touches. So, you have to do a lot of consensus building and change management, which are difficult to begin with, and when you have multiple constituencies, it just magnifies that challenge.

HOW IS WORKING ON AN SCM PROJECT VALUABLE TO AN IT PROFESSIONAL'S CAREER OVER THE LONG TERM? Clearly, "SCM" is a huge buzzword in the industry right now, so anyone having that on their résumé, with experience implementing Manugistics or i2 [software] is going to have some interesting career opportunities. These tend to be strategic projects with big business benefits, and it's good to be associated with something that brings a big return. Also, it's motivational; it makes you feel good when you work on something that has a big ROI for your company.

WHAT ARE SOME LOGICAL NEXT STEPS FOR IT PROFESSIONALS AFTER THEY'VE WORKED ON AN SCM PROJECT? It would be good for getting into IT management because of the visibility and complexity of these projects and because they're a big part of most businesses. If you prove that you can operate in that area, you've covered a lot of business ground. A new, related area that's getting some attention recently is continuing up the supply chain and going back into supporting product development; it's called product lifecycle management [PLM]. When you have the fulfillment side down, it's easy to go into product-development processes supporting design and manufacturing—you have the same concepts of collaboration, taking time and costs and waste out of the process by improving the manufacturability and distribution aspects of a product immediately in the design phase.

WHAT'S YOUR ADVICE TO SOMEONE WHO WANTS TO GET INVOLVED WITH SCM SYSTEMS? Getting experience and developing business expertise early on in inventory management planning and forecasting would be useful. Join professional societies like APICS [www.apics.org].

INDUSTRY FACT *The SCM market is expected to reach $7.8 billion in sales in 2001 with IT organizations ramping up inventory management, order-fulfillment and supply-chain planning applications, according to AMR Research, in Boston. Collaboration capabilities enabling companies to bring their distributors and suppliers into the process will comprise a key piece of those implementations, creating sustained opportunities for IT professionals with SCM-related experience. Looking forward, PLM, an extension of supply-chain management systems, is poised for significant growth. Licensing revenue for shrinkwrapped PLM applications will grow more than 50 percent in 2001 as manufacturers move to reduce time-to-market for new products, AMR projects. IT professionals looking for future growth following an SCM project are well advised to keep an eye on this new trend.*

Building a Knowledge Management System

BUSINESS OBJECTIVE   The overriding purpose of a knowledge management system is to connect people within an organization who need expertise in a particular subject with the ones who possess that expertise. "It has to do with getting everyone in a large, global organization to be able to work together," says Scott Beaty, a knowledge manager with the Leadership and Performance Operations (LEAP) group within Shell Oil, in Houston, Texas (www.shelloil.com). "It's connecting people to information and to other people. You know the knowledge is there somewhere in the organization, and KM enables you to get to it." But that aspect—managing what you know you know— is only one component of KM, Beaty adds. A truly robust KM system also enables organizations to get a handle on three other areas of knowledge: "Things you know you don't know but need to, or learning requirements; things you don't know you know, or capturing the tacit knowledge of the organization and the individuals in it; and things you don't know you don't know, or the process of discovery."

IT CONTRIBUTION   In KM, IT provides the roadmap and transportation that bring people and information together. Beaty notes that IT is an essential component underlying two guiding principles on a KM project. "Knowledge is information applied to work to add value, but information only becomes knowledge when a human being takes it and does something with it—you compare it with what you already know, understand the consequences of it, and connect it to different concepts and other pieces of information," he explains. "Having said that, the driving forces of information are speed and precision, and a way to achieve that is via computers and communication technologies. So the role that IT plays is connecting people to information and people to other people with the speed and precision they need to accomplish a business goal." Through data modeling, IT helps ensure the accuracy and consistency of the information; through user interface design, IT enables easy access to the data in relevant and meaningful ways; and through networking, IT facilitates the transfer of the information.

What It's Like to Work on a Knowledge Management System

Shell has a number of concurrent KM initiatives to improve access to the right people and the right information at the right time, leveraging the collaborative and document-management capabilities of Livelink software by Open Text Corporation. Beaty was the business sponsor for a KM system that enables his organization to share best practices across the company. Paul O'Sullivan, an information architect with Shell Shared Services (the company's IT arm) in Amsterdam was the application architect on a KM project dubbed Asset Hierarchy Application (AHA). That project, for a Shell engineering operations unit responsible for building power plants, aimed to improve document management. "Part of the problem in KM is enabling people to get to different types of documents," Sullivan says. "Taxonomies are kind of fixed, and you can only navigate via folders. But if you have massive amounts of data, that's not the most intuitive way to navigate." By customizing Livelink, Shell Shared Services built a user interface that allows multiple avenues into the data using metadata, he explains, and now offers that service in customized versions to all of Shell's business units.

What was the purpose of your KM system?

> **O'Sullivan:** The AHA project was an implementation of the document-management component of Livelink plus KM tools built for the engineering department to help them organize and manage the design phase of their plants. The users came to us with an open mind, and we spent a lot of time understanding what they were doing at the moment and looking at how we could automate the management of their drawings and blueprints and other documents.

> **Beaty:** LEAP functions as an internal learning-and-change management consultancy within Shell. There are about 55 of us located in offices in the Hague, the Netherlands, Kuala Lumpur, and Houston. And we operate in 140 countries delivering learning, leadership, business improvement, and change management programs throughout the company to effect quantum changes in the operation of the business. We have to continuously learn from each program we deliver and share

the knowledge we've acquired, new ideas, and best practices. So we needed a system to manage who knows what, where they are, and how they can be leveraged—a common set of templates and applications to deliver that knowledge.

What's involved, and how did the projects progress?

O'Sullivan: It entails a lot of analysis of business processes and dreaming up new workflows. There's lots of brainstorming and iterative prototyping and changes. The customer wanted a lot of options, so we would give them two or three alternatives for each decision they had to make. We'd get the requirements from them and the information that will go into the system, incorporate that into a data model, and test the integration of the data model with Livelink. A typical day would be one-third data modeling, one-third hands-on coding of the application, and one-third working out alternative solutions, brainstorming, and soliciting user feedback.

We started the AHA project in May 2000 and spent about six months getting requirements and doing the data models. We did a pilot implementation in November and started a live pilot in January 2001. After the system goes live, you start waiting on customer feedback because there are definitely shortcomings, and you hit a few walls with customer acceptance because we are giving them new ways in which they're going to do their work. So it takes a couple of months for them to reorient themselves and give us feedback, and that's when we'll be able to put together a system that will really be useful.

Beaty: In our LEAP KM system, the user interface was critical. We needed a system where users could control the content and not have to rely on IT to put all the information in it. A lot of KM efforts fail because they are dependent on people to write down what they know that they think would be interesting and useful, and then throw it over to IT to put it in a database in some form, some taxonomy that's accessible. A huge benefit of the Livelink software was that IT could customize it for us so we can put the information in ourselves, and tap into the global LEAP community to find what we need. The interface has two [onscreen] buttons. One is "How do I...?" and you can find out things like how to deliver a leadership model with focused results or how to operate your computer. The other is "Does anybody know...?" and that will help you find folks who can tell you about a customer or a product or how to find a doctor in Nigeria.

Who was involved on the KM project?

O'Sullivan: I was the application architect, responsible for translating business requirements to technical requirements and designing the prototype. I helped define the information requirements to meet the business processes we were automating; designed the application, its interface, and its interaction with traditional systems in place; managed the build, test, and deployment of the solution; and helped design a support structure. We also had a project manager, a data architect/data modeler, a document management expert, and a collaboration and KM consultant—a business analyst with a KM focus—and a customer representative.

We also consulted with other groups depending on when they were needed. For example, we had networking people at our disposal because this was an Internet-based system, we worked with the infrastructure group on the web servers, and we worked with the DBA group on setting up the databases.

What technical skills and prior project experience were you looking for in staffing the project?

O'Sullivan: Livelink, Oracle for the database, PowerBuilder for data modeling, and Internet Information Server, Active Server Pages, COM [component object model], Visual Basic, and [Oracle] PL/SQL for development. My prior project experience was in the installation, configuration, and extension of several other Livelink systems for the Internet collaboration and ecommerce solutions department within the IT Services group. I had experience building all types of applications before I got into knowledge management.

Beaty: KM is not the place for an entry-level person—you need people who have done a couple of large IT projects already because the KM piece is fairly sophisticated.

A really solid business background is essential. M.B.A. courses would be really good so you understand how the business operates. Also, industry-specific knowledge of what you are supporting, because the oil business is really different from, say, financial services. It's a commodity-based business vs. a transaction- and information-services-based business. So you need a deep understanding of the business drivers of the industry that you're in, and as subset of that, you should understand the value chain—how the business makes money and where this project can help the business generate revenue or cut costs.

What kind of business process and/or technical training did the team have to go through?

O'Sullivan: A lot of on-the-job learning. The previous KM projects I had worked on had really made me aware of the fact that KM project complexity does not usually lie in the technical aspects, but more in the information management aspects—metadata definition, taxonomy, security, etc. I had technical training in Livelink and data modeling. To understand KM, I did a lot of self-study. I had worked on various taxonomies in other Livelink implementations, and it was through that and keeping my eyes open and questioning people. There is not a lot of formal training you can do. I subscribed to newsletters, read *Fast Company*, used the Booz-Allen & Hamilton website (www.bah.com), which has a lot of case studies and profiles, and the *California Management Review*.

What were a couple of the major challenges—from a project perspective as well as a personal perspective—as you built the KM system?

O'Sullivan: On the project level, managing the customer as they realized the scope and complexity of the project in terms of internal ways of working and business process changes. The real nut to crack is convincing people that it's worth doing. Very often the person who is your primary client will become a champion of the project; for example, on this project an engineer was all gung-ho about making the change. But if you never get buy-in from the entire group, the systems crash and burn. The role of change management falls more to the management consultants and the business analysts, but IT can show them best practices and help identify taxonomies and meta data, and help build up support from that point of view.

On a personal level, it was moving from a development role to an architect, trying to manage the availability and timing of all the phases from concept through to deployment and support. I had much more interaction with other technical areas and people.

How is working on a KM project valuable to an IT professional's career over the long term?

O'Sullivan: KM covers a wide variety of IT fields, most importantly data and information modeling, and that is a cornerstone of most IT projects—it will always provide an alternative view on the problem at hand.

What are some logical next steps for IT professionals after they've worked on a KM project?

O'Sullivan: Movement toward a specialist's role such as data architect or data modeler on the technical side. On the business side, there's opportunity for movement into business-process modeling or creation, change management, or organizational behavior. You can also move into general project management. My goal is to move more into web-based portal applications to integrate all of the applications that people use into one space. I'm building toward that now by working for the systems integration department on the complete integration of legacy applications with our ERP system and providing a web-based face to those applications. My plan has always been to solidify my technical skills in information management and then try to leap into the more human side of things. I'd like to take training in human factors and human-computer integration.

Beaty: I recruited the guy who worked as the IT project manager on our LEAP project to come work for us in the business. Real professional growth from this area would be to go run a part of the business; that's when you really learn the role that IT can play. That would definitely put you on the fast track for the CIO's office. The people I know who best understand IT and business are those who have a deep IT background and have actually worked as business leaders.

What's your advice to someone who wants to get involved with KM systems?

O'Sullivan: Read about KM and understand its business principles and benefits, even if you're technical. The most important people, from a KM project team point of view, are those who can speak to and translate between the business and technical sides of the fence. Predominantly, it's the big consulting firms and really large companies like Shell that are doing KM, so look for opportunities in-house with a large company or target the consultancies.

 INDUSTRY FACT Corporate knowledge management initiatives are on the rise, driven by a desire to get the right information to the right people at the right time, according to International Data Corporation, Framingham, Massachusetts. The market research firm expects spending on KM services and software to increase dramatically by 2004. The KM services market will grow from $1.3 billion in 1999 to more than $8 billion in 2003, while the KM software market will increase from $1.4 billion in 1999 to $5.4 billion in 2004. Taken together, the projections promise viable prospects for IT professionals to get involved with KM.

Overhauling the Network Infrastructure

BUSINESS OBJECTIVE   As companies continuously extend their businesses to the Internet, they must persistently evolve their network infrastructures to keep up with the performance and content demands created by an ever-growing number of Internet users. For example, Weather.com, the companion website for the cable network The Weather Channel, completely redesigned its network architecture in 2000 to ensure better performance during the user-heavy hurricane months of August and September. "We wanted to improve performance so that if a server got loaded down with user requests, the network wouldn't continue to dispatch requests to that machine," explains Mark Ryan, CTO of Weather.com, based in Atlanta, Georgia. The revamped architecture provides better load balancing, better protection against physical outages, and improved speed. The business impact: "It ensures a more consistent, reliable end-user experience, and that boosts traffic to the site."

HOW IT CONTRIBUTES   While there are, as with any IT project, business drivers for rebuilding a network, IT owns the project from start to finish. The IT organization monitors and analyzes performance of the existing architecture, stays up-to-date with new technologies that can improve performance to meet the demands of the business, selects and manages the vendor relationships that keep the network up and running, and designs and implements the new architecture based on the sum of its expertise.

What It's Like to Work on a Network Infrastructure Overhaul

In preparation for hurricane season, when site traffic can swell from an average of 10 million page views per day to 40 million per day, Ryan and his team at Weather.com spent about four months in 2000 designing and deploying the new network at two hosting facilities. The new network would also lay the foundation for a site relaunch in February 2001. Working with its host provider, Exodus Communications, it moved one of its collocation facilities from Virginia to Douglasville, Georgia, where it built a new network from scratch. It also revamped the replicated network in place at Exodous' main facilities in Santa Clara, California. "We use a collocation arrangement for disaster recovery," Ryan says. "If one facility goes down, the workload automatically shifts to the other." As network host, Exodous supplies the company with the physical facility, power, and network security. "They're our big switch that hooks us to the Internet," Ryan explains. "We execute and manage the internal network."

WHAT WAS THE PURPOSE OF YOUR NETWORK INFRASTRUCTURE OVERHAUL?   To design the network in such a fashion where the dispatching was done in a systematic approach vs. a device-based approach. So instead of having work dispatched to individual boxes, we went to a round-robin approach. Now, any type of user request that comes into the site—for city forecasts, maps, ski information, any type of information—is better load balanced. That improves the user experience and also helps with any physical outages that might occur—if one server drops out of service, in the round-robin topology, the work can be redirected to another server. In the round-robin architecture, if a network server goes down, that's only about one tenth of our capacity. That was a guiding principal.

From a design perspective, our workload is extremely sensitive to natural events such as snowstorms and hurricanes, when users log on more to get weather information. So we run off the 55-percent rule—each hosting facility has 55 percent of the capacity we think we would need in a hurricane. So in a nonpeak month, we can actually shut one facility off.

WHAT'S INVOLVED, AND HOW DID THE PROJECT PROGRESS?   We did a technology refresh and redefined the network architecture at the same time. We actually moved the network from a different hosting facility and built it from scratch, so we replaced the majority of servers and networking equipment. We ran the site off of the network in Santa Clara while we were doing the work in the Douglasville facility, then went live with the Douglasville network, shut down Santa Clara to do the work there, and then brought both networks online in time for hurricane season. It took us about three-and-a-half months in Douglasville, and another month to execute in Santa Clara.

It's extremely critical to have a documented plan agreed to up front. If you have that, it's very easy to define the cost of change. One problem with these projects is that the scope creep is amazing. New requirements come up in the middle of the project … and with creep, either your cost or time to completion goes up. If you have a clearly defined deliverable upfront, then you can understand the cost of any change in scope, and then people will usually back off of scope creep. I didn't allow any changes once we agreed on the plan—any changes that came up got handed off to the network architect for consideration in the next iteration. If you have the leisure of not allowing change, that's a wonderful thing. But with longer projects that are a year long or more, scope creep is unfortunately inevitable because business requirements change over time.

WHO WAS INVOLVED ON THE NETWORK OVERHAUL?   A project manager, a network or infrastructure architect, network administrators and web server administrators, and network and operations engineers from [our] own staff [and] the hosting facility's staff. There's always an architectural review that involves the applications and database departments to make sure their needs and requirements are being addressed, but they don't have anything to do with the physical execution.

As CTO, I do the high-level stuff like identifying the business objective, evaluating the ROI, outlining the investment and payback, and describing what has to be done architecturally, and I need the architect's input on the product suite and the rationale, such as higher availability, increased speed of user experience, and cost savings.

The architect draws up the design, researches the product suites and tools, evaluates different network topologies, analyzes the pros and cons of all the options, and does capacity planning and disaster recovery planning. Once a design is approved, the architect is there for guidance and reference, but is generally starting to work on whatever the next release of the network will be.

The administrators, engineers, and operations folks execute the design. They do the actual physical work—cabling, configuring routers and hubs, moving ports, monitoring capacity and performance, and so forth. And the project manager ensures that the plan is on track and if not, gets it back on track, makes sure that all changes are documented and communicated, and sees that problems are resolved or escalated to the next level.

WHAT TECHNICAL SKILLS AND PRIOR PROJECT EXPERIENCE WERE YOU LOOKING FOR IN STAFFING THE PROJECT? The network architect had to be someone who had worked in the networking field for some time and understood the applications implications of what we were doing at the physical level—for example, how a request is dispatched to a server. A good understanding of load balancers, routers, hubs, switches, etc., was required, of course, by the architect and the network engineers. We used gear from Cisco and Foundry. We consider certification in those technologies critical. Certification describes a level of competency, like an apprenticeship, that says an industry has stated you are qualified to do X amount of work at a certain level of competency.

The systems and network administrators needed Unix and Linux expertise, and the project manager needed technical experience. A nontechnical project manager could do the job, but one who has worked in IT and understands all the terminology has a much easier time on a project like this. If we can get it, we like our project managers to be certified by the Project Management Institute.

WHAT KIND OF BUSINESS PROCESS AND/OR TECHNICAL TRAINING DID THE TEAM HAVE TO GO THROUGH? We didn't do any training per se. Where we needed additional expertise, like with the Cisco and Foundry gear, we worked with consultants. There weren't a whole lot of people with Foundry skills available on the open market, so we had to go with consultants from Foundry itself. Overall, the project team was 90 percent Weather.com and 10 percent consultants.

WHAT WERE A COUPLE OF THE MAJOR CHALLENGES—FROM A PROJECT PERSPECTIVE AS WELL AS A PERSONAL PERSPECTIVE—AS YOU REBUILT THE NETWORK INFRASTRUCTURE? The difficulty of finding people delayed the rollout. We also had challenges with language barriers—where people use the same term but it means different things to different people. For example, an applications developer and a systems administrator have different understandings of the word *object*. So a lot of times with new technologies, it's extremely important to have a definitions list and use a lot of pictures because that puts a physical layer on the definitions. We had a physical picture of what we were trying to accomplish that we put on the bulletin board and distributed to each person on the team.

HOW IS WORKING ON A NETWORK INFRASTRUCTURE OVERHAUL VALUABLE TO AN IT PROFESSIONAL'S CAREER OVER THE LONG TERM? It really gives you end-to-end experience with all of the elements required for an application to be supported: the connectivity of network gear to load balancing to servers to databases all the way through to the applications, and from an Internet perspective, all the way to the end-user. It's a major crash course in how an IT organization functions and the complete scope of product suites, from the [network equipment] suite to the Unix and Linux servers to the applications servers and the different infrastructure technologies that run across all those parts. When you get that end-to-end view, you aren't focused just on the individual technologies, but rather, you get a more philosophical view of the entire connectivity across the organization.

WHAT ARE SOME LOGICAL NEXT STEPS FOR IT PROFESSIONALS AFTER THEY'VE WORKED ON A NETWORK OVERHAUL? If you're the network architect, you can step up to infrastructure architect, who works not only at network level but also at the middleware level, which allows the transfer of data between two points. They make decisions on transport technologies, message queuing, and action activity queuing in a database; it's stepping up from the network hardware layer to the logical software layer. From there, they could move into applications architecture or development or into operations management. The network administrators and engineers, depending on their experience and desire, could eventually move into architecture or operations management. There are all kinds of career paths for them.

WHAT'S YOUR ADVICE TO SOMEONE WHO WANTS TO GET INVOLVED WITH A NETWORK INFRASTRUCTURE PROJECT? Ask management for the experience, and beforehand, get certification in your discipline to demonstrate that you're ready for the experience. Get some experience executing smaller, individual projects, like upgrading a departmental network, rolling out a network operating system upgrade, or performance monitoring. A project like this is very exciting, and if you get the chance, you should do it.

KING OF THE WHOLE WORLD WIDE WEB: BUILDING A DESTINATION WEBSITE

When Elvis Presley sang "King of the Whole Wide World" in the 1961 film *Kid Galahad*, little did he know that he would one day also be King of the whole World Wide Web. But today, more than 20 years after his death on August 16, 1977, the King of Rock and Roll is mentioned on more than 50,000 web pages, ranging from the reverent to the irreverent to the irrelevant. In August 2000, Elvis Presley Enterprises (EPE) relaunched the official Elvis Presley website, www.elvis.com, just as some 30,000 fans were expected to converge in Memphis, Tennessee, for the annual Elvis Week activities.

Key new features at the time of the relaunch included a Flash movie intro; a free downloadable screensaver featuring eight images of Elvis; E-cards (E for Elvis); a virtual Graceland tour using I-Pics 360-degree digital photos of favorite rooms in the mansion; a live webcast of the candlelight vigil held outside Graceland on August 15; new RealMedia features, including the video of Elvis' first interview after his discharge from the Army; an interactive Flash trivia game; subscriptions to a new email newsletter; and an upgrade of the site's ecommerce capabilities, including real-time inventory lookup and crisper product photos. Phase two of the relaunch began right after Elvis Week 2000; features added since then include a free email service, Flash E-Cards, additional video footage and songs, and ecommerce enhancements, such as wish-lists and other personalized features.

The relaunch and subsequent site updates have been a joint effort of EPE and its website design firm, Little Rock, Arkansas–based Aristotle. Following, Todd Morgan, Graceland's director of media and creative development, and Nancy Mitchell, Aristotle producer, discuss what it's like to work on the ultimate tribute site for the Artist of the Century.

KING OF THE WHOLE WORLD WIDE WEB: BUILDING A DESTINATION WEBSITE

What were the drivers behind the new iteration of the website?

Morgan: It was just part of the natural growth of the site—knowing what was out there, what was being done that we wanted to do, listening to our audience and what they expect, and making those things happen beautifully. We wanted to do a better job and reach more people.

Half of the visitors to Graceland are under 35, so there continues to be an unbridled passion and enthusiasm for discovering Elvis. You just have to get Elvis and his work in front of people, and he does the rest. He's our Marketing Director Emeritus, and he's still doing the job. Many times over the years we've been asked, "What is EPE's mission statement?" And we don't really have a formal one. In all seriousness, our CEO [Jack Soden] says it's simply this: "Don't screw it up." The Elvis phenomenon is so huge and has a life of its own. So it's about Elvis and his audience … and we just try to do good projects that enhance the power and the magic that's already there.

How do you distinguish the official Elvis.com site from the myriad Elvis fan sites and tribute sites on the Web?

Morgan: People connect with Elvis on so many different levels. Some have a favorite era—Elvis in the fifties, the '68 Comeback Special, the movies, the seventies concerts. Some are into all of it. We've tried to design our official site so that whatever Elvis you connect with, you'll find him when you come to our site.

Who's on the team at Graceland and Aristotle?

Morgan: Everything we do is an ensemble effort. Most areas of our company are involved in some way because we're presenting Elvis and our company on the Net. My focus is content—Elvis Himselvis. I have a designer on my staff who does a lot of Internet work, and we have an onsite tech person who handles email issues. The marketing director has a lot of Internet experience; the VP/GM [vice president and general manager] is heavily involved; the merchandising director; and to some degree, our licensing people because there are some [intellectual property] issues.

Mitchell: We have 16 people on the project, including 7 on the IT side: 2 applications developers, a network analyst, a systems administrator, an ASP programmer, and an HTML programmer. One of the programmers doubles as the DBA. We're using SQL 7 and also doing a lot of backend programming to enable EPE to make content updates without our help.

KING OF THE WHOLE WORLD WIDE WEB: BUILDING A DESTINATION WEBSITE

What was the timeframe for the site rebuild?

Mitchell: We signed the contract on June 7, 2000, and shortly after, we showed EPE two designs. They picked one and we were well into it when we showed it to four focus groups. And then we decided to change it. That was in July, and we threw out all the work we had done up to then.

So then we were putting in ten-hour days for three weeks, and the last week before the launch we were putting in about 14 hours a day. Normally, we put in about a 9-hour day. One night just before the soft launch, I was here to 4:00 A.M., and I was back that morning at 8:45. Programmers were developing the site and all the backend stuff with no graphics, and the last week started putting in all the last-minute pieces and capturing video.

How did you reward the staff for the time they put in over that summer?

Mitchell: We bought dinner for people every night and got them ice cream, sodas, whatever they needed during the day. The night before the soft launch we threw a surprise Blue Hawaii party. EPE sent us a cardboard standup of Elvis from *Jailhouse Rock*, and we drank blue margaritas, and ate blue food, and played Elvis music, and showed Elvis movies, and had an Elvis trivia game.

What were your criteria in choosing a design firm, and why did Aristotle get the job?

Morgan: All-around expertise, broad capabilities, and the staff support to make it all happen beautifully and quickly. And, with everything we do, it just has to feel right. When we sat down around our big conference table and met with [the Aristotle staff], it just felt right. We really connected and could communicate with one another—there was an instant ease of collaboration, and we got excited about them immediately.

Were you looking for a firm with Elvis fans on board?

Morgan: It isn't necessary to have the Elvis fever—we bring truckloads of that to the table. He's at the heart of everything we do. We really just needed the expertise to help us bring Elvis to the Internet. But it's a huge bonus any time a company has that great feeling, and we find that most people do—people from all over the

KING OF THE WHOLE WORLD WIDE WEB: BUILDING A DESTINATION WEBSITE

world and from all walks of life have some special feeling about him whether they're died-in-the-wool fans or not. And once you get Elvis into your life, and he gets ahold of you, you're gotten for life.

Mitchell: We bid on the project because we have a real Elvis fan on-staff who wanted to go for the job. And once we got it, our lead art director started listening to Elvis music nonstop to get inspired by Elvis. I've found it very interesting. I had never been to Graceland before, and after we landed the job, we had a tour and…that put a face on Elvis for me because as a person who wasn't a fan, I didn't understand where he came from or what happened to him. I don't know if I'll ever be a die-hard fan, but I now own ten Elvis CDs. I have a much deeper appreciation for Elvis and what he did. My email address is bluesuedeshoes@elvis.com.

What's it like to work at Graceland?

Morgan: A lot of the projects that we do on the hill [the site of the Graceland mansion] have to happen after hours—like shooting a TV special—and there are those moments late at night when it's really quiet, and you're in the house or in the Meditation Garden, and it's so peaceful. There's a warmth that the place has, the imprint of Elvis' spirit, of the life that was at Graceland when he was there. And in those quiet moments, you just shake your head at how privileged you are to be a small part of it every day. Whatever role we all play, we know that the effort matters to millions of people. It's a good gig.

Mitchell: It was a cool thing for us to go into Graceland after hours and take the I-Pics pictures. No one was there other than the crew and the security guard, and we got to go beyond the ropes and see the things that most people don't get to see from the tour. You can't sit on the furniture—I didn't even touch anything. But seeing the little details up close put even more of a face on Elvis for me.

Would Elvis have been a fan of the Web?

Morgan: Absolutely, without a doubt. Elvis was always aware of new technology and was usually among the first to have it. He had a telephone in a briefcase in the sixties, and a couple of sky-to-ground phones in his jets (*The Hound Dog II* and *The Lisa Marie*). He had a big-screen TV in the mid-seventies. So he definitely would have been online as soon as it was available. He loved anything new.

 NOTE *Excerpts from this interview appeared in* Computerworld *on August 14, 2000.*

Chapter 10

· ·

Hot Industries

Just as IT needs and requirements vary from project to project (as discussed in Chapter 9), they also change from industry to industry, and it pays to understand the differences. The critical systems in a retailer, such as integrated point-of-sale (POS) systems, are distinct from those in an insurance company, where automated claims processing goes straight to the bottom line. Even with applications that cut across different industries, like supply-chain management (SCM) systems, there will be variations given the differences in how each industry conducts business. Educating yourself in the specifics of an industry can make a dramatic difference in your IT career.

Knowing what's going on in your particular industry will make you a stronger IT contributor. It will enable you to anticipate and relate to your company's business objectives, even when they may not be clearly conveyed to IT by upper management. It will also help you articulate the IT perspective to business users and managers with authority and in language they can understand. That will be helpful to your career whether you decide to pursue an IT management track or a purely technical track. And fully understanding industry trends has the residual benefit of helping you make informed job choices over the course of your career. You'll know when it's time to make a change because the industry you're in is softening, and you'll be prepared to identify job opportunities where your IT skills can make a strategic business difference. Understanding where an industry is headed, and the role that IT will play in that direction, can also help you shape your training goals effectively.

Taking an industry-oriented approach to your IT career planning is a constructive way to distinguish your résumé from the rest. If you're an established IT professional, diversifying your résumé by working in several different industries shows that while you're a technologist, you're able to grasp many different types of business problems and have a well-rounded background. Career-changers, such as bank tellers or sales reps, for example, can leverage their experience within a specific industry to break into IT, where managers are always on the lookout to hire people with industry expertise. And if you're just starting out, targeting IT departments in an industry in which you have a personal interest is an effective way to focus your job hunting and kick off your career.

This chapter takes a look at some of the key trends in the top industries for IT professionals and the impact those trends are having on IT projects and priorities. Some common trends that are shaping IT across all industries include the following:

▶ A growing reliance on the Web to reach existing and new customers, as well as suppliers and employees.

▶ Alliances among competitors to codevelop business-to-business (B2B) websites and online industry marketplaces and exchanges.

▶ Industry consolidation through mergers and acquisitions, which puts pressure on IT to help combine business processes and eliminate redundancies.

▶ A focus on core enterprise-wide applications such as customer relationship management (CRM) and supply-chain management as companies move to get the right product or resource to the right people at the right time.

TIP In addition to reading computer publications, read The Wall Street Journal *and the trade publications that apply to your company's business. If you're working for a food and beverage company, read* Supermarket News; *if you're in the catalog division of a major retailer, read* Catalog Age; *if you're in publishing, read* MediaWeek. *Besides covering industry news, most trade publications now include a technology section. You won't want to rely on them exclusively for your technology news, but because they're generally written to appeal to executive readers, you'll get the technology angle with a heavy emphasis on the management whys and wherefores. Moreover, a number of computer publications cater to readers in specific industry niches, such as* Manufacturing Systems. *Industry organization websites can also be useful for keeping up with new trends and understanding management concerns. And stay clued in to your company's position within its industry by reading the annual report, attending shareholder meetings, and following news posted on the company intranet.*

Energy

The energy industry, including utilities and oil and gas companies, is an exciting, if unpredictable, one for IT professionals. Each niche is undergoing tremendous change with mergers and acquisitions and the energy crisis that hit in the winter of 2000–2001.

With the deregulation of gas and electric utilities ostensibly opening up both competition and opportunity, local utility companies are leveraging IT to distinguish themselves through superior customer service or to open up new business segments. Key IT systems in electric and gas utilities include customer relationship management, resource management systems, forecasting systems, data warehouses, web-enabled buying and selling of power capacity, and workflow automation tools to make them more efficient and more responsive in the newly competitive environment.

The use of IT in oil and gas companies is multifaceted. Key applications include SCM systems, geographic information systems and computation-intensive oil and gas exploration systems, as well as providing research and development (R&D) support systems for engineers, geologists, and others. As for hardware platforms, oil and gas companies typically have a highly heterogeneous environment with everything from supercomputers to mainframes to network servers and workstations. Conoco, for example, developed its own Linux-based supercomputer to analyze seismic data that aids in its exploration for oil and gas reserves. The company developed the computer in-house by integrating Intel microprocessors, a massive storage system, and proprietary analysis software. The project is a significant example of the industry's unique and complex systems requirements.

UTILITIES IT LEADERS   Reliant Energy., Houston, Tex.; Peco Energy, Philadelphia, Pa.; Avista Corp., Spokane, Wash.; Florida Power & Light, Juno Beach, Fla.; CP&L, Raleigh, N.C.

OIL AND GAS IT LEADERS   Enron Corp., Houston, Tex.; Chevron Corp., San Francisco, Calif.; Amerada Hess Corp., New York, N.Y.; Phillips Petroleum Co., Bartlesville, Okla.; ExxonMobil Corp., Irving, Tex.

INDUSTRY WEBSITES   ElectricNet, www.electricnet.com; Oil.com, News and Directory for the Oil and Gas Industry, www.oil.com; Platts, www.platts.com (includes a special section on IT in the energy business, www.platts.com/infotech/index.shtml); Power Marketing Association (PMA) Online, www.powermarketers.com; World Energy News, www.worldenergynews.com.

What It's Like to Work in Energy Industry IT

Kay Sallee, corporate IT services manager, Phillips Petroleum Co. (www.phillips66.com), Bartlesville, Okla.; October 2000.

NUMBER OF IT EMPLOYEES   About 400 in Bartlesville, plus 196 dispersed across oil refineries, rigs, and other business units worldwide.

NUMBER OF EMPLOYEES (END-USERS)   About 2,450 in Bartlesville; 12,110 worldwide.

MAJOR IT INITIATIVES   E-business (B2B and B2C), expanding the intranet, knowledge management, a Windows 2000 migration and, in 2001, an SAP upgrade.

WHAT'S UNIQUE ABOUT WORKING IN IT IN THE OIL AND GAS INDUSTRY?   "We have a lot of emphasis on the use of technology to help us improve exploration and production processes—seismic data collection and analysis, geophysics, geographic information systems, drilling information systems. There's a lot of number crunching; it's calculation-intensive. And we have a unique user base—lots of engineers and a big research and development community that's exploring alternate fuel technologies."

HOW IS WORKING IN CORPORATE IT DIFFERENT FROM WORKING IN THE VARIOUS UNITS? "We have to work harder here in Bartlesville to keep our focus on the business because we're not on a rig or in a refinery. Those folks—by virtue of where they are—their focus is very clearly on the business."

WHAT KIND OF WORK DOES IT DO IN A REFINERY?   "Process control work, lab information management systems, [creating] interfaces with real-time data collection from the instruments, data analysis."

IT TRAINING IN 2000   Windows 2000 network and systems administration, intrapersonal communication, knowledge management, web-related technologies, and SAP.

IT CAREER PATH OPTIONS   "We have various job models; most of my staff are 'business solutions providers.' We don't have a regimented progression plan, but we like to move people through the different business units."

WORK DAY   "It's a nine- to ten-hour day. Most people arrive between 7:00 and 8:00 A.M. and leave between 5:00 and 7:00 P.M. We also have flextime. In IT, we have a change weekend once a month where people work through a Saturday night on operating system upgrades, hardware change-outs, and preventative maintenance."

DRESS CODE   Casual.

CORPORATE CAMPUS   "We take up a pretty good portion of downtown Bartlesville with four buildings that are all connected by an underground tunnel system, plus a hospitality building that has the cafeteria and meeting rooms. And just on the edge of town is the R&D campus. IT is spread out, but most of us are in one building."

MUST PEOPLE CARRY BEEPERS? CELL PHONES?   "Yes, about 40 percent of the corporate IT staff does, including infrastructure staff or those who support 24/7 applications."

ONSITE AMENITIES "A recreation complex downtown for employees, retirees, and their families. It has a gym, a bowling alley, a swimming pool, and a recreation staff to coordinate activities like volleyball leagues, basketball games, and programs for kids like gymnastics and swimming."

LITTLE PERKS IT parties, such as a make-your-own-sundaes party and a Halloween pumpkin-carving contest, and recognition rewards. "Our CIO really believes in celebrating successes and recognizing people's contributions, and that takes on many faces. We keep a drawer full of things like Wal-Mart gift certificates, movie passes, and certificates for restaurants."

NOTE *An edited version of this interview appeared in* Computerworld *on October 23, 2000.*

Entertainment

Information technology jobs in entertainment can be as glamorous as the industry itself. Consider the web staff at Playboy Entertainment, Beverly Hills, California, which dons silk pajamas and smoking jackets for parties at the Playboy Mansion. They're invited not to mingle with the celebrity guests, but rather to produce cybercasts of the parties for Playboy's subscription-only website. They may not get friendly with Hef, but one former manager of technology services at Playboy Entertainment said that during his tenure, he frequently bumped into him.

But glamorous IT gigs are not guaranteed. Entertainment companies, with the exception of gaming developers and special-effects houses, traditionally haven't been the most aggressive users of information technology. Walk into a typical end-user's office at a television network, for example, and up until a few years ago, the PC was likely to be on a special table in the corner—not front-and-center on the user's desk. That's all changing now as the Web has emerged as a key platform for delivery of the industry's main product: content. As entertainment companies have learned to leverage the Web for content, they've also started to rely more on email and intranets for communicating internally and externally.

While that may not be as exciting as a night at a Playboy Mansion cybercast, perhaps even more alluring than that is seeing your name on the big screen as the credits of a blockbuster movie roll by. In special-effects houses and post-production studios, IT support is of the utmost importance. The artists and animators who are creating and manipulating the dinosaurs in *Jurassic Park* or the toys in *Toy Story* are under intense deadline pressure. They risk revenue and reputations if they fail to get a finished movie or commercial out the door on time. The IT staff supporting them has to be top notch, sure of their skills, highly motivated, and willing to do whatever it takes to keep its number-crunching systems up and running. "Not everyone in the world is cut out for the pressures of working in the movie business," says Andy Hendrickson, director of systems development at Industrial Light & Magic (ILM), San Rafael, California. "We have absolute deadlines, and some people are not used to that. Our people come out as a cut above on being able to do whatever's necessary to make deadlines happen. That's key to a successful business here."

TOP ENTERTAINMENT IT LEADERS* CBS Corp. (wholly owned by Viacom Inc.), New York, N.Y.; Industrial Light & Magic, San Rafael, Calif.; Walt Disney Co., Burbank, Calif.; Home Box Office Inc. (wholly owned by AOL Time Warner), New York, N.Y.; NBC, New York, N.Y.

NOTE **List derived from various sources.*

INDUSTRY WEBSITES ShowBizJobs.com, www.showbizjobs.com; 365Broadcast, 365Post, and 365ProAudio, interactive community sites for broadcast, post-production, and audio recording professionals, www.365broadcast.com, www.365post.com, and www.365proaudio.com; *CGI* magazine, www.cgimag.com; *Multichannel News*, trade publication for cable television industry, www.multichannel.com; *Entertainment and the Digital Economy*, monthly publication covering the entertainment companies on the Internet, ev.variety.com.

What It's Like to Work in Entertainment Industry IT

Andy Hendrickson, director of systems development, Industrial Light & Magic (www.ilm.com), a division of LucasFilms Ltd., San Rafael, Calif.; October 1999.

ILM is the visual-effects studio that helped create such films as *Star Wars: Episode I*, *The Mummy*, *Saving Private Ryan*, *Men in Black*, *The Lost World: Jurassic Park*, and *Twister*, among others.

NUMBER OF IT EMPLOYEES Just over 45.

NUMBER OF EMPLOYEES (END-USERS) About 1,000.

WHAT KINDS OF PROJECTS DO END-USERS WORK ON? "Everything from commercials to big budget feature films. The scope of images is from big explosions and spaceships and dinosaurs all the way down to more subtle effects like background scenery replacement—like the jungle scenes in *Forest Gump*."

WHAT IS IT RESPONSIBLE FOR?   "We support the people designing the special effects. We're a 24/7 facility; photorealistic computation is going on night and day here—rendering, compositioning. Making the visuals we see on the movie screen takes hours and hours of computation. We're a very large site, and we have a number of supercomputers here—Silicon Graphics Origin 2000s—that we keep busy chewing away on these problems. Any time any of these systems fails, we might not get an image out the next day, and we have severe drop-dead dates for deadlines. Slipping on any of those would be disastrous. When you see a trailer in the movie theater, the movie is still not done. And [the trailers] are telling viewers when the movie will open, and we have to have it out the door on that date. We have to finish it about three weeks before the opening so the distributor has time to make prints and send it out."

WHAT'S THE IT MISSION?   "The systems development mission is to provide next-generation computing facilities on which the images can be made. That includes evaluating and building new clusters of supercomputers; evaluating and modifying new types of file systems in which to hold these images; and designing and constructing business logic solutions for motion picture image generation—like job control, process monitoring, data center–type stuff. But it's an interesting environment because we're not a transaction processing–oriented house.

"We also do all our own payroll, financial, and backend systems. There are two divisions—graphics and image generation support, and business applications support."

WORK DAY   About 9:00 A.M. to 6:00 P.M. "There's overtime if we're [trying] to get a show out the door. The typical work day consists of going to dailies and screening what happened the night before, working on any number of long-term projects, and the inevitable short-term emergency."

DRESS CODE   "You can't come to work naked. Shoes are optional. Jeans and a button-down shirt [are] about as formal as it gets. I've never seen anyone wear a tie here since I came on board in 1989."

KIND OF OFFICES   A campus environment with 22 buildings. "We don't have cubes, but rather, a maze of 5.5- and 6-foot-tall walls and individual work areas. We specifically avoid the Dilbert cubicle look. Because we have very creative people here, a lot of the offices are creatively outfitted—we're encouraged to customize our workspace."

DÉCOR   "Wild. We have some deep purple walls, red walls, yellow walls, white walls. The color scheme is all over the place, and the offices are decorated with models from past films, like R2-D2 prototypes, Imhotep statues from *The Mummy*, dinosaur reference models from *Jurassic Park*. We have an antique mummy sarcophagus. There's a life-sized Darth Vader in the reception area. It's a very organic work environment. It's not a rigid, structured environment—ILM abhors that."

LITTLE PERKS   Free weekend screenings of new movies; impromptu, catered parties on Friday afternoons; wrap parties held offsite when a production is completed; an annual offsite Christmas party; and an annual Halloween party. "You can imagine the costumes people put together. They're spectacular, and the company gives great prizes like a trip to Hawaii or an SGI [Silicon Graphics Inc.] workstation to take home. The costumes are always a big secret until the party."

DOES THE IT STAFF EVER GET SCREEN CREDIT?   "Some of us get our names on the screen—listed as 'production support' or 'production engineering and systems development.' I've had mine listed many times, and it's always a thrill."

NOTE *An edited version of this interview appeared in* Computerworld *on October 18, 1999.*

Financial Services

As a group, investment firms, consumer banks, the various stock exchanges, and credit card companies are among the most cutting-edge users of IT. In fact, among the *InformationWeek* 500 list, an annual listing of leading IT users, 37 of the publication's picks for 2000 were in banking and financial services, giving those two segments one of the best representations of the 24 industries covered. The leaders of the pack were those who had most aggressively leveraged the Internet for doing business with customers.

In fact, the Internet has enabled the development of a whole new class of financial services firms: the online trading firms like Etrade, cyber banks like WingSpan, and more. NextCard, a company specializing in online credit services, went public in just under three years and grew to over 500 employees in only four years.

At the same time, with financial services firms among the oldest users of information technology, this industry still has its fair share of legacy mainframe systems, as well as a plethora of industry-specific software and applications, like trading systems and online quote systems. In addition, they typically have a healthy amount of original applications development underway, and their online trading sites, such as Charles Schwab & Company's Schwab Online and Fidelity Investment's Powerstreet, have become key platforms for future growth. The bottom line: Whatever technology you're interested in working with, any given financial services firm is likely to be using it.

In consumer banking and credit card companies, major applications include loan and credit-line processing, CRM, and data mining. Especially with mergers and acquisitions, the ability to give customer service reps (CSRs) a full picture of a customer's various accounts, investments, and credit cards is key to cross-selling products and services and lowering customer attrition.

Because the IT requirements are so all-encompassing in financial services, investment firms, banks, and credit card companies are fertile ground for beginning IT professionals. They tend to invest in a lot of training, and on the whole, their corporate cultures have become somewhat less formal over the past few years. On the other hand, when the going gets tough economically or during mergers, financial services firms have been known to have massive layoffs.

BANKING IT LEADERS ABN Amro Holding N.V., Amsterdam; J.P. Morgan Chase & Co., New York, N.Y.; Mellon Financial Corp., Pittsburgh, Pa.; PNC Financial Services Group Inc., Pittsburgh, Pa.; First Union Corp., Charlotte, N.C.

INVESTMENT SERVICES IT LEADERS CIT Group Inc., New York, N.Y.; FMR Corp., Boston, Mass.; CountryWide Credit Industries Inc., Calabasas, Calif.; Charles Schwab & Co., San Francisco, Calif.; Capital One Financial Corp., Richmond, Va.

INDUSTRY WEBSITES American Bankers Association, www.aba.com; America's Community Bankers, www.acbankers.org; *Bank Systems & Technology*, www.banktech.com; *Wall Street & Technology*, www.wallstreetandtech.com.

What It's Like to Work in Financial Services IT

Vincent Phillips, vice president of web systems, Electronic Brokerage Technology, Charles Schwab & Co. Inc. (www.schwab.com), San Francisco, Calif.; September 1999.

NUMBER OF IT EMPLOYEES Almost 300 in the electronic brokerage group; 1,600 in the entire IT organization, including a data center in Phoenix, Arizona, and three regional processing centers.

NUMBER OF EMPLOYEES (END-USERS) Around 12,000.

NUMBER OF REGISTERED USERS AT WEBSITE Over 2 million.

DRESS CODE "It depends on who you ask. The chairman certainly thinks there is one, but if you look closely at what employees are wearing, you'd think there's not. It's very lax—no holes in your clothes and nothing obscene written on your t-shirts. I have one guy [who] has a different pair of eyeglasses and shoes to go with each outfit.

And then I have people with wildly colored hair and pierced body parts. There's a number of Silicon Valley–type programmers here, too."

WORK DAY "The typical programmer saunters in between 9:00 and 10:00 A.M. or later, and god knows when they go home. The quality-assurance folks either come in really early or really late so they can test things without interference from the developers. The day-to-day production support folks come in just before the market opens, around 6:00 A.M., and go home just past the close."

MUST PEOPLE CARRY BEEPERS? CELL PHONES? Most everyone carries a pager. Managers and production-support people carry cell phones.

PERCENT OF STAFF THAT TELECOMMUTES ON A GIVEN DAY Three to five percent. "The company has a fairly new formal telecommuting policy, but our group has always had an informal policy of allowing people to telecommute on demand. Our people are savvy Internet users and have good setups at home. [We have] a few who telecommute from long distances—one from Provo, Utah; one from the Sierra foothills; one from Southern California. They come into the offices three or four days a week."

ONSITE AMENITIES A concierge who takes care of dry cleaning, laundry, and just about anything else involving pickups and deliveries.

WHY DO YOU LIKE WORKING AT SCHWAB? "Everyone knows we are here to do something great for customers. People don't come to work to make a lot of money, but to work on cool stuff that real people use and that is useful to them. That's why I work here, and that's why people come here and stay. If it's not good for customers, we don't do it, and if something is good for customers, we figure out a way to do it."

 NOTE An edited version of this interview appeared in Computerworld *on September 13, 1999.*

Food and Beverage

If your interest lies in working within an industry that touches every person, every day, what could be more germane than working in food and beverage processing? And if food and drink are a preoccupation of the general public, IT is a preoccupation of food and beverage companies, which are constantly seeking ways to reduce costs, increase customer loyalty, make timely marketing decisions, and reinforce branding.

These companies, which in the seventies helped drive the use of the bar code as a means of identifying products (see Chapter 2), are now among the leaders in the formation of online B2B marketplaces, such as Transora.com. They've also been creative users of the Web to reach out directly to consumers, a smart move for companies whose products pass through many hands before actually making it into shoppers' grocery carts. The Pillsbury Company, for example, maintains myriad websites aligned with its various brands, from www.greengiant.com to www.haagendazs.com. Kraft Foods' website is chock full of recipe ideas—using Kraft ingredients, of course—ranging from a searchable cookbook to an interactive meal planner.

Large companies in this industry spent an average of 1.55 percent of annual revenues on IT in 1998, according to a 1999 study conducted by the Grocery Manufacturers of America (GMA) and CSC Consulting, an IT market research firm. The amount of spending wasn't expected to change much over the next few years, but IT priorities definitely shifted—from a focus on Y2K compliance and transaction-oriented systems to web initiatives and decision support systems. Small-to-medium companies, which are still playing catch-up on IT infrastructure and basic systems, are planning to increase IT spending from 1.12 percent of annual revenue in 1998 to 1.49 percent over the next several years, according to the study.

Key IT systems for food and beverage processors include supply-chain management, packaging and distribution, forecasting, and inventory management. They're big users of electronic data interchange (EDI), and if they maintain their own trucking fleets for shipping their products, then they have transportation scheduling and maintenance systems. And if the GMA has any sway (and it does), data mining will likely be a top IT project in the coming years. Another GMA report, released in April 2000, showed that data-mining partnerships between grocers and food companies could increase sales by as much as 10 percent by pinpointing specific consumer habits and buying trends.

FOOD AND BEVERAGE IT LEADERS   McCormick & Co., Sparks, Md.; Nabisco Inc., Parsippany, N.J.; Kraft Foods Inc., Northfield, Ill.; E & J Gallo Winery, Healdsburg, Calif.; General Mills Inc., Minneapolis, Minn.

INDUSTRY WEBSITES   Barbecue Industry Association, bbqind.org; The Food Institute, www.foodinstitute.com, Grocery Manufacturers of America, www.gmabrands.com; Institute of Food Technologists, www.ift.org; National Coffee Association, www.ncausa.org; National Food Processors Association, www.nfpa-food.org; *Supermarket News*, www.supermarketnews.com; Uniform Code Council Food and Beverage Page, www.uccouncil.org/focus_by_industry/fi_food_and_beverage.html.

What It's Like to Work in Food and Beverage Industry IT

Jason Womack, network services manager, Kendall-Jackson Winery Ltd. (www.kj.com), Santa Rosa, Calif.; July 1999.

NUMBER OF IT EMPLOYEES   18.

NUMBER OF EMPLOYEES (END-USERS)   About 550, including 150 remote users.

DRESS CODE   Business casual. "Jeans and a dress shirt are not uncommon, but t-shirts and tennis shoes are."

WORK DAY   "It varies by the season. There are people who come at 5:30 A.M. and leave at 7:00 P.M. They're responsible for a major in-house developed application [for] grape harvest season. Others are here 8:00 A.M. to 5:00 P.M."

WHEN'S THE HARVEST?   "It depends on the weather. It could start as early as July, but usually it starts between late August and mid-September. If it's very hot, we have to get [the grapes] off the vine early, or if it's really moist, we could have mold issues."

WHAT ISSUES DOES THE HARVEST RAISE FOR IT?   "Our end-users are monitoring the vineyards and logging data all the way from when we plant the seedlings to the harvest, but there's more of a hit on our system as we get ready for harvest. People are working frantically to monitor blocks [of grapevines] to determine their readiness, their expected harvest dates, what brands and bottles they might go into, etc., so there's a lot of additional input into the system as we ramp up. And a lot of our facilities are operating 24/7 during that time, and the system has to be available or we could have trucks with grapes just sitting on them. So we have to be on call and our support team has to be flexible and responsive."

WHAT'S IT LIKE TO WORK WITH WINEMAKERS?   "They're not shirt-and-tie number crunchers. They have less of an anal mentality, for lack of a better word. They perceive of themselves as creating art in a bottle, and they take great pride in their work. We [in IT] have a more personal relationship with them than I've had in my previous work experiences. They're less uptight about deadlines and are very agreeable and open-minded to new ideas. Generally speaking, they're early adopters of new technologies."

MUST PEOPLE CARRY BEEPERS? CELL PHONES?   "We all have beepers across the board. Some managers and tech support people have Nextel phones—they're kind of like walkie-talkies but with a 500-mile range. They also have cellular capability."

LITTLE PERKS   "The company gives away bottles of wine for Thanksgiving and other holidays for those who are interested. We try to have morale lunches when we complete a big project. And we have a harvest party after the harvest in the fall."

IS WINE SERVED AT STAFF MEETINGS?   "No. Pastry—the person who was on call over the weekend is responsible for bringing pastry to the staff meeting on the following Tuesday."

WHAT DO YOU LIKE ABOUT WORKING AT A WINERY?   "I came here from a mortgage company, and the environment there—where you're dealing with customers' personal finances—was a lot more stressful and hierarchical. Here, it's a lot more artistic and creative, so it's more relaxed in comparison."

NOTE   *An edited version of this interview appeared in* Computerworld *on July 26, 1999.*

Freight and Transportation

This is an industry marked by a relatively small number of dominant players: FedEx, UPS, and Airborne Express on the package delivery end; and J.B. Hunt Transport Services, Ryder, and Roadway Express, on the freight side. But it's one in which IT really packs a wallop and can quickly distinguish one player from the others. Without a doubt, FedEx is the industry leader when it comes to the use of IT, and it's exactly that fact that has made it the dominant player overall in package shipping. It was the first company, for example, to use bar coding to enable package tracking, now a commonplace application.

Key applications in both industry segments center around knowing what shipments are where at any given time. Superior customer service is the lifeblood of the industry, and the major players were among the first to offer self-service via the Web and now are racing to be first with wireless customer service offerings. Route planning, shipping, load balancing, and fuel and maintenance forecasting and planning are essential applications for smooth and cost-efficient operation. J.B. Hunt Transport Services, in Lowell, Arkansas, for example, uses its massive data warehouse to analyze such key operations data as mileage, pricing, costs of accidents, and more.

A unique aspect of IT in freight and transport is the prevalence of handheld devices used by drivers and field personnel for dispatching, routing, and package tracking. To gain a user's perspective on the technology being deployed and how it affects their jobs, Patty Conway, manager of field services technologies for Airborne Express, in Seattle, Washington, suggests "that all the IT support folks spend a day on the trucks to understand what the business is all about. That helps immensely."

FREIGHT AND TRANSPORT IT LEADERS   FedEx Corp., Memphis, Tenn.; United Parcel Service of America Inc., Atlanta, Ga.; CNF Transportation Inc., Palo Alto, Calif.; DHL Airways Inc., Redwood City, Calif.; Roadway Express Inc., Akron, Ohio.

INDUSTRY WEBSITES   Council of Logistics Management, www.clm1.org; The Internet Truckstop, www.truckstop.com; Layover.com, www.layover.com; Transport Link, www.transportlink.com; Transport World, www.transportworld.com; Uniform Code Council Industrial/Commercial Page, www.uc-council.org/focus_by_industry/fi_industrial_commercial.html.

What It's Like to Work in Freight and Transport Industry IT

Patty Conway, manager of field services technologies, Airborne Freight Corp., dba Airborne Express (www.airborne.com), Seattle, Wash.; April 2000.

WHAT IS THE FIELD SERVICES UNIT?   The liaison between central IT, the drivers (about 14,000), and the local dispatch stations (about 300 worldwide). "We're a hybrid of IT and functional experience, responsible for defining systems requirements for the field, working with IT to build the systems, and testing and deploying the systems."

NUMBER OF IT EMPLOYEES   "We have six now in field services, and we're ramping up for a wireless project, so we'll be 30 by spring 2001." Central IT has 440 employees.

NUMBER OF EMPLOYEES (END-USERS)   About 20,000.

MAJOR PROJECT (IN FIELD SERVICES)   "We just got funded [$50 million for 5 years] to do a wireless real-time dispatch and proof-of-delivery system, so we're in a ramp-up mode to get the development and deployment going. We also do the business case development and the financials, so we're part of a much longer life cycle than just the IT life cycle."

HOW WILL THE PROJECT CHANGE FIELD OPERATIONS?   "Right now, we have a very decentralized voice environment, using acoustic couplers to download information twice a day." The new system will use two-way Motorola pagers to relay information. "The benefit of this system will be moving to a paperless environment and getting information to our customers much more quickly."

TECHNOLOGY TRAINING PLANS FOR THE PROJECT   "Most of our training is hands-on. The technical groups doing the systems testing will get more technology training, but the deployment group will get more on-the-job, hands-on training."

WORK DAY   "Because we're an international company and we're on the West Coast, people come in early—between 6:30 and 7:30 A.M.—and they leave between 4:00 and 5:00 P.M., unless we're on a critical project. Then it's lots of hours all the time. During deployments, we work on weekends because we're a six-day-a-week operation."

BONUS PROGRAMS   "We have an annual bonus based on corporate performance, and we have the APEX [Airborne Project for Excellence] program, which is ongoing throughout the year. People are nominated for going above and beyond what would be considered normal performance, and winners are recognized with a cash award."

DRESS CODE   Business casual. "It tends to be more casual [in IT] than some of the traditional business units."

MUST PEOPLE CARRY BEEPERS? CELL PHONES?   "We wear pagers with real-time email, and we carry cell phones when we're doing deployments and rollouts. At this point, we don't have an on-call rotation, but we will have to work that out as we get further along in the project. We're not often called in after-hours because support for field systems is provided by central IT, so we only have to get involved if there's a major problem."

LITTLE PERKS   Discounts on major airlines; free passes to local attractions like zoos and museums.

WHAT DO YOU LIKE ABOUT WORKING AT AIRBORNE?   "It's a tremendous opportunity working with the field and ensuring that IT builds the systems that they require. I think we add a lot of value."

NOTE *And edited version of this interview appeared in* Computerworld *on May 1, 2000.*

Government

The federal government has downsized overall in the last eight years, and federal agency IT organizations have outsourced much of their analysis, development, and maintenance work. Nonetheless, federal agencies are looking to IT to enable them to carry on business with fewer people. So they find themselves in need of "experienced IT managers who can run a competition for services, manage a project, and make the business case for new efforts," says Sandra Gibson, chief information officer (CIO) and director of the information technology and communications division at National Aeronautics and Space Administration (NASA) headquarters, in Washington, D.C.

Moreover, an emphasis on using technology to bring government to the people pushed federal, state, and local government agencies onto the Web during the Clinton-Gore administration. With an increased reliance on the Web for communicating with the public and recent cases of hackers taking over government websites, Internet security specialists "can probably write their own tickets," Gibson says. As of this printing, it remains to be seen what changes the Bush-Cheney administration will bring to federal IT, but *Computerworld* reported in January 2001 that federal CIOs expect new online initiatives and a shift toward centralized, cross-agency IT management ("Bush Expected to Rattle Federal IT," by Patrick Thibodeau, January 22, 2001).

Some IT professionals say working in civil service IT carries a bias; those who choose to go the government route will inevitably face a general assumption held by other IT professionals that they just aren't sharp enough to cut it in private industry. While certain segments of government IT may lag behind the private sector, the overall move toward making government more efficient means that IT's role is more critical than ever.

In addition to project management and security skills, government IT agencies are in need of website development skills and systems integration skills to help them tie new front-end systems to legacy backend systems.

GOVERNMENT IT LEADERS   Top State and Local Applications of IT (according to Civic.com's "State and Local 50" at www.civic.com/supplements/SL50/2000/intro.asp): Madison, Wis., Online Property Information System; New York State Online Permit Database; Connecticut Department of Social Services Biometric Identification Project.

INDUSTRY WEBSITES   The Council for Excellence in Government, www.excelgov.org; *Federal Computer Week*, www.fcw.com; *Federal Employees News Digest*, www.FENDonline.com; *Government Technology*, www.govtech.net; Uniform Code Council Government Page, www.uc-council.org/focus_by_industry/fi_government.html.

What It's Like to Work in Government IT

Sandra Daniels-Gibson, director of the information technology and communications division of NASA and CIO of NASA Headquarters (www.nasa.gov), Washington, D.C.; August 1999.

NUMBER OF IT EMPLOYEES   Just over 20 permanent staff members and 300 contractors. "We outsource a lot of activities—that's a trend in federal government."

WHAT ARE SOME PERMANENT STAFF POSITIONS? "Contract technical representatives, who manage our contract support; service managers, who are like end-user liaisons; software engineers, who put together systems requirements and specs; the IT security manager; the acquisition manager for hardware and software purchases; and the person responsible for all of our internal communications."

NUMBER OF EMPLOYEES (END-USERS) Around 1,200 in Washington.

WHAT ACTIVITIES IS NASA HQ IT RESPONSIBLE FOR? "This is more of a corporate site, where all the administrators reside who have oversight for all NASA programs and centers. So we support financial and personnel systems, budgeting, the liaisons to Congress and the White House, the chief engineer, and the chief scientist. We also support all external communications, like the NASA home page and our kids-only website. We also help out at the White House if they are having a [NASA-related] function, like an event for the nation's teachers. We created a CD-ROM for the recent Apollo 11 anniversary. Or, if an administrator is going up to Capitol Hill to present our budget and wants a high-tech CD-ROM-based presentation, we would put that together."

DRESS CODE "It ranges from business to business casual, and we have dress-down Fridays."

WORK DAY "As early as 6:00 A.M. to 6:00 P.M. and later. We also have an alternate work schedule where you can work a nine-hour day and have one day off every other week."

MUST PEOPLE CARRY BEEPERS? CELL PHONES? Beepers.

ONSITE AMENITIES "We have an onsite fitness center, and that's of big interest here."

LITTLE PERKS "When you've done a good job on a project, you can go to a launch at the Kennedy Space Center at Cape Canaveral. We also get free tickets to events at the Air and Space Museum. And at any given time, one of the astronauts is likely to be here giving a presentation in the auditorium, and that's really nice."

WHAT DO YOU LIKE ABOUT WORKING AT NASA? "We're quite busy here because we have the customer focus of making sure our users' desktop requirements are taken care of as well as any number of special projects, like becoming ISO 9000–certified. That's a quality assurance stamp that says our processes and procedures are documented and consistent across NASA. And because we're NASA, a lot of what we do and support involves leading-edge technologies, like an intelligence synthesis environment—using virtual reality as a way of collaborating or having meetings without all being in the same place. So we get to support a lot of things that we wouldn't in other jobs. The variety of work keeps it interesting for us."

NOTE *An edited version of this interview appeared in* Computerworld *on August 23, 1999.*

Healthcare

Healthcare providers, such as medical centers, hospitals, and HMOs, and the products and services companies that furnish the equipment, supplies, lab work, and other essentials used by care providers comprise a highly IT-dependent industry. Given that the baby-boomer generation is aging, lifespans are lengthening, and government is pushing for healthcare reform, IT is critical to managing care, controlling costs, and ensuring continued advancements in medical technology.

The predominant IT skill set needed by healthcare providers is the ability to make disparate systems talk to each other. In hospitals, outpatient clinics, nursing homes, and other care facilities, where information for patient records must be pulled together from laboratory data systems, clinical systems, billing, pharmacy systems, and others, integration skills are essential. On top of that hard-to-find skill, medical institutions tend to use a lot of specialized industry-specific software, and a familiarity with those packages is a huge plus in hospital IT departments. Around-the-clock IT support is essential—the phrase "mission-critical system" takes on a whole new meaning when system downtime could result in diminished patient care.

In the product and services segment, IT provides support for manufacturing systems, research and development, sales and distribution, and, in laboratories, diagnostics facilities. Working for a healthcare products company would be good background for IT professionals who want to transition from manufacturing IT into medical center IT or vice versa.

HEALTHCARE PROVIDERS IT LEADERS CareGroup Healthcare Systems, Boston, Mass.; Sun Healthcare Group Inc., Albuquerque, N.M.; Quorum Health Group Inc., Brentwood, Tenn.; HCA-The Healthcare Co., Nashville, Tenn.; UPMC Health System, Pittsburgh, Pa.

HEALTHCARE PRODUCTS AND SERVICES IT LEADERS Laboratory Corp. of America, Burlington, N.C.; Becton Dickinson & Co., Franklin Lakes, N.J.; Quest Diagnostics Inc.,

Teterboro, N.J.; Dade Behring Holdings, Deerfield, Ill.; Cardinal Health Inc., Dublin, Ohio.

INDUSTRY WEBSITES   Advanced Medical Technology Association, www.himanet.com; American Hospital Association, www.aha.org; American Medical Informatics Association, www.amia.org; Federation of American Hospitals, www.fahs.com; *Healthcare Business*, www.healthcarebusiness.com; Medical Records Institute, www.medrecinst.com; *Modern Healthcare*, www.modernhealthcare.com; Uniform Code Council Healthcare Page, www.uc-council.org/focus_by_industry/fi_healthcare.html.

What It's Like to Work in Healthcare Industry IT

Steve Dlubala, database administrator (DBA), Johns Hopkins Medical Institutions (infonet.welch.jhu.edu), a teaching hospital, patient-care facility, and research center, Baltimore, Md.; September 1999.

NUMBER OF IT EMPLOYEES   "Just shy of 200 in central IT; several larger departments in the hospital that have specialized technology—like the Oncology Center or the pathology labs—have their own IT organizations."

WHAT GROUP ARE YOU IN?   "In central IT—in a DBA group supporting the clinical applications, mainly patient care–oriented systems."

NUMBER OF EMPLOYEES (END-USERS)   "In excess of 5,000; we also have remote physicians who are accessing patient data."

DRESS CODE   "Semi-business—shirts and ties, but suits or sports coats are not required. No jeans or sneakers, except on Fridays. Friday is an official casual day."

WORK DAY   "We're unofficially on flex-time. Most people arrive between 8:00 and 9:00 A.M. and leave between 4:30 and 6:00 P.M. But on a project basis, we often have application implementations or changes on Thursday mornings, so we'll have six to ten people here at 4:00 A.M."

WHAT IS MOST CHALLENGING ABOUT WORKING IN A MEDICAL CENTER?   "Support for the applications. Because we're a hospital, and a lot of data is critical data, we have care providers who are depending on [access to] it 24 hours a day. So we're very strong on the post-implementation support side. And it's my impression that because of that, proportionately, we have a larger number of 24-hour on-call support staff than other businesses would."

HOW MANY ARE ON CALL AT ANY GIVEN TIME? Fifteen to twenty people. "We'll have three to four people on call for specific application areas, and a rotation lasts one to two weeks. They all carry beepers and most have cell phones now, too. Most of us have company-supplied PCs at home, so unless you're responsible for the network or a specific piece of hardware, you should be able to handle most things from home. On rotation, you'll typically get called an average of six times a week after-hours."

HOW DO DOCTORS AND NURSES MEASURE UP AS END-USERS? "Considering the pressures they have on them in caring for patients and needing accurate data right away, they are fairly cooperative, intelligent, and responsive for the most part. Some are resistant to change, but you see that in any place."

WHAT DO YOU LIKE ABOUT WORKING AT JOHNS HOPKINS? "Being challenged by the diversity of applications and computer systems that we have here. I've spent a good amount of time on getting various hardware platforms to talk to each other and send data back and forth. I've been in the database group three years, and I started out as a mainframe systems programmer. So, over 18 years, I've had a range of opportunities to work with different hardware and software."

 NOTE *An edited version of this interview appeared in* Computerworld *on September 20, 1999.*

High Tech and Telecommunications

There was a time when working in the high-tech industry meant you had to live on one of the two coasts. That's not true today, when high-tech companies extend far beyond Silicon Valley or Boston's Route 128 area. Nor does working in the high-tech industry necessarily imply that you are working within the traditional computer and software industry. Corning, for example—a company that the general public commonly associates with Pyrex—has emerged as a high-tech industry leader, providing the majority of the fiber optics used to make fiber optic cables, as well as other high-tech materials and equipment. In fact, Corning, based in upstate New York, divested its Pyrex division in 1998.

The country's leading telecommunications companies also turn up in unlikely locations: Sprint is in Kansas City, Missouri, MCI-Worldcom is in Clinton, Mississippi, and Alltell is in Little Rock, Arkansas. And the telecommunications industry appears unstoppable in its growth with the explosion of new local and long-distance service providers, Internet service providers (ISPs), digital subscriber line (DSL) service providers, and developments in wireless communication.

Working in IT in high tech or telecommunications is a near guarantee of working with the latest and greatest that IT has to offer. Moreover, within software companies lie opportunities to move from internal applications development and support to working on a vendor's various product lines. And, because most high-tech companies now also have consulting arms—such as Oracle, Sun, and IBM—there's the chance of moving into one of those groups. In most cases, having a high-tech or telecommunications company on your résumé is likely to fast-track you for consideration by future employers.

High-tech and telecommunications companies are well known for their great benefits. Many of the cutting-edge benefits offered by leading employers today, such as onsite day care and health clubs, concierge services and casual dress, started in Silicon Valley companies like Apple, Hewlett-Packard, and Intel. (See Chapter 14.)

INFORMATION TECHNOLOGY IT LEADERS   3Com, Santa Clara, Calif.; Compaq Computer Corp., Houston, Tex.; Cisco Systems Inc., San Jose, Calif.; IBM Corp., Armonk, N.Y.; Lucent Technologies Inc., Murray Hill, N.J.

TELECOMMUNICATIONS IT LEADERS   Sprint Corp., Kansas City, Mo.; EchoStar Communications Corp., Littleton, Colo.; SBC Communications Inc., San Antonio, Tex.; World-Com Inc., Clinton, Miss.; Alltel Corp., Little Rock, Ark.

INDUSTRY WEBSITES   American Electronics Association, www.aeanet.org; Association of Communications Enterprises (ASCENT), www.ascent.org; Software & Information Industry Association, www.spa.org.

What It's Like to Work in High-Tech Industry IT

Greg Di Iorio, IT business manager, Telecommunications Products division, Corning Inc. (www.corning.com), Corning, N.Y.; May 2000.

Corning's Telecommunications Products division (www.corningfiber.com) makes the glass for fiber optic products, coats it in plastic, and sells it to the end customer, which uses it to create fiber optic cables.

IS CORNING A COMPANY TOWN?   "We were at one point. It was more of a factory, blue-collar town, but that has changed 180 degrees to more of a professional town. We actually have more Ph.D.s per capita than Silicon Valley. Corning [the company] is always reinventing itself; all of our businesses are in high-tech, fast-growth sectors. And part of our changing image is shedding the 'company-town' designation."

PEOPLE TEND TO THINK OF CORNING (THE COMPANY) IN TERMS OF PYREX AND CORN-INGWARE, BUT YOU ACTUALLY DIVESTED OF THAT BUSINESS IN 1998. WHAT'S THE COMPANY'S BEST-KEPT SECRET? "Corning has been as integral in laying the infrastructure for the Internet as the Ciscos of the world. So now we're emphasizing that we are a major player in the Internet space. Wall Street knows it, but the general public does not."

NUMBER OF IT EMPLOYEES Fourteen in the Telecommunications Products division headquarters office, colocated with the business unit; about 300 globally for the division, dispersed across five fiber optic manufacturing plants; 1,000 in Corning.

WHAT ARE THE DIFFERENCES IN WORKING IN IT AT HQ, AT THE PLANTS, AND AT THE DATA CENTER? "The cultures are somewhat different. At the plants, getting product out the door rules all. Here at headquarters, we're more focused on the sales side and strategic business issues. And at the data center, you're maybe one step removed from the [users]—you don't get that daily interaction with them like when you're sitting right in their lap. There it's more of a technical community, and here we're more involved in the business issues."

NUMBER OF EMPLOYEES (END-USERS) About 5,000 in Telecommunications Products, including 300 in headquarters; about 30,000 in Corning.

CAREER PATH Started as a telecommunications analyst in corporate IT, doing PBX and voice installs; named to lead a corporate messaging initiative in 1996 to implement one consistent email system across the company; next led an Internet infrastructure development project, followed by deploying a remote-access strategy and infrastructure; moved into current position in July 1999.

IS THAT TYPICAL? Yes. "Within Corning IT, there's tremendous opportunity to move around, learn new skills, and work in various divisions. We stress it to keep people fresh."

DRESS CODE Business casual. "It's not formal, but no jeans and sneakers."

WORK DAY "The work day isn't just the hours you put in at the office. We have a unique arrangement because we were one of the first towns in the country to get cable modems, and at Corning, we got secure access from a cable modem network into the Corning network that allows people to work a lot from home. So I usually do email from about 5:30 to 7:00 A.M. and get to the office about 7:30 A.M. I leave about 5:30 P.M., coach baseball, put the kids to bed, and then log in again at 9:00 or 10:00 P.M. to clean up more email or work on a presentation. I try to set a limit of 10:30 P.M. The cable modems are a pretty big perk for us, but sometimes it's a blessing, and sometimes it's a curse."

MUST PEOPLE CARRY BEEPERS? CELL PHONES? "Everybody in IT gets a beeper. We're always on call formally or informally."

CRITICAL IT PROJECTS IN THE TELECOMMUNICATIONS PRODUCTS DIVISION "We're trying to integrate all of our locations—the headquarters offices and the five plants—together with consistent systems. For that, we're depending a lot on the Web, some ERP technologies, some CRM software. We have a couple of major B2B ecommerce initiatives underway as well."

IT TRAINING "We have a unique orientation program in this division called a 'Smart Program' that you go through whether you're in engineering, sales, or IT. It orients you to every functional group in the division and includes presentations on how we develop new products, how we market them, how we do engineering, how we do IT, etc. So new IT people who come in learn exactly how the business runs before they even step up to a keyboard. Technical training will include database, E-applications, web-based applications development, and now that we're bringing ERP into the division, there may be some ERP training."

BONUS PROGRAMS "They're pretty lucrative. We have a company-wide goal-sharing bonus that's based on a mix of meeting corporate and divisional goals. And we have formal recognition programs throughout the year where anybody can nominate anybody else for a job well done. There are divisional cash awards and Individual Outstanding Contributor Awards that can be stock options or cash. So there are various levels of recognition, and it's very democratic."

DÉCOR Japanese-style water gardens and sculpture areas throughout the headquarters building. "It's very light and airy. I sit right by one of those meditation areas, but I'm so busy I don't have time to meditate. I guess maybe I should."

ONSITE DAYCARE? Yes. "Corning helped build two daycare centers, one downtown [near headquarters] and one up on the hill by the Sullivan Park data center. The company indirectly subsidizes them to keep the costs low."

FREE REFRESHMENTS Sodas, juice, water, and coffee, and snacks such as pretzels, Pepperidge Farm Goldfish, and donuts [bear claws and jelly donuts are IT favorites]. "They keep us geeks all wired up."

OFFICE MASCOT   Dilbert. "We have cartoons hanging up everywhere, and my kids gave me the Dilbert boss talking head for Christmas. It says things like, 'This won't look good on your performance review,' and 'It doesn't have to make sense; I'm the boss.'"

WOULD EMPLOYEES FEEL COMFORTABLE EMAILING THE CEO?   "Oh, yeah. As a matter of fact, Corning is a midsize town, and it's very family-friendly and close. So you'll see the [vice chairman, Norm Garrity] of the company in Kmart and say, 'Hey, Norm,' and he'll say, 'Hey, Greg, good to see you again.' Our executives are a very visible part of the community, which is a cool thing about working here."

WHAT DO YOU LIKE ABOUT WORKING AT CORNING?   "We have a very close-knit community of IT folks within the company. There's a healthy sense of competition among the various divisions, but at the same time, we respect each other and work very hard to make each other successful. If you're willing to learn and put out extra effort, the opportunities are endless."

NOTE *An edited version of this interview appeared in* Computerworld *on May 29, 2000.*

Insurance

Many consumers view insurance as a necessary evil and insurance companies as slow-moving behemoths, but IT in these organizations is just the opposite. Because insurance is an information-dependent product, the best insurance companies view IT as a strategic business partner and key contributor to gaining and servicing customers, controlling costs, determining risk, and processing claims. Insurance companies usually support large, thriving IT organizations and tend to be early adopters of new technologies. For example, they were among the first companies to adopt imaging technologies as a core application for claims adjustment and processing.

As insurance companies continue to diversify into financial planning and investment services in addition to personal and corporate insurance packages, the activities in IT are increasingly diversified as well. Customer extranets are a growing trend as insurance companies rely more on customer self-service to lower costs and speed up claims processing. Similarly, extranets to service independent agents and claims adjusters are also a key application. While insurance may not be a glamorous industry, the array of hardware, software, and networking technologies required in insurance

IT today means endless challenges, change, and opportunity for IT professionals who want exposure to myriad technologies and business problems. And the corporate benefits aren't bad, either—where else could you expect to get a better insurance plan?

INSURANCE IT LEADERS   Aetna Inc., Hartford, Conn.; The Hartford Financial Services Group, Hartford, Conn.; Aflac Inc., Columbus, Ga.; Progressive Insurance Casualty Co., Mayfield Village, Ohio; Allstate Insurance Co., Northbrook, Ill.

INDUSTRY WEBSITES   American Insurance Association, www.aiadc.org; Insurance Industry Internet Network, www.iiin.com; Insurance Research Council, www.ircweb.org; *Insurance & Technology*, www.insurancetech.com; National Association of Mutual Insurance Companies, www.namic.org.

What It's Like to Work in Insurance IT

Philip Smith, manager of client/server web development, Aflac Inc. (www.aflac.com), Columbus, Ga.; September 2000.

NUMBER OF IT EMPLOYEES   About 400 in the United States; about 20 in the web development group.

NUMBER OF EMPLOYEES (END-USERS)   About 4,900 in the United States and Japan.

WEBSITE TRAFFIC   "That's increased exponentially since the duck campaign started [the company's television advertising campaign featuring a duck quacking the company's name]. In August, we had 1.1 million hits on our home page vs. 98,000 in August of 1999. That's a 946 percent increase. It's amazing what a little duck can do for you."

WHAT KIND OF PRESSURE HAS THE DUCK PUT ON IT?   "Sales leads for the first three months of this year outpaced all of those for 1998 and 1999 combined. So we've had to beef up a lot of our extranet systems for our field sales associates. But we've had no major meltdowns, knock on wood."

WHAT ACTIVITIES FALL UNDER THE WEB DEVELOPMENT GROUP?   "The Internet site, the intranet, and an extranet for our 30,000-person independent field sales force."

MAJOR INITIATIVES   A website redesign to give it a "real fun" look-and-feel and a new email application that will enable Aflac to send mass emails to the field sales force and will reduce paper generation.

BONUS PROGRAMS "In the past couple of years, they've been incorporating more project-oriented incentives, like a $100 cash reward for meeting a project milestone. And we have a company-wide yearly bonus based on revenue."

DRESS CODE Business casual in IT; business with business-casual Fridays elsewhere in the company.

WORK DAY "My team gets here between 7:00 and 8:00 A.M. and leaves between 4:30 and 6:00 P.M. We're good about keeping normal, steady hours."

MUST PEOPLE CARRY BEEPERS? CELL PHONES? "Web developers only have to carry a beeper if you have a big application going up at the end of the week—then maybe you'll carry one that weekend or something. On the mainframe side, they're on call all the time."

KIND OF OFFICES "Cluttered, right now. The majority of IT is all together in an old building that was a dairy before, but we also have local IT support in each location."

ANY WINDOWS IN IT? "Unfortunately, that's not a luxury we have in IT because we're in an older building. In the new location, I think they're trying to give IT a happier feel."

ONSITE DAYCARE? Yes.

OFFICE MASCOT The duck. "There's been a craze to get stuffed animal ducks. The duck has made everyone a little more lighthearted. Everyone has something to laugh about—especially when one of the new commercials comes out."

LITTLE PERKS Restaurant gift certificates awarded spontaneously; team reward luncheons; annual company Christmas party.

LAST COMPANY-WIDE/DEPARTMENT PERK The annual employee appreciation week in May. "We have a dedicated week with events throughout the week and a big event for the grand finale—like taking your family to a Braves game or going to Six Flags."

HOW WORKING AT AFLAC COMPARES WITH MY PREVIOUS EMPLOYERS "I only stayed at my previous company for 18 months. I get bored easily, and if I didn't like it here, I'd be gone. But this has been a good experience so far."

NOTE *An edited version of this interview appeared in Computerworld on October 9, 2000.*

Manufacturing

Even though as a group, manufacturers were slow to test the value of the Internet to their internal business processes, e-business initiatives now are taking priority on the IT agenda across the industry. Competitors are becoming collaborators as online marketplaces crop up across all segments of manufacturing, from automobiles to widgets. To streamline the supply chain, manufacturers are scrambling to get their suppliers, distributors, and customers on extranets where they can enter invoices, purchase orders, sales forecasts, and more. And they are retooling corporate websites from brochureware to in-depth resources for customers who want detailed product information and adding ecommerce features. For example, Weber-Stephen Products, Palatine, Illinois, has no immediate plans to sell its barbecue grills online, but it is exploring the possibility of selling low-volume parts and accessories that its distributors don't carry, notes Bill Krieger, vice president of information services. In fact, 29 percent of leading manufacturers maintain profitable e-business operations, according to research by *InformationWeek*.

In addition to e-business initiatives, key information systems in manufacturing include CAD/CAM, forecasting systems, manufacturing automation (including robotics), automated warehousing, and inventory management. "Forecasting systems are big for us because we're a seasonal business," says Krieger of Weber-Stephen. "We do forecasting right at the beginning of the season to make sure we have enough inventory to meet projections and also at the end of the season to make sure we don't have huge amounts of inventory that we have to hold over until the next season begins. We're using the Net to let our reps enter their forecasts, and then we put it together for sales. And then they plunk it together with their own forecasts for manufacturing so they can do a build schedule."

Nonetheless, IT gets mixed marks in manufacturing. A study by the National Association of Manufacturers released in August 2000 indicates that more than 53 percent of small manufacturers do not have an internal IT staff; conversely, 96 percent of large manufacturers have an internal IT staff.

MANUFACTURING IT LEADERS Snap-On Inc., Kenosha, Wis.; General Electric Co., Fairfield, Conn.; 3M, Minneapolis, Minn.; United Dominion Industries Ltd., Charlotte, N.C.; Ingersoll-Rand Co., Woodcliff Lake, N.J.; Lockheed Martin Corp., Bethesda, Md.

INDUSTRY WEBSITES *Advanced Manufacturing* magazine, www.advancedmanufacturing.com; APICS, www.apics.org; Industrial Research Inc., www.iriinc.org; *Managing*

Automation, www.managingautomation.com; Manufacturing Central, www.manufacturingcentral.net; *Manufacturing News*, www.manufacturingnews.com; *Manufacturing Systems*, www.manufacturingsystems.com; National Association of Manufacturers, www.nam.org; Plant Automation.com, www.plantautomation.com.

What It's Like to Work in Manufacturing IT

Joel Albertson, senior computer analyst, tech support staff, Winnebago Industries Inc., a motor-home manufacturer (www.winnebagoind.com), Forest City, Iowa; May 2000.

NUMBER OF IT EMPLOYEES   35.

NUMBER OF EMPLOYEES (END-USERS)   About 3,200 in the Forest City headquarters plus 300 located in three manufacturing plants across the state.

CRITICAL IT INITIATIVES   About 20 programmers maintain and enhance a mainframe-based, homegrown manufacturing system for motor-home production; the remainder of the staff is in operations and PC tech support (supporting 800 PC users ranging from robotics and CAD/CAM users to field sales reps). "We recently completed an extranet giving our 340 dealers access to our mainframe to make it easier for them to enter warranty information and so forth. We also have an intranet that we'll be enhancing, and we recently upgraded our website."

WHAT IS YOUR ROLE?   "I wear many hats—tech support, network administration, the website. Right now, one of our [mainframe] programmers is handling most of the [helpdesk] calls on the extranet, but I'll be getting more involved."

DRESS CODE   Business casual, with casual Fridays.

WORK DAY   "We're a 24/6 shop, and we have three shifts in IT. The only day we're not staffed is Sunday. My office is mainly on from 7:30 A.M. to 4 P.M., but we usually stay longer than that because of demand for user support or project deadlines."

IS A SECURITY BADGE/CARD NEEDED TO GET INTO THE BUILDING OR OFFICE?   "We have three car gates into the complex with security when you drive in and one security dog. We have a tremendous amount of inventory here—both finished products and components—so we have to make sure things don't leave without authority."

IT FACILITY   A building known as the "dog house." "Back in the early seventies, Winnebago had 12 security dogs, and this is where they were housed. It was expanded and remodeled for IT, but it's still referred to as the dog house. And we can bark up a storm."

IT TRAINING   No ongoing training planned. "I always attend the big trade shows and all the Microsoft seminars."

BONUS PROGRAM(S)   Annual company-wide bonus based on operating profit.

MUST PEOPLE CARRY BEEPERS? CELL PHONES?   Yes. "I carry one if I go out of town. In operations and tech support, we're basically on call all the time." Programmers have an on-call rotation by day of the week.

LITTLE PERKS   "We have an employee fleet of Winnebagos, and in the summer, you can put your name in for drawings to use a motor home on the weekends." Employees can buy motor homes at cost, "but I don't think any IT employees own one." Company reimburses 75 percent of tuition costs, and "we have a few IT people who've gone for M.B.A.s, but the majority uses that for certification programs." A computer-purchase program allows employees to make interest-free payments on home PCs through paycheck deductions.

WHAT DO YOU LIKE ABOUT WORKING AT WINNEBAGO?   "It's always challenging, and two days are never the same. I asked my boss what our IT mission statement is, and he said, 'Well, I guess to keep users happy.' And that's really what it is. But it's difficult and challenging to cover all of our users."

NOTE   *An edited version of this interview appeared in* Computerworld *on June 5, 2000.*

Nonprofit Organizations

When measured against the criteria that earned the other industries in this chapter a place on this list—IT-dependent industries that offer job seekers great technological challenges, ample employment opportunities, and competitive salaries—nonprofit organizations fall somewhat short of the standard. While some nonprofits are quite innovative about using technology to forward their mission, they operate with smaller staffs and offer much lower salaries. But in terms of job satisfaction reported by IT professionals who work in nonprofits, the nonprofit sector may outrank all the others. "I think I'm making a difference. I have an idealistic streak ... and I have kids who I want to grow up in a natural world," says Dave Simon, director of information and communications systems at The Sierra Club, in explaining why he left Anderson Consulting 11 years ago to join the environmental conservation and activist organization. Prior to working at Anderson, Simon had been in the Peace Corps. While

Anderson "was a great place to learn the technology and project-management skills," Simon says, "after 11 years, I needed a change."

Similarly, Michael Belkin, CTO at the Metropolitan Museum of Art, says job satisfaction rather than salary and benefits motivated him to trade in commercial IT for nonprofit IT. He left a financial services firm in 1995 to work in the museum's IT organization. Later, he went to work for the nonprofit Metropolitan Opera, and he returned to the museum in 2000 as CTO. "In institutions like the museum, you deal with a lot of the same issues from a business and technology perspective as at any other organization," Belkin says. "But the omnipresent thing is that the results of my work have a very tangible and visible impact on thousands and thousands of people every day. That's what makes working in institutions like this very rewarding."

The primary applications in a nonprofit support fundraising and membership drives, but with the advent of the Internet, nonprofit organizations are adopting more leading-edge technology to get the job done. While they lag behind corporate IT on the industry pay scale, they offer saner hours and less demanding end-users. At the Met, for example, users are primarily involved in research and education. "Our departments may not see technology as necessarily the driving force behind what they do day-in and day-out," Belkin says. "They see IT as a necessary aspect of enabling them to do their work, but if we were to disappear tomorrow, their work would continue."

NONPROFIT IT LEADERS**   American Red Cross, Washington, D.C.; ASPIRA, Washington, D.C.; Goodwill Industries International, Bethesda, Md.; PBS, Alexandria, Va.; World Wildlife Fund, Washington, D.C.

NOTE ***List derived from various sources, including Microsoft Corporation's Technology Leadership Grant program and Npower, which provides technical assistance to nonprofit organizations.*

INDUSTRY WEBSITES   American Institute of Philanthropy, www.charitywatch.org; *The Chronicle of Philanthropy*, philanthropy.com; Council on Foundations, www.cof.org; The Foundation Center, fdncenter.org; INC: Internet Nonprofit Center, www.nonprofits.org; National Charities Information Board, www.give.org; nonprofit.about.com; Nonprofit-TechWorld.org, technology resources for the nonprofit sector, www.nonprofit-techworld.org; *Philanthropy News* Network, pnnonline.org.

What It's Like to Work in Nonprofit IT

Dave Simon, director of information and communications systems, The Sierra Club, (www.sierraclub.org), San Francisco, Calif.; February 2000.

NUMBER OF IT EMPLOYEES   Twelve, including one in the Washington, D.C., office.

NUMBER OF EMPLOYEES (END-USERS)   Around 300 employees, plus "several thousand" active volunteers supported with email lists, local websites, web-accessible membership databases, etc., for organizing outings, outreach campaigns, and more.

AS A NONPROFIT, WHAT IT SALARY CHALLENGES DO YOU FACE?   "Typically, our salaries were 10 percent to 20 percent below the market average, and the differential has grown in the last few years. With the dot-com thing sending local salaries through the roof, it's terribly difficult to get people. What works out best is when people are environmentally motivated because then they're willing to put up with less money."

WHAT MOTIVATES IT PEOPLE TO WORK THERE?   "I think people come to work here because they believe in the organization, but also because we're doing a lot of exciting things technically, and we're small enough that we can move quickly. For example, we were doing commerce on the Web in 1996, we have wide-area links, and we just implemented a PeopleSoft financial system. We're not the IT backwater that you might think of in a nonprofit. There's a lot of room to learn and grow."

MAJOR WEB INITIATIVES   "Time-keeping systems for tracking hours spent on conservation work, which are critical because since our activities are funded by grants, the government requires scrupulous tracking of how we spend our time; a membership information system to provide information about club members to our local leaders; and an up-to-the-minute trip reservation system. We're doing fun stuff and using the Web as free plumbing. It's wonderful for us because it lets us reach out to our staff and volunteers all over the country at very little cost."

TRAINING   Java programming, ASP programming for web masters, and NT Server administration.

EMPLOYEE REVIEWS   A formal annual performance review, and informal semiannual reviews. Reviews include feedback from the employee on the manager. "I'm from Anderson, and my boss, the COO [chief operations officer], is from American Express, so we have the same corporate structures as everyone else."

THE ONE THING EVERYONE COMPLAINS ABOUT   "I would say that even here, there's a little dot-com envy going on. I've had people leave because they got offered 60 percent more money at a dot-com. The job market in this city is so hot that people are really thinking twice about why they work here."

TURNOVER RATE   "About 20 percent, about the same as the IT average."

WORK DAY   "Pretty much 9:00 A.M. to 5:00 P.M., which is one of the perks for putting up with a lower salary in a nonprofit."

WHY DO YOU LIKE WORKING AT THE SIERRA CLUB?   "It sounds really hokey, but feeling that I'm working toward something that makes a difference to the planet and the people on it. In many of our conservation battles, the timely delivery of information plays a significant contributing role—like being able to generate several thousand emails from our website or being able to provide a local phone list for activists to call people about a key bill—and that's a good feeling."

 NOTE *An edited version of this interview appeared in* Computerworld *on February 28, 2000.*

Pharmaceuticals and Biotechnology

Like the healthcare industry, the pharmaceuticals and biotechnology segment is growing by leaps and bounds as baby-boomers get older and people live longer. But in terms of leveraging IT across their multifaceted operations, companies in this industry have not been particularly aggressive in the past. Of eight pharmaceuticals and biotechnology firms named as IT leaders on the annual *InformationWeek* 500 list, only one—number 9-ranked Bristol-Myers Squibb Company—made it into the top 100. But, like manufacturing and other industries, this industry is quickly discovering the benefits of the Internet in enabling companies to increase productivity, lower costs, and better manage information across divisions.

For IT professionals, there has never been a better time to get involved in pharmaceuticals and biotechnology. Research support, supply-chain management, regulatory compliance, manufacturing, and distribution are key areas for IT services and support in pharmaceuticals and biotech firms. A number of unique factors involved in how pharmaceutical companies manufacture and distribute products have made supply-chain planning systems critical. For example, there's the lapse between when a drug is initially developed and when it finally hits the market, while companies await government approval and then, given the green light, ramp up for production. Providing collaboration tools for researchers in different locations is also high on the IT priority list, as are massive data storage systems and database management.

PHARMACEUTICALS AND BIOTECHNOLOGY IT LEADERS   Bristol-Myers Squibb Co., New York, N.Y.; Eli Lilly Co., Indianapolis, Ind.; Abbott Laboratories, Abbott Park, Ill.; American Home Products Corp., Madison, N.J.; Johnson & Johnson, New Brunswick, N.J.

INDUSTRY WEBSITES   Consumer Healthcare Products Association, ndmainfo.org; National Association of Pharmaceuticals Manufacturers, www.napmnet.org; Uniform Code Council Pharmaceuticals Page, www.uc-council.org/focus_by_industry/fi_healthcare.html.

What It's Like to Work in Pharmaceuticals and Biotechnology IT

Jack Cooper, CIO, Bristol-Myers Squibb Co. (www.bms.com), New York, N.Y.; October 2000.

NUMBER OF IT EMPLOYEES   About 2,000, dispersed across 85 locations worldwide; about 50 in headquarters.

NUMBER OF EMPLOYEES (END-USERS)   About 55,000 worldwide, of whom 35,000 have PCs (the remainder are in warehouses, manufacturing, etc.); about 400 in headquarters.

MAJOR IT INITIATIVES   "Early this year, we completed a large SAP implementation aimed at increasing our overall productivity and consolidating services across the company. That has saved us well over $1 billion a year, which has enabled us to invest in our research systems, and we've done extensive work on directly supporting the discovery, development, and clinical trials associated with new pharmaceutical products. We've set up collaborative computing so that researchers can research a database of compounds and share information about them.

"Maybe someone researching the effect of a compound on the heart observes that the compound presents itself in the brain, and wants to send that information to someone doing brain research. We want to put all the information from the original discovery to development to manufacturing to approval by the FDA [Food and Drug Administration] in an electronic format. Using IT, we can go up in multiples of orders of magnitude in increasing the compounds researchers can observe and speeding up the delivery of drugs."

WHAT'S UNIQUE ABOUT WORKING IN PHARMACEUTICALS INDUSTRY IT? "We're primarily a research organization, and the mindset associated with research is to make change. And IT professionals like to see new ideas come forth. So it's a very fertile environment for an IT professional to work in."

IT TRAINING E-systems and databases, soft skills, and leadership development training. "Training and education is not a destination, but a journey—you must want to continually learn and use new technologies and create new ideas."

EMPLOYEE REVIEWS Annual 360-degree reviews and performance partnerships in which an employee assesses their skills and outlines goals.

CAREER PATH OPTIONS "Predominantly, we offer an IT management trail, and more and more, we are offering a technical trail with multiple steps."

BONUS PROGRAMS Presidential Awards—financial and recognition rewards decided by an executive committee; no IT-specific bonus programs.

DRESS CODE "It's very flexible. We feel very strongly that we want our employees to be highly motivated and comfortable. In the corporate offices, we have a tighter dress code than anywhere else; here it's more business dress, although few have to wear a coat and tie."

WORK DAY "IT hours are attuned to the user department's hours. If you work in finance, for example, it's normal business hours. The overall average is an eight-hour day. We also have flex-time, and in the summer, we have Friday afternoons off."

KIND OF OFFICES At headquarters, cubes for developers, systems analysts, and other IT staff positions; perimeter offices with windows for project managers and up.

MUST PEOPLE CARRY BEEPERS? CELL PHONES? Yes, "if they're on call. For example, we have to report results on a monthly basis, so those supporting finance are on call during that period, and they rotate the schedule month to month. But we find today that the wireless devices are consumed and used by nearly everyone—we encourage that."

PERCENT OF STAFF THAT TELECOMMUTES ON A GIVEN DAY "It's very low. It's not very popular. You have to be aligned with your users and your team."

PERKS An annual trip for the corporate IT staff to the Culinary Institute of America for a one-day team-building exercise. Morning classes are followed by an afternoon cooking contest. "It's all about learning to work together—the division of labor and how to cooperate and support each other. Last year, I won the contest with pork chops in mango sauce. Everyone said it's because I'm the CIO, but I think I'm just a quick study."

WHY DO YOU LIKE WORKING AT BRISTOL-MYERS SQUIBB?   "When you look at the excitement and the desire to use technology to increase productivity and research, this place is unique above any place I've ever worked. And the focus on making the company a desirable place to work is also unique."

NOTE *An edited version of this interview appeared in* Computerworld *on November 6, 2000.*

Publishing and Media

Even though its prime product is information, the publishing and media industry hasn't traditionally been aggressive about using information technology. Before the emergence of the Web, few publishing and media companies could have been viewed as IT leaders. Information technology was less a tool for competitive advantage than a necessary expense to enable reporters, editors, production staff, marketing managers, and others to get their jobs done.

But the Internet is transforming the publishing and media business, offering not just a new channel for content delivery, but giving rise to the creation of whole new products—such as electronic books sold online. And many publishers have been effective with web portals and community sites built around their brands and product categories.

Publishing and media companies can offer IT professionals a lot of room for movement, thanks to massive industry consolidation. The Tribune Company, in Chicago, for example, owns newspapers, radio stations, broadcast television stations, and the Chicago Cubs baseball team. Publishing company Simon & Schuster is owned by media conglomerate Viacom, which also owns cable television networks such as MTV and Nickelodeon, broadcast network CBS, television programming distribution arms, an interactive unit, and more. The line between publishing, media, and entertainment continues to blur.

PUBLISHING AND MEDIA IT LEADERS   Primedia Inc., New York, N.Y.; R.R. Donnelley & Sons. Co., Chicago, Ill.; Dow Jones & Co., New York, N.Y.; McGraw-Hill Co. (publishers of this book), New York, N.Y.; America Online Inc., Dulles, Va.

INDUSTRY WEBSITES Association of American Publishers, www.publishers.org; I Want Media.com, www.iwantmedia.com; *Journal of Electronic Publishing*, www.press. umich.edu/jep; Magazine Publishers of America, www.magazine.org; *Media Week*, www.mediaweek.com; The Newspaper Association of America, www.naa.org.

What It's Like to Work in Publishing and Media Industry IT

Kathy Ameche, CIO, Tribune Co. (www.tribune.com), a diversified media company encompassing publishing, broadcasting, and interactive businesses (also owns the Chicago Cubs), Chicago, Ill.; March 2000.

NUMBER OF IT EMPLOYEES About 125 in corporate IT plus 125 to 175 additional decentralized IT staff.

NUMBER OF EMPLOYEES (END-USERS) About 15,000.

TENURE Since 1997; promoted to CIO in June 2000 from director of the program management office for Year 2000.

WORK DAY About 8:00 A.M. to 6:00 or 7:00 P.M. for most IT staff, "but we're a 24/7 operation, so there are three shifts in the technical operations center."

MAJOR IT INITIATIVES A PeopleSoft financial systems implementation; ecommerce across the entire organization, including "increasing revenue from our sites and making it easier for viewers, advertisers, and subscribers to get the information they need. We want to get all our different groups together to work on an ecommerce strategy for the entire organization;" the convergence of voice and data over the corporate network; and broadband, because "the technology is moving so quickly that we need to support the media for that."

WHAT'S YOUR ROLE IN THESE INITIATIVES? "I'm responsible for the enterprise systems that touch all of our different business groups as opposed to the individual systems that run a publishing or broadcasting unit. Tribune IT is a combination of centralized and decentralized efforts, and 99.5 percent of my systems are centralized."

HOW IS WORKING IN CORPORATE IT DIFFERENT FROM DECENTRALIZED IT? "We're all working on new systems and innovations, but we all have different types of systems. And in the remote offices, the IT staff are more colocated with their users."

INTERNAL CAREER PATHS A Technology Leadership Development program accepts three internal IT candidates each year for a two-year rotation through each line of business to work on business and IT projects; a shorter technology rotation program is being developed for candidates interested in technical career paths. "Tribune is really good at promoting and cross-training and allowing people to move into other areas. You can start in IT and end up in a business role in broadcasting, for example."

BONUS PROGRAMS   Sign-on bonuses, spot performance bonuses, formal annual bonuses at certain management levels; and quarterly awards based on peer recommendations.

DRESS CODE   Business casual.

MUST PEOPLE CARRY BEEPERS? CELL PHONES?   Both; on-call staff has laptops and dial-up access from home paid for by the company.

FAVORITE GOSSIP TOPICS   "Where's the company headed? What's the latest rumor you heard? Will the Cubs win the pennant?"

LITTLE PERKS   "Access to Chicago Cubs tickets; hob-nobbing with *Tribune* reporters in the elevators; and quarterly communication meetings where we have food and games. A year ago, we had a push to increase quality, and after that, we all got to play baseball at Wrigley Field."

WHAT'S UNIQUE ABOUT WORKING AT TRIBUNE COMPANY?   "As a media company, we have to react quickly. In 150 years of publishing the *Chicago Tribune*, we've never missed getting the paper out the door. We're very proud of our history and who we are and what we do, and the IT staff supports that."

NOTE *An edited version of this interview appeared in* Computerworld *on April 3, 2000.*

Retail

A retail company's livelihood depends on two things: strong branding and customer loyalty. But neither of those is achievable unless a retailer ensures that the right amount of the right product is in the right place at the right time.

Making sure that Jcrew store shelves are stocked with ample cashmere sweaters for the holiday buying season or that Barnes & Noble has enough copies of the latest Harry Potter book is no small feat from the IT perspective. Supply-chain management, inventory management, warehousing and distribution, merchandising, sales forecasting and reporting, CRM, and point-of-sale (POS) systems must all be working in perfect harmony.

Major retailers have more than just their stores to worry about; they also have ecommerce sites and frequently also have catalog and mail-order operations, each of which has its own unique systems behind it that must integrate with the company's centralized IT systems. While brick-and-mortar retailers may have initially felt a threat from pure-play e-tailers, it is precisely the fact that click-and-mortar plays have all the backend systems in place that they are now starting to capture cyber customers as well as walk-in customers, while many e-tailers are dropping like flies.

Consequently, demand for IT professionals in the retail industry is extremely high. In the fall of 2000, the Gap, which has IT operations in New York, San Francisco, and remote facilities worldwide, had more than 80 IT positions posted at its website. At The Limited, Columbus, Ohio, the individual IT departments supporting its myriad brands—including Limited, Express, Structure, Victoria's Secret, Lane Bryant, and others—were consolidated into one centralized group, a wholly owned subsidiary dubbed Limited Technology Services (LTS). In a move to bring top-flight IT talent onboard, LTS created a comprehensive Reward and Development program for the newly formed subsidiary. The move highlights just how critical IT organizations are to retailers.

RETAIL IT LEADERS   Office Depot Inc., Delray Beach, Fla.; CDW Computer Centers Inc., Vernon Hills, Ill.; Staples Inc., Framingham, Mass.; Bed, Bath & Beyond Inc., Union, N.J.; Wal-Mart Stores Inc., Bentonville, Ark.

INDUSTRY WEBSITES   *Catalog Age*, www.catalogagemag.com; *Executive Technology*, www.executivetechnology.com; National Retail Federation, www.nrf.com; International Mass Retailers Association, www.imra.org; Uniform Code Council Merchandising Page, www.uc-council.org/focus_by_industry/fi_general_merchandise___appar.html.

What It's Like to Work in Retail IT

Greg Alexander, senior vice president of MIS, The Sharper Image (www.sharperimage.com), a cataloger, retailer, and e-tailer, San Francisco, Calif.; November 1999.

NUMBER OF IT EMPLOYEES   Thirty-six, including the website team, plus three to four contractors at any given time; staff includes programmers, web development group, and POS helpdesk.

NUMBER OF EMPLOYEES (END-USERS)   About 1,500, including retail-store and distribution-center personnel; the numbers go up during the holiday season.

DRESS CODE Tuesday–Thursday, "dressy casual," or slacks and collared shirts; Mondays and Fridays, "as casual as you want to be," but no jeans with holes or t-shirts with large logos.

WORK DAY Flexible. One senior programmer/analyst works from 6:00 A.M. to 3:30 P.M.; others work from 9:00 A.M. to 6:00 P.M. "As we gear up for the holidays, management ends up spending more time in the office. ... And coinciding with our monthly catalog drop, our web group is probably spending longer hours to get new products featured in the catalog posted to the website."

IT ENVIRONMENT "We're primarily an AS/400 shop, but we have 12 or 13 (dedicated) servers for various functions from voice mail to email to polling servers for our stores, to a couple of FedEx servers for rating our packages for mail order. We use an external host for our web servers. We need a lot of bandwidth, and we needed to be truly colocated to accommodate all the site traffic. So, we [have] servers on the East Coast and West Coast. That way, if there's any disaster—an earthquake in the West or a hurricane in the East—we'll still be up."

DÉCOR "We have a lot of one-of-a kind products around. A replica of Robby the Robot (from the 1956 sci-fi flick *Forbidden Planet*) greets people in the lobby. And there are two Sharper Image executive massage chairs in the lobby, so when vendors come in, they can lounge in those—and we have them where we want them for our meeting."

MUST PEOPLE CARRY BEEPERS? CELL PHONES? "A couple of managers, myself included, carry cell phones. Programmers who are on call get a cell phone and a beeper. And the POS support group, as well as the helpdesk, also rotate cell phones."

FAVORITE GOSSIP TOPIC "Speculation on how well a new product is going to do."

LITTLE PERKS Discounted tickets to local theme park Great America; discounted health club memberships; an employee purchase program for company products, as well as a direct at-cost purchase program with select vendors; and monthly birthday gatherings in the computer room to celebrate all the IT birthdays for that month.

WHAT'S YOUR BIGGEST CHALLENGE? "I don't want to say our staff is thin, but we do a good job of supporting a lot of people without a lot of staff. We run a tight ship. The IT budget, including the website, is seven-tenths of 1 percent of revenue. Some people would say we're nuts, but it's impressive to run IT on that budget."

WHAT DO YOU LIKE ABOUT WORKING AT SHARPER IMAGE?   "There's never a dull moment. We don't have a wild and crazy environment, but it is fun. We have a lot of sharing of knowledge, a lot of talking and communicating between the cubes. We don't want people to just sit in their cube and do their job."

 NOTE *An edited version of this interview appeared in* Computerworld *on November 22, 1999.*

Travel and Hospitality

Given that automated reservation systems were among the first large-scale commercial applications of information technology (see the story of the Sabre reservation system in Chapter 2), the travel and hospitality industry has a long legacy of leveraging IT for competitive advantage. While reservation systems certainly remain one of the dominant applications in the industry, IT in travel and hospitality goes much further than just automating the processing of an airline ticket purchase or a hotel room reservation. Reservation systems have enabled companies in this industry to collect vast amounts of information about their customers, which they leverage in myriad customer relationship management applications.

Harrah's Entertainment, for example, has earned patents for the technology it developed to support its Total Gold customer rewards program. Members of the program call in, and at the click of a mouse, the customer service rep (CSR) knows the customer's preferred property and type of room, how often the member stays in a Harrah's hotel or casino, and more. Not only does the system enable CSRs to provide a personal touch over the phone, but it also enables the company to offer holiday deals and special weekend packages to the right people at the right time, optimizing revenue flow as well as engendering loyalty among its customer base. The system can also generate such promotions and offers for direct mail or email campaigns.

These types of systems, in varying degrees of sophistication, are used across the travel and hospitality industry—by hoteliers, airlines, cruise lines, car-rental companies, and travel agents. While they seem straightforward on the surface, they require substantial underlying technology to make them work, including robust networks, extremely large data warehouses, and customized applications.

In addition to reservation and CRM systems, travel and hospitality companies maintain a wide range of complex systems, including POS systems, room-service systems (in hotels and on cruise ships), scheduling systems, fleet-management systems (for airlines, car rental companies, and cruise lines), supply-chain management systems, and more. Moreover, they have ported their reservation systems to the Web and are web-enabling their internal systems as well. In short, the travel and hospitality industry offers IT professionals opportunities to work with a vast array of new and legacy technology.

In a mere four years at Delta Airlines' Technology services arm, Delta Technology, Walter Leddy has managed to develop a new skill set every year. As a business analyst in the electronic ticketing group, he learned to build SQL databases. In the Gate and Boarding development team, he learned C++ and object-oriented programming. The following year, as that team ramped up for an Airport Renewal initiative (see "What It's Like to Work in Travel and Hospitality IT" later in this chapter), he was promoted to technical lead and learned project management skills. Next, for a new online initiative, he began learning Java development. "As any IT person has, I've certainly had opportunities to go elsewhere," Leddy says, "but I stay here because we get to touch any kind of technology that's currently available anywhere."

TRAVEL IT LEADERS   Avis Group Holdings Inc., Garden City, N.Y.; Continental Airlines Inc., Houston; Delta Air Lines Inc., Atlanta, Ga.; Galileo International, Rosemont, Ill; Royal Caribbean Cruises Inc., Miami, Fla.

HOSPITALITY IT LEADERS   Starbucks Corp., Seattle, Wash.; Wendy's International Inc., Dublin, Ohio; Carlson Companies Inc., Minneapolis, Minn.; Harrah's Entertainment Inc., Memphis, Tenn.; Marriott International Inc., Bethesda, Md.

INDUSTRY WEBSITES   American Gaming Association, www.americangaming.org; American Hotel and Motel Association, www.ahma.com; *eTourism Newsletter*, www.etourismnewsletter.com; *Hotel and Motel Management*, www.hmmonline.com; *Lodging News*, www.lodgingnews.com; *Restaurant Business*, www.restaurantbiz.com; Travel Industry Association of America, www.tia.org.

What It's Like to Work in Travel and Hospitality Industry IT

Walter Leddy, developer, Delta Technology Inc., the wholly owned IT subsidiary of Delta Airlines Inc. (dt.delta-air.com), Atlanta, Ga.; May 2000.

CURRENT PROJECT   MYOBTravel.com, a travel-planning and reservations site that will cater to small businesses with one to 50 employees.

NUMBER OF IT EMPLOYEES   Around 2,000 in Delta Technology; five on the MYOB.com project.

NUMBER OF EMPLOYEES (END-USERS)   Around 70,000 in Delta Airlines.

TENURE IN CURRENT POSITION   Since April 2000.

LAST POSITION HELD   Developer, Gate and Boarding team, Customer Experience Technologies group within Delta's Airport Renewal initiative. "We targeted areas where we were lacking in customer service, and one was the gate area in the airports. We analyzed their work processes and decided they needed new workstations and software that would let them manage passengers more efficiently so they could spend less time behind the computer and more time actually communicating with passengers. We put in [6,000 workstations with] Windows applications that let them monitor seat inventory in real time and allocate seats using a visual seating chart and an interactive passenger list."

NEW RESPONSIBILITIES   Overall design, coordinating the development with other team members, and eventually, the deployment of the site. "There isn't a designated team leader, but essentially that's what I am. I'll be spending 50 percent of my time on development and 50 percent on coordination between the developers and the deployment teams."

NEW SKILLS REQUIRED   "Java—I'm working with other developers to build that skill set. The learning curve is not that difficult because I've had previous object-oriented experience. My work will be on the user interface—building the web pages and handing the data for those pages off to another developer who will be parsing and inserting the data into a database. So I won't have to learn about the backend of the site."

WORK DAY   "I might not be the norm, but I get in about 7:30 A.M. and stay until 6:30 or 7:00 P.M. We have a ten-hour day, four-day week option here, but I work five days. My projects are usually cutting-edge, and you just have to do what it takes to meet the deadlines."

WHAT IMPACT DOES THE BUSY SUMMER TRAVEL SEASON HAVE ON IT?   "My [current] project is not affected. The big hit for small-business travel is from the end of the summer through Christmas. But when I was on the Gate and Boarding team, having more passengers going through the airports would impact the system. As long as it was running as it should, summer travel wouldn't have any adverse effect."

BONUS PROGRAMS   "We have an employee stock-purchase plan through payroll deductions. And I receive an annual bonus based on merit and company-wide performance. Spot bonuses are at managers' discretion."

MUST PEOPLE CARRY BEEPERS? CELL PHONES?   "I was required to wear a beeper [when] I was the primary contact for systems that went down in the field. When we were first deploying the 6,000 workstations, I'd get beeped every night, but by the time I left and the helpdesk had been trained, I got maybe two calls a month."

KIND OF OFFICES Standard cubicle layout. Delta Technology has its own building across the street from the main Delta headquarters, one exit down from the airport.

ANY WINDOWS? About 50 percent of the staff has windows; one side of the building overlooks the airport runways. "You definitely have the distraction of looking out there and thinking of all the places you'd like to fly off to."

DRESS CODE Business casual. "There are very few renegades; it's a fairly conservative atmosphere."

TRAVEL BENEFITS "We get a certain amount of free domestic and international flights each year, so you can jump on a plane whenever you feel like it if there's a seat available. I have a lot of friends in the company, and we've gone for weekends in Paris and Amsterdam. And I just went with a group to Machu Picchu [Peru]."

WHY DO YOU LIKE WORKING AT DELTA? "It's great to have a management team that makes sure you get to work with different technologies as you develop. My friends in other IT organizations say it's hard to find a manager who will accommodate that."

NOTE *An edited version of this interview appeared in* Computerworld *on May 22, 2000.*

NOTE *Unless otherwise noted, the IT leaders listed for each industry are taken from InformationWeek's annual* InformationWeek 500 *list, published September 11, 2000 (www.informationweek.com/500menu/500menu.htm).*

Chapter 11

· ·

Hot Locations

One of the advantages of an IT career is that you can live nearly anywhere and still find challenging work. Even in places as unexpected as Bozeman, Montana, and Forest City, Iowa, IT professionals are thriving. (Bozeman, population 41,000, is home to RightNow Technologies, an application service provider (ASP) employing about 200 people; Forest City, population 4,500, is home to Winnebago Industries, which has a 35-person IT shop, and is within commuting distance to several larger cities.) In small hamlets and urban areas alike, the IT supply-and-demand gap has driven most employers to actively recruit from outside their primary area, which opens up the playing field for IT job seekers.

In overall economic terms, smaller communities are prospering right along with larger ones; rustic areas like Northwest Arkansas and comfortable cities like Memphis, Tennessee, rank among metropolitan heavyweights like New York and Los Angeles on *Forbes* magazine's "Best Places" list for 2000, which identified 200 communities experiencing significant economic activity and growth. So, whether you adore a penthouse view or land spreadin' out so far and wide, a career in IT gives you considerable flexibility in choosing where you live.

How you choose where to live depends on your priorities, obligations, and how far along you are toward your professional goals. If you're just starting out and are not tied down by a family to support, you may want to consider voyaging beyond your home turf to a new location that will feed your personal interests. Early in your career, when you have nowhere to go but up, the choices are endless. If you've begun to climb the management ladder and have started a family, you will likely want to balance an area's employment outlook with quality-of-life factors such as population, local education, home prices, and cost-of-living index. Does the area have the right combination of employers you can grow with plus top-notch schools and low crime rates?

As you get closer to the executive level, with more discretionary income, you may find yourself relocating based solely on a strategic opportunity with your employer of choice. Whatever your lifestyle and career priorities are at any given time, you will want to balance those against an area's general economic and demographic picture. And even though the IT supply-and-demand gap will afford you a wider berth in determining where to live, you should nonetheless evaluate the sustainability of an area's IT job market.

One useful way for determining the long-range outlook for IT jobs in a given area is to evaluate how many high-tech employers have large facilities there. A concentration of high-tech employers often breeds a host of supporting IT consulting and outsourcing services; over time, the highly employable workforce that those types of companies draw tends to lure other types of employers into the area, creating even more jobs. "High-tech industries have a large direct economic impact on metro economies," stated The Milken Institute in a 1999 report: "America's High-Tech Economy: Growth, Development, and Risks for Metropolitan Areas" (www.milken-inst.org/poe.cfm?point=pub03). "They are determining which metropolitan areas are succeeding or failing." Based on the report, planting yourself in a high-tech corridor can create long-term career stability and growth. (Just keep in mind that a rising cost of living tends to accompany a rising economy.)

Consider, for example, the economic success of high-tech hotbeds that grew around Boston's Route 128, fed by the Massachusetts Institute of Technology, and Silicon Valley, fed by Stanford University and Xerox PARC (Palo Alto Research Center), where the first personal computer was prototyped. While the high-tech industry remains the dominant sector in both locations, both also support other healthy segments. Over the last 20 years, a number of other U.S. regions and cities have experienced similar growth and prosperity by attracting high-tech businesses, such as the following: Research Triangle Park, North Carolina; Austin, Texas; Washington, D.C.; and even New York City. In fact, many communities have avidly sought to promote themselves as high-tech havens, coining monikers to reflect a real—or hoped—high-tech economic burst: Silicon Hills (around Austin, Texas), Telecom Corridor (in Richardson, Texas, a Dallas suburb), Silicon Alley (in Manhattan), Multimedia Gulch (San Francisco's South of Market district), Silicon Prairie (around Chicago), Silicon East (around the Washington, D.C., metro area), and even Silicon Sandbar (in Cape Cod, Massachusetts).

A local economy driven by the high-tech industry will be a diverse economy, and that's an important factor in choosing a new location. If a community supports a variety of different industries, the long-term outlook for IT professionals will likely be more stable than it will in an area heavily dependent on one industry. For example, if you're working in an insurance company in an insurance town and the insurance industry takes a nosedive, where will you turn? In a more diversified region, you would simply import your IT skills to a local employer in another industry that's still flourishing.

In other words, in selecting the location for your next IT career move, keep in mind the notion that "All pigs are equal, but some are more equal than others." Following is a sampling of 20 towns, cities, and regions that each offer a range of different lifestyles *and* an outstanding IT job market.

INDUSTRY FACT *If you've got the itch to move, you're not alone: About 40 million people change addresses each year, and of those, 6.8 million move to another state, according to data from the U.S. Census Bureau.*

Atlanta, Georgia

General Tecumseh Sherman would hardly recognize the sleepy southern city that his troops burned to the ground during the Civil War. Today, the economy is on fire, and IT troops are cutting a path across the metro area.

The Home Depot, based here, ranked number 1 on *Computerworld*'s annual "100 Best Places to Work in IT 2000" list, released in June 2000, and four other area employers also made the list, including BellSouth Corporation, Aflac, Equifax, Georgia-Pacific Corporation, and Scientific-Atlanta. The latter four also garnered mention, as did The Home Depot and Delta Air Lines, on the *InformationWeek* 500 list of leading IT innovators, published in September 2000. The Internet economy is thriving here as well, with EarthLink, the number 2 Internet service provider in the country, iXL, a leading E-consultancy, CNN Interactive, and a number of smaller startups.

With its vigorous job market and low unemployment, Atlanta also ranks consistently on a variety of other "Best Places" lists. It ranked number 2 on *Forbes* magazine's second annual "Best Places" list for 2000, which examines communities with the most dynamic economic growth. Projected job growth through 2010 is 23.15 percent, ahead of the national average of 15.09 percent. Atlanta scores high marks for livability as well, with its lower-than-average cost of living, reasonable housing prices, World Series–winning major league baseball franchise the Braves, and 20 colleges and universities.

MAJOR EMPLOYERS   The Home Depot, Inc., Southern Co., Delta Air Lines, The Coca-Cola Co., United Parcel Service, Inc., BellSouth Corp., EarthLink, Inc., iXL, Inc., Turner Broadcasting System, Inc.

TYPICAL IT SALARIES   Systems analyst, $59,279; database administrator, $65,681; network/data communications manager, $86,947.

MEDIAN HOME PRICE $126,800.

COST-OF-LIVING INDEX   103.2.

POPULATION   3,857,097.

UNEMPLOYMENT RATE   2.4 percent (December 2000).

ONLINE EMPLOYMENT RESOURCES   www.atlanta.computerjobs.com, atlanta.techies.com, atlanta.computerwork.com.

Boston, Massachusetts/Route 128

In the sixties, Boston's MIT gave birth to the first major high-tech corridor, along Massachusetts Route 128, much as Stanford University would later feed Silicon Valley. While the old Route 128 companies don't hold the same industry sway that they once did—Digital Equipment Corporation was absorbed by Compaq Computer Corporation, Data General is now a division of EMC Corporation, and Wang was acquired in 1999 by Amsterdam-based Getronics, to name just a few examples—the area surrounding Boston is still largely high tech. But it's a lot more diversified now, and the IT job market is still plenty strong, fueled by a variety of manufacturers, financial services companies, retailers, and healthcare providers. Specialty chemical company Cabot Corporation ranked number 2 on *Computerworld*'s "100 Best Places to Work in IT 2000" list, and other area companies that ranked in the top 50 include State Street Corporation (number 10), FleetBoston Financial Corporation (number 20), and retailer Staples (number 27).

MIT also helped lay the groundwork for the Internet, back when it was a Department of Defense initiative known as Arpanet, and that legacy is also evident in the area, with a number of Internet-related companies. The state of Massachusetts has even moved to establish itself as the *.commonwealth* (dot commonwealth). And dot-com jobs in the .commonwealth are plentiful. A search for Internet-related jobs on bostonworks.com in March 2001 yielded over 500 openings. IT professionals here may not get a World Series win, but they can have the world.

MAJOR EMPLOYERS   FMR Corp. (Fidelity Investments), John Hancock Financial Services, Inc., Bose Corp., Staples, Inc., EMC Corp., RSA Security Inc., The Gillette Co., FleetBoston Financial Corp., Reebok International, Ltd., Lotus Development Corp., Verizon Communications.

TYPICAL IT SALARIES   Systems analyst, $65,719; database administrator, $72,544; network/data communications manager, $95,215.

MEDIAN HOME PRICE $255,100.

COST-OF-LIVING INDEX   143.

POPULATION   3,297,201.

UNEMPLOYMENT RATE   1.7 percent (December 2000).

ONLINE EMPLOYMENT RESOURCES   www.boston.computerjobs.com, boston.techies.com, boston.computerwork.com, newengland.computerwork.com, www.digitalmass.com/networking/jobs/.

Chicago, Illinois

Chicago employers are getting as extreme as the local weather in their efforts to recruit and retain IT professionals. Healthcare firm Baxter International, for example, pays $5,000 bonuses for employee referrals to the IT department. Walgreen Company, the pharmacy chain, launched an internal training program in 1998 to develop new IT professionals from within the corporate ranks, dubbed Employee Transition Into IT (ETIT). Allstate Insurance Company, which ranked number 16 on *Computerworld's* "100 Best Places to Work in IT 2000" list, spends $6,500 on training for each IT employee annually, according to *Computerworld*. Not only does that keep the IT skills portfolio up to date, but it keeps IT employees on deck.

With a diversified industry base encompassing retail, healthcare, financial services, manufacturing, insurance, oil and gas, publishing, hospitality and food manufacturing, plus a strong crop of Internet contenders, Chicago needs IT professionals like the Cubs need Sammy Sosa. In terms of IT salaries, the local unemployment rate, and the cost of living, Chicago is on par with the national average, but the lifestyle in the Windy City is far from average. *Money* magazine's "Best Places to Live 2000" report called it the "Best in the Midwest." The city's vibrant blues scene continues to thrive, and with pro teams in every major sport, as well as architectural landmarks and leading museums like The Field Museum and The Art Institute of Chicago, IT professionals who locate here have plenty to occupy them besides the numerous available jobs.

MAJOR EMPLOYERS   Sears, Roebuck and Co., The Tribune Co., Walgreen Co., McDonald's Corp., Abbott Laboratories, Sara Lee Corp., Baxter International.

TYPICAL IT SALARIES   Systems analyst, $64,219; database administrator, $70,998; network/data communications manager, $93,515.

MEDIAN HOME PRICE $170,200.

COST-OF-LIVING INDEX 111.3.

POPULATION 8,008,507.

UNEMPLOYMENT RATE 4.2 percent (December 2000).

ONLINE EMPLOYMENT RESOURCES www.chicago.computerjobs.com, chicago.techies.com, www.chicagojobs.com, www.chisoft.com/jobsearch, chicago.computerwork.com.

Florida

Florida is one of the fastest-growing U.S. states for employment, ranked third after California and Arizona for most new jobs created, according to a July 17, 2000, article in the *Miami Herald* ("The Herald 100: Florida's Leading Companies," by Cindy Krischer Goodman). And it's not all tourism-related; the state's economy is fairly diversified across the financial services, transportation, high-tech, medical-device manufacturing, and healthcare industries.

Moreover, the state government is working hard to attract more high-tech companies, launching an IT Florida Task Force that has had some success. Between Tampa and Orlando is a stretch referred to as the I4 Corridor, where the state has lured a number of high-tech companies to establish facilities. Plans to bring semiconductor manufacturing to the area raised environmental concerns, but three large IT-related businesses in the Tampa-St. Petersburg metro area are featured on the *Miami Herald's* "The Herald 100": Tech Data Corporation, a hardware and software distributor in Tampa (number 15) employing over 8,200 people, and two large IT outsourcers, Sykes Enterprises in Tampa (number 33), which employs more than 10,000, and IMRglobal Corporation, a Clearwater-based firm that employs 3,800 (number 76).

A number of Florida companies are considered leading IT users. Tech Data and Office Depot, in Delray Beach, made both "The Herald 100" and the *InformationWeek* 500 lists. Tampa-based TECO Energy, number 53 on "The Herald 100," ranked number 15 on *Computerworld*'s "100 Best Places to Work in IT 2000" list; and Home Shopping Network, in St. Petersburg, was number 41. While IT salaries across the state are a bit lower than in other areas, the cost of living is also lower, and the lifestyle is definitely more laid back.

MAJOR EMPLOYERS   Miami-Ft. Lauderdale: Florida Power & Light, Assurant Group, Office Depot, Inc., Carnival Corp., Ryder System, Inc., AutoNation, Inc., The Wackenhut Corp.; **Tampa-St. Petersburg:** TECO Energy, Inc., Tech Data Corp., The Tribune Co.,

Home Shopping Network; **Orlando:** Tupperware Worldwide, Walt Disney Co., Universal Orlando.

TYPICAL IT SALARIES   **Miami:** Systems analyst, $59,235; database administrator, $65,696; network/data communications manager, $87,158; **Ft. Lauderdale:** Systems analyst, $60,013; database administrator, $66,581; network/data communications manager, $88,396; **Tampa:** Systems administrator, $56,241; database administrator, $62,603; network/data communications manager, $83,738; **St. Petersburg:** Systems analyst, $56,051; database administrator, $62,390; network/data communications manager, $83,447; **Orlando:** Systems analyst, $57,562; database administrator, $63,895; network/data communications manager, $84,934.

MEDIAN HOME PRICE   **Miami:** $135,200; **Ft. Lauderdale:** $136,200; **Tampa:** $94,800; **Orlando:** $106,300.

COST-OF-LIVING INDEX   **Miami-Ft. Lauderdale:** 107.9; **Tampa:** 97.3; **Orlando:** 100.2.

POPULATION   **Miami:** 2,175,634; **Ft. Lauderdale:** 1,535,468; **Tampa-St. Petersburg-Clearwater:** 2,278,169; **Orlando:** 1,535,004.

UNEMPLOYMENT RATE   **Statewide:** 3.6 percent; **Miami:** 4.9 percent; **Ft. Lauderdale:** 3.3 percent; **Tampa-St. Petersburg-Clearwater:** 2.4 percent; **Orlando:** 2.3 percent (all data for December 2000).

ONLINE EMPLOYMENT RESOURCES   www.florida.computerjobs.com, centralflorida.techies.com, southflorida.techies.com, florida.computerwork.com, miami.computerwork.com, orlando.computerwork.com, tampabay.computerwork.com.

TIP *In evaluating the probability of landing a good job in a particular metropolitan area or region, weigh the unemployment rate against the caliber and number of the area's top employers. If the unemployment rate is very low, but the area boasts a number of leading-edge IT shops, you can safely figure that the IT shops have a difficult time recruiting and retaining IT pros simply due to a lack of available candidates on the job market.*

Hartford, Connecticut

Hartford appears here with some reservations. It's an insurance town—among the three cities with the most insurance company headquarters in the world—and insurance remains its largest single industry. But insurance companies are big users of information technology, and Hartford hosts some real standouts: Aetna, Travelers Property Casualty Corporation, Massachusetts Mutual Life Insurance Company (which is based in Springfield, Massachusetts, but has a sizeable IT operation in Hartford), and many others. Their operations are quite diversified, offering myriad lines of insurance products as well as financial services. That, plus the sheer volume of insurers in the area, ensures that despite slow jobs growth for Hartford overall, the IT job market should remain healthy.

Competition for IT staff among the insurers here is fierce, prompting employers to come up with some creative recruiting and retention techniques. The Hartford Financial Services Group, for example, formed an internal IT consulting arm, Hartford Technology Services, in the hopes of attracting entrepreneurial types into the corporate fold. The company also actively maintains an alumni network, keeping in touch with former IT staff members to get referrals to new employees as well as to keep the doors open should a former employee decide to return. Travelers has a similar program.

Hartford's central East Coast location—just about equidistant between New York and Boston, and close to the Connecticut and Rhode Island shorelines as well as the Berkshires of Southern Massachusetts—make it a livable city for those who appreciate the outdoor life. On the other hand, job growth in 2000 was a mere 0.17 percent, and the forecast through 2010 isn't spectacular either—only 9.18 percent vs. a 15.09 percent national average, according to *Money* magazine. So, while demand for IT professionals is outpacing the supply, the long-term economic outlook for the city is not insured.

MAJOR EMPLOYERS   Aetna Inc., United Technologies Corp., The Hartford Financial Services Group.

TYPICAL IT SALARIES   Systems analyst, $64,789; database administrators, $71,485; network/data communications manager, $93,728.

MEDIAN HOME PRICE $151,200.

COST-OF-LIVING INDEX   112.5.

POPULATION   1,147,504.

UNEMPLOYMENT RATE   1.6 percent (December 2000).

ONLINE EMPLOYMENT RESOURCES   hartford.techies.com, hartford.computerwork.com.

Las Vegas, Nevada

Who would have ever thought—other than perhaps Bugsy Siegel—that Las Vegas would one day make all the major "Best Places to Live" lists? And yet this once rough-and-tumble desert town is thriving, creating new jobs faster than they can be filled. The casino boom of the nineties, coupled with growing government services to support the ever-increasing population, has created IT jobs as varied as the themes of the new casinos. Jobs growth in 2000 outpaced the national average, at 4.54 percent vs. 1.68 percent, according to *Money* magazine's "Best Places to Live 2000" report. Moreover, jobs growth through 2010 is forecast at 42 percent—nearly triple the national average of 15.09 percent. Unemployment rates have kept pace with the national norm, at or around 4 percent.

Gaming, not surprisingly, is the biggest IT game in town. But the boom in gaming has also meant a boom in construction and related services. A friendly tax climate has also drawn call centers and distribution hubs to open here. Mayor Oscar Goodman is vigorously promoting his town among members of the high-tech community, hoping to establish a solid base of technology vendors in the area. In the meantime, Vegas is a big draw for independent consultants and startups. Bugsy Siegel's entrepreneurial vision survives. Viva Las Vegas; viva IT.

MAJOR EMPLOYERS Park Place Entertainment Corp., University of Las Vegas, the State of Nevada, Mandalay Resort Group, MGM Mirage.

TYPICAL IT SALARIES Systems analyst, $63,321; database administrator, $70,029; network/data communications manager, $92,311.

MEDIAN HOME PRICE $131,300.

COST-OF-LIVING INDEX 105.1.

POPULATION 1,381,086.

UNEMPLOYMENT RATE 4.1 percent (December 2000).

ONLINE EMPLOYMENT RESOURCES lasvegas.techies.com, lasvegas.computerwork.com.

Memphis, Tennessee

Elvis may have left the building, but Memphis still rocks. The hometown of the King of Rock and Roll is notable as the home base for two of the largest—and most employee-friendly—IT workplaces in the country. FedEx Corporation and Harrah's Entertainment ranked third and fourth, respectively, on *Computerworld*'s "100 Best Places to

Work in IT 2000" list. And each also was selected for the *InformationWeek* 500 list of IT innovators for 2000. FedEx's presence here, along with the city's location at the junction of two major interstates with the Mississippi River, has drawn a number of companies to set up major distribution and transportation centers here, among them Williams-Sonoma, Nike, and Northwest Airlines. Throw in several large hospitals and healthcare-related companies like Baptist Memorial Health Care Corporation and Schering-Plough HealthCare Products, the University of Memphis, and a number of brokerage firms, and the IT job market in this midsized city of the mid-South is as mighty as the Mississippi itself.

Memphis is also a downright livable city, with a strong sense of community and history, not to mention some of the best barbecue in the country. The annual month-long Memphis in May festival draws visitors from all over the country for the music and the food, and Graceland continues to lure Elvis fans from the world over for the annual Elvis Week activities each August. And in the spirit of southern hospitality, no one ever forgets to say, "Thank you. Thankyouverymuch."

MAJOR EMPLOYERS   FedEx Corp., Harrah's Entertainment Inc., Stream International Inc., Baptist Memorial Health Care Corp., Schering-Plough HealthCare Products, Inc., AutoZone, Inc., International Paper, Morgan Keegan & Co., Inc., University of Memphis.

TYPICAL IT SALARIES   Systems analyst, $58,659; database administrator, $65,054; network analyst, $68,558.

MEDIAN HOME PRICE $114,600.

COST-OF-LIVING INDEX   92.4.

POPULATION   1,105,058.

UNEMPLOYMENT RATE   3.6 percent (December 2000).

ONLINE EMPLOYMENT RESOURCES   midsouth.techies.com, memphis.computerwork.com.

Minneapolis and St. Paul, Minnesota

The Twin Cities may be in the coldest state in the lower 48, but the IT job market is anything but frigid. Minneapolis and St. Paul support a diverse array of industries, including high tech, healthcare, hospitality, retail, transportation, and grocery manufacturing, plus they have a remarkably high number of leading IT shops. Manufacturer

3M, hospitality firm Carlson Companies, retailer Best Buy Company, airline Northwest Airlines, and food company General Mills ranked on the *InformationWeek* 500 list for 2000; Best Buy, General Mills, and Minnesota Life Insurance Company turn up on *Computerworld's* "Best Places to Work in IT 2000" list; and healthcare company United-Health Group made both lists.

Despite the cold clime, the Twin Cities area gets high marks for livability, with one of the lowest cost-of-living indexes for all large U.S. metropolitan areas as well as one of the shortest average commute times, plus 27 hospitals, 2 major zoos, 1,000 parks, and several major pro sports teams. It ranked number 44 on *Forbes* magazine's "Best Places" list.

The area is also ripe with educational opportunities, and a number of area colleges have collaborated with local industry to tailor IT programs to meet the needs of the local market. The Carlson School of Management at the local campus of the University of Minnesota offers one of the leading techno-M.B.A. programs in the country. So if you want to work in IT and work on an IT degree at the same time, you'll find twin opportunities in the Twin Cities.

MAJOR EMPLOYERS   Carlson Companies, Inc., The Pillsbury Co., 3M, Target Corp., UnitedHealth Group, Northwest Airlines, Best Buy Co., Inc., General Mills, Inc.

TYPICAL IT SALARIES   **Minneapolis:** Database administrator, $70,180; webmaster, $71,143; network analyst, $73,827; **St Paul:** Database administrator, $69,455; webmaster, $70,419; network analyst, $73,108.

MEDIAN HOME PRICE $139,400.

COST-OF-LIVING INDEX   102.

POPULATION   2,872,109.

UNEMPLOYMENT RATE   2.1 percent (December 2000).

ONLINE EMPLOYMENT RESOURCES   www.twincities.computerjobs.com, twincities.techies.com, twincities.computerwork.com.

New York, New York

With one of the highest concentrations of financial services, publishing, music, entertainment, and media companies in the world, New York has long had a dynamic IT job market. But since the mid-nineties, when the city's Silicon Alley suddenly emerged as the dot-com capital of the world, the demand for IT professionals surged like the tallest skyscrapers over the bustling metropolis. It was just the shot in the arm New

York's economy needed at the time, and even though a number of the original Silicon Alley employers have disappeared or downsized, the IT job market appears to be surviving the crush—at least for now.

Largely because of high IT demand, unemployment in the Big Apple has steadily decreased since the mid-nineties. The new Internet-related businesses revitalized the city, and soon even so-called "old economy" employers were vying with dot-com start-ups to get up-and-coming dot-com kids onboard. But overall, unemployment here is still somewhat higher than the national average. While it dropped to an annual average of 5.7 percent for 2000 from 6.7 percent for 1999, the future is cloudy. New York's projected job growth rate through 2010 is only 4.54 percent, compared to a national average of 15.09 percent. Nonetheless, thanks to the city's economic diversity and the number of large employers across a diverse range of industries, New York–based IT professionals can still find ample opportunity.

While IT managers always say they need IT professionals who are good communicators, nowhere is the ability to talk a good game more important than in New York. The Big Apple has little tolerance for people who can't get right to the point. And the city that never sleeps lives up to its reputation for working hard and playing hard. Demand for IT professionals is high, but so are the cost of living, rent, crime, and other negatives. On the other hand, there's never a dull moment, and if you want to be *near* the city but not actually *in* the city, the metro area covers Westchester County, Long Island, Northern New Jersey, and Southern Connecticut, each of which also offers a robust IT job market.

MAJOR EMPLOYERS   New York City: Merrill Lynch & Co., Inc., UBS PaineWebber Inc., Viacom Inc., AOL Time Warner Inc., Pfizer Inc., Barnes & Noble, Inc., Colgate-Palmolive Co., PricewaterhouseCoopers, Avon Products, Inc., Metropolitan Life Insurance Co., The MONY Group Inc.; **Long Island:** Computer Associates International, Inc., Cablevision Systems Corp., 1-800-Flowers.com, Inc., Arrow Electronics, Inc.; **Northern New Jersey:** The Prudential Insurance Company of America, Toys R Us, Inc., Matsushita Corp. of America, Lucent Technologies, Inc., AT&T.

TYPICAL IT SALARIES   Manhattan: Database administrator, $76,315; webmaster, $77,350; network analyst, $80,234; **Long Island:** Database administrator, $75,266; webmaster, $76,290; network analyst, $79,143.

TYPICAL RENT ON A ONE-BEDROOM APARTMENT (MANHATTAN) $1,650–$2,694 (according to research by *Time Out New York*, Issue No. 255, August 10–17, 2000, page 27).

MEDIAN HOME PRICE $204,600.

COST-OF-LIVING INDEX   234.6.

POPULATION   Manhattan: July 1, 1998: 1,550,649; **New York City:** 8,712,600; **Greater New York metropolitan area:** 20,196,649.

UNEMPLOYMENT RATE   New York City: 5.2 percent; **Greater New York metropolitan area:** 4.8 percent (all data for December 2000).

ONLINE EMPLOYMENT RESOURCES   www.nynma.org/jobs/ (for Silicon Alley jobs), www.newyork.computerjobs.com, newyork.techies.com, newyork.computerwork.com.

Northwest Arkansas

The Fayetteville-Springdale-Rogers metropolitan statistical area is one of the best-kept secrets in the country: It's a utopia for IT professionals who want a challenging job but a laid-back lifestyle. Situated in the northwest corner of Arkansas in the Ozark Mountains, the area is home to three of the top IT shops in the country: Wal-Mart Stores, Tyson Foods, and J.B. Hunt Transport Services. Each has large implementations of leading-edge technology, and all three made the *InformationWeek* 500 list of leading IT innovators in 2000. Moreover, because the area is such a well-kept secret and unemployment is a low 1.7 percent (December 2000), finding qualified IT professionals is difficult. So each company goes out of its way to work on IT recruiting and retention, offering great benefits and a fun workplace.

J.B. Hunt, for example, which ranked number 60 on *Computerworld's* "100 Best Places to Work in IT 2000" list, pays relocation expenses and pays for temporary living expenses for up to 30 days. The company also organizes IT team outings such as golfing or canoeing. Tyson, which recently opened a cavernous new facility for its IT staff in an old supermarket, throws a number of parties each year, such as a Rodeo Day–themed barbecue complete with a country-western band, and a tailgate party to celebrate the college football season kickoff (in honor of the University of Arkansas Razorbacks, in Fayetteville). Wal-Mart is number 79 on *Computerworld's* "100 Best Places to Work in IT 2000" list.

Besides the three large IT shops in the Fayetteville-Springdale-Rogers metropolitan area, a number of large companies are located nearby in the Fort Smith metropolitan area, such as Beverly Enterprises, a leading provider of acute healthcare services, and beverage distiller Hiram Walker. Northwest Arkansas is even sprouting some software startups, like BAV Software, which develops and sells supply-chain software for retailers, and Apprentice Information Systems, which provides custom software and consulting to local government agencies. According to *Money* magazine's "Best Places to Live 2000" report, job growth through 2010 in the Fayetteville-Springdale-Rogers tri-city area is forecast at 31.52 percent, more than double the national average of 15.39 percent. Combine that with the local surroundings—the bucolic Ozark Mountains, the Buffalo National River, and the genteel university campus—and you start to wonder how this small metropolitan area has remained a secret so long.

MAJOR EMPLOYERS Wal-Mart Stores, Inc., J.B. Hunt Transport Services, Inc., Tyson Foods, Inc., the University of Arkansas.

TYPICAL IT SALARIES Fayetteville: Systems analyst, $54,042; database administrator, $60,141; network/data communications manager, $80,399; **Springdale:** Systems analyst, $53,440; database administrator, $59,460; network/data communications manager, $79,456; **Rogers:** Systems analyst, $52,653; database administrator, $58,584; network/data communications manager, $78,283.

MEDIAN HOME PRICE Fayetteville: $134,600; **Ft. Smith:** $98,400.

COST-OF-LIVING INDEX Fayetteville: 92.2; **Ft. Smith:** 86.6.

POPULATION 285,017.

UNEMPLOYMENT RATE 1.7 percent (December 2000).

ONLINE EMPLOYMENT RESOURCES www.whatajob.com.

Omaha, Nebraska

With economic growth higher than the national average and a cost-of-living index lower than the national average, Omaha is frequently cited as one of the best places to live in the United States. In fact, economic growth has been so steady and robust that the city has taken great strides to thwart a job market crisis. Unemployment has hovered around a low 3 percent for several years running, but employment since 1990 has increased 25 percent, with 85,000 new jobs created between 1990 and 1999. Local businesses, colleges and universities, and government have made a strong commitment to aggressively recruit out-of-state talent, particularly to fill IT jobs.

For example, The AIM Institute, a nonprofit consortium of 35 area businesses, 10 local and regional colleges and universities, the Greater Omaha Chamber of Commerce, and the State of Nebraska, was formed to coordinate community resources toward bolstering the local IT workforce. AIM's studies on the local IT skills gaps led to the creation in 1995 of the Creighton Institute for Information Technology and Management at Creighton University, to provide technology-training programs to local businesses and their employees.

There are plenty of IT jobs to merit all the effort. With 30 insurance firms making their headquarters here, and a plethora of call centers and services firms in the area, the number of unfilled IT positions just seems to keep increasing. For example, in late 1999, local IT staffing firm Data Processing Resources Corporation (DPRC) was acquired by Compuware, which announced plans to begin offering IT consulting services and to hire an additional 70 IT professionals over 18 months. First Data Corporation, a leading provider of credit card, debit card, checking, electronic funds transfer, and other payment-processing systems, built a new technology center in 1998, and in 2000, announced plans to build a new 200,000-square-foot office complex. First National Bank opened a new technology center in 1999 that will employ 350 IT professionals. And those are just a few examples. Omaha also has a number of manufacturing facilities, which collectively saw a 10.8 percent increase in employment between 1990 and 1999, compared with a decrease of 3.4 percent in the sector nationwide.

Despite the glowing economic picture, Omaha suffers from an image problem: It isn't likely to top most college graduates' or young professionals' list of cool places to live. But it hasn't gone unnoticed by outfits that research the topic, and it makes most of the major "Best Places to Live" and "Best Places to Work" lists, from *Money* magazine's to *Forbes.*' For IT professionals, it's a wild kingdom waiting to be inhabited.

MAJOR EMPLOYERS   ConAgra Foods, Inc., First Data Corp., Mutual of Omaha Cos., Union Pacific Corp.

TYPICAL IT SALARIES   Database administrator, $63,620; webmaster, $64,548; network analyst, $67,133.

MEDIAN HOME PRICE $109,600.

COST-OF-LIVING INDEX   94.

POPULATION   698,875.

UNEMPLOYMENT RATE   2.4 percent (December 2000).

ONLINE EMPLOYMENT RESOURCES   greatplains.techies.com, www.accessomaha.com/Jobs/jobs.html, www.omaha.org.

TIP *When assessing the salary you should negotiate in a new town, don't rely on a single source of information. Because the methods of gathering salary data, the organizations surveyed, and many other aspects of the research vary from survey to survey, it's best to eyeball three to five different surveys and come up with a salary range based on a combination of the data. First run your current salary through one or two of the salary and cost-of-living calculators available on the Web—they'll help you determine what you need to earn in a new city to maintain the same standard of living you have in your current city. (See the online resources at the end of this chapter.) Then compare that to the average salaries for your job title as stated by a few different IT salary surveys, such as the ERI data provided in this chapter and other surveys available online. (See Chapter 14 for links to IT salary information on the Web.)*

Pacific Northwest

Two things are certain in the Pacific Northwest: rain and IT employment. Both the Seattle and Portland metropolitan areas scored in the top 20 of *Forbes* magazine's "Best Places" list, and Portland garnered the distinction of best big city in *Money* magazine's "Best Places to Live 2000" report. Job growth in Seattle to 2010 is forecast at 20.06 percent, and in Portland at 26.59 percent, well ahead of the national average of 15.39 percent. The *InformationWeek* 500 list for 2000 ranked Seattle-area employers Microsoft Corporation number 88, Airborne Express number 462, and Portland's Tektronix number 135.

Both metropolitan areas are fairly well diversified, but each has a substantial number of high-tech employers. Seattle, in fact, has become something of a northern Silicon Valley, with not only Microsoft, but also RealNetworks, developers of the ubiquitous RealMedia player; a number of IT consulting and services firms; and dot-coms galore, most notably Amazon.com, which—despite its growing pains—has set the standard for ecommerce. And Portland counts some 1,200 high-tech employers among its corporate citizens.

Both areas are noted for their scenic beauty as well as their robust job markets. Seattle is perched on the Puget Sound in the shadow of the Olympic Mountains. Portland, dubbed the "City of Roses," is situated at the junction of the Willamette and Columbia Rivers, with the Cascade Mountains to the east and the Coastal Mountains to the west. Each city has revived its downtown area, offering all the urban amenities that draw young professionals to a city. When it's raining, it's pouring.

MAJOR EMPLOYERS   Seattle: Microsoft Corp., Airborne Express, Amazon.com, The Boeing Co., Starbucks Coffee Co., Costco Wholesale Corp.; **Portland:** Nike, Inc., Columbia Sportswear Co., Tektronix, Inc., Mentor Graphics Corp.

TYPICAL IT SALARIES   Seattle: Database administrator, $71,928; webmaster, $72,896; network analyst, $75,594; **Portland:** Database administrator, $68,368; webmaster, $69,317; network analyst, $71,961.

MEDIAN HOME PRICE   Seattle: $221,400; **Portland:** $165,700.

COST-OF-LIVING INDEX   Seattle: 130.2; **Portland:** 111.

POPULATION   Seattle: 2,334,934; **Portland:** 1,845,840.

UNEMPLOYMENT RATE   Seattle-Bellevue-Everett: 3.2 percent; **Portland, Oregon-Vancouver, Washington:** 3.2 percent (all data for December 2000).

ONLINE EMPLOYMENT RESOURCES   Seattle: www.seattle.computerjobs.com, seattle.techies.com, seattle.computerwork.com; **Portland:** www.portland.computer-jobs.com, portland.techies.com, portland.computerwork.com.

Philadelphia, Pennsylvania

More than 30 Fortune 500 employers have their headquarters in the birthplace of the constitution, which constitutes a strong IT job market in telecommunications, biotechnology, financial services, healthcare, and manufacturing. While projected job growth in the Greater Philadelphia area through 2010 is relatively low—7.71 percent, or about half the national average of 15.39 percent—a number of area employers are considered leading-edge IT users. E.I. du Pont de Nemours and Company, QVC, PECO Energy, Cigna Corporation, and Unisys Corporation all landed a place on the *InformationWeek* 500 list in 2000. The latter two also rank among *Computerworld's* "100 Best Places to Work in IT 2000" list.

The Greater Philadelphia area encompasses parts of Northern Delaware and Southern New Jersey—including Atlantic City, the East Coast's casino capital—adding to the diverse array of IT jobs. And owing to its history as the cradle of democracy, a fierce sense of independence runs through Philadelphia, and the metro area is home to a number of small IT consulting firms as well as large employers.

As for quality of life, Philadelphia offers all the amenities of any large city, with a lively arts and cultural scene, historic sites, the Ivy League school the University of Pennsylvania, and major league sports franchises. Just outside Philadelphia lie some of the most beautiful beaches on the Eastern Seaboard, in Southern New Jersey, offering prime recreational pursuits when the city's ample diversions just aren't enough. Let freedom ring.

MAJOR EMPLOYERS Cigna Corp., Towers Perrin, Verizon Communications, Comcast Corp., Bethlehem Steel Corp., E.I. du Pont de Nemours and Company, Motorola's Broadband Communications Sector (formerly General Instrument), MBNA Corp., PECO Energy, The Pep Boys, Sunoco, Inc., Unisys Corp., Urban Outfitters, Inc.

TYPICAL IT SALARIES Systems analyst, $63,981; database administrator, $70,630; network analyst, $74,274.

MEDIAN HOME PRICE $131,000.

COST-OF-LIVING INDEX 123.1.

POPULATION 4,949,867.

UNEMPLOYMENT RATE 3.4 percent (December 2000).

ONLINE EMPLOYMENT RESOURCES www.philadelphia.computerjobs.com, philadelphia.techies.com, philadelphia.computerwork.com.

Phoenix, Arizona

Given its proximity to California, coupled with a low cost of living, Phoenix has cooked up a spicy mix of IT employment opportunities. While not so many companies make their headquarters here, a number of leading firms maintain major data centers in the area, including American Express Company, Charles Schwab & Company, and Visa International; high-tech employers Motorola, Intel Corporation, and Honeywell International also have major operations here.

Together, these companies have drawn a substantial IT workforce from outside the area. But demand still outstrips the supply, with airlines, energy company Tosco Corporation (number 63 on *Computerworld*'s "100 Best Places to Work in IT 2000" list), and other manufacturing firms also competing for the available talent. Phoenix also supports a healthy healthcare-related sector, given the number of retirees and others who move to the area for the benefits of the desert climate. Hospital IT departments in the area are so strapped for talent to staff their software projects that they are turning to non-IT professionals who have clinical experience.

The Phoenix-Mesa metropolitan area came in at number 23 on *Forbes* magazine's "Best Places" list for 2000. Job growth is projected at 28.36 percent through 2010, according to *Money* magazine, and unemployment rates have held steady at between 2.3 and 3.3 percent since 1998, according to the Bureau of Labor Statistics. The climate may be arid, but the IT job market is an oasis.

MAJOR EMPLOYERS   America West Airlines, American Express Co., Charles Schwab & Co., Honeywell International Inc., Motorola, Inc., Southwest Airlines Co., Tosco Corp.

TYPICAL IT SALARIES   Database administrator, $65,317; webmaster, $66,243; network analyst, $68,823.

MEDIAN HOME PRICE $127,200.

COST-OF-LIVING INDEX   101.6.

POPULATION   3,013,696.

UNEMPLOYMENT RATE   2.4 percent (December 2000).

ONLINE EMPLOYMENT RESOURCES   www.phoenix.computerjobs.com, phoenix.techies.com, www.arizonajobs.com, phoenix.computerwork.com.

Research Triangle Park, North Carolina

Locals call the area surrounding Research Triangle Park, North Carolina, simply "The Triangle," referring to the triumvirate of Raleigh, Durham, and Chapel Hill, each of which boasts a major university. It could also refer to the triumvirate of market segments that dominate local employment, all of which have high demand for skilled IT professionals: high tech, government, and healthcare, including pharmaceuticals and biopharmaceuticals.

IBM Corporation, Cisco Systems, and Ericsson are just a few of the 29 high-tech companies that have large organizations based in Research Triangle Park (RTP), the largest research center in the United States, supporting 136 companies and research organizations. The 7,000-acre campus is also home to some 30 pharmaceutical- and healthcare-related companies drawn to the area by the presence of two medical schools and one of the highest concentrations of M.D.s in the country. The dynamic growth generated by RTP and the rich development work going on around the campus were major factors prompting *Money* magazine to confer "Best of the South" status on the area. Anticipated job growth of 24.8 percent by 2010 places the Triangle at number 25 in the nation.

With so much private-sector competition in RTP, the state government—the area's largest employer—struggles to get the IT professionals it needs. One recent ad in the *Raleigh News & Observer* posted by the state Court Management and Information Services Division sought to fill 11 IT positions at one time. Demand for IT professionals outside government and RTP is equally high, and a number of leading-edge IT shops call the metro area home, including utility CP&L (formerly Carolina Power & Light) and software developer SAS Institute, both of which were ranked on the *InformationWeek* 500 list of leading IT innovators for 2000.

The Triangle, with outdoor recreation in some of the most beautiful countryside in the country, also offers plenty of chances to unwind after a day on the job. Chapel Hill is full of the best charms that a college town has to offer, including top-flight college sports teams, an outstanding theater program, and lots of live music. Plenty of jobs, high pay relative to local expenses, and easy living make this growing metropolitan area a leading choice for IT professionals seeking a work/life balance.

MAJOR EMPLOYERS   GlaxoSmithKline, University of North Carolina, CP&L, IBM Corp., SAS Institute Inc., Duke University Medical Center, State of North Carolina.

TYPICAL IT SALARIES   **Raleigh:** Database administrator, $65,491; webmaster, $66,416; network analyst, $68,994; **Durham:** Database administrator, $65,225; webmaster, $66,149; network analyst, $68,726; **Chapel Hill:** Database administrator, $63,954; webmaster, $64,861; network analyst, $67,389.

MEDIAN HOME PRICE $164,600.

COST-OF-LIVING INDEX   100.6.

POPULATION   1,105,535.

UNEMPLOYMENT RATE   1.6 percent (December 2000).

ONLINE EMPLOYMENT RESOURCES   www.carolina.computerjobs.com, northcarolina.techies.com, triangle.computerwork.com, www.researchtriangle.com.

San Francisco and Silicon Valley, California

For IT professionals, there's probably little mystery about why *Money* magazine chose San Francisco as best large city in its "Best Places to Live 1999" report. Its proximity to Silicon Valley mixed with its lively social and cultural scene has spawned a multitude of dot-com startups, as well as software development companies and IT services firms. But the city is not merely the northern tip of the technological center of the universe;

the business environment in San Francisco is one of the most diversified in the nation, with financial services, national retailers, apparel manufacturers, and other large companies making their headquarters here.

It's not only the outstanding job market that makes San Francisco so appealing to so many. Each of its myriad neighborhoods has a distinct character and charm; Golden Gate Park is one of the most beautiful large urban parks in the country; and unparalleled outdoor recreation in a tranquil landscape can be found within an hour or two of the city—in any direction.

Stretching down the peninsula south of San Francisco to San Jose is Silicon Valley, the birthplace of myriad technological advances and major computer companies. The culture in the Valley is decidedly different than in San Francisco. The majority of the residents are involved in the computer industry in one way or another, and social lives tend to be defined by work. But whether you're interested in internal IT or developing the next generation of information technology products, the opportunities are as plentiful as they come. Not only does Silicon Valley offer challenging and demanding work, it also offers access to some of the most talented technologists in the world.

Eight area companies earned mention on *Computerworld*'s "100 Best Places to Work in IT 2000" list, including AutoDesk, DPR Construction, Cisco Systems, Silicon Graphics, Intel Corporation, Charles Schwab & Company, PG&E, and Hewlett-Packard Company. The latter six also appear on the *InformationWeek* 500 list for 2000, along with Chevron Corporation and Sun Microsystems.

MAJOR EMPLOYERS **San Francisco:** Gap Inc., Wells Fargo & Co., Charles Schwab & Co., Chevron Corp., Levi Strauss & Co.; **Silicon Valley:** Intel Corp., Hewlett-Packard Co., Cisco Systems Inc., Oracle Corp., Sun Microsystems Inc., Apple Computer Inc.

TYPICAL IT SALARIES **San Francisco:** Database administrator, $77,024; webmaster, $78,047; network analyst, $80,899; **Oakland:** Database administrator, $75,713; webmaster, $76,727; network analyst, $79,554; **San Jose:** Database administrator, $77,064; webmaster, $78,093; network analyst, $80,960.

MEDIAN HOME PRICE **San Francisco:** $372,700; **San Jose:** $327,800; **Oakland:** $273,600.

COST-OF-LIVING INDEX **San Francisco:** 187.1; **San Jose:** 193.4; **Oakland:** 147.5.

POPULATION **San Francisco:** 1,685,647; **San Jose:** 1,647,419; **Oakland:** 2,348,723.

UNEMPLOYMENT RATE San Francisco: 1.8 percent; **Oakland:** 2.2 percent; **San Jose:** 1.3 percent (all data for December 2000).

ONLINE EMPLOYMENT RESOURCES www.siliconvalley.computerjobs.com, bayarea.techies.com, www.californiajobs.com, bayarea.computerwork.com.

St. Louis, Missouri

The Gateway to the West is delivering on the promise symbolized by the famous arch that frames the city from its eastern border on the banks of the Mississippi River. Diversity is the defining adjective for St. Louis' business landscape; among the city's corporate residents are manufacturing, financial services, transportation, food and beverage distribution, and healthcare firms. Moreover, as one of the top five U.S. cities for Fortune 1000 corporate headquarters, St. Louis has a number of cutting-edge IT shops. Privately held Enterprise Rent-A-Car Company, which this year topped the *St. Louis Post-Dispatch's* list of leading private companies in the area, was cited on the *InformationWeek* 500 list of leading IT innovators for 2000, as were local employers Ralston Purina Company, Anheuser-Busch, The Earthgrains Company, and Sigma-Aldrich Company. Earthgrains and Sigma-Aldrich also ranked as two of *Computerworld's* "100 Best Places to Work in IT 2000."

Both the cost of living and unemployment in St. Louis are below the national average, and job growth of 3.25 percent in 2000 outpaced the national average of 1.68 percent. Job growth through 2010 is forecast at only 11.38 percent—below the national average. Still, with such a significant presence of Fortune 1000 companies and top IT shops, this midwestern hub remains a gateway to IT professionals.

MAJOR EMPLOYERS Monsanto Co., A.G. Edwards & Sons, Inc., Ralston Purina Co., Anheuser-Busch Inc., Enterprise Rent-A-Car Co., The Earthgrains Co., Sigma-Aldrich Co.

TYPICAL IT SALARIES Database administrator, $67,362; webmaster, $68,305; network analyst, $70,935.

MEDIAN HOME PRICE $105,300.

COST-OF-LIVING INDEX 97.8.

POPULATION 2,569,029.

UNEMPLOYMENT RATE 3.6 percent (December 2000).

ONLINE EMPLOYMENT RESOURCES www.stlouis.computerjobs.com, stlouis.techies.com, stlouis.computerwork.com.

TIP *If you're considering a job offer that involves relocating but you aren't sure whether the opportunity merits uprooting yourself and your family, you can minimize the risk by proposing a gradual relocation. Try to negotiate a three-month trial period, with temporary housing and travel expenses paid for or subsidized by the employer, before you make a permanent move. That will give you the chance to see if the job and the company are all that you expect, and it will afford your family an opportunity to explore the new city so that together you can arrive at a decision everyone feels good about.*

Southern California

While film and television studios tend to grab the spotlight in Southern California, the area is actually quite diversified. In and around Greater Los Angeles, large IT employers outside the entertainment and media industries include auto maker Toyota Motor Sales, USA, toy maker Mattel, and electronics distributor Ingram Micro, which ranked on the *InformationWeek* 500 list for 2000. Local government is also a significant employer of IT professionals.

The use of IT in entertainment companies varies. Post-production houses that offer special-effects design and editing are advanced technology users, and for a time, the studios were green-lighting web-related projects at a furious pace. But the Internet industry in the L.A. metropolitan area has been as shaky as in New York, and a number of high-profile Tinseltown web ventures have fallen to the cutting-room floor. Pop.com, a video and animation site announced by studios Dreamworks and Imagine Entertainment, ceased operations in early September 2000 before it even produced any significant content, laying off about 80 workers. At the same time, another venture backed by a Hollywood heavyweight, Michael Ovitz's multimedia site Scour.com, laid off all but 18 of its workers in 2000; most of those let go were software developers. And the Disney Internet Group has been decidedly on-again, off-again about its Go.com portal. Nevertheless, the Web will continue to play a key role in the industry, and it will drive much of the IT employment in the studios.

Due south, San Diego is a town of startups. Once dominated by large defense contracting and aerospace firms, today, San Diego has been revitalized by the spirit of entrepreneurship, spawning software development and IT services firms. Even larger companies have adopted new ways of doing business. For example, Science Applications International Corporation (SAIC) had been primarily known as a defense contractor, but has repositioned itself as a major IT outsourcer. The city's rebound from the recession of the early nineties earned it the number 6 place on *Forbes* magazine's "Best Places" list for 2000. All in all, the IT climate along the shoreline from L.A. to San Diego, sometimes called the Digital Coast, is as welcoming as the weather.

MAJOR EMPLOYERS **Los Angeles-Orange County:** Walt Disney Co., Metro-Goldwyn-Mayer Inc., Northrop Grumman Corp., Mattel Inc., Unocal Corp., Hughes Electronics Corp., Toyota Motor Sales, USA, Inc., Ingram Micro Inc.; **San Diego:** QUALCOMM Inc., Amilyn Pharmaceuticals, Jack In The Box Inc., Petco Animal Supplies, Inc., San Diego State University, Science Applications International Corp.

TYPICAL IT SALARIES **Los Angeles:** Database administrator, $73,413; webmaster, $74,418; network analyst, $77,219; **San Diego:** Database administrator, $69,098; webmaster, $70,058; network analyst, $72,735.

MEDIAN HOME PRICE **Los Angeles:** $200,600; **San Diego:** $230,700.

COST-OF-LIVING INDEX **Los Angeles:** 130.1; **San Diego:** 134.6.

POPULATION **Los Angeles-Long Beach:** 9,329,989; **Orange County:** 2,760,948; **Riverside-San Bernadino:** 3,200,587; **San Diego:** 2,820,844.

UNEMPLOYMENT RATE **Los Angeles-Long Beach:** 4.7 percent; **Orange County:** 2.0 percent; **Riverside-San Bernadino:** 4.0 percent; **San Diego:** 2.3 percent (all data for December 2000).

ONLINE EMPLOYMENT RESOURCES **Los Angeles:** www.la.computerjobs.com, losangeles.techies.com, losangeles.computerwork.com; **Orange County:** orange-county.computerwork.com; **San Diego:** sandiego.techies.com, sandiego.computerwork.com; **All cities:** www.californiajobs.com, california.computerwork.com.

Texas

From the state capital of Austin to Dallas to Houston, the high-tech industry has transformed the mix of companies and the job outlook in Texas. Most notably, the economy in Austin—a runner up for best large city in *Money* magazine's "Best Places to Live 1999" report—has been fundamentally reshaped by the presence of high-tech vendors, starting in the eighties when University of Texas (UT) college student Michael Dell founded Dell Computer Corporation. While the state government and UT are the two largest employers here, Austin is the address for a host of other hardware manufacturers, including National Instruments Corporation, Motorola, and Advanced Micro Devices, earning it the nickname Silicon Hills.

In addition to hardware makers, Austin also has IT consulting and services firms, software startups, and dot-coms. Dell, besides being a leading technology producer, is also a leading technology user. It ranks number 86 on the *InformationWeek* 500 list for 2000, and CIO Randy Mott was one of the key executives who helped align IT with business operations at Wal-Mart Stores. Job growth in the capitol city through 2010 is forecast at 33.19 percent, more than double the national average. Austin owes part of its high-tech success to UT, which has one of the top information technology degree programs in the country. The university also fuels the city's creative cultural and social milieu; Austin draws some of the best and most varied live music in the country.

Dallas also has generated its own small technology center, dubbed the Telecom Corridor, in nearby Richardson. With telecommunications heavyweights Samsung Telecommunications America, Nortel Networks, Nokia, and others establishing a presence, Richardson even went so far as to copyright its moniker. Consulting and outsourcing firm EDS, in Plano, was tapped for the *InformationWeek* 500 list of leading IT innovators in 1999, and local employers J.C. Penney Company, Brinker International, and AMR Corporation, parent of American Airlines, made the 2000 list. The latter three companies also earned spots on *Computerworld*'s "100 Best Places to Work in IT 2000" list, alongside Texas Instruments.

Houston is still an oil town, with 15 oil and gas companies, but as the home base for NASA, Houston also has its share of aerospace and engineering firms. In addition, more than 50 dot-com companies have been founded in Houston, employing 3,520 people, according to the *Houston Chronicle* ("52 New Dot-Com Companies Call Houston Home," by Rebecca Mowbray, May 15, 2000). PC manufacturer Compaq Computer Corporation is a major high-tech employer here. A number of leading IT shops are based in Houston, as well, including Enron Corporation, Continental Airlines, and Sysco Corporation, all of which ranked on the *InformationWeek* 500 list in 2000. While Texas tends to conjure up images of cowboys, longhorn steers, and oil magnates, IT professionals are staking their own brand of success here.

MAJOR EMPLOYERS   **Austin:** Dell Computer Corp., University of Texas, National Instruments Corp.; **Dallas-Ft. Worth:** Sabre Inc., EDS, J.C. Penney Co., Inc., Texas Instruments Inc., AMR Corp.; **Houston:** Compaq Computer Corp., Continental Airlines, Shell Oil Co., Methodist Healthcare System, Enron Corp., Sysco Corp.

TYPICAL IT SALARIES   **Austin:** Systems analyst, $57,047; database administrator, $63,375; network/data communications manager, $84,397; **Dallas:** Systems analyst, $60,537; database administrator, $66,992; network/data communications manager, $88,432; **Ft. Worth:** Systems analyst, $58,693; database administrator, $65,057; network/data communications manager, $86,196; **Houston:** Systems analyst, $60,986; database administrator, $67,263; network/data communications manager, $88,115.

MEDIAN HOME PRICE   **Austin:** $130,100; **Dallas:** $126,000; **Ft. Worth:** $104,100; **Houston:** $108,500.

COST-OF-LIVING INDEX **Austin:** 96.2; **Dallas:** 100.5; **Ft. Worth:** 91.1; **Houston:** 93.1.

POPULATION **Austin:** 1,146,050; **Dallas:** 3,280,310; **Ft. Worth-Arlington:** 1,629,213; **Houston:** 4,010,969.

UNEMPLOYMENT RATE **Statewide:** 3.4 percent; **Austin:** 1.6 percent; **Dallas:** 2.5 percent; **Ft. Worth-Arlington:** 2.6 percent; **Houston:** 3 percent (all data for December 2000).

ONLINE EMPLOYMENT RESOURCES **Statewide:** www.texas.computerjobs.com, www.texasjobs.com, texas.computerwork.com; **Austin:** austin.techies.com, austin.computerwork.com; **Dallas:** dallas.techies.com, dallas.computerwork.com; **Houston:** houston.techies.com, houston.computerwork.com.

Washington, D.C.

If you thought Washington, D.C., was all federal government jobs and defense industry–related work, it's time you looked at the nation's capitol with fresh eyes. While the federal government set about reinventing itself during the Clinton Administration, the metropolitan area reinvented its local economy. There's still a preponderance of government-related IT work going on here, but there's also an IT revolution, driven by such companies as AOL Time Warner, wireless communications company Nextel Communications, Internet service provider PSINet, and others. An entrepreneurial culture has emerged with technology and IT services startups in the Greater Washington area—which comprises parts of Maryland and Virginia as well as the Beltway. This area has "its first real claim to be counted as a center of commercial technology," according to an April 5, 2000, article in *The Washington Post* ("The Evolution of Wired Washington," by Peter Behr, page G11). Of 293 technology-related startups founded in and around D.C. since 1994, only 83 are focused on federal government contracting, the article stated.

Moreover, one in ten workers in the area is employed in a technology-related job, according to another *Washington Post* article ("For Tech Workers, It's Destination D.C.," by Peter Behr, April 24, 2000, page F07). Among the largest users of IT in the area, financial services firms Freddie Mac, Fannie Mae, and Capital One Financial Corporation were all tapped for both *Computerworld's* "100 Best Places to Work in IT 2000" list and the *InformationWeek* 500 list of leading IT innovators for 2000. IT professionals can give Washington a vote of confidence.

MAJOR EMPLOYERS AOL Time Warner, Mariott International, Inc., U.S. Airways, Inc., Nextel Communications, Washington Post Co., General Dynamics Corp., Fannie Mae, Freddie Mac, Capital One Financial Corp., the U.S. Government.

TYPICAL IT SALARIES   Database administrator, $69,487; webmaster, $70,441; network analyst, $73,098.

MEDIAN HOME PRICE $176,400.

COST-OF-LIVING INDEX   124.

POPULATION   4,739,999.

UNEMPLOYMENT RATE   D.C.: 6.1 percent; **Greater Washington, D.C.:** 2.1 percent (December 2000).

ONLINE EMPLOYMENT RESOURCES   www.dc.computerjobs.com, dc.techies.com, dc.computerwork.com.

NOTE *Unless otherwise indicated, all data in this chapter comes from the following sources. IT salary data comes from ERI Economic Research Institute, Redmond, Washington (www.erieri.com), and represents median base salaries on August 15, 2000, across all industries, assuming an average tenure in each position. All unemployment rates come from the U.S. Bureau of Labor Statistics (www.bls.gov). The national unemployment rate in December 2000 was 4 percent. Population data, unless otherwise indicated, comes from the U.S. Census Bureau (www.census.gov), and represents the estimated population as of July 1, 1999; unless otherwise indicated, the population figures are for the greater metropolitan statistical area, not just the primary community. Median housing prices and cost-of-living index figures come from Money magazine's "Best Places to Live 2000" report. The national median price for a three-bedroom home, according to the report, is $128,572; the baseline for the cost-of-living index is 100, and the national average is 104.*

Best Places Lists on the Web

***COMPUTERWORLD'S* 100 BEST PLACES TO WORK IN IT 2000**   www.computerworld.com/computerworld/records/images/pdf/000605bp.pdf

***MONEY* MAGAZINE'S BEST PLACES TO LIVE 2000**   www.money.com/money/depts/real_estate/bplive

***FORBES* MAGAZINE'S BEST PLACES**   www.forbes.com/tool/toolbox/bestplaces

***EMPLOYMENT REVIEW'S* BEST PLACES TO LIVE AND WORK 2000**
www.bestjobsusa.com/~candidate/bestplaces/index.asp

Relocation Tools

Use the following online salary calculators, cost-of-living calculators, and community reports for more information to help you assess the pros and cons of a move:

Fast Forward's BestPlaces.net

www.bestplaces.net

Here's a variety of relocation tools offered by the research firm that partners with *Money* magazine on its annual "Best Places to Live" report; the site features cost-of-living and salary calculators, crime statistics for 2,500 U.S. cities, information on 87,000 public schools in 16,000 school districts, climate data for 2,000 cities worldwide, detailed profiles of 1,000 cities, and an interactive "Find Your Best Place to Live" tool—enter your lifestyle preferences, and generate a list of communities that fit your profile.

MonsterMoving.com's ReloSmart

www.monstermoving.com/Relosmart

This site features city profiles (including housing information, cost-of-living analysis, and quality-of-life statistics), including a tool to generate side-by-side comparisons, plus a salary calculator and other tools; registration is required.

Homefair.com

www.homefair.com

A range of tools is available here, including an international salary calculator, moving calculator, community calculator (for researching ZIP codes with similar demographics), and report generators for cities, crime statistics, school information, home prices by street and community, and more; registration is required to use some features.

NewsEngin's Cost-of-Living Inflation Calculator

www.NewsEngin.com/neFreeTools.nsf/083c35bcd0562e26862565af0057ad64?Open-View&Start=1

This is a useful calculator for determining how the cost of living has increased city-by-city; for example, it shows that $100 in New York City in 1995 had the same buying power as $102.90 in 1996. Use it to evaluate how quickly the cost-of-living is rising in your target city.

BestJobsUSA.com City Outlines

www.bestjobsusa.com/careerguide/comap/comap.asp

These profiles of major U.S. cities feature a sprinkling of demographic data (some of it is several years old), a listing of major employers, and a brief rundown on the quality of life.

Part IV

How to Get There from Here

In this Part

Chapter 12

· ·

The Skills that Thrill: Getting the Training You Need to Maintain Your Marketability

After three years as a programmer, Ted Pulliam started to feel that his skills were stalling. His employer, a large bank, had given him some opportunities for on-the-job skills development, and he was working with newer technologies—Visual Basic, Active Server Pages, HTML, and C++—but he'd had little formal training and feared that he'd fall behind his peers. When he began looking around for a new position, his priority was to find an employer committed to regular IT training. "Knowing that a company thinks enough of you to invest in you and have high expectations of you is about 75 percent of job satisfaction in IT," Pulliam explains.

He accepted a position at Republic Mortgage Insurance Company (RMIC), in Winston-Salem, North Carolina, in June 2000 largely because the company pledged that he'd be trained for new projects. "That's what pulled me over—they made it clear that they would help me achieve my objectives," he says. RMIC made good on its promise within three months. That September, Pulliam traveled to Massachusetts for a two-week bootcamp in Siebel Call Center, part of Siebel Systems' e-business applications suite. Comprised of one-third class lectures and two-thirds hands-on lab work, the bootcamp extended his applications development skills into the customer relationship management (CRM) arena and enabled him to immediately start creating new CRM applications for RMIC's call center, he says. His ability to quickly transfer what he had learned into a live production environment paid off: Less than a year after joining RMIC, Pulliam earned his first promotion. In the spring of 2001, he took up development on a high-visibility application that will enable RMIC customers to submit mortgage insurance applications online.

"I feel like I'm making a bigger impact on the company because the sale of loan insurance is our bread and butter," Pulliam says. "And I'm helping our sales people increase their productivity."

Pulliam's burst of professional growth highlights that continuously upgrading your skills is a never-ending necessity in an IT career. "It's incredibly important in this profession to be a lifelong learner," says Phil DeKok, manager of IT training and sourcing at catalog company Lands' End, based in Dodgeville, Wisconsin. "There is no such thing as having arrived. Because of the pace at which technology is moving and changing, if at any point you sit back and say, 'I'm comfortable with what I know,' you'll quickly become obsolete. You need to be able to react to new technologies in the enterprise and make sure you continue adding value to the business's ability to maintain its competitiveness."

Plotting Your Training Roadmap

Navigating through all the training possibilities is a tricky proposition: How do you decide what training to take, and how do you go about getting it, especially if your employer doesn't have an ongoing commitment to training? Do you go for the top-paying skills or concentrate on the technologies your current employer is using? Do you stay within your comfort zone or strike out on something entirely new? Do you wait for your employer to pay for it or do you spend your own money? Can you get by on self-study, or do you need formal classroom training?

The answers come down to an assessment of your current skills, where you see yourself a year from now, and where you see yourself headed in the future. If you plan to seek corporate support for your training goals, you must also factor in the direction that IT is taking in your company.

"Weigh the business needs of your company against your own personal goals and, keeping both in mind, try to plot a career track," Pulliam suggests. "And then take the training to help move you along that track." In approaching your manager to request training, "always justify the business need," he adds. "Definitely make your interests known, but keep the needs of the company in the forefront."

Unfortunately, not all employers are proactive about training, nor are they all on the leading edge of technology. If your skills are growing obsolete in a slowly changing environment, and you've received little indication that your employer would support your efforts to update your skills, you should bite the bullet and pay for your own training. Your expenditures may even be tax-deductible (check with your accountant first); even if they're not, it's more a question of whether you can afford not to bring your skills portfolio up to date. "IT professionals must keep their skills current with market trends," says Sherry Lucki, president and owner of ABT Solutions, an IT recruitment agency in Orlando, Florida. "If you don't, you'll be in serious trouble. That's what makes IT so different from other careers—you can be obsolete in six months because technology changes so rapidly."

BEST EMPLOYERS FOR IT TRAINING

Continuous training is a high priority for some IT organizations, where staff development is seen as a key retention tactic as well as an essential ingredient for business competitiveness. Here's a look at the cream of the crop for their demonstrated commitment to training.

Company	Days of Training/Year	Annual Training Budget/Person
Computer Associates International	21	$24,000
CDW Computer Centers	18	$20,000
First Third Bancorp	45	$7,585
The Home Depot	17	$9,000
Price Waterhouse-Coopers	19	$7,500
Capital One Financial Corporation	20	$6,500
Cisco Systems	10	$10,000
Avon Products	12	$10,000
Harley-Davidson	20	$4,000
Wal-Mart Stores	20	$4,500

Source: *Computerworld's "100 Best Places to Work in IT 2000" annual report, published June 2000.*

Whether you have the support of your IT organization or you're going solo, use the following checklist to help you develop a training action plan:

✓ What are your company's upcoming projects, which ones do you want to be assigned to, and how does your skills profile match up against the requirements for the projects?

✓ What are your personal goals over the next year or two, and how does your skills profile match up against those goals?

✓ What are your weaker areas in terms of technical skills that would be complementary to your primary responsibilities? For example, if you're doing web-based applications development, and you aren't well versed in networking, consider taking an overview of Internet networking principles. Even though you aren't dealing with routers and switches yourself, understanding network concepts will make it easier for you to communicate with the operations and networking staffs, which will make you more valuable to the IT organization overall.

✓ In terms of long-range career development, where do you see yourself in five years? If you intend to climb the management ladder, it's never too early to take project management, leadership, and soft skills training. DeKok says professional development courses, such as conflict management, contract negotiation, supervisory effectiveness, and the like, should make up about 10 percent of your formal training efforts. You might also consider pursuing an M.B.A. (See "M.B.A. Programs" later in this chapter.) And, if you want to enter a particular industry that you've never worked in before, look for industry-oriented seminars. If you plan to stick with a technical track, focus on certifications. (See "To Certify or Not?" later in this chapter.)

✓ What is your preferred method for learning and absorbing new material? Your training efforts should comprise active, on-the-job training, formal classroom training, and self-study using CD-ROM courseware, online tutorials, books and manuals, and other self-paced training aids. DeKok suggests that formal instruction should account for about 20 percent of your overall training plan, and he recommends taking a blended approach of live instruction and distance learning. "I don't believe you can depend totally on e-learning because the instructor-to-student and student-to-student interaction that you get in the classroom can't be replicated in an e-learning environment," he explains. Successful IT professionals typically spend five to ten hours a week immersed in self-study, including reading and surfing the Web. (See Chapter 15 for a complete listing of resources to assist you in self-study.)

✓ When will you need the skills you are pursuing? As much as possible, you should plan your formal training so that it coincides with an opportunity to apply what you've learned on the job immediately afterward. (This is known as just-in-time training.) "Training has to take place just before you are going to use it or it's absolutely worthless," DeKok says. "One theory that's prevalent in adult learning is that if you don't apply what you've learned within one week, you'll lose 90 percent of your knowledge gained." RMIC's Pulliam concurs: "At my previous employer, I went through some applications training that I never used on the job, and if I were to start using that application now, I'd have to dig out my books to be productive."

TIP *If you're trying to break into IT from another profession, try to find a mentor within your company's IT organization to help you plot a training roadmap. An IT mentor can advise you of upcoming projects that could benefit from your business perspective and identify the technical skills that will be needed. Also, explore your corporate intranet. Many leading employers maintain free online courses that employees can take on their own time. Another option, if your employer offers tuition reimbursement, is to enroll in an introductory IT course at a local college.*

Online Resources: IT Training Information

If you're looking for training in a specific technology or product, the best way to ensure that you get authorized live classes, online courses, CD-ROMs, and other self-study materials is to check the vendor's own website. That will be the most reliable source for finding authorized training centers, third-party training partners, traveling seminars, and other options. But if you're looking for training in technology concepts, development techniques, or other topics that aren't vendor-specific, or if you want to do one-stop shopping, use the following training search sites:

Go For IT!

www.go4it.gov

Search for a wide variety of IT training and degree programs offered by corporations, industry-academic partnerships, government-industry partnerships, commercial training vendors, and more.

Seminar Information Service

www.seminarinformation.com

This site lists over 360,000 courses, seminars, conferences, and workshops in a wide range of subjects; it isn't IT-specific, but has plenty of information on IT training. Browse by category or use the advanced search to look for courses by keyword, location, dates, and/or topic.

Thinq

www.thinq.com/main_default.asp?

Literally thousands of live classes, online courses, CD-ROMs, tapes, and other training options are listed here from over 1,200 providers. Browse IT and business training by category or search by keyword. Maintain a personal Learning Portfolio to track courses.

The Training Registry

www.trainingregistry.com

This training search site can be cumbersome and tedious to use, but with patience, it can yield a number of training options, including live classes, online learning, CD-ROM courseware, and more. Optimize your time by clicking Registry Search at the top of the main page, and search for courses by keyword.

TOP SKILLS PREMIUMS

Hard-to-find technical skills that are essential to the development and support of mission-critical systems can generate significant boosts in salary. "More and more, such skills are being isolated and rewarded by employers," notes David Foote, president of Foote Partners LLC, an IT management consulting firm based in New Canaan, Connecticut. Following is a look at some of the top-earning skills.

Technology	Skill Set	Premium Paid*
Development tools and languages	Rapid Application Development (RAD) experience	16%
	Visual C++	11%
	Oracle Developer	10%
	C++	10%
	Java	9%
Web/ecommerce development	XML	13%
	Java Server Pages (JSP)	12%
	Scripting languages	11%
	Active Server Pages (ASP)	10%
	Web server administration	10%
Databases	Oracle	12%
	Microsoft SQL Server	12%
	DB2	9%
	Microsoft Exchange 2000 Server	9%
	Visual SQL	9%

TOP SKILLS PREMIUMS

Technology	Skill Set	Premium Paid*
Networking and infrastructure	Security skills	18%
	Routing	15%
	Gigabit Ethernet	13%
	Microsoft NT Server administration	12%
	TCP/IP	12%
	Wireless Application Protocol (WAP)	11%
Enterprise-wide application suites	Lawson	13%
	J.D. Edwards	13%
	PeopleSoft	13%
	Oracle Enterprise Apps	12%
	SAP	10%
Operating systems	Windows 2000/ME	13%
	Linux	10%
	Sun Solaris	9%
	Windows NT	9%
	Other Unix	8%

* Median bonus paid to permanent employees, as a percentage of base pay, for high-value technical skills; data collected from a survey of 22,000 IT professionals conducted January 1–March 31, 2001; released April 27, 2001.

Source: Foote Partners LLC (www.footepartners.com).

To Certify or Not?

Whatever your area of specialization within IT, obtaining certification should be part of your overall training agenda. That said, keep in mind that certification alone is not going to forward your IT career. While it signals to employers that you are serious about your skills development—after all, it takes a certain level of dedication and commitment to complete a certification—it won't automatically move your résumé to the top of the stack or place you in a higher tax bracket.

"It seems a lot of people who have their MCSE [Microsoft Certified Systems Engineer] think that piece of paper alone makes them deserving of $100,000 salaries," says John McNamee, director of operations at ASP-One, an applications service provider based in Chicago. "Back in the real world, it's experience that counts."

On the other hand, real-world experience backed up by current certifications will make you a strong contender for promotions and new positions. "I wouldn't make a determination on a candidate based solely on their certification status, but it might push someone over the top if they are in all other respects equal to other candidates," says Phil DeKok of Lands' End. Typically, certification matters most in highly technical areas, like networking, systems administration, and security. "Those are becoming more and more important because it helps managers, when reviewing dozens of résumés, to know that the candidate has had a certain set of experiences," DeKok says. "It's helpful to the initial screening."

For that reason, certification is particularly useful to career-changers and independent consultants. If you're new to IT, or you're an unknown quantity trying to sell your services to an IT organization, certification is like your calling card. Newcomers to IT might want to consider the A+ or Network+ certification from the Computing Technology Industry Association (CompTIA) (www.comptia.com) or some other vendor-neutral certification. Independent consultants should be certified in their domain of primary expertise.

Although it won't, in and of itself, guarantee you the job of your dreams, pursuing certification is an effective way to bring focus to your training goals. But be prepared to pay for certification out of your own pocket. Many employers, even those committed to training, are at times reluctant to support certification because it potentially increases your marketability. "It's a question a lot of companies are wrestling with," DeKok says. "From one perspective, if you support people in achieving certification, it's almost an incentive for them to go out looking for another job. But we try to look at it in terms of the extra value it provides to the company. We try to encourage it where it makes sense, not just for the sake of getting certified."

TOP TEN PAYING CERTIFICATIONS

Certification	Premium Paid*
Microsoft Certified Systems Engineer+Internet (MCSE+I)	15%
Microsoft Certified Trainer (MCT)	14%
PMI Project Management Professional (PMP)	13%
Cisco Certified Network Associate (CCNA)	13%
Cisco Certified Network Professional (CCNP)	12%
Cisco Certified Internetwork Expert (CCIE)	12%
Oracle Certified Professional (OCP)	12%
Certified Information Systems Auditor (CISA)	10%
Certified Network Professional (CNP)	10%
CompTIA Network+	10%

* Median bonus paid to permanent employees, as a percentage of base pay, for high-value technical certifications; data collected from a survey of 22,000 IT professionals conducted January 1–March 31, 2001; released April 27, 2001.

Source: Foote Partners LLC (www.footepartners.com).

TIP *Given that one of the most common reasons for IT project failures is mismanagement, IT organizations are placing more and more emphasis on project management certification. In many companies, it's required to move into the PM role; at the very least, it will increase your chances of gaining a PM position and will also boost your salary (see "Top Ten Paying Certifications"), whether you plan to continue on the management track or opt for a technical track. If you're a career-changer with a solid business background, obtaining a PM certification would nearly guarantee your transition into IT, as project managers are hard to find and usually delegate most of the hands-on technical work. Some companies don't even require their IT project managers to have come up through the IT ranks. The leading certification is the Project Management Institute's PMP program (www.pmi.org/certification). Other project management certifications are available from the Gartner Institute (www.gartnerinstitute.com), which offers three PM options.*

Online Resources: Certification Information

If you're contemplating certification or trying to navigate through the often-confusing volumes of information about how to get certified, use the following sites as a guide:

Brainbench

www.brainbench.com

This vendor-independent online certification center offers over 40 free tests (and growing) and countless fee-based skills tests (at $19.95 each) in programming, database administration, technical support, telecommunications, and other IT categories. You won't get an MCSE test here; rather, you'll get a certificate validating that you have a certain level of skill and proficiency in a given technology. After completing the tests, you receive a certificate and can post your transcripts for review by employers of your choice. Online preparatory materials and practice exams are available for $25 each.

BrainBuzz.com

www.brainbuzz.com

This may be the most comprehensive online resource for free IT certification information, study aids, and preparatory materials. Check out the listing of more than 250 IT certifications from over 100 IT vendors, training companies, and professional associations (complete with links to their official websites). Use the "Cramsession" section of this site to download your choice of nearly 200 study guides to prepare for various certification exams, get tips and tricks for passing the exam, and more. The "Skills Drill" section offers a number of interactive tests, consisting of 45 questions each, to help you assess what you know and what you don't about databases, operating systems, networking, programming, and web development. (Tests are free, but registration is required.) Discuss certification pros and cons, training tips, testing tips, and more with other IT professionals in the online forums. Click IT Resources to conduct time-saving technology research and to browse the Tech Library, which contains how-tos, tutorials, product reviews, programming scripts, and more.

CertifiedComputerPro.com: The Computer Professional Certification Resource

www.certifiedcomputerpro.com

This well-maintained homegrown site offers a nearly complete listing of certifications offered by more than 85 IT vendors, professional associations, and training vendors. It links to dozens of sites offering self-study materials and sample tests as well as myriad web resources for certifications from Microsoft, IBM, CompTIA (A+ and Network+), Cisco, and Novell.

GoCertify

www.gocertify.com

Maintained by Anne Martinez, author of *Get Certified and Get Ahead* (Osborne/McGraw-Hill, Third Edition, 2000), this is among the best resources for IT certification information online. Browse by topic for information on over 500 certification and training programs from more than 90 vendors. Unfortunately, the site is lacking a keyword search, and the program descriptions don't link to the vendors' websites, but use the site to get a nearly comprehensive overview of what's available.

M.B.A. Programs

If you have your sights set on the chief information officer (CIO) position, or if you are merely trying to navigate the waters between a nontechnical career and an IT career, you may want to consider obtaining an M.B.A. to further you along toward your goal. Obtaining an M.B.A. demonstrates your commitment to business goals and objectives, while getting a techno-M.B.A.—a degree that fuses technology and information management studies with the business perspective—can be a highly effective way for a career-changer to break into IT.

Tom Popp, formerly public relations manager at Matsushita Electric Corporation of America in Secaucus, New Jersey, became interested in IT when he began managing content for the company's website. Seeing that, because he was already on a management track, a deeper understanding of technology could take his career in a new direction, he enrolled in a part-time techno-M.B.A. program. His commitment was noticed, and while he was still in school, Matsushita management tapped him for a new web development team. After obtaining his degree in May 1999, he was named project manager in the interactive media services group.

"I wanted some new opportunities at work, and I wanted to pursue something that would expand my knowledge," Popp says. "I weighed whether I wanted to be more technical, but I was already a departmental manager. I saw that my skills were more in organization and planning than hands-on technical work, and I didn't want to start over completely."

The techno-M.B.A. program, combined with his on-the-job experience as part of the web development team, gave him the right blend of technology and business expertise to move fully into the IT organization. An M.B.A. can open new doors for established IT professionals as well. "It will help you see the bigger picture, and that will help your individual performance," says George Slogik, ecommerce manager at Lincoln Electric Company, in Cleveland, Ohio. Slogik returned to school for an M.B.A. after ten years in the IT organization at Lincoln. "It won't help you design a web page, but it may give you a broader perspective of what's important on a web page from a customer's point of view. It will broaden your horizons." But, he cautions, don't expect an immediate raise or promotion the day after you get your diploma: "It will be noticed, but your advancement still goes back to your individual performance."

In fact, the ultimate value of an advanced degree to an IT professional's career is a hotly debated topic. A survey by the Graduate Management Admission Council of M.B.A. graduates from the class of 2000 found that techno-M.B.A.s were the fourth most popular of all M.B.A. programs (following finance, general management, and marketing), with 12 percent of the M.B.A. grads specializing in IT. But Phil DeKok at Lands' End notes that it isn't a universal requirement for moving up the IT management ranks.

"In some circles, IT management would see an M.B.A. as more and more essential," DeKok says. "In my company and others, it is not—we place a lot more value on what people bring to the job based on their experience. An M.B.A. is great, but there's a difference between the school of experience and the school of theory. If you don't translate theory into on-the-job performance well, your M.B.A. would be of little value to an employer."

From that perspective, it's generally agreed that it's best to get at least several years of real-world experience before enrolling in an M.B.A. program. With time spent in the trenches, you'll have more to contribute in the highly collaborative environment of an M.B.A. program, and you'll also be more focused on what you want to gain from the program.

In deciding whether to pursue a traditional M.B.A. or a techno-M.B.A., consider your background and experience compared with where you see yourself down the line. If you have a strong background in IT, including a Bachelor's degree in Computer Science or MIS, a straight M.B.A. might round out your credentials more—especially if you see yourself expanding from IT management into executive business management or starting your own company. On the other hand, if your undergraduate education was in liberal arts or business administration, a techno-M.B.A. would probably be the most appropriate choice to close any gaps in your background and experience.

Once you've decided which type of degree to pursue, you must choose whether to immerse yourself in a fulltime program or attend school part time. That decision will largely come down to your familial obligations, how far along you are in your career, and whether you require tuition reimbursement from your employer. (The GMAC study found that 52 percent of students who attended part time were sponsored by their employers, while only 4 percent of full timers had corporate support.) If you opt to continue working full time while you pursue your degree, a number of techno-M.B.A. programs offer a combination of live courses with a distance-learning environment to accommodate working professionals. Southwest Missouri State University in Springfield, Missouri, and the Keller Graduate School of Management, which is based in Chicago but has campuses nationwide, are just two examples of these hybrid programs. And Capella University (www.capella.edu) is a fully accredited online university that offers several different techno-M.B.A. programs.

TOP TEN TECHNO-M.B.A. PROGRAMS

Northeastern University, Boston, Massachusetts, www.cba.neu.edu/htmba

University of Texas, Austin, Texas, texasmba.bus.utexas.edu

University of Maryland, College Park, Maryland, www.rhsmith.umd.edu

University of Alabama, Tuscaloosa, Alabama, www.cba.ua.edu/mis

University of California at Irvine, California, www.gsm.uci.edu

University of Illinois at Urbana-Champaign, Illinois, www.mba.uiuc.edu

Purdue University, West Lafayette, Indiana, www.mgmt.purdue.edu/programs

Southwest Missouri State University, Springfield, Missouri, www.coba.smsu.edu/mba/Techno-MBA.htm

Carnegie Mellon University, Pittsburgh, Pennsylvania, www.gsia.cmu.edu

University of Florida, Gainesville, Florida, www.floridamba.ufl.edu

Source: Computerworld, September 27, 1999; for the full article and a complete list of the top 25 programs, see "Techno-MBA Top Dogs: Computerworld's Third Annual Top Techno-MBA Survey," by Bronwyn Fryer, at www.computerworld.com/cwi/story/0,1199, NAV63-131_STO42377,00.html.

Online Resources: M.B.A. Program Information

The following websites feature searchable databases of M.B.A. programs nationwide plus information on applying, taking the GMAT, seeking financial aid, and more:

Business Week B-Schools Guide

www.businessweek.com/bschools/index.html

Search profiles of 225 full-time and 250 part-time M.B.A. programs by school name, or any combination of ranking, location, topic of study, cost, GMAT score requirements, and more. Check out the ranking of top 30 U.S. business schools and top 7 business schools abroad, and use the site's interactive tools to compare various programs and calculate the return on investment in an M.B.A.

Graduate Management Admission Council

www.gmac.com

Register to take the GMAT, and review this site's comprehensive advice on selecting a program, searching for the right school, the career benefits of obtaining an M.B.A., and more.

GradSchools.com

www.gradschools.com

Search for full-time, part-time and distance learning programs by area of study or institution name; this site is quick and easy to use, but it doesn't offer much valuable information about the schools.

The MBA Channel at Petersons.com

www.petersons.com/mba

Search for graduate school programs by topic of study and location; online application available (registration required for this service).

U.S. News & World Report Grad School Guide

www.usnews.com/usnews/edu/beyond/bchome.html

Search for M.B.A. programs by school name or any combination of location, distance from your home, part-time or full-time programs, average starting salaries of graduates, GMAT score requirements, ranking, and cost. This site also features "America's Best Graduate Schools," a ranking of the 50 leading U.S. business schools by academic reputation, graduates' starting salaries, graduate employment, and more.

Chapter 13

- -

On the Market: Finding and Pursuing Your Next Opportunity

Like many dot-commers in the latter months of 2000, Rebecca Moss found herself attending pink-slip parties and applying for unemployment after the startup she'd been working for went through a series of staff cuts. And like many, even though she'd seen it coming, she was unprepared when the ax fell: Her résumé was out of date, she had not aligned with a recruiter, and she had not been seeking potential new opportunities.

Aside from the fact that she now had some management experience to add to her résumé, she was starting from scratch—in a soft job market besotted by available candidates and with only two weeks' severance pay and her unemployment checks to support herself in the meantime.

Despite the circumstances, she was optimistic that she'd find a new position within a month. After all, she had solid, proven skills in project management, website production, HTML, and interface/navigational design. But six weeks and numerous fruitless job interviews later, with the crowds at those pink-slip parties growing larger by the week, the doldrums hit. "When the end of the first month came, I realized that finding a new job would be harder than I had thought," she says. "It was a passing feeling, but I got a bit discouraged and depressed." It was then that she temporarily put the brakes on her job search and embarked instead on some serious soul searching about what she wanted from her career. She came up with four key criteria that she methodically applied to her subsequent search efforts:

► The employer must have a clear business focus, with definite goals and priorities that are consistent with those goals. "My former employer had changed their story every two months as it suited investors," she explains.

► The employer must be committed to growing IT employees' skills and responsibilities. "Whether through informal mentoring or formal training, I had to know I wasn't just going to be left hanging out there," Moss says.

▶ The position must offer a clear path toward personal long-range goals. "I want a job that will enable me to do what I want in the long-term—increase my technical skills and ultimately move from site production into information architecture," she says.

▶ The employer should be a good cultural fit. "That comes down to intuition, to the vibe," Moss explains. "How does the company feel? Would I fit in culturally?"

"Arriving at those four criteria was a breakthrough," Moss adds. "As my job search drew out longer, I knew I might not be able to be too picky. But what was important was realizing that even if I had to take a job that wasn't perfect, it didn't have to be permanent and that it was up to me to do more to make sure I'm following a path that will develop my skills."

The lesson that Moss learned from being an unemployed dot-commer is a valuable lesson for anyone in the IT job market, whether you're seeking your first professional job, trying to break into IT from another career field, or trying to take your established IT career to the next level. You have to do more than just give lip service to some vague, far-off goal; you have to know what you really want and focus your efforts around that. It isn't about finding the perfect job, but rather, the job that will take you where you want to go.

Even under the best market conditions, creating a résumé, job-hunting, and interviewing are among the most stressful parts of launching or repositioning your career. But once you know what you really want, those tasks are not really so intimidating. You don't have to wait until you're collecting unemployment checks to go through the self-assessment that Moss went through. In fact, performing a concerted evaluation of your skills, considering what you enjoy about your job and what you don't, and deciding what you expect from an employer and from yourself can be a liberating and motivating exercise that will see you through any IT job search, even in the weakest market.

While the IT job market in 2001 looks somewhat different than in many previous years, demand for skilled IT professionals continues to outpace the supply. Demand for IT workers in 2001 fell 44 percent from 2000, according to a survey of 685 companies by the Information Technology Association of America (ITAA) that was released in April 2001. But even with the falloff in demand, the ITAA found that 425,000 IT jobs—or nearly half the projected 900,000 new IT jobs—will go unfilled in 2001 as companies struggle to find the skills and experience they need.

Moreover, many observers feel that even though layoffs and dot-com closures have put more IT people on the market recently, the increased supply of available workers for a shrinking number of jobs is only a short-term situation, and that the urgency will return to previous levels. "This current supply of IT people is only a temporary situation due to the shake-out as we continue to move toward the new economy," says Dr. Robert Zawacki, Professor Emeritus at the University of Colorado and an IT human resources consultant. "I predict in another year or two [employers] will again be competing for the critical skills, and the supply will not even meet half of the demand, given the growth in IT and the new economy. All paradigm shifts, such as the movement from the agricultural economy to the industrial economy, have had these consolidations and ups and downs."

You may have to work a little harder and wait a little longer to land a career-building IT position in the market of 2001. But if you focus on identifying your priorities and attaining your goals instead of finding the ideal job, you'll be well armed for job hunting, résumé writing, and interviewing, whether the IT job market is up or down.

Effective IT Job-Hunting Tactics and Strategies

How you conduct your IT job search depends partly on why you're in the job market. If you're unemployed, you should use every resource available to look for a new job. If you're a student trying to line up your first post-graduation position, leverage on-campus resources like the career counseling center. If you're currently employed but seeking a change, you can afford to take your time and pursue select opportunities. But a general rule of thumb is, don't put all of your eggs in one basket. Use a variety of channels.

Students should really begin their IT job search in their sophomore or junior year. By securing full-time summer internships, you'll have a huge leg up in the market when you graduate—perhaps even a firm offer by the beginning of your senior year. If your schedule allows, you should also consider working for a local IT organization or your campus computer center part time during the school year. Any experience you can gain during school will put you ahead of other entry-level job seekers when you hit the market.

If you're a career-changer trying to break into IT from another field, the first place you should look is within your own company. Try to get involved as an end-user on a new technology rollout. That will help you make connections with people in the IT organization in addition to exposing you firsthand to the role IT plays in the company. With your business experience and some technical training, you'll be an ideal candidate for new openings in IT because you already have a firm grasp of your company's goals, objectives, work processes, and initiatives.

If you're an established IT professional seeking career advancement, what's motivating you? Before you start sending out your résumé and calling up all your colleagues, you should identify why you're feeling dissatisfied in your current position and pinpoint what you want from a new job. If your main complaint is that you aren't earning enough money, maybe you can address that without changing jobs. If the problem in your current position is a lack of training or opportunity to develop new skills, and you see no change on the horizon, it's definitely time to start looking.

Following is a look at some of the most effective resources and tools you can apply to your IT job hunt. Take a best-of-breed approach, depending on your situation, and pursue all channels that are relevant to your circumstances and goals.

TIP *In addition to the job-hunting tactics covered here, don't overlook the tried-and-true Sunday classifieds. IT job fairs also offer a way to put yourself in front of several employers in one day.*

Pursuing Employers of Choice

If you have the luxury of taking your time finding a new position, or if all your other efforts to find a new job have stalled, consider taking a deliberate, methodical approach to pursuing your personal employers of choice. Identify companies that you're interested in working for and contact them directly.

This approach will require time, patience, and the thorough self-assessment that Moss went through. To come up with a list of employers to target, you must first understand your own goals and objectives. Is your priority to work for a leading user of information technology? Do you have family obligations that require a work/life balance and family-friendly benefits? Do you want to work for a company that will support your efforts to pursue new training or an advanced degree? Do you want to relocate? Develop a list of key criteria that reflect your personal and professional needs.

At the same time, make a list of employers that appeal to you for whatever reason: You've heard positive things about them from colleagues, they are leaders in their market, they produce a product that you respect, they're known for great benefits, or they're growing quickly. Then research each company against your list of criteria. Start with the companies' websites. Read about their products and customers, and check their career pages for information about benefits, policies, and available jobs. Research their IT environments by searching IT trade publication websites and IT portal sites. (See Chapter 14 for websites and tips on researching companies and IT organizations, and see Chapter 15 for additional online resources.)

If a company's corporate culture and IT environment match your criteria, determine its level of IT hiring activity. This is the ideal time to leverage your network of colleagues. (See the next section, "Networking.") If you know someone else who works for the company, find out whether there are openings and ask for a referral. And if you have a relationship with a reputable recruiter, ask whether the recruiter has placed people with the employer before. (See "Selecting and Working with a Recruiter" later in this chapter.)

If you don't have an inside track to the company via a colleague or recruiter, return to the company's website to search for jobs, and also check the IT job search sites for potential listings. Concurrently, call the company's human resources department. Ask to speak with the IT recruiter (most major companies have a dedicated IT recruiter these days) and try to find out if they work with outside recruitment firms. Alternately, if you've been able to identify company IT managers through your research, call them directly. It's most likely that the company has open IT positions, even if they're not posted anywhere on the Internet. Even if there are no available positions, sell yourself on your interest in the company and request an informational interview. Have a "pitch" ready—one that reflects the research you've done on the company—to convince the company's HR department to see you.

With the current shortage of IT professionals and the challenge for companies of hiring IT workers who will stick around for the long haul, it shouldn't be difficult to get a foot in the door when you can demonstrate that the company is among your employers of choice.

Networking

Never underestimate the value of who you know as well as what you know. Networking among your peers is one of the most effective means to finding a new position, especially now that so many companies pay referral bonuses to employees who help fill a job. But, like continuously updating your skills so you're prepared to act on a new opportunity, networking is something you should do on an ongoing basis—not just when you're anxious to land a new position. Here are some ways to network your way to a new job:

▶ Participate in user group and professional association meetings. In addition to meeting fellow professionals with whom you can compare skills and trade ideas, you will inevitably forge relationships that could have an impact on your career now or down the road. For example, John Goodhue, an independent Oracle DBA based in Minneapolis, Minnesota, who serves as treasurer of the Twin Cities Oracle Users Group, says his fellow members have become valuable contacts for finding contract gigs. "If you think about your future career development, attending a user group meeting is a small investment up against the rest of your day," notes Linda Meserve, lead programmer/analyst at a large insurance company and president of the Rocky Mountain Lotus Notes User Group in Denver, Colorado.

▶ Strike up conversations at trade shows and industry conferences. Go to the cocktail parties and after-hours events as well as the seminars and panel discussions. "The best part of attending conferences is meeting people who do what you do and sharing the war stories," says Ric Goldman, an IT consultant based in Palo Alto, California. "But it definitely also generates business leads. The more you interact, the more the potential benefits."

▶ Attend free vendor seminars. You'll learn something new and useful, plus you'll inevitably encounter someone whose company is about to launch a new project using the technology being covered in the seminar. And where there are new IT projects, there are nearly always new job opportunities.

▶ Get involved with the local chapter of your college alumni association. That's an ideal way to expand your professional network. Who wouldn't be willing to recommend a fellow graduate for a job when they can personally vouch for the quality of your education? And alumni associations often maintain job boards and offer other career-related services.

Selecting and Working with a Recruiter

Recruiters get a bad rap, especially among IT professionals. Unfortunately, much of their poor reputation is well founded. They frequently fail to keep up-to-date on technology, they don't truly understand IT organizational requirements, they mass mail résumés to employers with whom they don't have direct relationships, and they aim more for their finder's fee than for a great match between a candidate and an employer. But a good recruiter can be a huge asset in an IT job hunt, helping you to identify your goals and priorities as well as strengths and weaknesses, and matching opportunities to those instead of blindly trying to place you anywhere that happens to have an open slot to fill. Moreover, a good recruiter will be frank with you, offering concrete advice on ways to improve your prospects.

The challenge for IT job seekers is separating the wheat from the chafe and finding a recruiter with whom they can build a mutually committed, beneficial relationship. "Select your recruiter as carefully as you select the company you work for," advises Deron Streitenberger, CIO of Republic Mortgage Insurance Company (RMIC), Winston-Salem, North Carolina.

"The relationship needs to be based on trust and openness," says Sherry Lucki, president and owner of ABT Solutions, an IT placement firm in Orlando, Florida. "You should think of your recruiter as an agent—your conduit into the marketplace who is going to represent your interests."

Just as a sports agent has one-on-one relationships with team managers and coaches, an effective IT recruiter "should have real relationships with the companies they are presenting you to," Streitenberger says. "Otherwise, they can hose a potential opportunity." A busy IT hiring manager generally isn't going to view a candidate presented by an unknown recruiter very favorably, he notes. "The classic example is when they say they've screened a candidate for me, and he has four years of Visual Basic [VB] experience. Well, I don't need them to screen anyone for me, and just because a candidate has four years of VB doesn't make him an expert."

Another risk of working with a recruiter who doesn't have solid industry connections is overexposure, Lucki notes. If the recruiter is just mining the Internet for job openings and sending your résumé out for any job that matches a few keywords, the relationship will ultimately be unproductive. Moss says that this was her experience with many recruiters: "I felt more like they were just trying to meet a monthly quota of candidates." You want to work with someone whose priority is quality, not quantity. "You should be able to rely on the recruiter to show you only the best opportunities in the local marketplace for your skills and experience," Lucki says.

Other hallmarks of a recruiter whose work ethic is rooted in quality, not quantity, include the following:

Ability to offer sound advice regarding your skills   "A good recruiter is in the market every day talking to high-level IT managers about what the trends are and can counsel you on what you need to do to maintain your edge in the marketplace," Lucki says.

Candor   "Look for a relationship where the recruiter will address potential problems before you start interviewing—like unrealistic salary expectations or problems on your résumé like job-hopping," Lucki says. "If you're looking to make a move because of problems at your current employer, a good recruiter may actually direct you back to your current company to try to address the problems. They'll try to understand what's really motivating you."

Willingness to get personal   "A recruiter should try to understand the personal parameters that would affect your job search," Lucki explains. "What are your family obligations? Are you in a position to relocate? What would the ramifications of a relocation be in terms of your home, your spouse, and your kids? Are you willing and able to work overtime? They'll make things real on a personal level."

Will establish a long-term relationship with you   "A good recruiter isn't just going to help you find a job, but will help you with career planning," Lucki says. "The ultimate goal shouldn't be placing you in a job, but building a relationship with you."

CHECKLIST: QUESTIONS TO ASK A PROSPECTIVE RECRUITER

When evaluating prospective recruiters, you should interview them as thoroughly as they should interview you, notes Sherry Lucki, a recruiter with 20 years of experience placing IT professionals and president of ABT Solutions in Orlando, Florida. Ask questions that will reveal how they work, their industry connections, the breadth of their experience, and the depth of their knowledge of the IT market, technology trends, and IT career and salary trends. The following is a list of some sample questions:

✓ Which employers do you have direct relationships with that you work with regularly?

✓ How do you go about placing a candidate? What's your process? Will you be sending out my résumé, or do you have one-on-one relationships with IT hiring managers that will enable you to present me verbally?

✓ What niche do you service? Do you have a geographic or technology focus?

✓ How much experience do you have in the IT industry?

✓ What's the typical salary range for someone with my skills and experience?

✓ What types of openings do you typically see for someone with my skills and experience?

✓ In what areas would you suggest that I bolster my skill sets? Have you noticed any new types of IT projects coming up that I could be preparing for?

✓ Can you provide me with references to other IT professionals you've worked with?

There's No Place Like Home

Sometimes you needn't look any further than your own company for your next career-building position. With the high cost of IT turnover, most companies are eager to move IT professionals into new positions rather than risk losing them. If your reason for wanting a change has to do with needing a new challenge rather than frustration with your employer, start thinking about new ways you could contribute and apply your skills while at the same time taking on something new. If you have a formal or informal mentor, this is a perfect time to solicit feedback on appropriate avenues for your continued growth; if not, pay attention to water-cooler talk for a heads-up on someone who may be leaving or a new project coming up that might translate into an internal opportunity for you, Streitenberger advises. Once you've identified some potential options, figure out what additional training you would need, and take steps to get it formally or through self-study.

An internal move is an especially useful career tactic if you're trying to garner a position for which you have little or no prior experience; your current employer is more likely to take a chance moving you into a new area than an employer that doesn't know you. For example, Aroon Mital says he had hit a roadblock in his career after three years as a Lotus Notes administrator. "I felt I had maxed out, and I was interested in doing development work," he recalls. He started studying the Notes development manuals and developing test databases in Notes in his spare time. He also taught himself JavaScript, a language used in the Notes environment. His big break came when a colleague who did Notes development decided not to return from maternity leave, he recalls. "I went to my boss and volunteered to take over her responsibilities and hire a junior administrator to take over mine," he explains. The move had a practical benefit to the IT organization, which Mital used persuasively: It would be cheaper and easier to hire a junior admin than a senior developer, and Mital was already familiar with the company's key development initiatives. But it wasn't just his sound business argument that won him the new position—it was also that he'd been preparing himself for such an opportunity before it came along. Once granted the promotion, he took formal classes in Notes development.

Mital's planning, preparation, and go-for-it attitude had unforeseen long-term benefits. When his company was acquired in the summer of 1999, he knew it was time to launch an external job search. His move into development proved instrumental in landing his current position as a Notes developer at Samsung Telecommunications America in Richardson, Texas. "It definitely would have been harder to find a new job—especially a development job—with only admin experience," Mital says. "Having both made me more marketable."

Contrary to a prevailing impression in the market that building a long-term IT career with one employer is detrimental to your future prospects, it can actually be a challenging, invigorating experience—as long as the employer supports your continued development and growth in a variety of areas. Carla Woods, a senior business consultant responsible for a supply-chain management initiative at Tyson Foods, Springdale, Arkansas, has rotated through positions in Cobol programming, middleware applications development, software release management, an HP OpenView implementation, disaster recovery, and upper operations management since joining Tyson in 1990. Now her career path has come full-circle back into applications development. "Since I've been exposed to different applications and hardware issues, I can see how things are interrelated and how important the pieces are to the whole," she says. "I told my bosses years ago that I have a low threshold for boredom, and they have always managed to put something new on my plate when I've gone looking for it and even when I haven't."

When she first started getting restless as a Cobol programmer, she took the initiative of going to the department head and requesting a move. Rather than reacting defensively, he put out the word to his management colleagues that she was looking for something new. She interviewed for several different positions before settling on middleware applications development, which took her programming skills into the client/server arena. Next, she identified a specific available position, as software release manager, and pursued it. After that, her career at the company developed a momentum of its own. Seeing that she adapted easily to new challenges, management began seeking her out for new projects. "I've never felt that I wouldn't get new opportunities here," Woods says. "Management believes in letting people bloom. I've been treated well, with respect, and have had no reason to go looking anywhere else."

The Best IT Job Search Sites

Looking for a job is a job in itself, especially if you opt to conduct your search on your own. The Internet has made the process much easier, especially for IT professionals—IT organizations were among the first to do online recruiting, and they are by now well practiced at it. No longer do you have to wait for the Sunday classifieds to come out; you can mine opportunities and apply online whenever you want. And if you're seeking to relocate, the Internet is an ideal resource for finding jobs outside of your local market.

But don't be lulled into complacency because the Web puts opportunities at your fingertips. Online job hunting should not be a substitute for cold calling, networking, seeking a reliable recruiter to represent you or, other IT job-hunting tactics. "It really is an easy way to feel like you are doing a lot to find a job," Moss says, even when it can often be unproductive. Moreover, the great advantage of an Internet-based job search—instant access to scores of IT job listings from around the country any time of day—is also its Achilles' heel for job hunters: You're in competition not just with fellow subscribers to your local Sunday paper, but with the worldwide community of IT job seekers. Moss notes that one interviewer told her he'd received over 100 résumés for a single online job posting. After two months of working the Web, Moss ultimately decided to restrict her online searches to one day a week as a supplement to face-to-face networking and contacting employers of choice. "I placed less emphasis on applying to online postings and more on researching companies that I would like to work for and approaching them directly," she says. "I made my efforts more focused rather than scattershot."

While it can be effective, as Moss concluded, online hunting should be only part of a multifaceted job-search strategy. Here are some additional guidelines to optimize your online job search efforts:

▶ Don't use your office PC to conduct a job search or use your office email address to respond to jobs posted on the Web. Do it from home with your private email address. If your regular email address uses a nickname or clever handle, set up a new address using your proper name: It's more professional.

▶ Keep in mind that job-search sites often have redundant listings—two or three or more recruiters may all be advertising the same position on behalf of one employer. So screen online ads carefully before responding to avoid the risk of overexposure.

▶ Beware of ads placed by recruiters or staffing agencies that allow only an online response; when recruiters don't provide contact information in the job description, it may be a sign that they are simply trying to get a lot of résumés on file. As Moss found in her job hunt, recruiters sometimes place enticing ads for jobs they aren't actually trying to fill. "It felt like there was a bait-and-switch thing going on because I would get callbacks [after submitting an online application], but as I talked to the recruiter, it was clear that the job didn't really exist," she says.

Following are some of the most reliable IT job search sites:

BrainBuzz

jobs.brainbuzz.com
This favorite among IT professionals, part of the BrainBuzz.com training and certification site (see Chapter 12), lives up to the hype. It's easy to navigate, features a wide range of employers and job types, and job listings are updated 24/7.

SEARCH OPTIONS   Search by keyword, location, and job duration (permanent, contract, contract-to-hire), or see all jobs by date posted; the search engine allows you to eliminate listings from staffing agencies; search locally or globally, from Albania to Zimbabwe.

JOB DESCRIPTION INFO   Postings contain the date posted, responsibilities, years of experience/technology skills/education and certification required, salary, benefits offered, contact information, and links to company information and other jobs posted by the employer.

RÉSUMÉ POSTING   Registration is required; cookies must be enabled in your browser.

EXTRA FEATURES   Bar your current employer from seeing your résumé with Boss-Blocker; use JobScout to be notified of new jobs that match your keywords; browse employers by company name; join the UltraShare network of IT consultants to be contacted by an UltraShare project manager for contract opportunities; apply to jobs online; email listings to a friend.

DRAWBACK(S)   Employers are allowed to conceal their identity; while most don't, without the employer information, you may as well be scanning the classifieds.

BrassRing
www.brassring.com
Search job listings from over 1,200 employers at this comprehensive IT job-search site.

SEARCH OPTIONS   Use skills, job title, or employer as keywords; add location information for a narrower search; sort listings by date or by relevance; click Who's Hiring to browse employers by company name.

JOB DESCRIPTION INFO   There isn't a standard format for job descriptions, so the depth and detail depends on the employer; link to information about the employer or to a listing of all jobs posted by the employer.

RÉSUMÉ POSTING   Create and post a full résumé or a skills profile; post résumé publicly or confidentially; post up to five customized résumés and multiple cover letters for review by employers; registration is required.

EXTRA FEATURES   Apply for jobs online, even if you're not registered; customize agents to email you job listings and articles that match your criteria; search for IT career events by location, type, and/or date; establish a free email account; click Company Research to link to profiles and other information from WetFeet.com (reviewed in Chapter 14). The Career Guidance Center offers articles, one-click job searching across multiple sites, and links to online training from KaplanCollege.com.

DRAWBACK(S)   Depending on the employer, some job descriptions leave a lot to be desired.

ComputerJobs.com
www.computerjobs.com
While in many ways, this site seems designed more for the employer than the job seeker, it offers myriad options for narrowing down your job search, and it hosts a lot of jobs.

SEARCH OPTIONS   Start your search by clicking one of the 19 metro areas and regions or one of the 18 skills areas, or use a pull-down menu to search for jobs by state; from the metro pages, point and click to drill down by skills category, do a keyword search, or conduct a power search that combines keyword, state, job title, skills, job description, city, and employment type (registration required); from the skill sites, browse the entire listing or narrow down the options using keywords plus pull-down menus for regions and specific skills; from either, browse jobs by employer.

JOB DESCRIPTION INFO   Job listings are fairly consistent, including a summary of responsibilities, skills/experience required, benefits offered, salary (often, not always), travel required, employment type, location, contact information, and date posted; link to other jobs requiring similar skill sets or other jobs listed by the same employer or recruiter; link to the employer's website; save the job to a personal folder or get a printer-friendly version.

RÉSUMÉ POSTING   Build a résumé for review by employers who subscribe to the site; note that once you post your résumé, your options are limited for controlling who accesses it or what they do with it—you can set a filter to block certain employers, but you can't make it completely confidential.

EXTRA FEATURES   Each metro page contains links to local user groups and associations, technology publications (but not local newspapers or magazines), training providers, insurance companies, and relocation resources; some—not all—employers accept online applications; additional starting points for job searches are the Startups page and the Consultants Corner; compare your salary with others' using the interactive salary survey; create a skills profile to have jobs matching your criteria automatically saved to your personal job-search page; track your online applications; email jobs to a friend.

DRAWBACK(S)   The majority of jobs here are posted by recruiters, IT services firms, and staffing agencies; the PowerSearch feature doesn't really offer too many additional options for searching than pointing and clicking your way through the site does—it's hardly worth the registration if you're not planning to post your résumé; there's no shortcut between the various metro and skills sites—if you want to move from the data warehouse site to the Denver site, you must return to the home page; you might think twice before posting your résumé because many employers at the site don't take online applications.

ComputerWork.com

www.computerwork.com

This site stands out for its ease of use and localization. It features separate pages for 52 cities and regions, including cities often overlooked by other sites, like Nashville, Memphis, Charlotte, Cincinnati, and Indianapolis, plus ten IT skills categories.

SEARCH OPTIONS   Use skill, job title, or location as keywords.

JOB DESCRIPTION INFO   Listings include date posted, responsibilities, years of experience/technology skills required, salary, relocation benefits offered, contact information, and links to company information and the employer's website.

RÉSUMÉ POSTING   Use the menu-driven form to create a résumé available for review by employers; posting your résumé activates the Job Tracker, which emails you jobs matching your designated keywords.

EXTRA FEATURES   Each local site features links to area newspapers and city guides, while each technology site links to relevant technical publications; apply to jobs online or save them to a shopping cart for future reference; email listings to a friend.

DRAWBACK(S)   Nearly all the jobs are posted by IT services firms, recruiters, or staffing agencies. If you're set on finding a job directly with the employer of your choice, this isn't the place to look.

Dice.com

www.dice.com

This popular site offers myriad options for optimized online job searching. It is especially useful to consultants and contractors because it allows you to restrict searches by the complete range of available job types, including full-time, contract, or contract-to-hire (including W2, independent, or corp-to-corp).

SEARCH OPTIONS   Do a quick keyword search from the home page or click Advanced Search to search by multiple combinations of keywords, states (up to five at once), job types, area codes (up to five at once) and/or date posted; use the Metro Pages to search for jobs in one of 27 U.S. cities and regions; metro pages allow you to restrict your search to specific area codes, a particularly useful feature for large metro areas with multiple codes, such as Boston, Chicago, and Los Angeles; browse employers by region and company name; from the employer pages, link to the company's website, display all jobs listed, or search for specific jobs by keyword, job type, date posted, location (including area code), and telecommuting options.

JOB DESCRIPTION INFO   Get a summary of responsibilities, skills, and experience required, salary/pay rate, job type, location, contact information, and links to the employer's website.

RÉSUMÉ POSTING   Posting your résumé creates a unique web page with your own URL, which you can control access to; announce your immediate availability with a personal profile, including contact information, position and pay desired, skills and experience, desired location, work status, and your résumé (optional); registration is required for these features.

EXTRA FEATURES   Get a reality check on your salary expectations with the interactive salary survey, which allows you to narrow your salary criteria by skills, experience, location, and job type; apply for jobs online; email jobs to a friend.

DRAWBACK(S)   While major employers do list jobs here, the great majority of jobs are posted by IT services firms, recruiters, and staffing agencies.

HotJobs.com Technology Channel

www.hotjobs.com/htdocs/channels/tech

Despite a couple of major drawbacks, the ease of searching and sheer quantity of IT jobs posted merit bookmarking this site, the technology section of all-purpose job-search site HotJobs.com. The majority of jobs are posted by high-tech companies, IT services firms, and dot-coms, but a significant number of heavyweight "old economy" companies list jobs here as well. Other HotJobs channels of interest to IT professionals are the Internet/New Media, Startup, Tech Contract, and Telecommunications channels.

SEARCH OPTIONS   Search by any combination of keywords, location, and up to three job-title categories at a time; filter searches to exclude search firms; search for international jobs in 58 countries (click Search By Location on the main page, www.hotjobs.com); browse jobs by employer (company names are listed in alphabetical order).

JOB DESCRIPTION INFO   The depth and detail of job descriptions varies; a summary of responsibilities, skills/experience required and contact information are generally included; link to all jobs posted by the employer; get a printer-friendly version of the job description.

RÉSUMÉ POSTING   Create a résumé in three steps when applying to jobs online or cut and paste your existing résumé.

EXTRA FEATURES   Career discussion boards (registration required); apply for jobs online (registration required); email jobs to a friend.

DRAWBACK(S)   Job descriptions don't link to the employer's website, a huge oversight; nor are employers required to post company profiles—some do, many don't; a FAQ for job seekers would be a useful addition (there's no information about what happens to your résumé, for example); a job-tracking email agent is not offered.

JustTechJobs.com
www.justtechjobs.com
If you are interested only in jobs that leverage your key skill sets, use this family of technology-specific job search sites for 47 IT skills areas, from Access to XML. Start from the generic site or go to the site of your choice by entering the URL www.justSKILL-NAMEjobs.com, e.g., www.justcoldfusionjobs.com, or www.justecommercejobs.com, etc.

SEARCH OPTIONS   Search by job title and/or location from the QuickSearch box or use the advanced search form to search by title, date posted, city, employer, job type (contract, H1B Visa, entry-level, etc.), and/or keyword.

JOB DESCRIPTION INFO   The depth and detail of job descriptions is inconsistent, depending on employer; job summary, required skills, job type, travel requirements, and contact information are usually included; jobs are clearly marked with an icon to indicate H1B Visa sponsorship, entry level, startup, or contract.

RÉSUMÉ POSTING   Registering at the site automatically creates and posts a résumé.

EXTRA FEATURES   Five top-paying jobs posted are listed on the main page; apply online or save searches for future reference (registration required for this feature); AutoNotify emails job listings matching your criteria; validate your salary requirements using the interactive salary survey.

DRAWBACK(S)   Most employers decline to list salary information in their job descriptions; sites are heavier with recruiters, services firms, and staffing agencies than major employers, and although you can search internationally, don't count on finding exotic opportunities here; while navigating the sites is fairly easy, a FAQ with navigation tips would be a useful addition.

Monster.com's IT Jobs Page

technology.monster.com

Fortune 500 companies list jobs right alongside small staffing agencies at this site, the IT-specific area of mega-job-search site Monster.com.

SEARCH OPTIONS   Search by city or region, job category and/or keyword; browse employer profiles by company name and/or location.

JOB DESCRIPTION INFO   The depth and detail here varies with each employer; a summary of responsibilities, skills/experience required, and job type (full-time, contract) are generally included; some employers list salary information; some list contact information, while others allow only online applications; link to all jobs posted by the employer as well as an employer-produced company profile.

RÉSUMÉ POSTING   Create up to five résumés and cover letters; résumés can be stored confidentially for personal use only or publicly for viewing by employers (registration required).

EXTRA FEATURES   Search for news articles by company name or stock symbol to get information on stock performance and quarterly and annual financials; company information includes lists of key executives and competitors; save your search criteria to act as a custom job-tracking agent to have matching jobs emailed to you; get IT certification information.

DRAWBACK(S)   Neither job descriptions nor employer profiles consistently link to the employers' websites.

Techies.com

www.techies.com

This highly customizable job-search site is geographically oriented, with dedicated pages for most of the 50 states plus major metro areas. When you register—which is required for most of the features—you designate a primary area plus as many additional areas as you like from which to launch your research. Log in at the main page or go straight to the local site of your choice by entering this URL in your browser: LOCATION.techies.com.

SEARCH OPTIONS   Do a QuickSearch by keyword or conduct an advanced search by keyword, job function, job type (full-time, contract, etc.), location, and industry, (registration required to launch the advanced search feature); browse employers by location and company name; contractors can register for the Net-Strike Service, which matches freelancers with projects that fit their skills profiles (click the Projects tab).

JOB DESCRIPTION INFO   Listings are typically detailed, covering responsibilities, skills/experience required, salary and perks, and employment type (full-time, contract); link to a detailed employer profile; contact information is not included—candidates must apply for jobs online (registration required).

RÉSUMÉ POSTING   Create a résumé upon registration that you can designate as confidential or make available for viewing by employers; you have the opportunity to customize your résumé each time you apply for a job online.

EXTRA FEATURES   Detailed employer profiles include a corporate snapshot (number of employees, year founded, work environment, primary business, customer base, and technology skills needed), a long overview, benefits, testimonials from current employees, photographs of the workplace and employees, and a link to all jobs posted by the company; get email notification of online Internet job fairs in the cities of your choice; receive weekly career newsletters; maintain a list of preferred employers to be notified when they post new jobs; use the TechBroker to create a job-matching profile that emails you with relevant new job listings; track your online applications.

DRAWBACK(S)   The only discernible fault with this site is the lack of a quick pull-down menu for navigating among the various city and regional sites—you must click to a separate page to request a new city section; some may feel hindered by the online-only application process.

The Wall Street Journal's CareerJournal

www.careerjournal.com

Even though this is the only job-search site on the list that isn't IT-specific, it may well be the best in terms of the caliber of jobs and employers represented. This is the place to find some of the best IT jobs with leading employers posted on the Net.

SEARCH OPTIONS   Do a quicksearch by keyword or use a detailed form to search by keyword, location, distance you're willing to commute, employer, and/or industry; search for jobs in the United States, Europe, and Asia.

JOB DESCRIPTION INFO   The depth and detail of the descriptions varies; at a minimum, a summary of responsibilities and skills required are included, plus a statement from the employer about the company; link to a listing of all jobs posted by the employer; click Obtain A Briefing Book to link to a *Wall Street Journal* (WSJ) profile of the employer and its business initiatives, as well as current stock information, detailed quarterly and annual financial data, and graphs depicting long-term stock performance.

RÉSUMÉ POSTING   Create a personal skills profile that can be viewed by employers or create a confidential online résumé to use in replying to job postings.

EXTRA FEATURES   Create a personal page customized with job listings and articles that match your criteria; use the JobSeek Agent to have opportunities matching your criteria emailed to you; read career articles and columns from the *WSJ* and other sources, including salary information and negotiating tips; apply online; email jobs to a friend.

DRAWBACK(S)   Serious, committed job-hunters will be hard-pressed to find any drawbacks here.

Quick Hits: Searching for Consulting Gigs

ContractJobHunter

www.cjhunter.com

This fee-based résumé-posting and job-search site costs $20 per year.

EXP.com

www.exp.com

Register as an IT expert at this site, which aims to connect people needing expertise in a subject with the folks who can provide it; create a skills profile that potential clients can view when seeking an expert, and respond to public questions or private requests for proposals; the site takes a 20-percent commission on the fee paid to the expert by the client.

FreeAgent.com

www.freeagent.com

Post a skills profile for review by potential clients, plus browse and bid on open projects; the number of available IT projects at any given time varies.

Guru.com

www.guru.com

Search for and bid on freelance IT projects; post your skills profile for review by potential clients; you must register to use all features at this site.

HelloBrain: The World's Intellectual Capital Exchange

www.hellobrain.com

Search for and bid on a wide range of requests for proposals (RFPs) for IT consulting projects; HelloBrain, which handles the billing and payment, takes a commission of 15 percent to 25 percent of the project fee.

SmarterWork

www.smarterwork.com

Browse and bid on projects to be conducted online; IT project categories include software development and website development; when the buyer and seller agree on a fee, the payment goes into an escrow account that pays out when the client signs off on the completed work; the site takes a 10 percent commission on the fee paid.

Software Contractors Guild

www.swguild.com

Search contract jobs for free; post your résumé and create a skills profile for $20 per year.

Talent Market at Monster.com

www.talentmarket.monster.com

Auction off your skills or bid on open projects at this auction-style marketplace; fees, ranging from $250 to $1,000 depending on the value of the project, are paid by the clients.

Quick Hits: Searching for Jobs Abroad

GoJobsite

www.gojobsite.com

Search for jobs in France, Germany, Ireland, Italy, Spain, and the United Kingdom.

IT-WebForum

www.it-webforum.com

Search for jobs by employer or job category, or use the PowerSearch feature to search by keyword, country, skills category, and date posted.

OverseasJobs.com

www.overseasjobs.com

Winner of the "not the sharpest tool in the shed" site award, this database of international jobs nonetheless features solid opportunities and employers; search by keyword and/or country.

Top Jobs on the Net

www.topjobs.net

Search for jobs in Ireland, the Netherlands, Norway, Poland, Spain, Sweden, Switzerland, the United Kingdom, and Thailand; each local site features local business news, employer profiles, local salary ranges, and information on working in the country; some of the sites are presented in the local language.

TIP *Should you post your résumé online at job search sites? That depends on how much privacy the website offers. Read both the job seeker's and employer's FAQs to determine whether you can store your résumé confidentially, for use only when you want a specific employer to review it, or whether it's stored in a public database that any employer can access. Ultimately, you want to control the use of your résumé; you don't want to end up with the online equivalent of your name and number scribbled on the bathroom wall. If your résumé goes into a public database, unscrupulous or inexperienced recruiters may then mass mail it to employers, which eventually can harm your credibility and good standing, warns Lucki of ABT Solutions. "If a company gets multiple submissions of your résumé, it will back off from you because issues will arise regarding who represents you or else they'll get a sense of you as a little desperate," she says. "Either way, it's not good to lose control of your résumé." RMIC's Streitenberger concurs. Both online and off, he says, "Be very judicious about who you give your résumé to."*

Effective IT Résumé Tactics and Strategies

No one likes putting together a résumé; deciding what to say, and what not to say, can be disconcerting and, at times, tedious. One advantage of working with a reliable, reputable recruiter is that you shouldn't even need a formal résumé because the recruiter will be representing you directly to the hiring manager, Lucki notes. Nevertheless, you should keep your résumé up-to-date with new skills and experience so that if you ever need it, it's ready to go.

One advantage IT professionals have in writing a résumé is the common language of IT: technologies, acronyms, products, and certifications that everyone recognizes at a glance. While you should "get rid of as much jargon as possible," you should list relevant skills and tools that you've used, advises Phil DeKok, IT training and sourcing manager at catalog company Lands' End, in Dodgeville, Wisconsin. Highlight your technical skills in a "Skills Profile" section at the top of your résumé. List certifications as well as software and hardware with which you've had direct, hands-on experience. Be concise, using strong, clear keywords, and list the skills categorically, in order of strength. For example, the skills profile on a developer's résumé might look like this:

SKILLS PROFILE: Certifications: MCSD; **Languages and Tools:** Visual Basic, ASP, Java, Perl, CGI; **Databases:** Access, Oracle, ColdFusion; **Operating Systems:** Windows NT 4.0, Windows 2000, Unix, Linux.

The section of your résumé detailing your professional experience should then reflect how you've used the technologies listed in your skills profile. This is the most important part of your résumé, and it should detail your accomplishments, not merely your work history and job descriptions. While you should include a one- or two-sentence summary of your overall responsibilities in each position held, follow that with bullet points; use the limited space you have to nail down your exact contribution to major initiatives and the measurable results. "Focus on the value you delivered," DeKok advises. "Give examples of how you've used tools or skills in a successful project that added value to the business." For example:

Instead of: Participated on project to upgrade manufacturing line systems.

Write this: Implemented system enhancements that increased productivity on the manufacturing line by 30 percent as measured in monthly production statistics analysis.

Instead of: Led project to create data warehouse for sales and marketing department.

Write this: Built Oracle-powered data warehouse, designed using Microsoft InterDev, that enabled national sales and marketing managers to respond to RFPs on average three weeks faster than before.

Instead of: Worked on deployment of new corporate WAN.

Write this: Deployed Cisco routers and hubs for new corporate WAN supporting 200 users in five locations nationwide that increased throughput and reliability by 50 percent, as measured in monthly performance reports.

How you organize your professional history depends on the extent of your experience and the type of position you're applying for. In most cases, the traditional backward chronological order is appropriate, Lucki says. Sometimes, however, organizing your experience topically, by functional experience, is useful, notes Streitenberger of RMIC. "You want your résumé to show where you've been and where you're going," he says, "but if you've had relevant past experience like managing multinational projects, that doesn't necessarily belong in chronological order. You would want to highlight that." In that case, you might separate work experience into two sections on your résumé: Under the heading "Functional Experience," spotlight your most high-profile, relevant projects and experience, and under "Career History," give a backward chronological account of positions held. Don't hesitate to customize your résumé for each potential opportunity. "Have a standard résumé ready, but be ready to tailor it so that it is most effective for a particular position," Lucki says.

Unless you are a recent college grad or have only a few years of professional experience, place your educational background at the end of the résumé. An exception to this rule would be if you recently completed an advanced degree, such as a techno-M.B.A.; that would merit listing your education and training following the skills profile, Lucki says. List your technical training as well as your college degree. If you have an advanced degree, list your academic credentials first; if you've been out of school a number of years and don't have an advanced degree, highlight technical and management training first. Your academic credentials should include the degree earned, the school, and year of graduation; if you have multiple degrees, list the most recent one first and work backward in chronological order. Your grade point average isn't necessary, unless it's outstanding (say, a 3.6 or higher) and you are just starting out or have very little work experience to detail. Training information should include course name, training vendor, and date completed. If you don't have a college degree but you've had substantial IT training, list the key courses that show the progression of your skills development.

Finally, don't overlook the value of dotting all your Is and crossing all your Ts. Before you send out a single copy of your résumé, whether online or in hard copy, proofread it closely. "When I see spelling errors, the first thing that crosses my mind is, 'Here's an IT professional who doesn't bother to use the spell checker,'" DeKok says. "If they are not even using the most basic tool available to them in their word processor, how will that translate into the larger IT arena? And above that, it shows me that they aren't paying attention to details, and that's extremely important in IT."

WWW.YOURNAMEHERE.COM

A personal website can be a tremendous marketing tool during an IT job hunt. You can use it as your virtual calling card, as a show-and-tell aid, and as an extension to your résumé. Moreover, if you are trying to learn or improve your web development skills, building the site and thinking about how to present yourself online is a practical exercise with a definite return on investment. "When a candidate has taken time to create a web presence, that's a plus," says Deron Streitenberger, CIO of Republic Mortgage Insurance Company (RMIC), Winston-Salem, North Carolina. "If they are taking advantage of all the tools available to represent themselves, that says something."

If you have work experience that won't fit on your hard-copy résumé, you can post a full-length résumé at the site to reference during phone screenings. Also store show-and-tell materials, like code you've developed (including a summary of how the code solved a particularly vexing technical problem), schematics of networks you've built or supported, or other documentation that illustrates your expertise in action. If you've developed web-based applications or designed web pages, link to the sites and include a summary of your exact contribution. If you've been quoted or profiled in any professional publications, link to the articles.

Aside from pointing interviewers to the website during phone screenings, you can also refer to it during in-person interviews. You can include the URL on your résumé and cover letters, and pass it along as you network. But, as Streitenberger notes, "You have to be careful about not letting your quirky side out." To make your website the best online representative of your work and experience, follow these guidelines:

▶ Keep it strictly professional; do not include personal information. Potential employers do not care about your hobbies, how many cats you have, how charming your dog is, how cute your kids are, where you spent your summer vacation, or your favorite bookmarks.

▶ Use the main page to introduce yourself, with a brief summary of your career history, your area of expertise, and your current position. Include any links to articles in which you're featured here; you may also want to link to other websites you've worked on from the main page. And include an email link.

WWW.YOURNAMEHERE.COM

▶ In the interest of maintaining control of your résumé, do not post it on a public area of the site. Store it in either a password-protected or hidden area of the site that is accessible only when you provide the password or URL extension to someone you want to see it.

▶ Take the same care to protect code documents, schematics, drawings, or any other proprietary show-and-tell material you store on the site. If your résumé is stored in a protected or hidden area, consider linking to those documents from your résumé. If you view the work you did on other websites as proprietary, you may also want to store those links in a private area.

▶ If you are seeking e-business or web-related work, or you are an independent consultant, spend the money to have your own URL, and choose one that sounds professional. Otherwise, if you will be using the site only during your job hunt or have no need to demonstrate web development skills, a free website is acceptable. Free website space is available at Yahoo!, Netscape, and myriad other sites, and it is generally available from your ISP as well.

What Not to Do on Your IT Résumé

After you've put together what you think is the perfect IT résumé, go back over it carefully with the following points in mind and delete any inappropriate material:

▶ Don't include in your skills profile technologies that you haven't had hands-on experience using. If you've taken a Java course but haven't used Java on the job, leave it off. Instead, list the class in the education section. If you've only been doing self-study to come up to speed, save that point for the interview.

▶ Don't put an objective on your résumé; it will only serve to possibly exclude you from opportunities that you may be perfectly qualified for.

▶ Don't put personal information such as hobbies and interests, marital status, age, race, or religion on your résumé. But do list any activities that are germane to the job, such as membership in professional associations, titles held in user groups, or volunteer work related to IT (e.g., teaching a weekend PC course for young students). List these activities at the end of your résumé under the heading "Professional Affiliations."

▶ Don't get creative with the formatting of your résumé. Use a conventional format. Busy IT managers want to scan it quickly and easily.

▶ Don't go over two pages. If your résumé runs long, consider listing jobs going back only ten years. Another option is to elaborate on your last three positions and cover the others in a quick summary listing employer, title, dates and, if space allows, responsibilities.

Effective IT Interview Tactics and Strategies

Regardless of how intrepid you've been in tracking down job opportunities, or how alluring your résumé is, whether you get the job will ultimately boil down to how well you navigate the interview process. From the initial phone screening to the final interview, you want to project an enthusiasm for the employer, the position, and the technology. And above all, be honest. An unemployed mainframe programmer, lamenting that an interview didn't go well, surmised, "I guess I didn't lie enough." In his conclusion is a clue to the real reason his interview was unsuccessful: The employer likely picked up on the fact that he was lying a little.

Preparing for the Interview

Don't walk into an interview unprepared, thinking your technical brilliance alone will see you through. Anticipate potential questions, and have some answers at the ready. You can expect general questions about why you're leaving your current job, what you like and dislike about your current position, your strengths and weaknesses, your short-term and long-term goals, and why you're interested in the job at hand. If you've put yourself through a self-assessment at the beginning of your job hunt, you already know the answers to those questions. But, just as you should customize your résumé for different types of opportunities, so should you tailor your answers to common interview questions. Prior to your first interview, whether it's onsite or a phone screening, you should nail down the specifics of the position, and thoroughly research the employer. Both will help you frame your answers to general queries and technical questions in the context of the opportunity.

A recruiter, if you are working with one, should fill you in on all the details about the job at hand. If you are going solo, try to get a written job description prior to the interview; if that's not possible, ask as many questions as you can when setting up the initial interview. You should know which department of the IT organization or the company the position is in, how the company defines the job title, overall responsibilities, and, if possible, day-to-day responsibilities. Also try to find out if the position is a new one created by a specific project need or new technology implementation, and, if so, the goals and objectives of the project.

The more you know about the job, the better you will be able to position your skills and experience in the course of the interview; for example, a helpdesk job in a call center entails different demands than a helpdesk job in corporate headquarters. In interviewing for the former, you would want to emphasize that you can handle a high-volume, fast-paced environment; for the latter, you would want to demonstrate that you have a strong end-user service ethic and that you're comfortable dealing with all types of end users, from administrative assistants to executives.

If you can picture yourself in the job beforehand and anticipate the day-to-day requirements, you'll come across in the interview as someone ready to hit the ground running—a huge asset. Yssa Bobrow, formerly vice president of IT at an ecommerce consulting firm and now an independent IT consultant, recalls a candidate who quickly jumped to the top of her list because "he was already envisioning himself in the position—what he would have to deal with and who he would be supporting," she says. "He was already thinking in terms of solutions and was gauging his own skill level to our environment."

Likewise, researching the employer's corporate culture, products and services, business initiatives, recent news announcements, competitors, and market position will also enable you to shape your answers appropriately for the opportunity at hand. If you know, for example, that the company is launching a new product line, when the interviewer asks, "Why are you interested in working for us?" your reply can reflect that: "Well, I want to work for a company that's continuing to grow, and this company has consistently identified viable new opportunities to increase its market share, such as with the new product line you're rolling out this year."

At the very least, you should review every section of the employer's website; ideally, you should go the extra mile and find out what others are saying about the company as well as unfavorable news that the company's website will usually omit. If you're working with a recruiter, you should get "a good technical breakdown of the company so you understand how your background fits in," says Lucki of ABT Solutions; if not, check computer trade publications for any mention of the company's IT environment. (Again, see Chapter 14 for websites and tips on researching companies and IT organizations, and see Chapter 15 for additional online resources; also see Chapter 10 for industry-specific resources.) From your research, you can pick up details that you can use to formulate questions to ask the interviewer about the IT environment. (See "Interviewing the Interviewer" later in this chapter.)

TIP *Develop some show-and-tell materials to bring to the interview. They help bolster your credibility and show that you've thought through the value you bring to the position, RMIC's Streitenberger says. If you've created a web presence (see "www.YOURNAMEHERE.com"), use that as your show-and-tell. If not, bring along some documentation that illustrates your contribution to a successful project and reinforces the points that you'll make about your technical expertise in the course of the interview. But don't get carried away. Streitenberger notes that he was less than impressed by a candidate who brought to an interview a Power-Point presentation on his career history. Appropriate materials include screen shots from websites you've developed, network schematics, code samples, project plans, etc.*

Acing the Technical Interview

The IT technical interview is like taking the SATs: You know there will be verbal and math, and you can run through practice tests to get familiar with the terrain, but you can't anticipate the exact questions. You can review what you know, but you can't learn everything you don't know the night before. You're never going to know all the answers anyway, so it's more a matter of how well you think on your feet. "Specific technical knowledge is relatively important, but more important is a solid expression of what you know and don't know," Streitenberger says. "If a candidate thinks they know a lot but they don't, or if they know a lot but can't convey what they know—both are problematic."

The interviewer's goal in the technical interview is to assess both the depth and breadth of your knowledge of particular technologies. Your goal should be to show, not tell. Translate your technical experience into a meaningful context by discussing specific projects you've worked on and how you've used your technical expertise to solve a problem for your company. "If a candidate gets too focused on the technology alone, I get nervous," Streitenberger says. If the interviewer is exploring your knowledge of Oracle, for example, highlight how you enhanced the scalability of a database to allow more transactions per second without having to add new hardware, which generated both additional productivity and cost savings. Such an answer demonstrates both an awareness of business concerns and your expertise with the technology. The worst thing you can do is fake it in a technical interview. If you don't know the answer, acknowledge that you're not sure, and ask follow-up questions that reflect how you would troubleshoot an unfamiliar technical problem on the job. That will at least demonstrate to the interviewer that you're not intimidated by new challenges.

Following are some favorite interviewing techniques used by IT managers:

▶ Gregor Cranz, chief technology officer at e-tailer iBeauty.com in New York, likes an empirical demonstration of a candidate's skills. For example, he gives applications developers a copy of the Level I Java certification exam, which consists of 60 questions. Candidates can answer their choice of 30 of the questions. "It's a real litmus test," Cranz says, because it separates those who say they know Java from those who really do. "A lot of people have the title senior Java programmer, but all they've actually done are Java applets," Cranz explains. "I need true senior programmers who know server-side Java."

▶ Bobrow poses hypothetical technical conundrums that don't have a definitive answer; moreover, in laying out the scenario, she provides only a few of the details that would be required to solve the problem in a live situation. "I want to test their troubleshooting ability and see how well they do fact-finding," Bobrow explains. "They may not have the exact skills to solve the problem, but the point is, do they ask me more questions? The red flag for me is if they look like they have no idea, and don't even ask me follow-up questions to at least try to figure it out. If they don't, I know they won't respond well in a crisis."

▶ Streitenberger favors simulations that test not only the candidate's problem-solving skills, but also how well they respond to changing project requirements. The exercise may not even involve technology, but rather, a complicated challenge, such as planning a reception for a foreign dignitary. "Problem-solving is our core competency, so I give them a set of circumstances and tell them they have 30 minutes to come up with a plan," he explains. Then, with only 10 or 15 minutes to go, he returns and throws a curve ball into the situation, giving them a change in the details that would alter the scope of the hypothetical event. "That's really valuable for seeing how well they cope with change," Streitenberger says. "It's easy to see if they can use Visual Basic; it's much harder to see if they can translate business requirements into code and cope with change."

Interviewing the Interviewer

The interview should be a mutual exploration of whether you're a good fit for the position and the organization and whether they're right for you. So be prepared to ask some thoughtful questions about the position, the IT organization, and the company. "Your questions should demonstrate that you've taken time to learn about the company before the interview," advises DeKok of Lands' End. For example, if you're interviewing for a network administrator job, and through advance research you know that the employer has 25 offices nationwide, you can demonstrate what you know by asking how the company handles remote access to servers and applications. Moreover, your questions should reflect that you are evaluating the overall opportunity—not just the particulars of title, responsibility, salary, and perks. "Make sure your questions don't make you look like you're only interested in your personal gain," Lucki says. "Tailor your questions and answers to show that you're interested in what's best for both of you."

To that end, questions about the company's stability are fair game, IT hiring managers say. If the company is private, ask if it's profitable and, if not, when it anticipates profitability. Ask a startup how much it has raised in venture capital and who its major backers are. Ask whether there have been company-wide and/or IT layoffs; if so, ask why, and how often layoffs have occurred in the past. And ask for customer references. "I would respect that—I'd think I'd like that person to work for me because they're going the extra mile of finding out how the company is perceived in the market," Streitenberger says.

Some general questions to raise include these:

▶ What is the relationship of IT to the business units? To whom does the CIO report?

▶ How aligned is IT with the goals and objectives of the company? How do your mission-critical systems contribute to the business?

▶ What are the major IT initiatives scheduled for this year?

▶ What are the goals and objectives of the department or project I'd be working with?

IT Interview Faux Pas

Job interviews can get off track at any point. Sometimes, it may be because the hiring manager doesn't really know what he wants in a candidate; sometimes, the company just isn't a good cultural fit for you, and your style of communicating doesn't mesh with the interviewer's. Those are things that you can't really control. On the other hand, candidates often make mistakes that are all their own. Here are some IT interview faux pas to avoid:

▶ While you want to demonstrate a passion and enthusiasm for IT and your career during the interview, don't lose your composure in the process. One candidate for a development position at See's Candies, South San Francisco, California, got so carried away in describing why he was leaving his current employer that MIS director Greg Gibbons immediately moved his résumé to the reject pile. "He was objecting to a project that had been canceled, and he got so adamant about it that he started pounding his fist on my desk," Gibbons recalls. Not only did the candidate come across as potentially volatile, but his actions indicated that he probably wasn't a team player.

▶ Similarly, don't complain about your current or former employers. Interviewers will inevitably ask why you are changing jobs, and you should be careful to frame your answer in positive terms. Don't say: "They made promises that they didn't fulfill," "I didn't get a raise I was promised," or "I had to work too much overtime," Lucki advises. "A lot of people badmouth their former employers, and that's completely inappropriate," she adds. "Hiring managers don't like to hear negatives because there is no Eden. A litany of complaints is offensive."

▶ Even though IT departments typically have a low-key dress code, don't show up for the interview in anything less than business casual. DeKok recalls an IT candidate who arrived for an interview wearing jeans and a rock band t-shirt. "Not only that, he had on sunglasses that were so dark you couldn't see his eyes, and he never removed them during the entire interview," DeKok adds. While Lands' End has a casual work environment, the choice of attire raised a red flag that was reinforced in the course of the interview. "As I talked with him, it was clear that he had an attitude of 'Take it or leave it—this is who I am,'" DeKok explains. "And we didn't take it."

▶ Don't misrepresent yourself. An experienced IT manager will know right away when you are less than truthful about your skills and background. "The moment that you say you have 12 years of Java experience, your credibility is shot," Streitenberger says. (Java hasn't been on the market for 12 years.)

▶ Don't ask about compensation in the initial interview. "That can convey that you're more interested in your own personal benefit than in working for the company," DeKok explains. Naturally, salary, bonuses, and benefits are important issues to any candidate, but save those questions for a second interview, DeKok advises. Raising those issues too early in the interview process will undermine your efforts to project an enthusiasm for the position at hand. Likewise, if the interviewer asks about your desired compensation, be prepared to respond but don't get pulled into salary negotiations on the spot. "Try to defer negotiations away from interview process," Lucki advises. "You want to make sure it's a good position and a good match before you resolve salary issues." She suggests answering with, "I am currently making X dollars a year, and I'm open to a fair offer." And be honest about what you are currently earning.

► Don't display technical arrogance or reveal your technology biases. "If you come across as too opinionated or limited in scope, you won't be considered an asset," Lucki warns. For example, Eric Kidd, former CTO at online pet store PetSmart.com, declined to make an offer to a candidate for a software engineering position even though he had stronger Java skills than any of the other candidates for the job. "He made it clear that he was not willing to work with any other programming language," Kidd recalls. "His interests were very self-centered. It was as is he were saying, 'I only want to work somewhere that benefits me, and I don't care if I benefit you.'" While Java was the primary development language in use at PetSmart.com, Kidd notes that flexibility and the willingness to contribute wherever help is needed "is what makes a strong contributor invaluable." Kidd adds that if the candidate had stated a preference for working with Java, but had been less adamant, he probably would have offered him the job. "We were doing a lot of work in Java, and with his skills in that area, it would have been unlikely that he'd have been called upon to work with other programming languages. But it wasn't clear to me that he understood the concept of a team."

► Never rule out an opportunity in the course of an interview. Even if by the end, you're thinking you don't want the position, Lucki suggests closing the interview with a simple, "Thank you for your time; I enjoyed meeting with you." That leaves the door open, which is important "because later you may find in thinking about it that it isn't the type of job you originally wanted, but it's the right job for you today," she explains. Conversely, if by the end of the interview, you definitely want the job, ask for it, Lucki says: "Tell the interviewer, 'I'd really like to come work for you. I'd like to pursue this opportunity to the next step.'"

Chapter 14

Land of Opportunity: Evaluating IT Job
Offers, Employers, and Prospects

Dave Dierolf wanted to get back to his IT roots. After a long stint doing procurement research for the Institute of Defense Analysis, he was ready to take up applications development work again. And, after many years of living inside "the concrete jungle of the Beltway" around Washington, D.C., he says he was ready to move his young family to a more tranquil burg. When he landed a position with a CD-ROM developer nestled in the foothills of the Blue Ridge Mountains, he thought he'd found his dream job.

"It was 1990, very early on in the development of CD-ROMs, and I got enamored of the technology because it was leading-edge," Dierolf recalls. "Plus, the company was in a 200-year-old farmhouse, but it was fully wired and had the most cutting-edge networking available at the time. So it all seemed great."

Unfortunately, it all looked so appealing that Dierolf failed to see beyond the down-home surroundings and the trend-setting technology. "I didn't practice good due diligence in researching the company, its viability, or how it was viewed by its parent company," he says. "And it turned out that there was no job security." The manager who hired him was let go before the end of Dierolf's first week on the job. Within a month, there were rumors that the parent company planned to shut down the division. Then came talk that it was moving the operation from Charlottesville, Virginia, to Colorado. A management consultant was sent in to study the situation. Employees were being cut out of the loop. One by one, Dierolf's coworkers left for greener pastures.

Dierolf spent nine months in the job, which he says was an "emotionally exhausting" time. "I had moved my wife and daughter, leaving a very solid job behind, and I'd also taken a reasonable cut in pay. We had landed in a nice part of the country, but there weren't nearly as many other job opportunities in Northern Virginia as there had been in the D.C. area." He managed to mobilize his remaining coworkers into convincing the powers that be to keep the organization intact, but says, "We lost all confidence over time about how they were treating us." Six months into the job, he began casting his net again, and eventually found a new position as head of research and development for a computer sales organization within Crutchfield Corporation, a consumer electronics catalog business.

Edward Jackson found himself in a similar situation in 1997, when he left a lucrative, $175-an-hour independent consulting project with Deloitte & Touche to join a pre-IPO Silicon Valley startup selling a database reporting tool. "If you imagine the classic Silicon Valley success story, this seemed to be it," Jackson says. "It had all the right signs of being a successful, well-positioned startup that would soon have an IPO [initial public offering] and go to the moon. The management team had years of experience in the software industry. They showed me the financials, and they looked great. They had some very big-name customers in the Fortune 2000, and I actually had been using their product." The company offered Jackson $95,000 in base compensation plus a $20,000 performance bonus and a $5,000 signing bonus. It added up to less money than he was making as a freelancer, but the recruiter convinced him that, in a market that was hot for startups, he was missing out by remaining a consultant. When the company offered to throw in 12,000 stock options, which it priced at about $4 a share, Jackson thought "it all sounded like the right package," he says.

But less than a month into the job, Jackson already suspected he'd made a grand mistake. His coworkers, who he reasoned should be eager to make the company a success so they'd all score big in the IPO, seemed under-motivated. He was traveling back and forth from the West Coast to the East Coast, working 14- to 16-hour days, and could never get anyone from the home office on the phone when he needed them. Meanwhile, key customers were breathing down his neck—the product wasn't working properly and the company's development team wasn't delivering promised functionality. Jackson says he was perplexed and frustrated.

"No one seemed to have the same sense of urgency as I did," he explains. "At first I thought the difference was because of my consulting background—as a high-priced consultant, you can't fail, and I brought that intensity with me to this new job." Then he uncovered the truth of the matter. "I discovered that the founder of the company actually owned 80 percent of the equity—the stock was extremely diluted, so my options were not worth very much, and neither were anyone else's," he says. "No one had the equity incentive to go for broke."

Jackson cut his losses early. He quietly put out the word among his former clients that he was available, lined up a new freelance gig within a day, and quit the company without giving notice. In the two months he had worked for the startup, he'd garnered only $16,000 in salary compared with about $50,000 he could have earned on the Deloitte & Touche contract, and he forfeited his bonuses by leaving before the customary waiting period was up. But he couldn't in good conscience stay with a company that he felt had flim-flammed him, and he recouped his losses in due time back on the consulting market. He doesn't put the job experience on his résumé.

Both Jackson's and Dierolf's experiences prove that career missteps don't have to spell the end of your IT career. Whether you've made a poor job choice or simply find yourself in an unlucky situation, you can still bounce back and even end up better off than you were before, more resilient and self-aware for having made the mistake and learned from it. Today, Jackson is chief technology officer (CTO) and cofounder of his own startup, SkillsVillage.com, an application service provider (ASP) that assists human resources departments with hiring and managing contractors and consultants. Dierolf is vice president of information technology at Crutchfield, which has grown to a $200-million-a-year business.

But you can minimize the risk of making a misguided career move by heeding the lessons they learned: Practice due diligence; don't allow yourself to be blinded by cutting-edge technologies, false promises, or cushy perks; and thoroughly review whether a company and its IT organization provide the right environment for you and your goals. Would an employer misrepresent the facts to get you on board? Dierolf and Jackson would certainly answer yes to that question.

Their experience illustrates that training for new IT opportunities, finding them, and acing the interview constitute only two-thirds of the battle; the next step is evaluating and selecting which opportunities to pursue and, ultimately, which offer to accept. Given that it's an IT job seeker's market, you owe it to yourself to carefully assess available jobs and firm offers in terms of both your short-term and long-term objectives. (See "Ten Things I Wish Someone Had Told Me Before I Went Out into the World" later in this chapter.) It's part of any job-hunting process to research the company before you interview (Chapter 13), but you should check out the company on the back end as well. Verify that the way your interviewers have positioned the company reflects the way it really is. Confirm that you'll be working with technologies that will forward your skills, not stagnate them. And bear in mind that IT frequently has its own unique subculture within the overall corporate culture.

Of course, you can never be 100 percent sure that a job is for you until you've taken it on. But, with a reasonable amount of research and forethought, you'll increase the probability of selecting an IT job that will please you now and put you on the path toward where you want to be in the future. "Keep your feet on the ground, and don't get too carried away with the promising aspects of a job," Dierolf advises. "Don't try to avoid all the risks, but don't be blind to the risks, either."

Throughout this chapter, you'll find suggested online websites for researching IT career information, IT organizations, companies, and IT salary and benefits information. As you use these resources to garner information and make career decisions, always consider the source: Who is producing the website? Who's contributing to it? What potential biases might it have? For example, at WetFeet.com, billed as "Helping you make smarter career decisions," your initial impression will be that you've found the mother lode of company research. Each corporate profile features "insider information" on the corporate culture, a description of the company's mission and business, and potential career paths within the company. But as you drill down into the individual profiles, it becomes clear that much of the information is provided by the companies themselves—it has been put through their PR machines for the best possible spin. That doesn't mean you might not pick up some good insights, but just be aware that the information isn't necessarily objective.

The best way to determine a site's potential biases is to first read through the "About Us" section of the site. Click About WetFeet, for instance, and you'll learn that WetFeet's main business activity is recruiting—and from that, you can infer that the companies it profiles are no doubt its clients. Naturally, the corporate profiles aren't going to tip you off to the drawbacks of working for those companies. Take a "Buyer beware!" approach to discussion boards as well. Even though the comments you'll find about companies in newsgroups or at forums like The Vault are not screened or edited by employers, consider that discussion boards tend to draw more complaints than praise. It's just human nature that people tend to sound off more when they're unhappy than when they're happy. So, while a company might seem to be generating a lot of negative comments among its employees, keep in mind that there may be thousands of content employees out there who just aren't posting in the forum.

Bottom line: Consider the source and don't rely too heavily on the information at any one site; always try to get a well-rounded picture by pulling together information from several different resources.

Evaluating the Opportunity

As you start to evaluate prospective IT job opportunities, don't just think about the job at hand, the day-to-day ins and outs, and the immediate prospect of a promotion or higher salary. Think instead in terms of both your current priorities and long-term goals. While that advice could apply to any job in any field, it's especially critical in IT, where technology, projects, and job descriptions change so rapidly. Consider that in the applications development realm, for example, the position of Java developer—an essential mainstay in leading IT organizations today—started to take off only in 1997 and has become commonplace only in the last two years. Likewise, jobs within the IT operations area were considered rather unglamorous until recently. But today, given companies' reliance on 24/7 uptime, a stint in the IT operations group can be a key stepping stone to the CIO's office. So, when faced with prospective opportunities, making sound decisions will be easier if you have a clear yet flexible idea about your long-range IT career path.

Flexibility is key so that you don't inadvertently miss out on emerging new career opportunities that may not exist today. It would be foolhardy to have a rigid ten-year plan that's fixated on attaining a certain IT position, because even if that position is strategic in 2001, it may be obsolete by 2011. Try to think in broad terms, such as the type of contribution you'd like to be making five years from now. And don't expect to reach your career apex in just a few years, no matter how bleeding-edge your skills may be. A recent study by JobTrak.com, an entry-level job recruitment site, found that 81 percent of college students and recent graduates expect to reach their career goals in under ten years; of those, 48 percent think they'll reach their goals in five years or fewer. Either their goals are shortsighted or their expectations are unrealistic.

Once you have a flexible long-term plan in place, and you're weighing your immediate opportunities, remember that there are no hard-and-fast rules for IT career advancement. Neither is there a formula to guarantee that an opportunity in front of you will be a good one. So apply some creative thought to different kinds of career moves that might propel you toward your next goal or your end goal. Some examples include the following:

▶ If you think that two years from now you'd like to be project managing strategic IT initiatives, try to identify opportunities that will put you in day-to-day contact with business units, working side-by-side with end-users.

▶ If you think that you'd ultimately like to be vice president of IT operations, seek opportunities to work outside of headquarters, such as in IT support at a manufacturing facility or a remote sales office, to gain experiences that will give you insight into the big picture.

▶ If you prefer to remain in hands-on tech work, try to identify opportunities that would enable you to stay on the leading edge with your skills, like participating in an upgrade to a new application, operating system, or network infrastructure. Find out if the company offers a purely technical career path in addition to an IT management path. How are techies recognized in terms of promotions, added responsibility, and financial incentives?

With a crystal ball in one hand and a serious self-assessment in the other, analyze any new opportunity in the context of the current IT job market as well as where the market might be going a couple of years from now, and balance that against your personal goals.

RESEARCH TIP *Mapping out a long-term career strategy requires more than just understanding technology trends. You must also assess what impact those trends will have on the IT organizational structure, IT positions, and job descriptions. So in addition to keeping up with emerging technologies and how they're being applied, spend some time researching the impact of the technology on the structure of the IT organization. Read IT career features and news stories for analysis of how new trends in IT are creating new IT career opportunities.*

Ten Things I Wish Someone Had Told Me Before I Went Out into the World

With nearly 30 years of IT experience behind him, Carl Wilson, executive vice president and CIO of Marriott International, Bethesda, Maryland, shares the advice he wishes someone had given him at the outset of his career. His ten recommendations for IT career planning serve as criteria you can use for evaluating potential job opportunities. As you weigh various offers, use these points to judge an opportunity in the context of your long-term career.

1. Carefully pick your company and boss.

Does the company you're considering conduct its business in a manner that you are comfortable with? Is its main line of business one that you'll feel comfortable supporting? "It's very important that you can personally identify with what that company is trying to achieve, its products and services," Wilson advises. "You will not achieve full success working in an environment that runs counter to your values." For example, Wilson notes that he "would have a very hard time working for an arms dealer, but it feels great to be working for a hospitality company that is trying to make travelers' experiences wonderful." Likewise, you will likely not feel you are meeting your full potential working for a boss whose values do not mesh with your own. Look for bosses who can serve as mentors, not just in terms of developing technical skills or management techniques, but in broader terms such as how they conduct themselves with colleagues and subordinates and how they manage their professional and personal lives.

2. Only work for a firm that reinvests in you.

Will the employer's policies, practices, and IT budget support your further skills development and career advancement? "Look for a company that has a career path you can progress through based on your own acquired and demonstrated skills, especially in the early stages, when you are as much a student as a worker," Wilson says. "If a company is not reinvesting in you, eventually, that will impact your career negatively." In each round of interviews you go through with an employer, ask for concrete examples of IT staff members who have progressed through different jobs in the organization, training that others in your position have attended, and skills development opportunities that would be available to you.

3. Build your network early and grow it over time.

Does the employer support participation in professional associations and industry groups? Is the environment one in which you can foster a variety of different relationships? Because you never know where a colleague—within your company or without—is going to end up, it always pays to build relationships with other professionals in your field, Wilson says. "Most major jobs in really good companies are filled by word-of-mouth and recommendations by employees," he explains. Start developing a network of people you respect as early as college. Get involved in professional associations as soon as you enter the workforce or launch a new career path. Not only will a solid network help you uncover viable new career opportunities, it will also expose you to new ideas, technologies, and approaches to your work. "I have seen people who are so insular within their companies that they don't broaden themselves," Wilson says. "It's good to get involved in [professional activities] outside your company because you'll bring a fresh perspective to your job."

4. Don't repeat a work experience more than two or three times—aim to have a different role with each new job.

Does the employer seem to pigeonhole IT professionals or does it regularly provide opportunities to pursue new challenges? "Make sure your role changes over time so you keep growing," Wilson says. "You don't want to accumulate 20 years of experience that is really just four years' experience repeated five times." If, for example, you're an applications developer, don't get stuck building one particular type of application, such as sales force automation systems. "Go through that experience once to learn it, do it again to refine your skills, but if you're asked to do it a third time, your role should be as team leader or project manager so you get a new perspective," Wilson says. Another approach, if you don't want to tackle management, is to ask to be assigned to a new area that leverages and expands your acquired skills, such as (in this example) a customer relationship management system.

5. Don't be afraid to take a lateral or lower graded job for more experience.

Does the company offer flexible career paths? Would it support unconventional moves that could benefit your long-term career development? Sometimes, the best career moves for your future are those that don't necessarily advance you from your current position, but will expose you to new ways of thinking about IT. Wilson says his career has profited several times over from a willingness to step down the ladder rather than up it. In the mid-seventies, as a top mainframe programmer at Bendix Corporation, he took a 6 percent pay cut to move into a business process reengineering job because he "wanted the opportunity to have a direct influence on the design of systems and not just be a top coder." The experience broadened his perspective on how IT could be applied to the business, and nine months later, Bendix recognized his efforts by moving him into a key project management position. While you want to assess the pros and cons of an unconventional move carefully, don't rule out what may be a good opportunity simply because it doesn't fit a traditional model. "I've noticed that IT professionals have a tendency to develop along very narrow lines—once they develop an expertise in an area, they just follow that path," Wilson observes. "And I've seen people get so narrowly focused in their careers that they never could see their full potential."

6. Don't be afraid to take on tough assignments that no one else wants.

Does the company recognize and reward employees for taking risks and accepting challenges that have a high potential for failure? Does management provide a soft landing if you fail? "That should be part of the leadership role in IT because it's not always an individual's fault when a project isn't successful," Wilson says. "There may be extenuating circumstances or it just turned out not to be a good idea." Management should encourage staff to take on risky assignments—and IT professionals should seek challenging opportunities—because "you learn at an accelerated rate when you take those on," he says. "And once you conquer the assignment, you develop a certain amount of confidence that will play well in other areas of your career."

7. You will not be promoted by your boss, but by your peers and subordinates.

Does the job give you the opportunity to interact with colleagues up, down, and across the organization? Does the environment support peer feedback and 360-degree reviews (in which leaders and subordinates review each other)? "The way bosses know who to promote and move forward is based on what they hear from an employee's peers and subordinates," Wilson says. "A lot of people try to manage their careers by ingratiating themselves with upper management, but it's more important to focus your time on developing strong relationships with your peers and being an advocate and supporter of your subordinates. If you do those two things well, management will notice, and upward movement will come automatically."

8. Acquire project management skills.

Does the IT organization follow sound project management methodologies? Does it advocate project management training? "This is the most sought-after skill set within most companies today," Wilson says. "People who can organize work, break it into chunks, influence and get work done by others, and define deliverables that produce value are very, very valuable to any company." Even if you don't plan to become a project manager, Wilson still recommends project management training because "it helps you to be a better team player and understand the demands of the project; you'll contribute more to the team's success." It's never too early to start project management training, and Wilson advises pursuing certification from an organization such as the Project Management Institute. (See Chapter 12.)

9. Learn from your mistakes. If you don't make any, you haven't done anything.

Does the company's management style make room for you to learn from your mistakes? Does it foster a generous, risk-tolerant environment, seeking to turn errors into opportunities for growth instead of admonishments and recrimination? "Celebrate your failures as much as your successes," Wilson says, because that's how you learn and grow. Wilson's favorite interview question is, "Tell me something that you really screwed up badly," he says, because people reveal a lot about themselves in how they respond. "If they say they've never made any mistakes or had any problems, then they probably haven't done a lot," he says. "If they say it was everyone else's fault, they probably didn't learn anything. But if they say, 'Yes, I had this project, and I messed it up, and in retrospect, I should have done this,' then I know I've found a star."

10. Live a balanced life, because your work is what you do, not what you are.

Does the company expect you to always put your job first, or does it promote policies and practices that will help you strike a balance between your professional and personal lives? Wilson quotes an adage from Indian folklore: "A continuously bent bow ceases to shoot straight." In other words, "If we become too absorbed in our work, and identify ourselves so closely with our work that it's all we think about, we cease to be effective, and that's where burnout comes from," Wilson explains. "You have to have a life outside of work." Build time into your day that belongs to you, and "vigorously protect and defend it," Wilson says. For example, he gets to the office around 7:00 A.M., but he avoids taking meetings before 8:00 or 9:00 A.M. so he can use mornings for thinking and strategizing; likewise, he clears his calendar after 4:30 P.M. because that's when he wraps up the day's to-do lists. By 6:00 P.M., he's headed home for family time. "It requires some prior planning, and there are times that the job demands that you step out of the lines," Wilson says, "but you have to maintain time for you."

Online Resources: Researching IT Careers

Computerworld Careers Page

www.computerworld.com/careers/

This is the page for one-stop shopping for *Computerworld*'s careers coverage, including weekly stories and major features dealing with emerging job titles, hiring and recruiting trends, career paths, and more.

InformationWeek Careers Page

www.informationweek.com/career2

Read various weekly articles and use career tools, including training and education guides, a career advice column, and more, at this page; note that there are some broken links.

InformationWeek Research IT Staffing Report

http://img.cmpnet.com/infoweek/799/graphics/itstaffing.pdf

Turn to this report when mapping out your job-search strategy to find out what's motivating employers to hire IT staff and to uncover recent trends in IT recruiting and retention (requires Adobe Acrobat).

IT Careers.com

www.itcareers.com

This service of ITWorld.com features relevant articles from a wide variety of sources and webcasts on IT career topics (as well as job postings). It features special reports for both job seekers and employers—find out what recruiters and hiring managers are thinking by checking out the content aimed at them.

 NOTE *For more IT career-related sites, see Chapter 13 and the "IT Publications and Portal Sites" and "IT Community Sites" listings in Chapter 15.*

Evaluating the Workplace

Gauging whether you'll feel fulfilled and productive in a new workplace is one of the trickier aspects of making an IT career decision. Just as you put your best foot forward in a job interview, HR and IT managers will highlight only the best aspects of the company and the IT environment. In discussing the company, they'll draw attention to the most attractive points—an on-site health club, free breakfasts for employees who arrive early, and ethnic diversity in the workforce. What you won't hear is that last year, they shut down three facilities and axed 1,500 workers. In your IT department interviews, you'll hear a lot about exciting upcoming projects, but little about how dissatisfied end-users are with the new enterprise resource planning (ERP) system or how the next iteration of the website is woefully behind schedule.

Even if you're invited to speak with your potential colleagues in the IT department, it's unlikely that they'll tell you, "Look, our boss is a moron who can schmooze upper management but doesn't know the first thing about Java," or that "Except for the drive to the office, I haven't seen daylight in six months." It's up to you to surmise what life in that IT environment is *really* like. Use your interviews and company visits to do a little detective work, and snoop around the Web for clues as well.

Judge the company on its viability, prospects, corporate culture, and people. While the IT department may seem like the kind of place you want to work, remember that it's part and parcel of a larger entity. Chapter 13 discusses how company research before your job interview will help you tailor your responses to questions to reflect the interviewer's concerns. Likewise, you'll be prepared to assess whether the way your interviewers pitch the company matches up against external reports and research. If the interviewer talks about how much the company is growing, but you've just read that it is dropping several product lines, tactfully ask about that. Don't be challenging—keep your voice in a neutral tone and couch your question in positive terms: "That's exciting that the company sees a lot of growth ahead. How does the discontinuation of your X product fit into the company's growth projections?" How willing the interviewer is to answer a difficult question, and how well he or she does, will give you some insight into whether this is a company that walks the walk or merely talks the talk. And the fact that you asked the question will signal to the interviewer that you are taking your job search, and thus your career, seriously. So even if you catch someone off guard, the impression you'll leave is of a candidate who's thorough and prepared.

Among the salient points about a company that you want to cover in your research and in your interviews are the following:

✓ Is the company profitable or on its way to profitability? If it's a public company, review its quarterly earnings reports in the "Investor Relations" section of its website and look up its Securities Exchange Commission (SEC) filings on the Web.

If it's privately held, try to uncover financial information from industry trade journals, Hoover's Online (see "Online Resources: Researching Potential Employers" later in this chapter), and other resources. And don't hesitate to bring up the company's financials in an interview, especially at a startup. Questions could include these: Do you anticipate going public? When do you expect to reach profitability? When was your last round of venture capital?

✓ Has it had recent layoffs? You can try looking this up on the Web, but it's also a fair question to ask in an interview. Start with a softball question like, "What's the company's policy regarding layoffs?" and then if necessary, follow up with, "When was your last round of layoffs, and what drove the decision?"

✓ How is the company viewed in its marketplace? How does it measure up to its competitors? This isn't a question that you want to come right out and ask in an interview, but you can get an idea of the company's take on this by asking, "What do you think is the biggest public misconception about your company?" The answer will reflect the company's own research into how it's viewed by outsiders.

✓ How is the corporate culture manifested in the company's policies and physical environment? This is largely subjective, and you can rely at least partly on your own observations. Are office doors open or closed? What's the office décor (or lack thereof)? Do employees seem engaged with each other, either in impromptu hallway conferences or in water-cooler conversation?

Just as important as evaluating the company's success and culture is evaluating the IT organization's success and culture. One thing you want to determine right away is how IT is viewed by the rest of the company. Is it essentially a reactive service and support organization, or is it a key partner in establishing and pursuing the corporate mission? You can get some clues about this from the corporate reporting structure and the physical environment as well. For example, if the CIO reports to the chief financial officer, that can be a sign that the company views IT as a cost center rather than a strategic asset. The preferable model is that the CIO reports directly to the CEO or president.

Also, where in the company is IT located? Are IT staffers dispersed so that development and support teams are colocated with the end-users they support? If the IT staff is centralized, are they in the basement or in the one area of the company overlooked by the last remodeling? Or do they have a comfortable space with lots of light and ergonomically correct furniture? These things may seem merely cosmetic, but they can be valid indicators of how IT is perceived and valued by the company.

Within the IT department itself, what's the cultural vibe? Owing to IT's unique function, the IT organization may develop its own subculture within the overall corporate culture, so again, take the opportunity to make some personal observations about the environment. Is there an ambience of "it's us against them" or a sense of connectedness to the rest of the company? Do people seem excited about new technologies or bored by their work? Is new skills training a high priority, and do IT managers set aside the time for it as well as the budget? Does the staff have up-to-date workstations on their desks with large monitors and lots of technology books?

Look for nonverbal clues about how IT employees feel about their jobs, like whether they have personal items in their workspaces (a subtle indicator of how free they feel to express themselves) or if they have merchandise with the company logo (pride in their employer and connectedness to the business). And, because the key ingredient in the IT organization isn't merely the technology, but the people, try to learn as much as you can about who you would be working with.

To uncover information about the IT culture and your potential coworkers, you may want to ask IT managers and staff the following questions:

▶ Where were you working before coming here? Why did you take the job here?

▶ How long have you worked here? What position were you hired for here and what has your career path been so far?

▶ How is this IT department different than others you've worked in?

▶ What was the last training that you took, and when? What are your upcoming training plans?

If it feels difficult to ask the more personal questions, look for opportunities to ask them off-handedly and casually, when you're not in "official interview" mode, such as during the IT tour or when you're walking to the cafeteria for a cup of coffee. How open the interviewer is about answering the questions can be one sign of what the atmosphere is like within the IT organization—are the people open, friendly, communication-oriented, confident?

Finally, don't expect every IT organization to be a utopia of leading-edge technology, workplace fun and games, and constant catering to your every need. Unfortunately, given the intense media coverage of IT careers in recent years, and the ballyhoo surrounding the dot-com revolution, a general impression has emerged that IT pros are universally treated like company royalty. But as in any job in any field, that isn't necessarily the case. (See the following section.)

RESEARCH TIP *For an idea of the IT organization's initiatives and culture, search for articles about the company at your favorite IT trade publication websites. Just because a company hasn't been featured in Internet Week or InfoWorld doesn't mean it's a bad place to work, but you may turn up some revealing information.*

The Myths and Realities of IT Workplace Perks

Information technology organizations are so desperate for talent that they'll invite you to bring your dog to the office and do your dry cleaning for you. That is, on the days you're not telecommuting from home.

Don't count on it. While many IT organizations do offer unique perks perhaps not found in other workplaces, the supply-and-demand frenzy of recent years has given rise to a number of exaggerations about what you can expect in the IT workplace—such as pets roaming the office and fulltime telecommuting arrangements.

"There are so many myths flying around out there, and some of them became validated because of the supply-and-demand frenzy in 1999–2000," says Shelley Morrisette, senior vice president and director of research at Darwin Partners, an IT human resources management consulting firm based in Wakefield, Massachusetts. Morrisette notes that three simultaneous trends in IT created a swell of demand for IT professionals: the build-up of dot-com startups, the Year 2000 remediation problem, and a rapid move to implement ERP systems. Collectively, those "just sucked up all the IT talent and put the IT labor market on its ear," Morrisette says.

Recruiting and retention became the new workplace holy grail. Many companies moved to create more benevolent working environments for their hard-to-find, harder-to-hold IT employees, implementing workplace policies that catered to IT employees' personal needs and fostered greater balance between home and work. Some of the perks were so unusual—revolutionary, even—that they generated a lot of buzz in the media and were, perhaps, over-reported in comparison to how often they were actually offered.

The new IT workplace trends first emerged in Silicon Valley's technology hotbed. Innovative companies like Hewlett-Packard Company, Tandem Computers , and Apple Computer created camaraderie and engendered loyalty by hosting Friday afternoon beer-busts, creating on-site daycare centers, offering sabbaticals, and more. Those kinds of workplace innovations caught on in the exuberant high-tech startup environment of the mid-to-late nineties. The dot-com companies of the East and West Coasts—with their barrels of venture capital, hipster cache, and determination to bust old paradigms—recreated the workplace to draw legions of Gen X and Gen Y workers away from the esteemed Fortune 1000. To compete, even the so-called "old-economy" companies began extending similar workplace benefits to their IT organizations.

But as those by-now-legendary dot-coms have gone belly-up or moved to put a more corporate face on their image and exercise greater financial restraint to please shareholders after their IPOs, you're a lot less likely to see Rover padding around the office. That said, companies aren't likely to withdraw reasonable workplace perks that they extended to IT workers. Many of the perks have proven to help retention, and have been so successful that they in fact have spread beyond just the IT department. But if you're expecting an IT environment to be a freewheeling playground, keep in mind the reality behind these common IT workplace myths:

Myth: Bring your pet to work.

Reality: A number of startups bent on changing the corporate rules and catering to small staffs that were putting in 20-hour days often allowed pets to accompany their owners to work. But that benefit has slowly fallen off as coworkers complained of allergies or the VP's cute little pooch became too much of a distraction. Not even IT workers at The Humane Society get to bring their pet to work.

Myth: Work from home full time.

Reality: Despite charming commercials featuring pajama-clad telecommuters videoconferencing with the corporate office, daily telecommuting is by no means common in IT. The truth is, many IT positions require hands-on work that can't be done remotely. And while part-time telecommuting options are gaining in popularity, old management paradigms persist. Even though a Darwin Partners study indicates that the majority of IT workers would take 15 percent less in salary for the privilege of working from home, Morrisette says, managers still feel they can better manage employees when they are in the office along with everyone else. While you can expect to work from home on an occasional, as-needed basis, flexible schedules are much more common than daily telecommuting.

Myth: Wear whatever you want!

Reality: This is nearly true. Throughout the late nineties, IT organizations realized that one simple way to attract IT professionals was to give them more flexible wardrobe options, and the policy leaked into other areas of the company. Nonetheless, don't think you're going to get away with walking down corporate corridors in shorts and Birkenstocks. The "business" in business casual means that you can get away with nice sportswear—chinos, shirts with collars, etc. Don't plan on dressing like it's a day at the beach except in the most liberal companies. Morrisette notes that corporate dress policies tend to mirror the region the company is based in—Silicon Valley is more laid back and Silicon Alley is trendy, while Dallas is still a little dressier, for example. Dot-coms and startups are exceptions to the business casual standard.

Myth: A concierge is at your service.

Reality: This is a perk offered in more companies than you might imagine. Like business casual dress, it started partly in reaction to the IT labor supply-and-demand gap, but the benefit isn't necessarily limited to the IT staff. Concierge services can include dry cleaning pickup and delivery, film drop-off, catered lunches, take-out food available to pick up on your way home, and more. "Companies want to help employees out as much as possible, but the idea is to make employees more productive—I don't think they're just being altruistic," Morrisette says. Nonetheless, with IT employees putting in more than 2,100 hours a year, according to Darwin, an onsite concierge can make a big difference in one's quality of life.

Myth: You can go for new skills training whenever you want.

Reality: Company-paid training is definitely on the rise among IT shops as they move to increase IT retention rates to counter the supply-and-demand gap. But while many companies have the best intentions for training—and the budgets to match—overworked IT professionals may still find it difficult to budget the time for new skills training. One way to test how high a priority an IT organization places on ensuring that employees get time off for training is to ask about their turnover rate, Morrisette says. If it's higher than 20 to 25 percent, be wary—that could be a sign that employees are dissatisfied with training opportunities. An IT professional who isn't challenged and fears his or her skills are becoming obsolete isn't likely to stick around too long.

Online Resources: Researching Potential Employers

Researching IT Shops

Computerworld's 100 Best Places to Work in IT 2000

www.computerworld.com/cwi/story/0,1199,NAV64_STO45408,00.html

To find the leading IT shops based on salary, benefits, bonuses, training, diversity, and other workplace factors, check out this annual listing; published June 2000.

Computerworld's Premier 100 IT Leaders

www.computerworld.com/premier100

While this annual listing focuses on people and not places, use the content here to assess which IT shops tap and develop today's IT leaders; then get some insight into how those leaders rose to the top.

The *InformationWeek* 500

www.informationweek.com/500menu/500menu.htm

Get the low-down on the 500 "most innovative users of information technology," as pegged by *InformationWeek*; 12th annual edition published September 11, 2000.

Researching Companies

100 Best Companies for Working Mothers

www.workingwoman.com/wwn/article.jsp?contentId=4085&ChannelId=208

Were this annual listing of the top companies for moms who work not compiled by the editors of *Working Mother* magazine, it might be more aptly titled "100 Best Companies for Working Parents"; published October 2000.

America's Most Admired Companies

www.fortune.com/fortune/mostadmired

Fortune magazine's assessment of the most highly thought of U.S. companies is based on quality of management and products or services, innovation, financial stability, employee talent, and other factors; link from here to *Forbes'* "100 Best Companies to Work For" list; published February 19, 2001.

The *Forbes'* 500 Top Private Companies

www.forbes.com/private500

This searchable listing of the leading 500 privately held companies in the United States is based on revenue, size, and financial performance, according to the editors of *Forbes* magazine; published November 27, 2000.

The *Forbes'* Platinum 400

www.forbes.com/platinum400

Search this listing, the "400 Best Big Companies in America," for corporate leaders as measured by financial performance, according to the editors of *Forbes* magazine; published January 8, 2001.

The Fortune 500

www.fortune.com/fortune/fortune500

The venerable grand-daddy of all corporate lists, these are the top U.S. companies ranked by revenue; be sure to check out the accompanying articles; published April 16, 2001.

Working Woman Magazine's Top 25 Companies for Executive Women

http://www.workingwoman.com/wwn/article.jsp?contentId=5904&ChannelId=208

Find the best companies for women striving for the executive suite using this annual ranking based on the companies' efforts to advance women in the workplace and the value they place on diversity, according to the editors of *Working Woman* magazine; published December 2000/January 2001.

Hoover's

www.hoovers.com

Get corporate profiles, IPO news, business analysis, and more. While a paid subscription (pay-per-view is also available) is required to access the most in-depth research here, nonsubscribers can review company capsules, financial news, and other features for free.

The Industry Standard's Layoff Tracker

search.thestandard.com/texis/trackers/layoff

If you're targeting dot-com companies, check this searchable listing to see which ones have had layoffs, how many, when, and why.

TheVault.com Company Research

www.vault.com/nr/researchhome.jsp

Access reader-written profiles and other research on over 3,000 employers, from AAA to Zurich Reinsurance. Then surf over to the site's Top 20 Message Boards at www.vault.com/community/mb/mb_top20.jsp and use the Companies message boards to ask questions—anonymously—about prospective employers or simply browse the boards for insider gossip. For example, one recent topic of discussion about a leading consulting firm that promotes its gay-friendly benefits revealed that in the office, the attitude was more like don't ask, don't tell.

WetFeet.com Company Research

www.wetfeet.com/research/companies.asp

Although the 1,600-plus profiles here are supplied by the employers themselves—and thus are typically glowing descriptions—the presentation merits a look; each profile features descriptions of the business, the corporate culture, and the interviewing process, as well as job information.

Evaluating the Job Offer

If you've determined that a potential IT opportunity aligns with your short-term and long-term goals, and that the IT workplace is one in which you'll be happy, then it's time to assess the actual offer. While the salary will certainly be a big part of the package, remember not to focus on salary alone. Instead, judge its fairness in terms of the overall compensation package, including bonuses, benefits, vacation time, stock options, 401K plans, and the like—plus how well the opportunity and the workplace match up with your needs and desires for your career. Your long-term satisfaction with the job—and with your compensation—will rest in the big picture, not the line-item details.

Surprisingly enough, despite all the media hoopla over IT salaries, it seems that as many IT pros feel underpaid in IT as in any other field. The IT job-search site ComputerJobs.com found in its year-long 2000 salary survey that only about one-third—32 percent—of IT professionals feel they are adequately paid. The majority, 67 percent, say they're underpaid, while a mere 1 percent feel overpaid. The numbers shift somewhat with salary bracket—among those making between $44,000 and $100,000, satisfaction goes up to 58 percent of respondents, whereas among those making less than $44,000, only 17 percent are satisfied. Not surprisingly, the highest paid have the highest satisfaction, with 65 percent of those making over $100,000 reporting that they feel adequately paid. The seemingly widespread dissatisfaction with salaries may stem from the fact that too many IT professionals make job decisions based on salary alone without looking at the big picture before accepting the offer. Perhaps at the outset, $50,000 a year sounded like a great deal, but once they're putting in 60 hours a week on the job, it doesn't seem so fair.

If the salary you're offered is less than you wanted, or even less than you are making now, your first instinct may be to dismiss the offer as not worth your time. In many case, that instinct might prove correct, but don't decline the offer without thinking about it first. Try to come up with a value for the overall compensation and benefits package, using these points to guide you:

✓ Will you qualify for bonuses and financial incentives?

✓ Is there a tax-free savings plan?

✓ Does the company offer tuition reimbursement, and if so, how flexible are the terms? Some companies require minimum grades and will cover the cost of the course only, while others are more generous. Also keep in mind that some companies have pay-back policies should you leave the company within a year of completing the course.

✓ How much vacation time will you get? Typically, companies offer two weeks to newcomers; if a company offers you more, factor that in.

✓ Do the insurance benefits cover domestic partners as well as spouses and children? What about same-sex partners? Will the insurance plan enable you to keep your current doctors?

✓ Is there a daycare subsidy? Does the company offer onsite daycare, and if so, how long is the waiting list?

✓ Are there benefits for elder-care or child-adoption assistance programs?

While perks developed to recruit and retain IT professionals frequently drive overall corporate benefit policies (see "The Myths and Realities of IT Workplace Perks," earlier), IT professionals can expect to receive the same insurance benefits, 401K plans, and vacation time extended to all employees. Bonus programs, on the other hand, are often tailored for the unique work processes and retention challenges involved in IT. Employers that place a high value on IT as mission-critical recognize that IT work is by nature different, more deadline-driven, and more project-oriented. These companies concede that financial incentives can increase productivity and decrease turnover. When interviewing, be sure to ask if the company offers IT-specific bonus programs and, if so, what's required to qualify for bonuses.

Among the various IT bonus schemes are spot bonuses for outstanding contributions, milestone bonuses for making a project deadline, and project-based bonuses given for completing projects on time and on budget with all the expected functionality. Spot bonuses and milestone bonuses usually involve small cash awards or gift certificates, while project completion bonuses may be a larger fixed amount of cash or a percentage of base salary. In terms of annual bonuses, CIOs and IT directors can expect to receive an average bonus of 22 percent of their base salary; middle managers, 9 to 11 percent; and staff, 4 to 5 percent, according to the 2001 salary survey by Datamasters, a Greensboro, North Carolina, IT consulting firm.

Some examples of companies that have devised IT-specific bonus programs include the following:

▶ Marriott International: IT managers and senior technologists qualify for varying types of bonuses, while lower-level employees qualify for recognition rewards such as a cash award or a free weekend at any Marriott property.

▶ Aflac: In recent years, the company has experimented with project-oriented incentives, like a $100 cash award for reaching a project milestone.

▶ Reebok International: IT staff members can earn spot bonuses upon project completion.

Stock options, once a big draw for pre-IPO dot-coms and other startups, don't seem nearly as glamorous now as they did before the big dot-com bust. But even though the IPO environment is less friendly than before, and overall stock-market performance has been wavering, IT job seekers shouldn't completely distrust stock options as long as they are not offered in place of fair and reasonable salary and benefits. If you decide to accept an offer that entails options, keep in mind that the earlier you join a startup, the more options you'll likely receive because you'll be viewed as taking on more of the risk.

As time goes by, the value of the options will depend on how many have been issued, how they've been distributed, and other factors. Their value once the IPO arrives will vary according to filing price, actual opening price, and closing price. And from there, it's a game of wait-and-see. A number of the record-breaking IPOs of 1999 and 2000 were penny stocks in danger of losing their NASDAQ listing by 2001. Considering that company officers are required by law to wait at least a year before they can sell their stock, a lot of paper millionaires were paper paupers seemingly overnight. Among larger corporations, stock options are uncommon except at the senior management and executive level, although they are sometimes awarded as bonuses to lower-level employees.

After you've arrived at a value for the overall compensation package, weigh the entire package against the other aspects of the job:

✓ Would it put you on a management track faster than in your current job or other offers you have in hand?

✓ Would it take you out of an aging technology into a new one?

✓ Would it get you into a company or industry that you've always wanted to work for?

✓ Would your opportunities to make a visible contribution increase?

✓ Would your job satisfaction increase?

✓ Would you be working fewer hours than you are now? Would your overall quality of life improve?

If, based on everything you've uncovered about the job, you can answer yes to several or all of these questions, you can consider the job offer to be worth a great deal even if the actual salary isn't what you were hoping for.

As for salary parity between men and women, IT is one of the most equitable fields today. A study by job-search site Techies.com analyzing salary data gathered from 106,133 members (87,075 men and 19,058 women) found male and female IT professionals nearly on par in the first five years of their IT careers, with women earning 92 cents for every dollar that men earn. That's considerably better than the national average: The U.S. Census Bureau reports that for all full-time positions, women earn less than 75 percent of what their male counterparts earn. As men and women move up the IT ladder, however, the salary gap widens to a range of 7 to 16 percent depending on job title.

RESEARCH TIP *As advised in Chapter 11, don't rely on one salary survey alone to determine what you should expect in a job offer. Establish an appropriate salary range for a job, based on your skills and years of experience, by culling the relevant data from three to five different surveys.*

The Myths and Realities of IT Job Offers

Just as the IT supply-and-demand gap has given rise to a number of urban legends about IT workplace perks, so has it generated some unrealistic expectations about IT job offers—like a free BMW as a signing bonus. Like the media buzz surrounding the IT workplace, myths about IT compensation and benefits are grounded in a grain of truth, arising from reports of extravagant offers made to what Darwin Partners research VP Morrisette describes as IT gurus—"the pace-setters who are among the early adopters of new technologies."

"A lot of IT people get paid these outrageous salaries because they have taken huge risks," Morrisette explains. "When a new hot technology comes along—say, Java—

they take time to become proficient in it, and are spending valuable resources becoming knowledgeable without knowing whether the opportunities will be there to make huge money. It could be that a technology doesn't pan out, and those newly acquired skills wouldn't be worth anything. So it's a game, and those who play it right will be worth a lot of money for a while, and then the salary premiums will level off."

For several years running, thanks to the IT supply-and-demand gap, the unusually high salaries being extended to the IT gurus raised the bar for everyone else, right down to IT newbies. But as the IT trends that sent compensation out-of-whack have stabilized (see "The Myths and Realities of IT Workplace Perks," earlier), IT recruiting and job offers are returning to saner standards.

"Companies were promising the moon to get people on board, but the IT labor market is like anything else: it peaks and ebbs and flows," Morrisette says. "Now we see the dot-coms going south, the Y2K problem has been resolved, and ERP demand has leveled off, and so we're seeing a much more realistic market. The demand is still there, but there's a better supply of workers."

Job seekers are more plentiful, with dot-coms and consulting firms announcing significant layoffs in late 2000 and early 2001. One outplacement firm, Challenger, Gray & Christmas, notes that dot-com layoffs increased 600 percent in the second half of 2000, to 36,177 job cuts from July to December compared with 5,097 from January to June. And TheStandard.com, the website for the Internet business publication *The Industry Standard*, reports that 48,692 dot-commers lost their jobs between December 1999 and the end of January 2001. Keep in mind that not all of those laid off were IT professionals, and the overall IT market remains robust. But while the demand still outpaces the supply, even the IT gurus will be less likely to see the unusual, highly publicized benefits of 1999–2000. The bottom line: If you're expecting an employer to offer you the sun, the moon, and the stars, bear in mind the realities behind some common IT job offer myths:

Myth: Get a free BMW as a signing bonus.

Reality: Morrisette notes that he only verified this happening at one company—a Silicon Valley startup with a treasure trove of venture capital that *leased* BMWs for some employees. Even auto companies like Saturn and Toyota don't just give away cars—they offer employee discounts, and the benefit extends to all employees, not just IT workers.

Myth: Get 100-percent coverage of your relocation expenses.

Reality: While companies in tight housing markets often offer financial incentives, in the form of signing bonuses, to workers who must move, don't expect a company to cover all of your relocation costs. The truth is, IRS regulations permit employers to deduct only certain percentages of relocation costs, and a company isn't likely to absorb nondeductible costs. For example, Morrisette says, there are caps on how much a company can pay to cover closing costs on the purchase of an employee's new home and to cover losses on the sale of the home left behind. You can reasonably expect the company to cover the actual moving costs and provide some temporary housing assistance as you get established in your new community. Also, some larger IT organizations have become so accustomed to hiring transplanted IT workers that they have instituted buddy systems and other programs to help new arrivals and their families settle in.

Myth: Get a 50 percent salary increase just by changing jobs.

Reality: Unless your current salary is exceedingly low or a revolutionary new technology emerges that only you and a few dozen others have mastered, don't expect extravagant salary boosts from changing jobs. With the supply-and-demand gap at more manageable proportions, and companies tightening their belts as the stock market continues its roller coaster ride, salary increases will be much more modest than in recent years. "In an economic slowdown, we'll still see increases in IT salaries, but they won't be phenomenal," says Dan Simmons, president of Continental Search, Baltimore, Maryland, an IT recruiting firm that specializes in the Lotus Notes market. In that segment, for example, Simmons notes that in 2000, new recruits were getting as much as 15 percent additional salary when they changed jobs; in 2001, he expects they'll see increases of 8 to 10 percent. "And as more companies and candidates focus on quality-of-life issues, employers may not shell out an extra $10,000 in a job offer," Simmons adds. "Maybe they'll only offer $6,000 extra, but they have an unbeatable benefits package or they'll let you telecommute once a week."

Myth: Leap three rungs on the organizational ladder in a single bound.

Reality: If a potential employer is willing to make you a project manager when you haven't even yet been a team leader, or make you a VP when you've had only nominal management experience, you owe it to yourself to question why. It isn't that you should doubt yourself or feel undeserving—you may be undervalued at your current employer and finally getting the recognition your skills and experience should command. But it might be an indication that the IT organization trying to hire you is desperate. You could be walking into a lion's den of unhappy workers and high IT turnover. The reality is, even if you're perceived as a potential star contributor, a prudent IT hiring manager will take a more measured approach to your job offer. So, without diminishing yourself or what you can bring to a new employer, take a closer look at the IT environment before you jump at that big promotion—and consider asking for the offer in writing along with details about the authority and resources you'll have.

Online Resources: Researching IT Salaries

ComputerJobs.com 2000 Salary Survey

www.computerjobs.com/salary2000

Based on the responses of 43,000 IT professionals, this survey breaks out results by age, certification, company size, education, experience, gender, location, region, state, and job title.

Computerworld's 14th Annual Salary Survey: "Rising in Riches," September 4, 2000

www.computerworld.com/cwi/story/0,1199,NAV47_STO49353,00.html

Along with an article analyzing IT salary trends for 2000, this survey breaks the figures down by job title, company size, industry, region, and more (Adobe Acrobat required).

Dice.com 2000 Salary Survey

marketing.dice.com/rateresults

The best feature here is an interactive query tool that finds average salaries based on job title, skill sets, and location; results are broken down by full-time salaries and hourly contracting rates.

Datamasters 2001 Regional IS Salary Survey

www.datamasters.com/survey.html

Datamasters, a consulting firm in Greensboro, North Carolina, breaks down annual salaries by region and job title, and shows median low, median, and median high salaries; the company's annual surveys dating back to 1990 are available online.

InformationWeek's 2001 Salary Survey: "Salary Strongholds," April 30, 2001

www.informationweek.com/835/salary.htm

This detailed analysis of *InformationWeek* Research's National IT Salary Survey of nearly 20,000 IT staff and managers includes charts illustrating IT workers' average work week, IT managers' base pay, and IT salaries by gender. Also check out an interactive Salary Advisor that generates reports benchmarking IT salaries by job function and job title, as well as best raises by job function, best-paying locations, and best-paying industries (based on the publication's 2000 salary survey, salaryadvisor.informationweek.com/ibi_html/iwsal00/).

Monster.com's Salary Center

salarycenter.monster.com/index.asp

Plug in your field, job category, job title, and location, and get a salary range for any IT job; this site also contains advice on negotiating salaries, how to boost your salary, and more.

Salary.com

www.salary.com

This isn't an IT-specific site, but the Salary Wizard enables you to create salary reports by job title and location for seven different Internet- and IT-related categories; reports include low, median, and high salaries, plus a job description. The site also features general compensation news and advice.

Techies.com Salaries and Benefits Page

home.techies.com/Common/Content/Infocenters/salary_index.html

Get a wealth of salary and benefits information and advice here; for the study on salary parity between men and women, "Salary Gap Smaller for Tech Women," see home.techies.com/Common/Content/01-01/Articles/Html/1career_womenin-tech.html.

The Vault's IT Comp and Benefits Page

www.vault.com/nr/newsmain.jsp?ch_id=409&nr_page=13&cat_id=1263

Peruse articles and advice on negotiating IT salaries, bonus trends, and more, including a brief salary survey listing job titles by technology specialty.

 NOTE *For more salary information on IT jobs in major cities, see Chapter 11.*

Chapter 15

- -

Keep IT Rolling: Sustaining Your Career Momentum

Over his 20-year IT career, Vincent Phillips has seen his share of IT acronyms come and go. He started out as a systems programmer working with IBM's MVS mainframe operating system at Charles Schwab & Company, the San Francisco–based brokerage firm. Working with MVS, he was involved with Customer Information Control System (CICS), an older IBM transaction processing system. Later, he got involved in mainframe networking, when the big acronym of the day was SNA, which stands for IBM's Systems Network Architecture (originally introduced in 1974). By the mid-nineties, Phillips was moving up the management ranks, reaching the position of senior manager of software engineering. But the future of mainframe programming was looking somewhat dim, and Phillips was ready to move on. "I felt like I had done all the things I could do in mainframes," he recalls, "and I was looking for something new and interesting and challenging."

Schwab had already launched a private dial-up network that customers could log onto to make their own trades, and in 1995, began preparing to launch an online trading site on the then-fledgling World Wide Web. Management approached Phillips about helming the project, but it meant he'd have to take a step down the management ladder to project manager. Nonetheless, "it looked like the Net was the future," Phillips says. "The job felt like a big strategic opportunity because the electronic brokerage enterprise was a startup venture within the company." He accepted and began leading a small team in developing what would become www.schwab.com.

Little formal training in Internet technologies was available at the time, and Phillips had no time for it anyway, so he brought himself up to speed on Internet technologies through self-study. "I began reading things like crazy, and I became an Internet junkie for a while, discovering what was available, what was special," he says. Using the Internet and books, he quickly learned about Internet protocol (IP) networking principles, web applications development in C++, HTTP protocols, common gateway interface (CGI), and Internet security, including public key encryption and Secure Sockets Layer (SSL) technology.

The online trading site launched five months after Phillips accepted the project management role. Three months later, he was promoted to director of systems engineering. Today, he's vice president of web systems for the electronic brokerage technology group, an organization of 300 IT staff members, and Schwab.com boasts over 4 million registered users.

Phillips' journey from mainframe programmer to web systems VP illustrates that it is incumbent on IT professionals to take responsibility for their continued career development and to keep their technology skills on the leading edge. His tenacity is proof that even if formal training isn't available, the resources are out there so that with sufficient self-motivation, IT professionals can manage their own skills retooling. You've been through the wringer establishing your IT career or taking it to the next level. Now you have to sustain the momentum. Fortunately, even though technology is changing at a faster rate today than ever before, thanks to the Web, it's also easier to keep up with those changes, stay in touch with your colleagues, and get the information you need to remain highly employable. Previous chapters of this book provide resources for finding jobs and training on the Web. Following is a compendium of resources that will help you, like Phillips, keep your IT career moving forward.

IT Publication Sites and Portals

Turn to the following resources for IT news and views.

IT Professional Journals

cNET

www.cnet.com

This is the definitive site for technology professionals and aficionados. Its news section contains some of the best technology and industry reporting on the Web; its technology sections and buyers guides are deep resources for both the novice and the experienced. Use the main page as a front door to all sections, and bookmark the ones you like best—once you find them, you'll use them regularly.

IT World

www.itworld.com

The umbrella site for International Data Group's IT publications, including *CIO*, *Network World*, *Computerworld*, *JavaWorld*, and more, this site features news and analysis, a careers section, email newsletters, discussion forums, and more.

Linux Journal

www.linuxjournal.com

This in-depth technical journal for Linux users offers news, trends analysis and reviews.

SlashDot

www.slashdot.org

The tagline for this supremely independent site, "News for Nerds," says it all; the amount of content here can be overwhelming, but there's something for everyone in IT.

TechWeb

www.techweb.com

The umbrella site for CMP Media's IT publications, including *InformationWeek*, *Internet Week*, *Byte*, and others, this site also features the PlanetIT portal to original IT news, analysis, and advice.

ZDNet

www.zdnet.com

The umbrella site for Ziff Davis IT publications, including *PC Magazine*, *MacWorld*, *Inter@ctive Week*, and others, this site is also a portal to an array of IT information on the Web.

Internet News and Features

Business 2.0

www.business2.com

Get news, analysis, commentary, and research on e-business, marketing, investing, and technology.

The Industry Standard

www.thestandard.com

This is one of the most plugged-in publications around today, featuring news, analysis, commentary, and research on all things related to the Net, e-business, and new media; stay current by signing up for its daily and weekly email newsletters.

Internet.com

www.internet.com

Use the 16 channels at this site to get news and features on all things related to Internet-related development, services, technology, and investing.

IT Business and Culture

Red Herring

www.redherring.com

Offering technology news aimed at an audience with a financial interest, the content at this site is more concerned with IPOs and company analyses than the details of technology. But it publishes several issues a year that are good for keeping up with emerging companies in the high-tech industry and other topics that will help you stay abreast of industry developments that could have a direct or indirect impact on your IT career.

Salon Magazine's Technology Section

www.salon.com/tech/index.html

The technology section of this successful online magazine features daily news updates but is most valuable for its thought-provoking features on technology topics; while it's not designed to help you forward your career, checking in here regularly will make you smarter about what's going on in the IT world at large.

Upside

www.upside.com

With probing, hard-hitting, and irreverent coverage of the high-tech industry, *Upside* is not about providing technical information; rather, it's an insider's view of what motivates the companies that drive IT.

Wired

www.wired.com

Business, politics, culture, and technology collide in the content at this site; while it's aimed at a larger audience than IT professionals, anyone with an interest in the larger issues shaping IT today and tomorrow should check in here regularly.

IT Community Sites

Turn to the following resources to interact with colleagues and get career advice.

BrainBuzz

www.brainbuzz.com

This favorite of IT professionals features myriad discussion boards, IT job-searching, industry news, and training and certification guides.

CIO Resource Centers

www.cio.com/forums

CIO magazine's resource centers are useful guides to a range of IT subjects, from application service providers to the Web, all from a management perspective; also included are career development sections for IT professionals and up-and-coming IT managers who see themselves headed for the executive suite.

EarthWeb

www.earthweb.com

One of the best IT portals on the Web, addressing technology, careers, and management issues of concern to IT professionals, this site encompasses JavaScripts.com, Datamation.com, Gamelon.com, PracticallyNetworked.com, and other IT-related sites, plus myriad email newsletters.

Systers

www.systers.org

This informal organization of women in IT and high tech maintains a private, women-only discussion list and newsletter dubbed *Mecca*; sign up here.

TechRepublic

www.techrepublic.com

Billed as a site for IT professionals by IT professionals, this community has special sections for CIOs, IT managers, developers, network administrators, support professionals, trainers, and consultants; it features news, IT research, technical Q&As, vendor links, discussion forums, and more.

Tek-Tips

www.tek-tips.com

Join an array of discussion forums covering all major technologies and IT management and career issues; it's all talk, all the time.

Technology-Specific Sites and Portals

Turn to the following resources for tutorials, how-tos, and advice related to top technologies.

HINT *If you don't find what you're looking for under a specific technology category, check the general resources section for portal sites that likely cover what you need. Also check the "IT Community Sites" and "IT Professional Journals" sections.*

General Resources

The Computer Information Center

www.compinfo-center.com

This is a comprehensive, A to Z resource for IT professionals covering artificial intelligence, computer-aided design, chip technology, computers and telephony, data capture, data warehousing, ecommerce, electronic publishing, enterprise information systems, general office systems and software, geographic information systems, graphics and multimedia, groupware and document management, hardware of all varieties, intelligent agents, Internet and intranets, IT management, large-scale computing, mobile and wireless computing, networks and data communications, operating systems, software of all types, system security, web development, and more.

The Fan Club Sites

This group of sites features technical advice, discussion forums, FAQs, news, links, and more for a number of products.

▶ The Baan Fan Club: www.baanfans.com

▶ The ERP Fan Club: www.erpfans.com

▶ The Oracle Fan Club: www.oraclefans.com

▶ The PeopleSoft Fan Club: www.peoplesoftfans.com

▶ The SAP Fan Club: www.sapfans.com

▶ The Windows NT Fan Club: www.windowsntfans.com

IT Toolbox

ittoolbox.com

Enter the front door to another family of portal sites on key technology and product areas, including Baan, CRM, data warehousing, enterprise application integration, e-business, ERP, networking, Oracle, PeopleSoft, SAP, and supply-chain management. New topics are added regularly.

TechGuide.com

www.techguide.com

Check in here for over 70 white papers on five key IT topics: communications and networking, Internet technology, data warehousing, document management, and enterprise solutions, plus discussion forums for each.

TechTarget Portal Sites

This family of web portals enables one-stop searching of all websites related to a particular technology as well as original content and news coverage, technology tips, and career advice. New sites are added regularly. Among the current sites are the following:

▶ ASPs: www.searchasp.com

▶ Customer Relationship Management: www.searchcrm.com

▶ Databases: www.searchdatabase.com

▶ Hewlett-Packard: www.searchhp.com

▶ IBM System/390: www.search390.com

▶ IBM AS/400: www.search400.com

▶ Linux: www.searchenterpriselinux.com

▶ Lotus Notes/Domino: www.searchdomino.com

▶ Microsoft Windows 2000: www.searchWin2000.com

▶ Microsoft Visual Basic: www.searchVB.com

▶ Networking: www.searchnetworking.com

▶ Security: www.searchsecurity.com

▶ Sun Solaris: www.searchSolaris.com

▶ Storage: www.searchstorage.com

▶ Web hosting: www.searchwebhosting.com

▶ XML: www.searchxmlresources.com.

Tech Tutorials

www.techtutorials.com

Whatever topic you need to tackle, you're sure to find a number of relevant tutorials here that are designed specifically for IT professionals; the site covers applications software, major hardware platforms, networking, programming languages, wireless devices, and more.

Technology Dictionaries and Encyclopedias

TechEncyclopedia

www.techweb.com/encyclopedia

Search for definitions of over 14,000 technology terms and concepts with this online database, a TechWeb network site.

Webopedia

www.pcwebopaedia.com

This searchable online dictionary defines IT terms in plain English and includes a detailed background on each term.

WhatIs.com

www.whatis.com

Use this online IT dictionary to get easy-to-read definitions and links to further information; it's part of the TechTarget family of sites.

Database Technology Resources

The Oracle User Forum and Fan Club

www.orafans.com

A virtual community with advice columns and original content in addition to online discussion groups, this is a much more robust fan site than OracleFans.com (listed earlier).

OTN Xchange: The Oracle Technology Network

otnxchange.oracle.com

At this official Oracle community site, Oracle pros can search for jobs, share code, and get information on Oracle-sponsored conferences and training.

ERP Resources

ERP Central

www.erpcentral.com

Bookmark this portal site for links to news and resources dealing with enterprise resource planning systems.

Hardware Resources

Smaller.com

www.smaller.com

Check out reviews and information on personal digital assistants, laptops, cell phones, and other wireless and mobile devices.

SysOpt.com: System Optimization Information

www.sysopt.com

The ultimate site for hardware jockeys and operations and support professionals, this site features hardware reviews, optimization techniques, price guides, and more; it's part of the EarthWeb family of sites.

Networking Resources

CommWeb Tutorials

www.commweb.com/tutorials

Use this collection of tutorials to come up-to-speed on various aspects of data communications, telecommunications, and the Internet.

The Information Technology Professional's Resource Center

www.itprc.com

Find networking- and operations-related information on the Web, including wireless, TCP/IP, network management, and more, at this well-organized portal; a careers development section offers training and certification information, as well as a guide to trade shows and conferences. Check out the active discussion forums.

Stardust.com

www.stardust.com

This guide to the latest advances in Internet infrastructure technology covers Ipv6 (Internet 2), IP Multicast, quality of service, and more.

Wireless LAN.com

www.wirelesslan.com

This site offers a quick-hitting overview of wireless LANs, why and how they're used, and requirements.

Operating System Resources

Frank Condron's World O'Windows

www.worldowindows.com/index.asp

This homegrown Windows portal has gained quite a following since it was established in 1995; it's maintained by Frank Condron, a Windows 2000 and Internet technologies consultant.

Linux Enterprise Computing

linas.org/linux

Use this vast homegrown site to link to online publications, how-tos, technical information, tools and applications, and more; it's focused on Linux in business and ecommerce.

Linux Help Online

www.linuxhelp.org

Get a rundown of the origins of Linux, plus links to vendors, technical information, and major publications, and "Top Headline" news alerts.

Linux Now

www.linuxnow.com

Check in here for Linux documentation, FAQs, links to related sites, and discussion forums.

Linux Online

www.linux.org

This comprehensive site features book reviews and an online bookstore, a vendor and distribution guide, user group listings, links to free downloads, history, tutorials, FAQs, how-tos, and more.

Linux Resource Exchange

www.linuxrx.com

If you're wondering about Linux, check out the interactive chart comparing its performance to other operating systems, plus get kernels, patches, how-tos and FAQs, security alerts, a listing of newsletters and mailing lists, and more.

Microsoft TechNet

www.microsoft.com/technet

This is the official Microsoft resource for IT professionals using the company's products.

Windows Users Group Network

www.wugnet.com

This online community supporting IT professionals involved with Windows and other Microsoft-related technologies and products features shareware, software reviews, tip of the day, and more.

WHO YOU KNOW, WHAT YOU KNOW

The most unlikely connections can lead to careers in IT—when backed up with self-motivation, tenacity, and a willingness to learn. Darren Nelson, the chief technology officer (CTO) at Hecklers Entertainment in Birmingham, Alabama, was working in a Sherwin Williams store before joining a dot-com and working his way up to CTO. John Atkinson was a political aide in the nation's capitol before becoming vice president of technology services at a San Francisco–based Internet startup. Both got to where they are today by maintaining good contacts and by doing whatever it took to educate themselves in IT.

After college, where he'd earned a B.S. in Commerce and Business Administration from the University of Alabama, Nelson had embarked on a career in the retail industry, working in a management trainee program with Sherwin Williams in Houston, Texas. In the meantime, two old friends from college were starting up Hecklers, a comedy content site within AOL. The two-man operation needed a third person who could be a jack-of-all-trades, Nelson recalls. "They hired me because they knew I had a strong work ethic," he says. "Hecklers didn't have a lot of resources, and they knew I would work long hours and do whatever it takes to get the job done."

After six months of doing everything from fielding phone calls and sending out press kits to sitting in on strategy meetings with AOL and resolving technical problems, Nelson's interests turned more and more toward the IT side of the company. "I enjoyed the problem-solving challenges that it presents," he explains. "I've always been a hands-on guy who likes to know how things work." Through avid reading, web surfing, and drawing on the technical support offered by AOL, he started teaching himself the nuts and bolts of "how to turn content into an entertaining website." Within two years, he was named CTO; today, he manages a staff of three and makes all the major technology decisions for six AOL content areas and five destination websites.

Atkinson leveraged two unlikely contacts to finally arrive as vice president of technology services at extension11, an ecommerce strategy and technology consulting firm in San Francisco. Having majored in political science at the University of California at Davis, following graduation, he took a job in Washington, D.C., as an intern to a California congressman. From contacts he made inside the Beltway, he was asked to be the project coordinator for Oliver North's Senate campaign against Charles Robb in Virginia in 1993. Shortly, he was moved into the role of deputy communications manager, and he determined that the only way North would have a prayer against Robb was if the campaign was able to get out one consistent message and get it out faster than Robb's campaign could get out theirs.

WHO YOU KNOW, WHAT YOU KNOW

"We learned that technique from the Clinton campaign in '92," Atkinson says. "They had a notorious sign in their headquarters that said 'Speed Kills Bush,' and we adopted that rapid-response philosophy. To execute that, we decided to … build our own fax network with servers and modems and some clever software that could blast 100 faxes in half an hour." The campaign brought in an IT consultant to provide the technical know-how, and Atkinson worked side-by-side with him, learning how to configure servers and manage the network. "I didn't see much sunlight that year," he says.

The "rapid-response" network helped the campaign close its gap from 35 polling points to a mere 2.5 points by the time of the election, but Robb edged North out, and Atkinson was in limbo. He accepted the position of press secretary to Congressman Frank Riggs of California, but by that time, he was growing disillusioned with politics. Fortuitously, the IT consultant he'd worked with on the North campaign had been tapped to overhaul the IT infrastructure at the House of Representatives, and he asked Atkinson to join him. "I was part of a four-man tech support team that they called the 'Dream Team,'" Atkinson says. "We had about 700 end-users. We upgraded all their PCs, took out all the dumb terminals, and gave them email and Internet access. I didn't have a chance to do any training—I read like crazy, and I learned everything on the job." Later, he proposed and built the House's first intranet, managing a team of 22 people.

Ultimately, Atkinson moved to the Bay Area to pursue his growing interest in the Internet, where a random pairing on a golf course landed him his next big opportunity. His golfing partner turned out to be a cofounder of a fledgling online credit card services venture, who asked Atkinson about his background and then invited him to interview at the company. Within two months, the company tapped Atkinson as director of technology infrastructure.

The company was NextCard, which now employs over 500 people. Atkinson, NextCard's seventh employee, set up the original network, coordinated applications development, oversaw the installation of two PBX phone systems, and deployed a 24/7 data center. NextCard went public in May 1999; Atkinson says he left "to move on to the next big challenge," landing at extension11 in October 1999.

For both Nelson and Atkinson, the transition to their newfound IT careers started with whom they knew, but their continued success was a direct function of what they learned and applied on the job. Self-study, late hours, trial and error, and leveraging all the technology information available to them on the Web and from coworkers propelled them to top jobs in the field. "Knowing the cofounders of Heckler's definitely was what got me in the door," Nelson says. "But afterward, my success was based on results. I wouldn't have been here very long if I hadn't produced."

Programming Languages and Platforms Resources

The Development Exchange

www.devx.com

A cybercommunity for applications developers offering code samples, tips and techniques, discussion forums, and how-tos, this site is organized by zones covering the leading development languages and platforms, including Visual Basic, Java, C++, and more; it's subscription-based, but new visitors can sign up for a 30-day free trial. This site also incorporates Inquiry.com, where developers answer each other's toughest questions.

Java Boutique

javaboutique.internet.com

Get free Java applets and source code, plus tutorials, reviews, and more. This site, which also features discussion groups, is aimed at those with at least some Java experience, but beginners can use it to detect what lies ahead on their Java learning curve.

Java Lobby

www.javalobby.org

The name spells it out: This is a group that lobbies on behalf of a completely open Java; but the site is much more—a portal to other Java sites, Java news, discussion forums, etc.

Java Ranch

www.javaranch.com

Although the cowboy theme of this site wears thin after a bit ("Saddle up, greenhorn! We're gonna write some actual Java code," the home page announces), it's nonetheless a useful watering hole for learning more about Java, connecting with other Java programmers, and getting the lowdown on Java certification.

Sun's Official Java Page: The Source for Java Technology

java.sun.com

Straight from the source, this site features Java news, APIs and documentation, discussion groups, case studies, applets, and more.

Notes.net

www.notes.net

This is a comprehensive technical resource featuring downloads, documentation, discussion forums, and more for users of Lotus Notes/Domino; it's maintained by Iris Associates, the wholly owned subsidiary of Lotus Development Corp. and IBM that develops Notes, Domino, and related products.

MCPCentral.com

www.mcpcentral.com

Just launched in August 2000, this site aims to be a one-stop resource for developers working within the Microsoft environment. It features articles, how-tos, and downloads for Active Server Pages, Visual Basic, Visual C++, SQL Server, and more. Unfortunately, it doesn't seem to be updated frequently, but nonetheless contains some useful tutorials.

Just PowerBuilder Information

www.justpbinfo.com

PowerBuilder (PB) pros share tips and advice at this site, which also includes technical documents and PB job listings.

Programming Tutorials

www.programmingtutorials.com

Use this portal to find more than 150 links to programming tutorials across the Web; languages covered include Java, XML, Active Server Pages, C, C++, CGI, Cobol, Perl, and more.

Programmers' Heaven

www.programmersheaven.com

Featuring message boards, more than 2,600 links, over 500 articles, and more, this is a comprehensive resource on programming for all experience levels.

Carl and Gary's Visual Basic Home Page

www.cgvb.com

Considered one of the definitive VB sites, this collection of resources put together by developers Carl Franklin and Gary Wisniewski has been around since 1994 and has value for VB programmers of all experience levels.

Visual Basic Explorer

www.vbexplorer.com

This site for beginning-to-intermediate VB developers features tutorials, source code, downloads, message boards, and more.

VBXML.com

www.vbxml.com

This guide to programming for the Net using XML is aimed at developers using Microsoft Visual Basic and Active Server Pages.

XML.com

www.xml.com

Use this collection of primers, FAQs, how-tos, and other resources to come up to speed on XML development.

Security Resources

CERT Coordination Center

www.cert.org

Maintained by the Computer Emergency Response Team at Carnegie Mellon University's Software Engineering Institute, this site contains security-related research, security advisories, incident reports, recovery procedures, and more; it's a critical resource for anyone who needs security information.

The SANS Institute

www.sans.org

SANS, a research and education cooperative for systems and network administrators and security professionals, offers research reports, news analysis, a salary survey, training and certification information, and other security-related resources at this site.

Web Technologies

ProjectCool

www.projectcool.com

This site offers tutorials, FAQs, reference materials, and more for web designers and developers, from the novice to the experienced; sign up for newsletters or connect with other web developers in the PeopleSphere section.

Web Developer

www.webdeveloper.com

If you're just starting to build Web pages and need to learn the basics plus some useful tips and tricks to help you scale the learning curve, check out this site.

IT Research Sites

Turn to the following resources for IT research, statistics, and analysis.

AMR Research

www.amrresearch.com

Free "Executive Views," analysis of top industry news stories, and other research is available here.

eIT-Forum: The IT Management Knowledge Portal

www.eitforum.com

Use this compendium of IT management research, papers, and articles when you need strategic IT information.

Forrester Research

www.forrester.com

The emphasis is on ecommerce, IT management, and various technology segments; registration is required to access the free IT research reports available here.

Gartner Group Online

www.gartner.com

One of the leading IT research firms offers substantial free reports and other content at its website.

International Data Corporation's IT Advisor

www.idc.com/ITAdvisor/default.htm

Check out the research aimed at IT professionals from market research firm International Data Corporation (IDC); the site contains executive summaries of IDC reports available to subscribers, as well as free samples of complete reports (registration required to download freebies).

Jupiter

www.jup.com

Get research on Internet-based commerce; guest registration is required to access free sample reports.

Knowledge Centers

www.knowledgecenters.org

This site is a vast repository of market research, white papers, articles, and more organized into five different centers of expertise: Internet, data warehousing, telecommuting, ecommerce, and small office/home office.

Microsoft Research Home Page

www.research.microsoft.com/home.htm

Check in here for details on advanced research at Microsoft.

ResearchPortal.com

www.researchportal.com

The primary research areas here include notebook PCs, handheld computing, SmartPhones, messaging tools, and wireless data equipment and services; registration is required to access free reports and data, and parts of the site require paid subscriptions.

TradeSpeak: The Knowledge Resource for Professionals

www.tradespeak.com

This is an online library of white papers on enterprise solutions, application-enabling technologies, and network and telecom infrastructure, as well as IT business and management issues; keep in mind that most of these papers are prepared by vendors who have a related product to sell; that said, the papers can still provide useful background on a wide array of IT subjects, from asset management to virtual private networks.

The Yankee Group

www.yankeegroup.com

The emphasis here is on new economy research of interest to IT strategy planners; substantial free content is available without a subscription.

BOUNCING BACK

When David Zimmer struck out on his own as a strategic IT consultant back in 1992, it seemed like he was looking at a sure thing. His expertise was in electronic messaging systems, and he planned to parlay that to position himself as an expert in unified messaging—the concept of integrating voice mail, fax, email, and other forms of electronic communication in the same mailbox with accessibility from either PCs or telephones. Corporate email was just starting to take off, and companies frequently had a hodge-podge of incompatible email systems in place, making corporate-wide messaging extremely difficult to achieve. They needed help integrating their disparate email systems, and Zimmer's then hard-to-find skills were in high demand. But he miscalculated the timeframe in which standard, centralized email would become an easy-to-offer corporate system.

"I should have seen that email was becoming more commonplace," says Zimmer, president of American Eagle Group, Warrington, Pennsylvania. "The demand for my skills dried up very quickly, and the demand for unified messaging was not picking up as fast as I expected. So there was a major gap in between." When a major contract ended in May 1997, Zimmer found himself out of work with few prospects of maintaining his cash flow. Companies began funneling their consulting budgets into website development and Y2K remediation projects, and Zimmer's business remained flat for 20 months. Very few gigs came his way and he was dipping into his savings accounts.

Zimmer concedes that he had his days when all looked bleak. But he was resolved to remain an independent consultant, even turning down some high-paying fulltime positions during those dark days. Instead, he pulled himself up by his bootstraps and spent his ample free time diversifying his skill sets. He focused on acquiring ecommerce and knowledge-management expertise, and he took steps to position himself not only as a unified messaging expert, but as a market leader. He began devouring books and magazines that covered ecommerce and knowledge management. Having learned his lesson that specific technology solutions come and go, he focused on the strategic issues.

"Everything changes so quickly that half of what you read is out of date before you get to use it," Zimmer explains. "So I was trying to figure out what companies were doing and see where the market was going and how my types of services and skills could fit in. And ecommerce and knowledge management were related to the messaging skills I already had because they're all about communicating."

BOUNCING BACK

He began publishing papers, meeting with vendors, organizing conferences, and making presentations nationwide. In 1998, he cofounded the Unified Messaging Consortium, which was funded by nine major vendors. As the consortium gained visibility through all of his presentations and papers, several companies approached him about doing cost-of-ownership studies, and he was able to start rebuilding his consulting practice. Today, with businesses looking to access corporate data, applications, and email from cell phones and handheld devices, the unified messaging market is going full-steam ahead, and Zimmer is helping lead the way. He's repositioning the Unified Messaging Consortium into a nonprofit industry association, the Unified Communications Consortium (www.unified-communications.com), with a broader focus that reflects the shift of the market toward unified communications.

"When people talked about messaging before, they didn't think about the real-time component of it, but now we're evolving into unified communications, which can encompass real time and asynchronous messaging," Zimmer says. "We need to consider [the integration of] a range of communication services, such as call forwarding, instant messaging, voice-over IP, wireless devices. It doesn't matter where I am, I can still get to all the information in my email, calendar, to-do lists, address book—whatever is stored on my corporate servers."

Instead of scrambling for gigs, Zimmer is working with communications industry vendors and service providers to devise strategies and strengthen their brand position; he also consults with end users on how to leverage unified communications in their organizations. "A dry period can be very good for you," he says, reflecting on how he turned his career around. "When the money dries up, you get a clarity of focus."

Sites for IT Consultants and Contractors

Turn to the following resources for information on independent IT consulting and contracting.

The Contract Employee's Handbook

www.cehandbook.com

Here's a comprehensive guide to the legal ins and outs of independent contracting, plus information on how to negotiate rates, taxes, and more.

Contract Employment Daily

www.cedaily.com

This collection of discussion forums—of varying quality—deals with consulting and contracting issues; the site includes a section where users post their hourly rates.

CPUniverse: The Online Resource from *Contract Professional* Magazine

www.cpuniverse.com

Get news and advice for IT contractors.

Independent Computer Consultants Association

www.icca.org

Connect with other consultants, find local chapters, join discussion groups and more at this site for the leading organization for independent IT professionals.

RealRates

www.realrates.com

The main feature here is a live, real-time IT consulting salary survey, but even better is the bulletin board, which hosts a number of lively, pointed discussions on all issues relevant to IT contracting and consulting.

Vendor- and Technology-Related User Groups

Turn to the following resources, organized alphabetically by vendor name or technology category, for user-group information.

Cisco Users Groups

www.cisco-users.org/other_cugs.htm

The Dallas-Ft. Worth chapter of the Cisco Users Group maintains this portal to 19 other local and regional Cisco user groups across the country.

International DB2 Users Group

www.idug.org

This is an independent nonprofit group supporting users of IBM's DB2 and related products.

International Association of Hewlett-Packard Computing Professionals

www.interex.org

This is a complete resource for HP users.

International Informix Users Group

www.iiug.org

Check in here for information on the official Informix user group.

Sun's Java User Group Guide

industry.java.sun.com/jug/

Get links to over 1,800 Java user groups worldwide, including more than 500 established groups, more than 1,300 forming groups, and over 25 online groups.

Linux User Groups Guide

www.linux.org/users/index.html

There are more than 500 Linux user groups worldwide from Algeria to Zambia, including over 400 in the United States. To find one near you, check out this handy guide at Linux Online.

VALU.org: The International Lotus User Group

www.valu.org/valu/home.nsf

This is the Lotus-endorsed international umbrella association for local user groups and regional special interest groups; its site features a user-group guide, an events calendar, discussion forums, and more.

Microsoft User Group Search Page

msdn.microsoft.com/resources/usergroup/find.asp

Microsoft's TechNet website lists nearly 1,000 local and regional user groups affiliated with the company's various products. Use this page to search by location, product, and other criteria to find a user group that suits your needs.

Microsoft Healthcare Users Group

www.mshug.org

This is the official group for Microsoft users working within the healthcare industry.

NT*Pro: The Association of Windows NT System Professionals

www.ntpro.org

Personally launched by Bill Gates in 1993, this group, based in the Greater Washington, D.C., metro area, caters to IT professionals involved with Microsoft's BackOffice products.

Worldwide Association of NT User Groups

www.ntpro.org/wantug

Check out this portal for links to all Windows NT– and Windows 2000–related user groups around the globe.

NetWare Users International

www.novell.com/community/nui

This is the umbrella group for Novell NetWare user groups around the world; click Membership to find a listing of individual chapters with links to their websites.

International Oracle Users Group - Americas

www.ioug.org

The official Oracle user group home page is a portal to all things Oracle; it includes links to local and regional chapters.

Oracle Development Tools User Group

www.odtug.com

This is a special interest group for users of Oracle's Internet Development Suite of tools.

Oracle User Resource (OUR)

www.oracle-users.com/index.html

This is an independent Oracle user group based mainly on the East Coast that sponsors an annual technical developers conference; its site includes links to myriad local and regional Oracle and Oracle-related user groups worldwide (www.oracle-users.com/links.htm).

SAS Users Group International

www.sas.com/usergroups/sugi/

For users of SAS Institute's data-mining software and other packages, this is a complete guide to local and regional SAS user groups worldwide.

International Sybase User Group

www.isug.com

Get information on the worldwide group for users of both the Sybase and Power-soft databases and tools.

Unix Users' Groups

www.sluug.org/~newton/othr_uug.html

This page at the independent St. Louis Unix Users' Group website features a nearly comprehensive set of links to Unix user groups associated with vendor distributions of the operating system as well as platform-independent Unix user groups.

IT Professional Associations

Turn to the following resources, organized alphabetically by the association name, for opportunities to further your professional development.

Association of Computing Machinery

www.acm.org

The ACM is a technically inclined organization for IT professionals and students.

Association of Information Technology Professionals

www.aitp.org

This professional group promotes career-oriented education and networking with peers.

Association of Internet Professionals

www.association.org

The membership comprises over 9,500 individuals working in the Internet arena, including senior managers, technologists and designers, independent Internet consultants, and others.

Association of Support Professionals

www.asponline.com

This is a worldwide organization for technical support professionals.

Association for Women in Computing

www.awc-hq.org

This professional association promotes the advancement of women in IT and the high-tech industry.

Black Data Processing Associates

www.bdpa.org

The BDPA provides professional development programs, services, and community outreach to its members.

Help Desk Institute

www.HelpDeskInst.com

This is the association for customer support professionals who work on internal and external helpdesks.

Network Professionals Association

www.npa.org

This organization for networking professionals aims to set standards for education, certification, and professionalism; members must be certified or working toward certification.

Network and Systems Professionals Association

www.naspa.net

NASPA aims to promote skills development and advancement among its members.

SAGE: The Systems Administrators Guild

www.usenix.org/sage

A special-interest group of the Usenix Association, this is a professional group for systems administrators.

Society of Information Management

www.simnet.org

This professional association for IT managers and executives promotes research and education in IT management.

Software Support Professionals Association

www.sspa-online.com

This is another organization catering to IT helpdesk professionals.

UniForum

www.uniforum.org

UniForum supports open systems and has deep roots in the Unix community.

Usenix: The Advanced Computing Systems Association

www.usenix.org

This association for IT professionals and computer scientists and engineers promotes open systems development; for Unix and Linux user-group information, click User Groups; site also includes links to SAGE: The Systems Administrators Guild.

The WITI Foundation (Women in Technology International)

www.witi.org

WITI is dedicated to advancing women in IT.

Major Annual Conferences and Trade Shows

Turn to the following resources, organized alphabetically by show name, for information on industry confabs.

Comdex

www.key3media.com/comdex

The annual confab in Las Vegas provides vendors a forum for major new announcements and for IT professionals to see the latest and greatest in IT.

Internet World

events.internet.com

This series of conferences and trade shows, including two in the United States, is held worldwide throughout the year.

JavaOne

java.sun.com/javaone

This is the ultimate annual conference for Java developers.

LinuxWorld Conference and Expo

www.linuxexpo.com

This is a new annual event for the Linux user community.

Lotusphere

www.lotus.com/home.nsf/welcome/lotuspherehome

Lotus sponsors two popular annual conferences in Orlando, Florida, and Berlin, Germany; for users of Notes, Domino, and related products.

MacWorld

www.macworldexpo.com

Check out the leading annual conference and trade show for Apple Computer, including shows in San Francisco, Boston, and New York.

NetWorld + Interop

www.key3media.com/interop

Get information on the annual conference and trade show for networking professionals.

PC Expo

www.pcexpo.com

This is an annual business technology conference and trade show held each June.

Books

The number of IT-related books on the market today could fill entire libraries; clearly, not even a fair representation of the vast number of titles can be listed here, but following is a sampling of series that are popular with IT professionals, plus a handful of titles for readers who want to know more about the history of the industry.

Technology Books

The Dummies Guides

Published by Hungry Minds (formerly IDG Books Worldwide)

www.dummies.com

Pick your topic, and there's a Dummies guide to see you through. Positioned mainly for novices, these guides can also be useful when you want to get a broad overview on a new technology or application.

The O'Reilly Guides

Published by O'Reilly & Associates

www.oreilly.com

The O'Reilly titles are among the most popular technology books for the experienced IT professional. They cover every major programming language and technique, operating system, database technology, networking technology, and application you can think of. The "In a Nutshell" series offers quick overviews, while the O'Reilly imprint offers a more in-depth look.

The Get Ahead Guides

Published by Osborne/McGraw-Hill

www.books.mcgraw-hill.com

The new Get Ahead series of career development titles for IT professionals includes *Get Certified and Get Ahead*, *Get Linux Certified and Get Ahead*, *Get Cisco Certified and Get Ahead*, *Get Your IT Degree and Get Ahead*, and others.

Books on the History of Computers and IT

Computer: A History of the Information Machine

By Martin Campbell-Kelly and William Aspray

1996, BasicBooks (a division of HarperCollins Publishers, New York)

Don't be misled by the rather dry title of this book; it's a fascinating account of the history of the computer industry.

Engines of the Mind: The Evolution of the Computer from Mainframes to Microprocessors

By Joel Shurkin

1996, W.W. Norton & Company, New York

This book is a fine companion to *Computer* (previous listing); it's another authoritative history of the development of computers from the ENIAC to the personal computer, with a focus on the pioneers who laid the groundwork for where IT stands today.

Fire in the Valley: The Making of the Personal Computer, Second Edition

By Paul Freiberger and Michael Swaine

1999, Osborne/McGraw-Hill, Berkeley, California

This edition of the detailed chronicle of the birth of the PC includes new material covering the years since its original publication in 1984.

Insanely Great: The Life and Times of Macintosh, the Computer That Changed Everything

By Steven Levy

1994, Viking-Penguin, New York

Levy, a *Newsweek* columnist, chronicles the development of Apple Computer and the impact of the Macintosh on the industry in this highly readable book.

The Silicon Boys and Their Valley of Dreams

By David A. Kaplan

1999, William Morrow & Company, New York

The already-legendary transformation of the peninsula that stretches from San Francisco to San Jose from fruit orchards to high-tech hotbed is explored in this timely account.

Weaving the Web: The Original Design and Ultimate Destiny of the World Wide Web by Its Inventor

By Tim Berners-Lee

1999, Harper, San Francisco

Berners-Lee offers an autobiographical account of how he fathered the World Wide Web.

Where Wizards Stay Up Late: The Origins of the Internet

By Katie Hafner and Matthew Lyon

1996, Simon & Schuster, New York

Hafner, who cowrote *Cyberpunk: Outlaws and Hackers on the Computer Frontier*, a lively look at the hacker subculture, here delves into the earliest days of the Internet before the World Wide Web made it a household word.

Index

INTERNATIONAL CONTACT INFORMATION

AUSTRALIA
McGraw-Hill Book Company Australia Pty. Ltd.
TEL +61-2-9417-9899
FAX +61-2-9417-5687
http://www.mcgraw-hill.com.au
books-it_sydney@mcgraw-hill.com

CANADA
McGraw-Hill Ryerson Ltd.
TEL +905-430-5000
FAX +905-430-5020
http://www.mcgrawhill.ca

GREECE, MIDDLE EAST,
NORTHERN AFRICA
McGraw-Hill Hellas
TEL +30-1-656-0990-3-4
FAX +30-1-654-5525

MEXICO (Also serving Latin America)
McGraw-Hill Interamericana Editores S.A. de C.V.
TEL +525-117-1583
FAX +525-117-1589
http://www.mcgraw-hill.com.mx
fernando_castellanos@mcgraw-hill.com

SINGAPORE (Serving Asia)
McGraw-Hill Book Company
TEL +65-863-1580
FAX +65-862-3354
http://www.mcgraw-hill.com.sg
mghasia@mcgraw-hill.com

SOUTH AFRICA
McGraw-Hill South Africa
TEL +27-11-622-7512
FAX +27-11-622-9045
robyn_swanepoel@mcgraw-hill.com

UNITED KINGDOM & EUROPE
(Excluding Southern Europe)
McGraw-Hill Publishing Company
TEL +44-1-628-502500
FAX +44-1-628-770224
http://www.mcgraw-hill.co.uk
computing_neurope@mcgraw-hill.com

ALL OTHER INQUIRIES Contact:
Osborne/McGraw-Hill
TEL +1-510-549-6600
FAX +1-510-883-7600